The #1 Cooking Magazine in the World Brings Great Taste Home

WHY HAVE cooks from all around made *Taste of Home* the world's most popular cooking magazine? Because it's packed with recipes that bring great taste into the kitchens of families everywhere.

In *2011 Taste of Home Annual Recipes*, you'll find all-new favorites sure to please your own family. This 18th edition of our best-selling cookbook series gives you an entire year's worth of scrumptious recipes published in *Taste of Home* magazine.

What's more, you get more than 90 bonus dishes never before seen in *Taste of Home*. That's a total of 512 recipes—all here at your fingertips!

Brimming with color photos and helpful tips from our kitchen experts, each chapter in this collection is designed to fit your lifestyle. On hectic weekdays, turn to "Quick Fixes" to get dinner on the table in a snap. Or impress at your next church supper with the take-along favorites in "Potluck Pleasers."

We've also featured special-occasion treats in "Holiday & Seasonal Celebrations"...slimmed-down dishes in "Cooking Lighter"..."Entrees on a Budget" to save you money...party menus in "Getting in the Theme of Things"...plus 12 other tasty chapters.

You'll even enjoy the winners from *Taste of Home's* six 2010 national recipe contests:

• **Cakes and Tortes.** Any way you slice it, this sweet contest whipped up layers of luscious entries. Our judges awarded the Grand Prize to Chocolate Truffle Cake (p. 108) and gave the Second Prize to Apricot Almond Torte (p. 108).

• **Ground Beef.** Where's the beef? Right here in this meaty competition full of big burgers, chili and more. Pound for pound, nothing could top winning Tacoritos (p. 57) and second-place Roadside Diner Cheeseburger Quiche (p. 54).

• **Lighten Up.** Eating healthier doesn't have to mean sacrificing taste—this competition proved it! You'll satisfy everyone in your family with Chicken Florentine Meatballs (p. 264), the Grand Prize dish, and second-place Sensational Tiramisu (p. 273).

• **Chicken Champs.** For a family dinner tonight or anytime, wing it with these flavorful entrees. Grilled Tomatillo Chicken (p. 62) garnered first place, while Open-Faced Chicken Avocado Burgers (p. 32) came out as the runner-up.

• **Slow Cooker.** The Grand Prizer winner, Slow Cooker Tamale Pie (p. 286), and second-place Spiced Cran-Apple Brisket (p. 60) were fast favorites in this contest. Simply pull out your slow cooker, add the ingredients and let it do the rest of the work for you!

• **Holiday Cookies.** Festive baked treats such as Extra-Special Cashew Crescents (p. 92)—the top winner—and second-place Molasses Cookies with a Kick (p. 96) add a fun, yummy touch to Christmas or any special occasion.

You get all of those prize-winning delights, plus hundreds of other family-favorite appetizers, main courses, side dishes, soups, breads, sandwiches and desserts in *2011 Taste of Home Annual Recipes*. So make this indispensable cookbook part of your own kitchen library, and you'll always have exactly the recipes you need right at your fingertips.

TANTALIZING TREATS. The recipe for cherry-topped Chocolate Malt Desserts (pictured above) was a runner-up in *Taste of Home* magazine's "Lighten Up" recipe contest. That delectable dessert is just one of the better-for-you menu choices featured in this book's "Cooking Lighter" chapter (p. 262).

taste of home
2011 ANNUAL RECIPES

Editor in Chief Catherine Cassidy
Vice President, Executive Editor/Books
Heidi Reuter Lloyd
Creative Director Howard Greenberg
Senior Editor/Books Mark Hagen
Editor Michelle Rozumalski
Art Director Gretchen Trautman
Content Production Supervisor Julie Wagner
Layout Designer Kathy Crawford
Proofreader Linne Bruskewitz
Recipe Asset System Manager Coleen Martin
Administrative Assistant Barb Czysz

North American Chief Marketing Officer
Lisa Karpinski
Vice President/Book Marketing Dan Fink
Creative Director/Creative Marketing James Palmen

taste of home

Executive Editor Christian Millman
Food Director Diane Werner RD
Editor Barbara Schuetz
Food Editor Patricia Schmeling
Associate Editor Cheri Mantz
Recipe Editors Mary King, Christine Rukavena
Copy Editor Susan Uphill
Contributing Designer Dana Borremans
Editorial Assistants Jane Stasik, Joanne Wied
Executive Assistant Marie Brannon

Test Kitchen Manager Karen Scales
Associate Food Editors Alicia Bozewicz RD,
Tina Bellows, Marie Parker, Annie Rundle
Recipe Specialists Jenni Sharp RD, Katie Bartnicki
Test Kitchen Coordinator Kristy Martin
Test Kitchen Associates
Rita Krajcir, Laura Scharnott, Jenny McCarthy
Photo Studio Business Manager Kimberly Gohr
Photographers Rob Hagen, Dan Roberts,
Jim Wieland, Lori Foy
Set Stylists Jenny Bradley Vent, Stephanie Marchese,
Melissa Haberman, Dee Dee Jacq, Deone Jahnke
Food Styling Manager Sarah Thompson
Food Stylists Kaitlyn Besasie, Alynna Malson,
Shannon Roum, Diane Armstrong,
Ronne Day, Kathryn Conrad
Food Stylist Assistant Leah Rekau
Photo Studio Coordinator Kathy Swaney

The Reader's Digest Association, Inc.
President and Chief Executive Officer Mary G. Berner
President, North American Affinities
Suzanne M. Grimes

Taste of Home Books
©2011 Reiman Media Group, Inc.
5400 S. 60th St., Greendale WI 53129

International Standard Book Number (10):
0-89821-823-3
International Standard Book Number (13):
978-0-89821-823-7
International Standard Serial Number: 1094-3463

PICTURED AT RIGHT: Clockwise from upper left:
Greek Deli Kabobs (p. 248), Cashew Curried Beef
(p. 302), Blue Cheese and Bacon Stuffed Mushrooms (p. 15), Coconut Almond Bombs (p. 92) and
Scallops in Sage Cream (p. 246).

2011 taste of home
ANNUAL RECIPES

Snacks & Appetizers 4

Special Salads 16

Soups & Sandwiches 28

Side Dishes & Condiments.....................40

Main Dishes 52

Breads, Rolls & Muffins 76

Cookies, Bars & Candies 90

Cakes & Pies 104

Just Desserts 118

Potluck Pleasers 134

Cooking for One or Two 146

Holiday & Seasonal Celebrations 158

'Mom's Best'..192

Field Editor Favorites 218

Quick Fixes...244

Cooking Lighter 262

Entrees on a Budget..............................276

Getting in the Theme of Things 288

The Cook's Quick Reference.................304

Index 307

PICTURED ON FRONT COVER. Clockwise from upper left: Chocolate-Strawberry Celebration Cake (p. 107), Roasted Vegetable Salad (p. 140) and Herbed Standing Rib Roast (p. 68).

PICTURED ON BACK COVER. Blackberry Cobbler (p. 235).

Front cover photo by Rob Hagen. Food styled by Diane Armstrong. Set styled by Stephanie Marchese.

For other *Taste of Home* books and products, visit *www.ShopTasteofHome.com*.

Snacks & Appetizers

Whether you're hosting a dinner party or just need something wholesome to tide the kids over before dinner, you'll find the perfect finger foods here.

Mamma's Caponata 6
Tapas Meatballs with Orange Glaze.......................6
Bacon Blue Cheese Appetizer 7
Shrimp on Rosemary Skewers 7
Grilled Glazed Drummies..7
Asparagus, Brie & Parma Ham Crostini 8
Seafood & Cream Cheese Stuffed Shells 8
Stuffed Artichoke Bottoms 8
Savory Stuffed Figs 9
Kids' Favorite Pumpkin Seeds................................9
Chicken Salad Caprese 10
Fire-Roasted Tomato Salsa 10
Pretty Stuffed Spring Peas....................................10
Fiesta Shrimp Cocktail..11
Havarti Shrimp Quesadillas 11
Rosemary-Parmesan Popcorn 12
Sweet-Tooth Popcorn..12
Gingerbread Caramel Crunch 12
Tex-Mex Popcorn..13
Buffalo Ranch Popcorn 13
Grilled Greek Crostini Topping 14
Chocolate-Covered Bacon.....................................14
Blue Cheese and Bacon Stuffed Mushrooms 15
Hot Ham & Cheese Slices......................................15

FUN TO MUNCH. Clockwise from top left: Hot Ham & Cheese Slices (p. 15), Mamma's Caponata (p. 6), Chicken Salad Caprese (p. 10), Asparagus, Brie & Parma Ham Crostini (p. 8) and Blue Cheese and Bacon Stuffed Mushrooms (p. 15).

Add the olives, vinegar, sugar, capers, salt and pepper. Return to a boil. Reduce heat; simmer, uncovered, for 20 minutes or until thickened. Serve warm or at room temperature with baguettes. **Yield:** 6 cups.

Nutrition Facts: 1/4 cup (calculated without baguette) equals 57 calories, 4 g fat (1 g saturated fat), 0 cholesterol, 134 mg sodium, 6 g carbohydrate, 2 g fiber, 1 g protein. **Diabetic Exchanges:** 1 vegetable, 1/2 fat.

Tapas Meatballs with Orange Glaze

(Pictured below)

PREP: 25 min. + chilling **BAKE:** 20 min.

Crisp on the outside but moist on the inside, these cheese-stuffed baked hors d'oeuvres are drizzled with a sweet-sour glaze.
—*Bonnie Stallings, Martinsburg, West Virginia*

- 1 egg, beaten
- 1/4 cup ketchup
- 1 small onion, finely chopped
- 1/2 cup soft bread crumbs
- 1/4 cup minced fresh parsley
- 3 teaspoons paprika
- 2 garlic cloves, minced
- 1/2 teaspoon salt
- 1/2 teaspoon pepper
- 1 pound lean ground beef (90% lean)
- 2-1/2 ounces feta cheese, cut into sixteen 1/2-inch cubes

Mamma's Caponata

(Pictured above and on page 5)

PREP: 30 min. **COOK:** 40 min.

My Italian mom has been making this recipe for years. You could also serve the eggplant mixture over warm pasta as an entree.
—*Georgette Stubin, Canton, Michigan*

☑ This recipe includes Nutrition Facts and Diabetic Exchanges.

- 1 large eggplant, peeled and chopped
- 1/4 cup plus 2 tablespoons olive oil, *divided*
- 2 medium onions, chopped
- 2 celery ribs, chopped
- 2 cans (14-1/2 ounces *each*) diced tomatoes, undrained
- 1/3 cup chopped ripe olives
- 1/4 cup red wine vinegar
- 2 tablespoons sugar
- 2 tablespoons capers, drained
- 1/2 teaspoon salt
- 1/2 teaspoon pepper

French bread baguettes, sliced and toasted

In a Dutch oven, saute eggplant in 1/4 cup oil until tender. Remove from the pan and set aside. In the same pan, saute onions and celery in remaining oil until tender. Stir in tomatoes and eggplant. Bring to a boil. Reduce heat; simmer, uncovered, for 15 minutes.

GLAZE:
- 1 jar (12 ounces) orange marmalade
- 1/4 cup orange juice
- 3 green onions, chopped, *divided*
- 1 jalapeno pepper, seeded and chopped

In a large bowl, combine the first nine ingredients. Crumble beef over mixture and mix well.

Divide into 16 portions; flatten. Top each with a cheese cube; form beef mixture around cheese into meatballs. Place on a greased rack in a shallow baking pan. Bake, uncovered, at 400° for 20-25 minutes or until no longer pink.

In a small saucepan, heat the marmalade, orange juice, half of the green onions and the jalapeno.

Place meatballs in a serving dish; pour glaze over top and gently stir to coat. Garnish with remaining green onions. **Yield:** 16 meatballs.

Bacon Blue Cheese Appetizer

PREP/TOTAL TIME: 5 min.

What's easier than a five-minute, three-ingredient recipe? Salty and sweet, this cracker-topper always goes over well with guests.
—Jake Haen, Ocala, Florida

- 1 wedge (8 ounces) blue cheese
- 1 tablespoon honey
- 3 bacon strips, cooked and crumbled
- Assorted crackers

Place blue cheese on a serving dish. Drizzle with honey. Sprinkle with bacon pieces. Serve with crackers. **Yield:** 8 servings.

Shrimp on Rosemary Skewers

PREP: 30 min. **GRILL:** 10 min.

Fresh sprigs of rosemary are the unusual skewers for these tasty kabobs. They can be presented as an appetizer or a main course.
—Amber Joy Newport, Hampton, Virginia

- 8 fresh rosemary sprigs, about 6 inches long
- 1/2 cup orange marmalade
- 1/2 cup flaked coconut, chopped
- 1/4 teaspoon crushed red pepper flakes
- 1/4 teaspoon minced fresh rosemary
- 1-1/2 pounds uncooked large shrimp, peeled and deveined

Soak the rosemary sprigs in water for 30 minutes. In a small bowl, combine marmalade, coconut, pepper and minced rosemary; set aside 1/4 cup for sauce.

Using long-handled tongs, dip a paper towel in cooking oil and lightly coat the grill rack. Thread shrimp onto rosemary sprigs. Grill, covered, over medium heat for 3-4 minutes on each side or until the shrimp turn pink, basting occasionally with remaining marmalade mixture. Serve with sauce. **Yield:** 8 skewers.

Grilled Glazed Drummies

(Pictured above)

PREP: 10 min. + marinating **GRILL:** 15 min.

Ever since I first made this recipe, my family has preferred these mild-tasting chicken wings over traditional hot wings. They're a great choice for a sports party, neighborhood get-together or any casual gathering. Plus, cleanup is a breeze—a nice bonus!
—Laura Mahaffey, Annapolis, Maryland

- 1 cup ketchup
- 1/3 cup soy sauce
- 4 teaspoons honey
- 3/4 teaspoon ground ginger
- 1/2 teaspoon garlic powder
- 3 pounds fresh *or* frozen chicken drumettes, thawed

In a small bowl, combine the first five ingredients. Pour 1 cup marinade into a large resealable plastic bag. Add the chicken; seal bag and turn to coat. Refrigerate for at least 4 hours or overnight. Cover and refrigerate remaining marinade for basting.

Drain chicken and discard marinade. Grill, covered, over medium heat for 15-20 minutes or until juices run clear, turning and basting occasionally with reserved marinade. **Yield:** about 2 dozen.

Asparagus, Brie & Parma Ham Crostini

(Pictured below and on page 4)

PREP/TOTAL TIME: 25 min.

This appetizer is sure to impress—but guests will never guess how easy it is to prepare. The combination of crusty bread, melted Brie cheese and in-season asparagus is out of this world.
—*Karla Johnson, East Helena, Montana*

- 12 **fresh asparagus spears**
- 2 **tablespoons olive oil, *divided***
- 1/8 **teaspoon salt**
- 1/8 **teaspoon pepper**
- 12 **slices French bread baguette (1/2 inch thick)**
- 3 **thin slices prosciutto *or* deli ham, cut into thin strips**
- 6 **ounces Brie cheese, cut into 12 slices**

Cut asparagus tips into 2-in. lengths. Place asparagus tips in a 15-in. x 10-in. x 1-in. baking pan lined with foil. Drizzle with 1 teaspoon oil and toss to coat. Sprinkle with salt and pepper. Bake at 425° for 10-15 minutes or until crisp-tender.

Brush baguette slices on both sides with remaining oil. Place on a baking sheet. Broil for 1-2 minutes on each side or until toasted.

Top each slice with asparagus, prosciutto and cheese. Broil 3-4 in. from the heat for 2-3 minutes or until cheese is melted. **Yield:** 1 dozen.

Seafood & Cream Cheese Stuffed Shells

(Pictured at right)

PREP: 50 min. + chilling

Of all the hors d'oeuvres I've served, this recipe is one of the most popular. Cool, pretty and simple to fix, the stuffed shells have a lovely seafood flavor. Green onions add a nice crunch, too.
—*Suzy Horvath, Sheridan, Oregon*

- 1 **package (12 ounces) jumbo pasta shells**
- 2 **packages (8 ounces *each*) cream cheese, softened**
- 1/3 **cup mayonnaise**
- 2 **teaspoons sugar**
- 1-1/2 **teaspoons lemon juice**
- 1/8 **teaspoon salt**
- 1/8 **teaspoon coarsely ground pepper**
- 1/8 **teaspoon cayenne pepper**
- 3 **cans (6 ounces *each*) lump crabmeat, drained**
- 1/2 **pound frozen cooked salad shrimp, thawed**
- 12 **green onions, finely chopped**

Cook pasta according to package directions; drain and rinse in cold water. Cool to room temperature.

In a large bowl, combine cream cheese, mayonnaise, sugar, lemon juice, salt, pepper and cayenne. Gently stir in the crab, shrimp and onions. Stuff shells, about 2 tablespoons in each. Cover and refrigerate for at least 1 hour. **Yield:** 3 dozen.

Stuffed Artichoke Bottoms

(Pictured above right)

PREP: 15 min. **BAKE:** 25 min.

These creamy, quick bites are really yummy and fuss-free for the hostess. I like to stuff the artichoke bottoms ahead of time, then pop them in the oven and serve them with cocktail forks.
—*Sandi Vanthoff, Henderson, Nevada*

- 2 **cans (14 ounces *each*) artichoke bottoms, drained**
- 2 **packages (one 8 ounces, one 3 ounces) cream cheese, softened**
- 3 **garlic cloves, minced**
- 2 **teaspoons minced chives**
- 1 **teaspoon minced fresh oregano *or* 1/4 teaspoon dried oregano**
- 1/2 **cup grated Parmesan cheese**

Cut a thin slice from bottoms of artichokes to level if necessary. Place in a greased 15-in. x 10-in. x 1-in. baking pan.

In a small bowl, combine the cream cheese, garlic, chives and oregano. Spoon into artichokes; sprinkle with Parmesan cheese. Bake at 350° for 22-26 minutes or until cheese is golden brown. **Yield:** 1-1/2 dozen.

Savory Stuffed Figs

(Pictured above)

PREP: 30 min. **GRILL:** 5 min.

Figs may not come to mind when you think of mouthwatering munchies, but they will after you sample these! The little grilled morsels are delicious. —Maggie Zabinko, Anchorage, Alaska

☑ **This recipe includes Nutrition Facts and Diabetic Exchanges.**

  12 bacon strips
  24 dried figs
  24 pecan halves

Cut bacon strips in half widthwise. In a large skillet, cook bacon over medium heat until partially cooked but not crisp. Remove to paper towels to drain; keep warm.

  Cut a lengthwise slit down the center of each fig; fill with a pecan half. Wrap each with a piece of bacon.

  Grill, covered, over medium heat or broil 4 in. from the heat for 5-8 minutes or until bacon is crisp, turning once. **Yield:** 2 dozen.

  Nutrition Facts: 1 stuffed fig equals 80 calories, 2 g fat (1 g saturated fat), 3 mg cholesterol, 75 mg sodium, 13 g carbohydrate, 2 g fiber, 2 g protein. **Diabetic Exchanges:** 1 fruit, 1/2 fat.

Kids' Favorite Pumpkin Seeds

PREP: 5 min. **BAKE:** 45 min. + cooling

My children love these pumpkin seeds and want them every fall. A little bit of pulp in the mix really adds to the flavor, so don't rinse the seeds. —Gwyn Reiber, Spokane, Washington

  2 cups fresh pumpkin seeds
  1/4 cup butter, melted
  1/2 teaspoon garlic salt
  1/4 teaspoon cayenne pepper
  1/4 teaspoon Worcestershire sauce

In a small bowl, combine all ingredients; transfer to an ungreased 15-in. x 10-in. x 1-in. baking pan.

  Bake at 250° for 45-50 minutes or until lightly browned and dry, stirring occasionally. Cool completely. Store in an airtight container. **Yield:** 2 cups.

baking sheets. Bake at 425° for 2-4 minutes or until lightly browned. Cut garlic in half lengthwise; rub over bread. Cut tomatoes into quarters; rub over bread. Brush with oil and sprinkle with salt. Bake 2-3 minutes longer or until crisp. Serve crostini with salad. **Yield:** 8 cups salad (6-1/2 dozen crostini).

Fire-Roasted Tomato Salsa

PREP: 30 min. + chilling

I love the smoky kick this salsa gets from the chipotle pepper. The recipe makes a big batch, but it doesn't last a day in our house.
—*Pamela Paula, Weeki Wachee, Florida*

- **2 pounds tomatoes (about 6 medium)**
- **1 jalapeno pepper**
- **1/2 cup fresh cilantro leaves**
- **2 green onions, cut into 2-inch pieces**
- **4 garlic cloves, peeled**
- **1 chipotle pepper in adobo sauce**
- **1 can (4 ounces) chopped green chilies**
- **2 tablespoons lime juice**
- **1 tablespoon olive oil**
- **1/4 teaspoon salt**
Tortilla chips

Grill tomatoes and jalapeno, covered, over medium-hot heat for 8-12 minutes or until skins are blistered and blackened, turning occasionally. Immediately place in a large bowl; cover and let stand for 20 minutes.

Peel off and discard charred skins. Discard stem and seeds from jalapeno; cut tomatoes into fourths. Set jalapeno and tomatoes aside. Place the cilantro, onions and garlic in a food processor; cover and process until blended. Add chipotle pepper, tomatoes and jalapeno; cover and pulse until blended.

Transfer to a bowl; stir in the chilies, lime juice, oil and salt. Cover and refrigerate for at least 1 hour. Serve with chips. **Yield:** 4 cups.

Editor's Note: When cutting hot peppers, disposable gloves are recommended. Avoid touching your face.

Chicken Salad Caprese

(Pictured above and on page 5)

PREP: 40 min. **BAKE:** 5 min.

You may need a fork to eat this hearty appetizer. With tomatoes, Greek olives and more, it's loaded with Mediterranean flavor.
—*Frances Pietsch, Flower Mound, Texas*

- **2 cups shredded rotisserie chicken**
- **1 pound fresh mozzarella cheese, cubed**
- **2 cups grape tomatoes, halved**
- **1 can (14 ounces) water-packed artichoke hearts, rinsed, drained and coarsely chopped**
- **1/2 cup pitted Greek olives, thinly sliced**
- **1/4 cup minced fresh basil**
- **1/4 cup olive oil**
- **2 garlic cloves, minced**
- **1/2 teaspoon salt**
- **1/2 teaspoon coarsely ground pepper**
TOMATO CROSTINI:
- **2 French bread baguettes (10-1/2 ounces *each*)**
- **4 garlic cloves**
- **2 small tomatoes**
- **1/4 cup olive oil**
- **1 teaspoon salt**

In a large bowl, combine the first six ingredients. In a small bowl, whisk the oil, garlic, salt and pepper; drizzle over the chicken mixture and toss to coat. Refrigerate until serving.

Cut baguettes into 1/2-in. slices. Place on ungreased

Pretty Stuffed Spring Peas

PREP: 30 min. + chilling

These yummy stuffed peas are the perfect way to welcome spring. I serve them on a platter surrounded by fresh strawberries.
—*Phyllis Cooper, Yarmouth Port, Maryland*

- **1 package (8 ounces) cream cheese, softened**
- **2 teaspoons minced chives**
- **1 teaspoon dried basil**
- **1 garlic clove, minced**
- **1/2 teaspoon caraway seeds**
- **1/2 teaspoon dill weed**
- **1/4 teaspoon lemon-pepper seasoning**
- **36 fresh snow peas (about 1/4 pound), trimmed**

In a large bowl, combine the first seven ingredients. Cover and refrigerate overnight.

Let filling stand at room temperature for 30 minutes. Meanwhile, in a large saucepan, bring 6 cups water to a boil. Add snow peas; cover and boil for 1-2 minutes. Drain and immediately place peas in ice water. Drain and pat dry. Gently split the peas open; pipe about 1 teaspoonful of filling into each pod. **Yield:** 3 dozen.

Fiesta Shrimp Cocktail

(Pictured below)

PREP: 20 min. + chilling

I make this zippy hors d'oeuvre when I have dinner parties, and it's always a hit. Impress guests by serving it in a martini glass or other fancy stemware. —Linda Stemen, Monroeville, Indiana

- 1 **pound cooked medium shrimp, peeled and deveined**
- 1 **medium tomato, chopped**
- 1/2 **cup Italian salad dressing**
- 1 **can (4 ounces) chopped green chilies**
- 3 **green onions, thinly sliced**
- 2 **teaspoons honey**
- 1/8 **teaspoon hot pepper sauce**
- 2 **tablespoons minced fresh cilantro**

Romaine leaves

In a large bowl, combine the first eight ingredients. Cover and refrigerate for at least 1 hour.

Arrange romaine in eight cocktail glasses or serving dishes. Using a slotted spoon, add about 1/2 cup shrimp mixture to each. **Yield:** 6 servings.

Havarti Shrimp Quesadillas

(Pictured above)

PREP/TOTAL TIME: 25 min.

Apricot preserves bring a touch of sweetness to the mushrooms, shrimp and Havarti cheese inside these grilled quesadillas. You could also cook them in a hot skillet until lightly browned. —Susan Manning, Burlington, North Carolina

- 1/2 **pound fresh mushrooms, chopped**
- 1 **tablespoon canola oil**
- 1 **tablespoon butter**
- 6 **tablespoons apricot preserves**
- 6 **flour tortillas (10 inches)**
- 6 **ounces Havarti cheese, thinly sliced**
- 1/2 **pound cooked peeled deveined shrimp, chopped**
- 2 **tablespoons butter, melted**

In a large skillet, saute mushrooms in oil and butter until tender. Spread 1 tablespoon preserves over half of each tortilla; top with cheese, shrimp and mushrooms. Fold tortillas over. Brush both sides with melted butter.

Grill quesadillas, uncovered, over medium heat for 1-2 minutes on each side or until golden brown and cheese is melted. Cut each quesadilla into four wedges. Serve warm. **Yield:** 2 dozen.

Popcorn with Pizzazz

OCTOBER is popcorn month...but you don't need to wait for the fall season before enjoying these peppy recipes. Each one jazzes up plain popcorn in a flavorful new way.

Just choose your favorite variety, from ranch and caramel to rosemary-Parmesan and Tex-Mex. Whether you're craving something sweet or spicy, you'll find the perfect choice here.

So why settle for boring corn when you can munch a special treat? Surprise everyone during your next movie night, sports party or lazy weekend afternoon with an eye-popping snack they'll grab by the handful.

Rosemary-Parmesan Popcorn

(Pictured below)

PREP/TOTAL TIME: 20 min.

Adults are sure to enjoy the savory herb and cheese flavor of this gourmet-style popcorn, but you might have to share it with the kids, too! —Dan Kelmenson, West Bloomfield, Michigan

- 1/4 cup fresh rosemary leaves
- 10 cups popped popcorn
- 1/4 cup butter, melted
- 3 tablespoons grated Parmesan cheese
- 1/2 teaspoon salt
- 1/4 teaspoon coarsely ground pepper

Place rosemary on a baking sheet. Bake at 300° for 10 minutes or until crisp. Finely chop rosemary or crush using a mortar and pestle; set aside.

Place popcorn in a large bowl; drizzle with butter. Sprinkle with cheese, salt, pepper and rosemary; toss to coat. **Yield:** 10 cups.

Sweet-Tooth Popcorn

PREP: 25 min. + standing

I like to be creative with this recipe and add different ingredients to make it festive for holidays. The sweet and salty combination is addictive! —Daynna Puckett, Broken Bow, Oklahoma

- 1 package (3.3 ounces) butter-flavored microwave popcorn
- 1 pound white candy coating, chopped
- 1 cup peanut M&M's
- 1 cup Reese's pieces
- 1 cup salted cashews
- 1 cup pecan halves

Microwave popcorn according to package directions. Place in a large bowl. In a microwave, melt candy coating; stir until smooth. Pour over popcorn and stir until coated. Combine M&M's, Reese's pieces, cashews and pecans; stir into popcorn mixture. Immediately spread onto waxed paper; let stand until set. Break into pieces. Store in an airtight container. **Yield:** 4 quarts.

Gingerbread Caramel Crunch

PREP: 25 min. **BAKE:** 1 hour

If you love gingerbread, you won't be able to resist this crispy, crunchy corn. Munch it yourself or share it as a yummy gift. —Lynne Weigle-Snow, Alexandria, Virginia

- 14 cups air-popped popcorn
- 3/4 cup packed brown sugar
- 1/2 cup butter, cubed
- 1/4 cup light corn syrup
- 1/4 cup molasses
- 1-1/2 teaspoons ground ginger
- 1/2 teaspoon ground cinnamon
- 1/4 teaspoon salt
- 1/2 teaspoon baking soda
- 1/2 teaspoon vanilla extract

Place popcorn in a large bowl coated with cooking spray; set aside. Butter the sides of a small heavy saucepan; add the brown sugar, butter, corn syrup,

1 teaspoon chili powder
1/2 teaspoon garlic powder
1/8 teaspoon smoked paprika

In a Dutch oven over medium heat, cook the popcorn kernels, oil and cumin seeds until oil begins to sizzle. Cover and shake for 2-3 minutes or until the popcorn stops popping.

Transfer to a large bowl; spritz with butter-flavored spray. Add remaining ingredients and toss to coat. Continue spritzing and tossing until popcorn is coated. Serve immediately. **Yield:** 4 quarts.

Nutrition Facts: 1 cup equals 44 calories, 3 g fat (trace saturated fat), 0 cholesterol, 150 mg sodium, 5 g carbohydrate, 1 g fiber, 1 g protein.

Buffalo Ranch Popcorn

(Pictured below)

PREP/TOTAL TIME: 10 min.

This zippy recipe will perk up your favorite snack food with the taste of buffalo wings. Try it when friends come over to watch the big game on TV. —Jenny McCarthy, Sussex, Wisconsin

16 cups popped popcorn
1/3 cup buffalo wing sauce
2 tablespoons butter, melted
1/8 teaspoon cayenne pepper
1 tablespoon ranch salad dressing mix
Additional cayenne pepper to taste

Place popcorn in a large bowl. In a small bowl, combine the wing sauce, butter and cayenne; drizzle over the popcorn and toss to coat. Sprinkle with the dressing mix and additional cayenne to taste; toss to coat. **Yield:** 4 quarts.

molasses, ginger, cinnamon and salt. Bring to a boil over medium heat, stirring constantly. Boil without stirring for 5 minutes.

Remove from the heat; stir in baking soda (mixture will foam). Stir in vanilla. Quickly pour over popcorn and mix well.

Transfer to two greased 15-in. x 10-in. x 1-in. baking pans. Bake at 250° for 1 hour, stirring every 10 minutes. Remove from pans and place on waxed paper to cool. Store in an airtight container. **Yield:** 3-1/2 quarts.

Tex-Mex Popcorn

(Pictured above)

PREP/TOTAL TIME: 15 min.

A spicy Southwestern seasoning blend makes this snackin'–good popcorn ideal for any fiesta. —Katie Rose, Pewaukee, Wisconsin

✓ This recipe includes Nutrition Facts.

1/2 cup popcorn kernels
3 tablespoons canola oil
1/2 teaspoon cumin seeds
Refrigerated butter-flavored spray
1/4 cup minced fresh cilantro
1 teaspoon salt

POPPING IN. Remember these helpful hints when coating plain popcorn:
• Pour the coating over the popcorn while it's still warm so the popcorn coats more evenly.
• Before coating, sift through the popped corn for any unpopped kernels.

Chocolate-Covered Bacon

(Pictured below)

PREP: 20 min. **BAKE:** 20 min.

Chocolate and bacon might sound like a strange combination, but give these a try—you'll be glad you did! The home economists in the Taste of Home Test Kitchen got the inspiration for this fun-to-make-and-eat novelty from the Wisconsin State Fair. Use one of the toppings listed or experiment with your own.

- **12 thick-sliced bacon strips (about 1 pound)**
- **12 wooden skewers (12 inches)**
- **6 ounces white candy coating, chopped**
- **1 cup semisweet chocolate chips**
- **1 tablespoon shortening**
- **Optional toppings: chopped dried apple chips, apricots and crystallized ginger, finely chopped pecans and pistachios, toasted coconut, kosher salt, brown sugar, cayenne pepper and coarsely ground black pepper**

Thread each bacon strip onto a wooden skewer. Place on a rack in a large baking pan. Bake at 400° for 20-25 minutes or until crisp. Cool completely.

In a microwave, melt candy coating; stir until smooth. Combine chocolate chips and shortening; melt in a microwave and stir until smooth.

With pastry brushes, coat the bacon strips on both sides with the melted coatings. Top each strip as desired. Place strips on waxed paper-lined baking sheets. Refrigerate until firm. Store in the refrigerator. **Yield:** 1 dozen.

Grilled Greek Crostini Topping

(Pictured above)

PREP/TOTAL TIME: 20 min.

I came up with the idea for this easy appetizer while I was on vacation in Greece. The little topped toasts are ideal for summer because you can pop them on the grill at a backyard cookout. Plus, the recipe calls for only bread and five other ingredients.
—Stephanie Proebsting, Barrington, Illinois

- **9 slices tomato**
- **1/2 pound feta cheese, cut into six slices**
- **1 tablespoon minced fresh oregano or 1 teaspoon dried oregano**
- **1 tablespoon olive oil**
- **Ground pepper**
- **Sliced French bread baguette, toasted**

Arrange three tomato slices in a single layer on a double thickness of heavy-duty foil (about 12 in. square). Top with two slices feta cheese, 1 teaspoon oregano and 1 teaspoon oil. Sprinkle with a dash of pepper. Repeat layers twice.

Fold foil around the mixture and seal tightly. Grill, covered, over medium heat for 8-10 minutes or until heated through.

Open foil carefully to allow steam to escape. Transfer to a serving platter; serve with toasted baguette. **Yield:** 8 servings.

Stuff the mixture into the mushroom caps, a scant tablespoonful in each.

Place in a greased 15-in. x 10-in. x 1-in. baking pan. Sprinkle with remaining bacon bits. Bake, uncovered, at 375° for 18-22 minutes or until mushrooms are tender. **Yield:** 2 dozen.

Hot Ham & Cheese Slices

(Pictured below and on page 4)

PREP/TOTAL TIME: 10 min.

These crispy puff pastry pockets not only make great snacks, but they're also a nice dinner on busy nights because they go together in 10 minutes. Everyone loves this super-easy twist on traditional ham and cheese. —Pat Stevens, Granbury, Texas

- **1 cup sliced fresh mushrooms**
- **1 small sweet red pepper, chopped**
- **2 green onions, chopped**
- **2 tablespoons butter**
- **1 package (17.3 ounces) frozen puff pastry, thawed**
- **1/2 pound thinly sliced deli ham**
- **1/2 pound sliced Swiss cheese**

In a large skillet, saute the mushrooms, pepper and onions in butter until tender. Set aside.

Unfold pastry. Layer the ham, cheese and mushroom mixture off-center on each sheet of pastry. Fold pastry over filling; pinch the seams to seal. Place in a greased 15-in. x 10-in. x 1-in. baking pan.

Bake at 400° for 18-22 minutes or until golden brown. Let stand for 5 minutes. Cut each with a serrated knife into 4 slices. **Yield:** 8 servings.

Blue Cheese and Bacon Stuffed Mushrooms

(Pictured above and on page 4)

PREP: 30 min. **BAKE:** 20 min.

A rich, warm and cheesy version of classic stuffed mushrooms, this attractive appetizer is perfect for your next dinner party or other special event. —Kristen Woodburn, Atlanta, Georgia

- **24 large fresh mushrooms**
- **1 carton (8 ounces) reduced-fat spreadable chive and onion cream cheese**
- **1 cup (4 ounces) crumbled blue cheese**
- **4 green onions, chopped**
- **2 garlic cloves, minced**
- **3/4 cup bacon bits,** *divided*

Remove stems from mushrooms and set caps aside; discard stems or save for another use.

In a small bowl, combine the cream cheese, blue cheese, green onions, garlic and 1/4 cup bacon bits.

MUSHROOM METHOD. Want to serve tasty Blue Cheese and Bacon Stuffed Mushrooms (recipe above) at your next get-together? It's easy!

When making stuffed mushrooms, start by removing the stems. Then scoop out some of the inside of each mushroom with a small round teaspoon (1/8 or 1/4 teaspoon).

After making the stuffing mixture, use the same teaspoon to easily stuff the mixture into the caps.

Special Salads

Fresh greens are just the start of the mouthwatering medleys featured here, from meaty main dishes to creamy gelatin and picnic-perfect coleslaw.

Tangy Ginger Slaw.................................18
Three-Potato Salad................................18
Cranberry Broccoli Salad....................18
Garden Cobb Salad...............................19
Cheddar 'n' Pea Tossed Salad.............19
Ginger Salmon Salad...........................20
Honey-Mustard Turkey Salad 20
Greek Potato Salad 21
Cherry Wild Rice Salad 21
Spiced-Up Chicken Salad 22
Mom's Gingered Apple Salad 22
Italian Cucumber Salad........................23
Nectarine, Prosciutto & Endive Salad 23
Poppy Seed Chicken Salad 24
Horseradish Coleslaw...........................24
Tomato Tossed Salad............................24
Tossed Salad with Peaches..................25
Grilled Steak and Mushroom Salad.....25
Four-Berry Spinach Salad 26
Creamy Cranberry Gelatin 26
Pineapple Coleslaw 26
Tangy Potato Salad 27
Bean & Barley Salad.............................27

DRESSED-UP DELIGHTS. Clockwise from top left: Cheddar 'n' Pea Tossed Salad (p. 19), Tossed Salad with Peaches (p. 25), Mom's Gingered Apple Salad (p. 22), Poppy Seed Chicken Salad (p. 24) and Tangy Ginger Slaw (p. 19).

garlic, ginger, sugar, salt and pepper flakes. Pour over cabbage mixture; toss to coat. Cover and refrigerate for at least 1 hour. Sprinkle with sesame seeds just before serving. **Yield:** 2 cups.

Nutrition Facts: 2/3 cup equals 48 calories, 2 g fat (trace saturated fat), 0 cholesterol, 119 mg sodium, 7 g carbohydrate, 2 g fiber, 1 g protein. **Diabetic Exchanges:** 1 vegetable, 1/2 fat.

Three-Potato Salad

PREP: 30 min. + chilling

This picnic-perfect salad is among the most popular in our farm market deli. Sweet potato and dill make a great combination.
—*Pamela Hershey, Parkesburg, Pennsylvania*

- **3 medium potatoes, peeled**
- **3 medium red potatoes, peeled**
- **1 large sweet potato, peeled and halved**
- **1 cup mayonnaise**
- **2 tablespoons sugar**
- **1 tablespoon white vinegar**
- **1 teaspoon salt**
- **3/4 teaspoon dill weed**
- **1/2 teaspoon pepper**
- **1 medium sweet onion, chopped**

Place the potatoes in a large saucepan and cover with water. Bring to a boil. Reduce heat; cover and cook for 30-40 minutes or until potatoes are just tender.

Meanwhile, in a small bowl, whisk the mayonnaise, sugar, vinegar, salt, dill and pepper.

Drain the potatoes; cube and place in a large serving bowl. Cool slightly. Add onion and dressing; stir gently to coat. Cover and refrigerate for 2 hours or overnight. **Yield:** 12 servings.

Cranberry Broccoli Salad

PREP/TOTAL TIME: 15 min.

Our state is a top producer of cranberries, so I've nicknamed this recipe Wisconsin Salad. It features sweetened dried cranberries, which our family produces from the crop we harvest each fall.
—*Cheryl Urban, Wisconsin Rapids, Wisconsin*

- **4 cups fresh broccoli florets**
- **1 cup dried cranberries**
- **1/2 to 3/4 cup sliced red onion**
- **1/3 cup crumbled cooked bacon**
- **1/2 cup mayonnaise**
- **1/2 cup half-and-half cream**
- **3 tablespoons sugar**

In a large salad bowl, combine the broccoli, cranberries, onion and bacon. In a small bowl, combine mayonnaise, cream and sugar until smooth. Pour over the broccoli mixture and toss to coat. Refrigerate until serving. **Yield:** 6 servings.

Tangy Ginger Slaw

(Pictured above and on page 16)

PREP: 30 min. + chilling

Crunchy and tart with an Asian twist, this fresh-tasting slaw is ideal for a backyard barbecue or a lunch box. The recipe makes a smaller amount for just a few people, but you could easily double or triple it. —*Joanna Trupiano, Gloucester, Massachusetts*

✓ This recipe includes Nutrition Facts and Diabetic Exchanges.

- **2 cups shredded cabbage**
- **1 small carrot, shredded**
- **2 tablespoons finely chopped sweet onion**
- **1 to 2 radishes, shredded**
- **2 tablespoons white balsamic vinegar**
- **1-1/2 teaspoons lime juice**
- **1 teaspoon sesame oil**
- **1 garlic clove, minced**
- **1/2 teaspoon minced fresh gingerroot**
- **1/4 teaspoon sugar**
- **1/8 teaspoon salt**
- **1/8 teaspoon crushed red pepper flakes**
- **1/2 teaspoon sesame seeds, toasted**

In a small bowl, combine the cabbage, carrot, onion and radishes. In another bowl, whisk vinegar, lime juice, oil,

Garden Cobb Salad

(Pictured below)

PREP: 30 min. + chilling

This sensational salad is my favorite for a ladies' lunch...but men and kids eat it up, too. Serving it in a pretty flowerpot makes a festive presentation and emphasizes its garden–fresh goodness.
—Christine Panzarella, Buena Park, California

    1 cup (8 ounces) sour cream
  1/2 cup mayonnaise
  1/4 cup crumbled blue cheese
    2 teaspoons cider vinegar
  1/2 teaspoon salt
  1/4 teaspoon pepper
    8 to 10 romaine leaves
   12 cups torn mixed salad greens
    8 thick-sliced bacon strips, cooked and crumbled
    1 cup diced avocado
    1 cup finely chopped cooked chicken breast
    1 cup chopped seeded tomatoes
    2 hard-cooked eggs, chopped
Edible pansies, optional

For dressing, in a small bowl, combine the sour cream, mayonnaise, blue cheese, vinegar, salt and pepper. Cover and refrigerate for at least 1 hour.

Line an 8-in. decorative flowerpot with plastic wrap or use a serving bowl. Arrange romaine around the edge; fill with mixed greens.

Arrange the bacon, avocado, chicken, tomatoes and eggs in a spoke pattern over the greens. Garnish salad

with edible pansies if desired. Serve with the prepared dressing. **Yield:** 6 servings.

Editor's Note: Make sure to properly identify flowers before picking. Double-check that they're edible and have not been treated with chemicals.

Cheddar 'n' Pea Tossed Salad

(Pictured above and on page 16)

PREP/TOTAL TIME: 10 min.

My family says, "Yes!" when they see me preparing this easy, colorful salad full of cheese and veggies. We live on a farm, and our garden is a handy source for salad ingredients each summer.
—Mandy Cmoc, Yorkton, Saskatchewan

    5 cups ready-to-serve salad greens
    1 medium cucumber, sliced
    1 medium tomato, chopped
    1 cup cubed cheddar cheese
  1/2 cup frozen peas, thawed
    2 tablespoons vegetable oil
    1 tablespoon white vinegar
  1/4 teaspoon sugar
  1/8 teaspoon onion powder
Dash salt and pepper

In a large bowl, combine the salad greens, cucumber, tomato, cheese and peas.

In a jar with a tight-fitting lid, combine oil, vinegar, sugar, onion powder, salt and pepper; shake well. Drizzle over salad and toss gently. Serve immediately. **Yield:** 8 servings.

Ginger Salmon Salad

(Pictured below)

PREP/TOTAL TIME: 15 min.

After trying something similar at a restaurant, I duplicated this salad from taste and memory at home. It's a cinch to prepare and cooks in no time. If you prefer, you can easily replace the mango with another fruit depending on what's in season.
—*Nancee Melin, Tucson, Arizona*

- 2/3 **cup lime juice**
- 1/2 **cup honey**
- 1/2 **teaspoon minced fresh gingerroot**
- 4 **salmon fillets (6 ounces *each*), skin removed**
- 1/4 **teaspoon salt**
- 1 **package (5 ounces) spring mix salad greens**
- 1 **cup sliced peeled mango**

In a small bowl, combine the lime juice, honey and ginger; set aside 1/2 cup for serving.

Place the salmon fillets on a broiler pan coated with cooking spray. Spoon 1/2 cup lime juice mixture over salmon. Broil 4-6 in. from the heat for 4-5 minutes on each side or until fish flakes easily with a fork, basting occasionally with the remaining lime juice mixture. Sprinkle with salt.

Divide the spring mix salad greens among four salad plates; top each salad with a salmon fillet and mango. Drizzle the salads with the reserved lime juice mixture. **Yield:** 4 servings.

Honey-Mustard Turkey Salad

(Pictured above)

PREP: 25 min. **COOK:** 10 min.

Pecans break out of the dessert "shell" in this mouthwatering main-dish salad from our Test Kitchen cooks. The nutty crunch complements the mix of turkey, red onion, blue cheese and more.

- 1/2 **cup olive oil**
- 1/4 **cup honey**
- 3 **tablespoons white wine vinegar**
- 2 **teaspoons plus 2 tablespoons Dijon mustard, *divided***
- 1/2 **teaspoon minced garlic**
- 3/4 **teaspoon salt, *divided***
- 3 **tablespoons plus 1/4 cup all-purpose flour, *divided***
- 3 **egg whites**
- 2 **tablespoons water**
- 1-1/3 **cups ground pecans**
- 1 **package (17.6 ounces) turkey breast slices**
- 1/4 **cup butter, cubed**
- 1 **package (16 ounces) ready-to-serve salad greens**
- 3 **medium tart apples, sliced**
- 1 **medium red onion, sliced**
- 2 **cups salad croutons**
- 1 **cup (4 ounces) crumbled blue cheese**

For the dressing, in a jar with a tight-fitting lid, combine the oil, honey, vinegar, 2 teaspoons mustard, garlic and 1/4 teaspoon salt; shake well. Set aside.

Place 3 tablespoons flour in a shallow bowl. In a second bowl, combine the egg whites, water and remaining mustard. In a third bowl, combine the pecans and remaining salt and flour. Coat turkey with flour; dip into mustard mixture, then coat with pecan mixture.

In a large skillet over medium heat, cook the turkey slices in butter in batches for 2-3 minutes on each side or until no longer pink. Keep warm.

In a large bowl, combine the greens, apples, onion and croutons. Shake dressing and pour over salad; toss to coat. Divide among salad bowls. Cut turkey into thin slices; arrange over salads. Sprinkle with blue cheese. **Yield:** 7 servings.

Greek Potato Salad

(Pictured below)

PREP: 25 min. **COOK:** 15 min. + cooling

This is my original recipe, which was inspired by a salad I had ordered in a restaurant. I've served it to many friends, always with rave reviews. It's very flavorful and impressive.
—*Roberta Webster, Hampton, Florida*

    5 **cups cubed peeled potatoes**
  1/2 **cup white wine vinegar**
  1/3 **cup sugar**
    1 **tablespoon olive oil**
3-1/2 **teaspoons dried oregano,** *divided*
1-1/2 **cups mayonnaise**
  1/2 **teaspoon salt**
    1 **bunch leaf lettuce, shredded**
Cherry tomatoes, halved, optional

Place the potatoes in a large saucepan and cover with water. Bring to a boil. Reduce the heat; cover and cook for 10-15 minutes or until tender. Drain and cool to room temperature.

In a small bowl, combine the vinegar, sugar, oil and 1/2 teaspoon oregano; set aside. In a large bowl, combine the mayonnaise, salt and remaining oregano. Add potatoes and toss to coat. Cover and refrigerate until chilled.

Just before serving, toss lettuce with the vinegar mixture; place on a serving platter. Top with potato salad. Garnish with cherry tomatoes if desired. **Yield:** 10 servings.

Cherry Wild Rice Salad

(Pictured above)

PREP/TOTAL TIME: 25 min.

While touring Door County, Wisconsin, I sampled this salad. As soon as I got home, I wrote the lady who'd made it and requested the recipe! The blend of rice, veggies and orchard–fresh fruit is a tasty way to remember Wisconsin's premier cherry–growing area.
—*Yvonne Gorges, New London, Wisconsin*

    2 **cups fresh snow peas, halved**
    2 **cups cooked wild rice**
    1 **cup cooked long grain rice**
    1 **can (8 ounces) sliced water chestnuts, drained**
    1 **cup dried cherries**
  1/2 **cup thinly sliced celery**
  1/4 **cup chopped green onions**
DRESSING:
    6 **tablespoons sugar**
    6 **tablespoons vegetable oil**
    3 **tablespoons cider vinegar**
4-1/2 **teaspoons soy sauce**
    1 **to 2 garlic cloves, peeled**
  3/4 **teaspoon minced fresh gingerroot**
  3/4 **cup cashew halves, toasted**

In a large bowl, combine the first seven ingredients. For dressing, in a blender, combine the sugar, oil, vinegar, soy sauce, garlic and ginger; cover and process until blended. Pour over the rice mixture and toss to coat. Cover and refrigerate until serving. Just before serving, stir in the cashews. **Yield:** 6-8 servings.

In a small saucepan, combine the lime juice, brown sugar, basil, mint, soy sauce, 1/2 teaspoon garlic and ginger. Slowly whisk in oil; set aside.

In a large nonstick skillet coated with cooking spray, saute chicken until no longer pink. Add the jalapeno, salt, white pepper, paprika and remaining garlic; saute 1 minute longer.

Place salad greens on a large platter; top with red peppers, cucumber and chicken. Bring lime juice mixture to a boil; drizzle over salad. Serve immediately. **Yield:** 6 servings.

Editor's Note: When cutting or seeding hot peppers, use rubber or plastic gloves to protect your hands. Avoid touching your face.

Mom's Gingered Apple Salad

(Pictured below and on page 17)

PREP/TOTAL TIME: 15 min.

Here's a refreshing twist on the classic Waldorf salad. Seasoned with crystallized ginger, dried cranberries and water chestnuts, this combo is quick and tasty. Prepared with reduced-fat mayo, the creamy homemade dressing is also a little lighter.
—Rebekah Radewahn, Wauwatosa, Wisconsin

- 3 **medium apples, chopped**
- 1 **can (8 ounces) water chestnuts, drained and finely chopped**
- 2 **celery ribs, finely chopped**
- 1/2 **cup dried cranberries**
- 3 **tablespooons crystallized ginger, finely chopped**

Spiced-Up Chicken Salad

(Pictured above)

PREP/TOTAL TIME: 30 min.

The deliciously different combination of basil and mint in the made-from-scratch salad dressing adds fresh appeal to this outstanding chicken entree. The recipe comes tried-and-true from family cooks and is sure to please everyone at your table.
—Iola Egle, McCook, Nebraska

- 1/3 **cup lime juice**
- 2 **tablespoons brown sugar**
- 1 **tablespoon minced fresh basil** *or* **1 teaspoon dried basil**
- 1 **tablespoon minced fresh mint** *or* **1 teaspoon dried mint**
- 1 **tablespoon soy sauce**
- 1-1/2 **teaspoons minced garlic,** *divided*
- 1/4 **teaspoon ground ginger**
- 1/4 **cup olive oil**
- 1-1/2 **pounds boneless skinless chicken breasts, cut into strips**
- 1 **jalapeno pepper, seeded and chopped**
- 1/4 **teaspoon salt**
- 1/8 **teaspoon white pepper**
- 1/8 **teaspoon paprika**
- 1 **package (5 ounces) spring mix salad greens**
- 2 **large sweet red peppers, julienned**
- 1 **small cucumber, halved and sliced**

    1/2 cup vanilla yogurt
    1/4 cup reduced-fat mayonnaise
      2 tablespooons sugar
    1/4 to 1/2 teaspoon ground ginger
    1/8 teaspoon salt
    1/4 cup chopped pecans, toasted

In a large bowl, combine the first five ingredients.
Combine the yogurt, mayonnaise, sugar, ginger and
salt; pour over the apple mixture and toss to coat. Chill
until serving.
    Just before serving, sprinkle with the pecans. **Yield:**
6 servings.

Italian Cucumber Salad

PREP/TOTAL TIME: 10 min.

*This simple veggie side dish always goes over well. I came up with
the recipe after sampling a similar salad at a local cafeteria.
When you don't have a lot of time to spare, it's great to have a
five-ingredient, 10-minute option like this one on hand.*
    —Jane Nichols, Houston, Texas

☑ This recipe includes Nutrition Facts and Diabetic Exchanges.

      2 medium cucumbers, peeled and sliced
      1 cup halved cherry tomatoes
      1 cup sliced red onion
    1/2 cup chopped green pepper
    1/2 cup Italian salad dressing

In a large bowl, combine all of the ingredients; cover
and refrigerate until serving. Serve with a slotted
spoon. **Yield:** 6 servings.
    Nutrition Facts: 1 serving equals 106 calories, 8 g fat
(1 g saturated fat), 0 cholesterol, 341 mg sodium, 8 g
carbohydrate, 2 g fiber, 2 g protein. **Diabetic
Exchanges:** 1-1/2 fat, 1 vegetable.

Nectarine, Prosciutto & Endive Salad

(Pictured above right)

PREP: 50 min. + cooling

*A drizzle of tangy-sweet dressing wonderfully complements this
colorful combination of fresh nectarines, greens and ham. The
mint and crunchy toasted almonds make it even better.*
    —Laurel Leslie, Sonora, California

      7 medium nectarines, *divided*
      1 cup water
    1/4 cup sugar
      3 tablespoons olive oil
    4-1/2 teaspoons lemon juice
    4-1/2 teaspoons Dijon mustard
      1 tablespoon honey
    1/8 teaspoon salt

    1/8 teaspoon minced fresh thyme *or* dash dried
         thyme
Dash pepper
      6 heads Belgian endive, separated into leaves
      6 cups fresh arugula *or* baby spinach
    1/2 pound thinly sliced prosciutto *or* deli ham,
         julienned
    1/3 cup minced chives
    1/4 cup chopped almonds, toasted
      1 shallot, finely chopped
      8 fresh mint leaves, thinly sliced

Chop one nectarine; slice the remaining nectarines and
set aside. Place chopped nectarine in a small saucepan
with the water and sugar. Bring to a boil; cook until
liquid is reduced to 1/4 cup.
    Strain and discard the solids; cool liquid completely.
Whisk in the oil, lemon juice, mustard, honey, salt,
thyme and pepper.
    In a salad bowl, combine the endive, arugula,
prosciutto, chives, almonds, shallot, mint and sliced
nectarines. Add prepared dressing; toss to coat. Serve
immediately. **Yield:** 9 servings.

JUST GINGER. Used in Mom's Gingered Apple
Salad (recipe above left), crystallized or candied
ginger is the root of the ginger plant that has been
cooked in a sugar syrup. It's also used in dips,
sauces and fruit desserts. Larger grocery stores
will carry candied ginger in the spice section.

Poppy Seed Chicken Salad

(Pictured below and on page 16)

PREP: 30 min. + marinating **COOK:** 15 min.

Juicy strawberries, crisp sugar snap peas and crunchy pecans are so good alongside the strips of lime-marinated chicken in this pretty entree salad. The homemade dressing is simply delicious.
—Rebekah Radewahn, Wauwatosa, Wisconsin

- 3 tablespoons thawed limeade concentrate
- 1/4 teaspoon pepper
- 3/4 pound boneless skinless chicken breasts, cut into thin strips
- 1 tablespoon canola oil

DRESSING:
- 1/2 cup white vinegar
- 1/3 cup sugar
- 1 teaspoon dried minced onion
- 1 teaspoon ground mustard
- 1/2 teaspoon salt
- 1 cup canola oil
- 1 tablespoon poppy seeds

SALAD:
- 1 package (6 ounces) fresh baby spinach
- 2 cups sliced fresh strawberries
- 1 cup fresh sugar snap peas, trimmed
- 1 small red onion, chopped
- 1/2 cup pecan halves, toasted

In a large resealable plastic bag, combine limeade concentrate and pepper. Add the chicken; seal bag and turn to coat. Refrigerate for 2 hours.

Drain and discard marinade. In a large skillet, saute chicken in oil until no longer pink.

Meanwhile, in a blender, combine the vinegar, sugar, onion, mustard and salt. While processing, gradually add oil in a steady stream. Stir in poppy seeds.

Divide spinach among four salad plates; top with strawberries, peas, onion and chicken. Drizzle each serving with 2 tablespoons dressing; sprinkle with pecans. Serve immediately. Refrigerate leftover dressing. **Yield:** 4 servings + 1 cup leftover dressing.

Horseradish Coleslaw

PREP/TOTAL TIME: 15 min.

With prepackaged coleslaw mix, this dish comes together in a flash. I hope you'll enjoy this creamy coleslaw as much as I do!
—Tina Smith, Burtchville, Michigan

- 8 cups coleslaw mix
- 2 cups shredded carrots
- 1 medium onion, finely chopped
- 3/4 cup mayonnaise
- 1/3 cup sugar
- 1 tablespoon prepared horseradish
- 1 tablespoon lemon juice

In a large bowl, combine the coleslaw mix, carrots and onion. In a small bowl, combine the mayonnaise, sugar, horseradish and lemon juice. Pour over coleslaw mixture and toss to coat. **Yield:** 10 servings.

Tomato Tossed Salad

PREP/TOTAL TIME: 10 min.

I stir chives and thyme into a pleasant dressing and drizzle it over this simple salad. It's especially good with sun-ripened tomatoes right out of the garden.   —Edna Hoffman, Hebron, Indiana

☑ This recipe includes Nutrition Facts and Diabetic Exchanges.

- 6 cups shredded lettuce
- 2 medium tomatoes, cut into wedges
- 1/4 cup oil and vinegar salad dressing
- 1 teaspoon minced chives
- 1/4 teaspoon dried thyme

Place lettuce and tomatoes in a salad bowl. Combine salad dressing, chives and thyme; drizzle over salad and gently toss to coat. **Yield:** 4 servings.

Nutrition Facts: 1 serving equals 71 calories, 5 g fat (trace saturated fat), 0 cholesterol, 267 mg sodium, 6 g carbohydrate, 2 g fiber, 2 g protein. **Diabetic Exchanges:** 1 vegetable, 1 fat.

Grilled Steak and Mushroom Salad

(Pictured below)

PREP/TOTAL TIME: 30 min.

My husband loves this hearty main dish, especially on hot days during the summer. He says he feels like he's eating a healthy salad and getting his steak, too! I always serve it with some great homemade bread, and it makes a very satisfying dinner.
—Julie Cashion, Sanford, Florida

- 6 **tablespoons olive oil,** *divided*
- 2 **tablespoons Dijon mustard,** *divided*
- 1/2 **teaspoon salt**
- 1/4 **teaspoon pepper**
- 1-1/2 **pounds boneless sirloin steak (3/4 inch thick)**
- 1 **pound fresh mushrooms, sliced**
- 1/4 **cup red wine vinegar**
- 1 **medium bunch romaine, torn**

In a small bowl, combine 1 tablespoon oil, 1 tablespoon mustard, salt and pepper; set aside.

Grill the steak, covered, over medium-hot heat for 4 minutes. Turn; spread with the mustard mixture. Grill 4 minutes longer or until the meat reaches desired doneness (for medium-rare, a meat thermometer should read 145°; medium, 160°; well-done, 170°).

Meanwhile, in a large skillet, cook the mushrooms in 1 tablespoon oil until tender. Stir in the vinegar and remaining oil and mustard; mix well.

Thinly slice steak across the grain; add to mushroom mixture. Serve over romaine. **Yield:** 6 servings.

Tossed Salad with Peaches

(Pictured above and on page 17)

PREP/TOTAL TIME: 30 min.

This colorful salad has a wide range of flavors and textures that go together so well. You'll enjoy sweet peaches, tart lemon, tangy vinegars and plenty of crunch from greens, bacon and nuts.
—Denise Elder, Hanover, Ontario

- 4 **medium ripe peaches, peeled**
- 2 **tablespoons sugar**
- 2 **tablespoons lemon juice**
- 2 **tablespoons cider vinegar**
- 1 **tablespoon rice vinegar**
- 1/4 **teaspoon salt**
- 1/3 **cup vegetable oil**
- 6 **cups spring mix salad greens**
- 4 **cups torn romaine**
- 1 **small red onion, halved and thinly sliced**
- 1/2 **cup thinly sliced cucumber**
- 6 **bacon strips, cooked and crumbled**
- 1/3 **cup chopped pecans, toasted**

Slice three peaches; set aside. Cut the remaining peach in half; place in a blender. Add the sugar, lemon juice, vinegars and salt; cover and process until blended. While processing, gradually add oil in a steady stream.

In a large bowl, combine the salad greens, romaine, onion and cucumber. Pour about 2/3 cup dressing over salad and toss to coat.

Transfer salad to a serving platter; top with the sliced peaches and bacon. Drizzle with remaining dressing; sprinkle with pecans. Serve salad immediately. **Yield:** 12 servings.

Creamy Cranberry Gelatin

PREP: 15 min. + chilling

I picked up this recipe at the gas company when I was a teenager, in the 1950s. I modified it slightly, entered it in a newspaper contest and won $100! —Mary Fitch, Ransomville, New York

- 1 **cup orange juice**
- 1 **package (3 ounces) pineapple gelatin**
- 1 **package (3 ounces) cream cheese, softened**
- 1 **can (16 ounces) jellied cranberry sauce**

Bring the orange juice to a boil. Place the gelatin in a small bowl; add orange juice and stir until dissolved. Refrigerate until slightly thickened.

In a small mixing bowl, beat the cream cheese until fluffy. Add the cranberry sauce; beat until smooth. Beat in gelatin mixture. Pour into six 1/2-cup gelatin molds coated with cooking spray. Refrigerate for several hours or overnight. Unmold gelatin onto serving plates. **Yield:** 6 servings.

Pineapple Coleslaw

(Pictured below)

PREP/TOTAL TIME: 15 min.

Pineapple brings pizzazz to this traditional coleslaw, adding both color and sweetness. It's a fast side dish that's sure to be popular at your next barbecue.   —Cheryl Dolan, Innerkip, Ontario

- 3 **cups shredded cabbage**
- 3/4 **cup shredded carrot**
- 1 **can (8 ounces) unsweetened crushed pineapple, drained**
- 1/3 **cup mayonnaise**
- 4 **teaspoons sugar**
- 4 **teaspoons white vinegar**

In a small bowl, combine the cabbage, carrot and pineapple.

In another small bowl, whisk the mayonnaise, sugar and vinegar; pour over pineapple mixture; toss to coat. Serve immediately. **Yield:** 4 servings.

Four-Berry Spinach Salad

(Pictured above)

PREP/TOTAL TIME: 15 min.

"Nature's candy" abounds in this berry-filled salad. Its slightly tart dressing contrasts deliciously with sweet in-season fruit.
—Betty Lise Anderson, Gahanna, Ohio

- 1 **tablespoon vegetable oil**
- 1 **tablespoon orange juice**
- 1 **tablespoon red wine vinegar**
- 1 **tablespoon balsamic vinegar**
- 1 **tablespoon water**
- 2 **teaspoons lemon juice**
- 1/2 **teaspoon sugar**
- 1/2 **teaspoon poppy seeds**
- 1/8 **teaspoon ground allspice**

Dash ground cinnamon

- 4 **cups fresh baby spinach**
- 1/2 **cup *each* fresh raspberries, blueberries, blackberries and sliced strawberries**
- 2 **teaspoons chopped walnuts, toasted**

For dressing, in a jar with a tight-fitting lid, combine the first 10 ingredients; shake well.

Combine the spinach and berries in a small salad bowl. Drizzle with dressing and sprinkle with walnuts; toss to coat. **Yield:** 2 servings.

Tangy Potato Salad

(Pictured above)

PREP: 40 min. + chilling

When picnic season arrives, my family starts thinking about potato salad. This tangy side is also great in the winter served hot with cubed ham. —Peggy Gwillim, Strasbourg, Saskatchewan

- 4 pounds red potatoes, cubed
- 3 tablespoons plus 2/3 cup white wine vinegar, *divided*
- 8 hard-cooked eggs, sliced
- 6 radishes, thinly sliced
- 1/2 cup minced chives
- 1 cup buttermilk
- 1/2 cup mayonnaise
- 2 tablespoons prepared mustard
- 1 tablespoon dried minced onion
- 1 tablespoon dill weed
- 1/4 teaspoon salt
- 1/4 teaspoon pepper

Place the potatoes in a Dutch oven; cover with water. Bring to a boil. Reduce the heat; cover and cook for 10-15 minutes or until tender. Drain. Immediately sprinkle with 3 tablespoons vinegar; cool.

Place potatoes in a large bowl. Add the eggs, radishes and chives. In a small bowl, combine the buttermilk, mayonnaise, mustard, onion, dill, salt, pepper and remaining vinegar. Pour over potato mixture and gently stir to coat. Refrigerate until chilled. **Yield:** 13 servings (3/4 cup each).

Bean & Barley Salad

(Pictured below)

PREP/TOTAL TIME: 30 min.

Our cooking club meets once a month to taste-test each other's creations and then draw from a hat to see whose meal we get to take home. This hearty salad is so good and lasts for days in the refrigerator. We like to spoon it onto crumbled pita chips. —Janelle Lee, Appleton, Wisconsin

- 3/4 cup quick-cooking barley
- 1 can (16 ounces) kidney beans, rinsed and drained
- 1 can (15 ounces) black beans, rinsed and drained
- 1 can (11 ounces) whole kernel corn, drained
- 1 large sweet red pepper, finely chopped
- 6 green onions, chopped
- 1/3 cup minced fresh cilantro

DRESSING:
- 3/4 cup olive oil
- 1/3 cup red wine vinegar
- 2 garlic cloves, minced
- 1-1/2 teaspoons chili powder
- 3/4 teaspoon salt
- 3/4 teaspoon ground cumin
- 1/4 to 1/2 teaspoon crushed red pepper flakes
- 1/4 teaspoon pepper

Prepare the barley according to the package directions. Transfer to a large bowl; stir in the beans, corn, red pepper, onions and cilantro.

In a small bowl, combine the dressing ingredients. Pour over salad; toss to coat. Chill until serving. **Yield:** 12 servings (3/4 cup each).

Soups & Sandwiches

Whether you want a quick but delicious midday meal or a casual yet comforting dinner, enjoy the family-favorite wraps, chili, melts and more in this chapter.

Red Curry Carrot Soup 30
Ham 'n' Swiss Envelopes 30
Turkey Salad Croissants 30
Spicy Chicken Lettuce Wraps 31
Cheesy Cauliflower Soup 31
Open-Faced Chicken Avocado Burgers 32
Wild Rice and Barley Soup Mix 32
Herb & Cheese-Stuffed Burgers 33
Rootin'-Tootin' Cincinnati Chili 33
Gnocchi Chicken Minestrone 34
Grilled Veggie Tortilla Wraps 34
Tomato-Pesto Cheddar Melts 35
Mac 'n' Cheese Soup 35
Zippy Chicken Wraps 36
Cheddar Potato Soup 36
Double-Cheese Beef Panini 36
Philly Cheese Fakes 37
Chipotle Cheeseburgers 37
Salmon Bisque 38
Turkey White Bean Soup 38
Turkey Dijon Melts 38
Cranburgers with Sweet Potato Fries 39
Moroccan Vegetable Stew 39

FOR LUNCH OR LATER. Clockwise from top left: Zippy Chicken Wraps (p. 36), Mac 'n' Cheese Soup (p. 35), Red Curry Carrot Soup (p. 30), Gnocchi Chicken Minestrone (p. 34) and Grilled Veggie Tortilla Wraps (p. 34).

Red Curry Carrot Soup

(Pictured above and on page 29)

PREP: 20 min. **COOK:** 15 min.

With its mix of delicious colors, textures and tastes, this exotic soup is something special. The meatballs and veggies make it hearty, too.   —Dilnaz Heckman, Tacoma, Washington

> 5   **packages (3 ounces *each*) ramen noodles**
> 3   **garlic cloves, minced**
> 2   **tablespoons peanut oil**
> 1   **can (14 ounces) coconut milk, *divided***
> 2   **tablespoons red curry paste**
> 1-1/2 **teaspoons curry powder**
> 1/2 **teaspoon ground turmeric**
> 32 **frozen fully cooked homestyle meatballs (1/2 ounce *each*)**
> 4   **cups chicken broth**
> 1   **medium zucchini, finely chopped**
> 1   **medium carrot, halved and sliced**
> 1/4 **cup shredded cabbage**
> 2   **teaspoons fish *or* soy sauce**

Optional garnishes: bean sprouts, chow mein noodles, fresh basil and green onions

Cook the ramen noodles according to the package directions (discard the seasoning packets or save for another use).

Meanwhile, in a Dutch oven, saute the garlic in oil for 1 minute. Spoon 1/2 cup cream from top of coconut milk and place in the pan. Add the curry paste, curry powder and turmeric; cook and stir for 5 minutes or until oil separates from coconut milk mixture.

Stir in the meatballs, broth, zucchini, carrot, cabbage, fish sauce and remaining coconut milk. Bring to a boil. Reduce the heat; simmer, uncovered, 15-20 minutes or until carrot is tender and meatballs are heated through.

Drain noodles; stir into soup. Garnish if desired.

Editor's Note: This recipe was tested with regular (full-fat) coconut milk. Light coconut milk contains less cream. **Yield:** 8 servings (2-1/2 quarts).

Ham 'n' Swiss Envelopes

PREP/TOTAL TIME: 30 min.

Bring a little fun to lunch or dinner with these tasty hot pockets stuffed with a delicious ham–and–cheese filling. They're made with refrigerated dough that's folded to resemble an envelope.
                                        —Tammy Burgess, Loveland, Ohio

> 3/4 **cup diced fully cooked ham**
> 4   **teaspoons finely chopped onion**
> 1   **teaspoon vegetable oil**
> 3/4 **cup shredded Swiss cheese**
> 1   **package (3 ounces) cream cheese, cubed**
> 2   **tubes (8 ounces *each*) refrigerated crescent rolls**

In a large skillet, saute ham and onion in oil until onion is tender. Add cheeses; cook for 3-4 minutes or until melted. Remove from the heat; set aside.

Unroll the crescent dough and separate into four rectangles; seal perforations. Place 2 tablespoons of ham mixture in the center of each rectangle. Starting with a short side, fold a third of the dough over filling. On the other short side, bring both corners together in the center to form a point. Fold over to resemble an envelope. Pinch seams to seal.

Place the envelope on an ungreased baking sheet. Bake at 400° for 10-12 minutes or until golden brown. Serve immediately. **Yield:** 4 servings.

Turkey Salad Croissants

PREP/TOTAL TIME: 30 min.

I created this creamy, crunchy salad for a small tea party I was having one midwinter afternoon. It's a great way to use up your leftover holiday turkey.   —Karen Jantz, New Plymouth, Idaho

> 4   **cups cubed cooked turkey breast**
> 1   **can (8 ounces) sliced water chestnuts, drained and chopped**
> 2/3 **cup chopped pecans**
> 2   **celery ribs, sliced**
> 2   **green onions, sliced**
> 1   **cup mayonnaise**
> 2   **teaspoons prepared mustard**
> 1/2 **teaspoon garlic pepper blend**
> 1/4 **teaspoon salt**
> 8   **lettuce leaves**
> 8   **croissants, split**

In a large bowl, combine turkey, water chestnuts, pecans, celery and onions. Combine the mayonnaise, mustard, garlic pepper and salt; pour over the turkey mixture and toss to coat. Cover and refrigerate until serving. Spoon onto lettuce-lined croissants. **Yield:** 8 servings.

Spicy Chicken Lettuce Wraps

(Pictured below)

PREP/TOTAL TIME: 30 min.

This is one of my go-to recipes when I want a casual, easy meal. I love the spicy Asian flavors all wrapped up in lettuce leaves.
—*Brittany Allyn, Nashville, Tennessee*

- 1 **pound chicken tenderloins, cut into 1/2-inch pieces**
- 1/8 **teaspoon pepper**
- 2 **tablespoons canola oil, *divided***
- 1 **medium onion, finely chopped**
- 1 **small green pepper, finely chopped**
- 1 **small sweet red pepper, finely chopped**
- 1 **can (8 ounces) sliced water chestnuts, drained and finely chopped**
- 1 **can (4 ounces) mushroom stems and pieces, drained and finely chopped**
- 2 **garlic cloves, minced**
- 1/3 **cup stir-fry sauce**
- 1 **teaspoon soy sauce**
- 8 **Bibb *or* Boston lettuce leaves**
- 1/4 **cup salted peanuts**
- 2 **teaspoons minced fresh cilantro**

Sprinkle chicken with pepper. In a large skillet or wok, stir-fry chicken in 1 tablespoon oil until no longer pink. Remove and set aside.

Stir-fry the onion and peppers in the remaining oil for 5 minutes. Add the water chestnuts, mushrooms and garlic; stir-fry 2-3 minutes longer or until vegetables are crisp-tender. Add stir-fry sauce and soy sauce. Stir in chicken; heat through.

Place 1/2 cup chicken mixture on each lettuce leaf; sprinkle each with 1-1/2 teaspoons peanuts and

1/4 teaspoon cilantro. Fold the lettuce over the filling. **Yield:** 4 servings.

   Editor's Note: This recipe was tested with House of Tsang Saigon Sizzle Sauce.

Cheesy Cauliflower Soup

(Pictured above)

PREP: 25 min. **COOK:** 5-1/2 hours

On a cool day, this comfort food is sure to warm everyone heart and soul. Prefer chunky soup? Skip the blender step and stir the cheese and cream into the slow cooker mixture, then heat on high until the cheese is melted. —*Sheryl Punter, Woodstock, Ontario*

- 1 **large head cauliflower, broken into florets**
- 2 **celery ribs**
- 2 **large carrots**
- 1 **large green pepper**
- 1 **small sweet red pepper**
- 1 **medium red onion**
- 4 **cups chicken broth**
- 1/2 **teaspoon Worcestershire sauce**
- 1/4 **teaspoon salt**
- 1/8 **teaspoon pepper**
- 2 **cups (8 ounces) shredded cheddar cheese**
- 2 **cups half-and-half cream**

Place the cauliflower in a 4-qt. slow cooker. Chop the celery, carrots, peppers and onion; add to the slow cooker. Stir in the broth, Worcestershire sauce, salt and pepper. Cover and cook on low for 5-6 hours or until the vegetables are tender.

In a blender, process soup in batches until smooth. Return all to slow cooker; stir in the cheese and cream. Cover and cook on high for 30 minutes or until cheese is melted. **Yield:** 9 servings (2-1/4 quarts).

Open-Faced Chicken Avocado Burgers

(Pictured below)

PREP: 30 min. **COOK:** 15 min.

A creamy avocado spread and thick slices of fresh mozzarella and tomato really dress up these ground chicken patties. They make a terrific meal alongside potato wedges or a green salad.
—*Lisa Hundley, Aberdeen, North Carolina*

    1 **tablespoon lemon juice**
  1/4 **teaspoon Worcestershire sauce**
  1/2 **medium ripe avocado, peeled**
  1/2 **cup mayonnaise**
  1/4 **cup sour cream**
    4 **green onions, coarsely chopped**
  1/2 **teaspoon salt**
  1/2 **teaspoon cayenne pepper**
BURGERS:
  1/4 **cup shredded Parmesan cheese**
    2 **tablespoons prepared pesto**
    3 **garlic cloves, minced**
  1/4 **teaspoon salt**
    1 **pound ground chicken**
    4 **tablespoons olive oil,** *divided*
  1/2 **pound fresh mozzarella cheese, cut into 4 slices**
    4 **slices Italian bread (3/4 inch thick)**
    2 **cups fresh arugula** *or* **fresh baby spinach**
    8 **slices tomato**
  1/4 **teaspoon dried basil**
  1/4 **teaspoon pepper**

In a blender, combine the first eight ingredients; cover and process until smooth. Chill until serving. For the burgers, in a small bowl, combine the Parmesan cheese, pesto, garlic and salt. Crumble chicken over mixture and mix well. Shape into four patties.

In a large skillet over medium heat, cook burgers in 2 tablespoons oil for 5-7 minutes on each side or until a meat thermometer reads 165° and juices run clear. Top with cheese; cover and cook 1 minute longer.

Meanwhile, brush the bread with the remaining oil; place on a baking sheet. Broil 3-4 in. from the heat for 1-2 minutes on each side or until toasted.

Spread each slice of toast with 2 tablespoons avocado spread (refrigerate remaining spread for another use). Top with arugula, a burger and sliced tomato. Sprinkle with basil and pepper. **Yield:** 4 servings + 1/4 cup leftover spread.

Wild Rice and Barley Soup Mix

PREP: 10 min. **COOK:** 1 hour

From our Test Kitchen cooks, this stick-to-your-ribs soup mix packed into a jar is a great gift for Christmas or any time at all. Include a copy of the preparation instructions.

    1 **tablespoon brown sugar**
    2 **teaspoons Italian seasoning**
  1/2 **teaspoon dried minced garlic**
  1/2 **teaspoon ground celery seed**
  1/2 **teaspoon pepper**
  1/2 **cup medium pearl barley**
  1/3 **cup dried vegetable flakes**
    3 **tablespoons chicken bouillon granules**
  1/2 **cup uncooked wild rice**
  1/2 **cup dried minced onion**
ADDITIONAL INGREDIENTS:
    8 **cups water**
Real bacon bits

In a small bowl, combine the first five ingredients. In a pint-size jar with a tight-fitting lid, layer the barley, vegetable flakes, brown sugar mixture, bouillon, rice and onion, packing each layer tightly (do not mix). Cover and store in a cool dry place for up to 4 months.

To prepare soup: Pour soup mix into a large saucepan. Add 8 cups of water; bring to a boil. Reduce heat. Cover; simmer for 1 hour or until rice is tender. Garnish with bacon bits. **Yield:** 6 servings.

BEST BURGERS. While beef, pork and lamb burgers should be cooked to 160°, cook turkey or chicken burgers (such as Open-Faced Chicken Avocado Burgers, above left) to 165°. To test for doneness, use tongs to hold the burger while inserting an instant-read thermometer horizontally from a side. Make sure the thermometer is far enough in to read the temperature in the center.

Rootin'-Tootin' Cincinnati Chili

(Pictured below)

PREP: 25 min. **COOK:** 30 min.

The name of this recipe refers to a special ingredient—root beer! It adds a nice touch of sweetness to the spicy chili. Serve it over spaghetti and let everyone add his or her own favorite toppings.
—*Holly Gomez, Seabrook, New Hampshire*

- 1 **pound ground beef**
- 1 **small onion, chopped**
- 1 **small green pepper, chopped**
- 1 **garlic clove, minced**
- 1 **can (14-1/2 ounces) fire-roasted diced tomatoes, undrained**
- 1 **cup root beer**
- 2 **tablespoons chili powder**
- 2 **tablespoons tomato paste**
- 2 **tablespoons minced chipotle peppers in adobo sauce**
- 1 **tablespoon ground cumin**
- 1 **beef bouillon cube**

Hot cooked spaghetti
OPTIONAL TOPPINGS:
Crushed tortilla chips, chopped green onions, and shredded cheddar and Parmesan cheeses

In a large saucepan, cook the beef, onions, green pepper and garlic over medium heat until meat is no longer pink; drain. Add the tomatoes, root beer, chili powder, tomato paste, chipotle peppers, cumin and bouillon. Bring to a boil.

Reduce heat; cover and simmer for 20-30 minutes to allow flavors to blend. Serve over spaghetti. Garnish with the chips, green onions and cheeses if desired.
Yield: 4 servings.

Herb & Cheese-Stuffed Burgers

(Pictured above)

PREP/TOTAL TIME: 30 min.

Tired of the same old ground-beef burgers at your summertime cookouts? Shake things up a bit with this quick-fix alternative. The creamy cheese filling is sure to wake up your taste buds.
—*Sherri Cox, Lucasville, Ohio*

- 1/4 **cup shredded cheddar cheese**
- 2 **tablespoons cream cheese, softened**
- 2 **tablespoons minced fresh parsley**
- 3 **teaspoons Dijon mustard,** *divided*
- 2 **green onions, thinly sliced**
- 3 **tablespoons dry bread crumbs**
- 2 **tablespoons ketchup**
- 1/2 **teaspoon salt**
- 1/2 **teaspoon dried rosemary, crushed**
- 1/4 **teaspoon dried sage leaves**
- 1 **pound lean ground beef (90% lean)**
- 4 **hard rolls, split**

Lettuce leaves and tomato slices, optional

In a small bowl, combine cheddar cheese, cream cheese, parsley and 1 teaspoon Dijon mustard; set aside.

In another bowl, combine the green onions, bread crumbs, ketchup, salt, rosemary, sage and remaining Dijon mustard. Crumble the ground beef over the mixture and mix well.

Shape beef mixture into eight thin patties. Spoon cheese mixture onto center of four patties; top with remaining patties and press edges firmly to seal.

Grill burgers, covered, over medium heat or broil 4 in. from heat for 5-7 minutes on each side or until a meat thermometer reads 160° and juices run clear. Serve burgers on rolls with lettuce and tomato if desired.
Yield: 4 servings.

1/2 cup frozen peas
3 tablespoons tomato paste
1 package (16 ounces) potato gnocchi
1/2 cup shredded Asiago cheese
8 fresh basil leaves, thinly sliced

Sprinkle the chicken with oregano, salt and pepper. In a Dutch oven, saute chicken in 1 tablespoon oil until no longer pink. Remove from pan and set aside.

In same pan, cook the peppers, zucchini, portobello mushrooms and onion in the remaining oil until tender. Add the prosciutto and garlic; cook 1 minute longer. Add the chicken broth, tomatoes, beans, peas, tomato paste and chicken. Bring to a boil. Reduce heat; simmer, uncovered, for 20 minutes, stirring occasionally.

Meanwhile, cook the gnocchi according to package directions. Drain; stir into soup. Garnish each serving with cheese and basil. **Yield:** 8 servings (2-3/4 quarts).

Editor's Note: Look for potato gnocchi in the pasta or frozen foods section.

Grilled Veggie Tortilla Wraps

(Pictured below and on page 28)

PREP: 20 min. + marinating **GRILL:** 10 min.

You don't have to be a vegetarian to appreciate the wholesome goodness of these meatless wraps. Stuffed with marinated veggies and cream cheese, these tasty tortillas will have everyone singing their praises. —*Marta Northcutt, Lebanon, Tennessee*

3 tablespoons red wine vinegar
3 tablespoons olive oil
1 teaspoon lemon-pepper seasoning

Gnocchi Chicken Minestrone

(Pictured above and on page 28)

PREP: 30 min. **COOK:** 30 min.

The inspiration for this chunky minestrone came from my Italian heritage—my mom was a wonderful soup maker. Frozen potato gnocchi cuts preparation time and adds extra heartiness.
—*Barbara Estabrook, Rhinelander, Wisconsin*

1-1/4 pounds chicken tenderloins, cut into 1/2-inch pieces
3/4 teaspoon dried oregano
1/4 teaspoon salt
1/4 teaspoon pepper
2 tablespoons olive oil, *divided*
1 *each* small green, sweet red and yellow peppers, finely chopped
1 medium zucchini, finely chopped
1 cup chopped fresh baby portobello mushrooms
1/3 cup chopped red onion
1/3 cup chopped prosciutto *or* deli ham
4 garlic cloves, minced
2 cans (14-1/2 ounces *each*) chicken broth
1 can (14-1/2 ounces) Italian diced tomatoes, undrained
3/4 cup canned white kidney *or* cannellini beans, rinsed and drained

1 garlic clove, minced
1/2 teaspoon dried oregano
1/2 teaspoon dried basil
2 medium zucchini, cut lengthwise into 1/4-inch slices
1 medium yellow summer squash, cut lengthwise into 1/4-inch slices
1 medium sweet red pepper, cut into strips
4 ounces cream cheese, softened
1 tablespoon prepared pesto
4 whole wheat tortillas (8 inches), warmed

In a large resealable plastic bag, combine the first six ingredients; add the zucchini, yellow squash and red pepper. Seal bag and turn to coat; refrigerate overnight, turning once.

In a small bowl, combine the cream cheese and pesto; set aside. Drain and discard marinade.

Place the vegetables in a grill basket or disposable foil pan with slits cut in the bottom. Grill, covered, over medium-high heat for 3-4 minutes on each side or until tender.

Spread reserved pesto cream cheese over tortillas; top with vegetables. Fold sides over filling. Serve immediately. **Yield:** 4 servings.

Tomato-Pesto Cheddar Melts

PREP/TOTAL TIME: 15 min.

Give ordinary grilled cheese sandwiches a boost with this simple recipe. Prepared pesto and sliced tomato add an interesting and delicious twist. —Lil Morris, Emerald Park, Saskatchewan

1 tablespoon prepared pesto
2 slices white bread
1 small tomato, sliced
1/2 cup shredded cheddar cheese
1/8 teaspoon salt
1/8 teaspoon pepper
1 tablespoon butter

Spread pesto over one side of each slice of bread. Top with tomato and cheese; sprinkle with salt and pepper. In a large skillet over medium-low heat, melt butter; add sandwiches. Cover and cook until the bread is lightly toasted and the cheese is melted. **Yield:** 2 servings.

HOMEMADE HINT. Prepared pesto is available in many grocery stores and is a convenient choice when your schedule is full. If you have some time to spare, consider making your own fresh pesto. You'll find four easy yet delicious recipes on pages 46-47 of this book, and any would taste great on Tomato-Pesto Cheddar Melts (recipe above).

Mac 'n' Cheese Soup

(Pictured above and on page 29)

PREP/TOTAL TIME: 30 min.

I found this recipe years ago and made a few changes. Because it starts with packaged macaroni and cheese, the creamy soup is ready in a jiffy. —Nancy Daugherty, Cortland, Ohio

1 package (14 ounces) deluxe macaroni and cheese dinner mix
9 cups water, *divided*
1 cup fresh broccoli florets
2 tablespoons finely chopped onion
1 can (10-3/4 ounces) condensed cheddar cheese soup, undiluted
2-1/2 cups 2% milk
1 cup chopped fully cooked ham

Set aside the cheese sauce packet from the macaroni and cheese mix. In a large saucepan, bring 8 cups water to a boil. Add the macaroni; cook for 8-10 minutes or until tender.

Meanwhile, in another large saucepan, bring the remaining water to a boil. Add broccoli and onion; cook, uncovered, for 3 minutes. Stir in the soup, milk, ham and contents of cheese sauce packet; heat through. Drain macaroni; stir into soup. **Yield:** 8 servings (2 quarts).

Zippy Chicken Wraps

(Pictured below and on page 28)

PREP/TOTAL TIME: 30 min.

I love these Southwestern wraps for hot summer days or picnics. If you're in a hurry, use precooked chicken tenders to save time.
—Jackie Smulski, Lyons, Illinois

- 1/2 **pound boneless skinless chicken breast, cut into thin slices**
- 1 **tablespoon butter**
- 1 **garlic clove, minced**
- 1 **teaspoon chili powder**
- 1/2 **teaspoon ground cumin**
- **Dash cayenne pepper**
- 1 **package (3 ounces) cream cheese, softened**
- 1/2 **cup shredded cheddar cheese**
- 1/4 **cup sour cream**
- 1 **can (10 ounces) diced tomatoes and green chilies, drained**
- 2 **green onions, thinly sliced**
- 4 **flour tortillas (8 inches)**
- **Sliced avocado, sliced ripe olives and salsa**

In a large skillet, saute the chicken in butter until no longer pink. Add the garlic, chili powder, cumin and cayenne; cook and stir until heated through. Remove from the heat; cool.

In a small mixing bowl, beat the cream cheese, cheddar cheese and sour cream. Stir in the chicken, tomatoes and onions.

Spoon 1/2 cup chicken mixture down the center of each tortilla; top with avocado and olives. Fold sides over filling and secure with toothpicks if desired. Serve with salsa. **Yield:** 4 servings.

Cheddar Potato Soup

PREP: 25 min. **COOK:** 20 min.

Here's a recipe I created as an alternative to plain potato soup. Hearty and comforting, it disappears quickly whenever I make it for my family on chilly evenings. Serve it with fresh-baked bread and a tossed salad, and you'll have a complete dinner.
—Susan Peck, Republic, Missouri

- 1 **large onion, chopped**
- 3/4 **cup chopped celery**
- 1/4 **cup butter**
- 5 **cups cubed peeled potatoes**
- 3 **cups water**
- 3 **cups milk, *divided***
- 4 **teaspoons chicken bouillon granules**
- 1/2 **teaspoon salt**
- 1/2 **teaspoon pepper**
- 1/4 **cup all-purpose flour**
- 4 **cups (16 ounces) shredded cheddar cheese**
- 1/2 **pound sliced bacon, cooked and crumbled**

In a large Dutch oven or soup kettle, saute onion and celery in butter for 5 minutes. Add potatoes and water. Bring to a boil. Reduce the heat; cover and simmer for 15 minutes or until potatoes are tender.

Stir in 2 cups milk, bouillon, salt and pepper. Combine flour and remaining milk until smooth; gradually stir into soup. Bring to a boil; cook and stir for 2 minutes or until thickened.

Reduce heat. Add the cheddar cheese and bacon; stir until the cheese is melted. **Yield:** 10-12 servings (about 2-1/2 quarts).

Double-Cheese Beef Panini

PREP/TOTAL TIME: 30 min.

When it comes to a speedy yet satisfying lunch or supper, nothing beats a piping-hot panini fresh from the panini maker or indoor grill. Blue cheese and horseradish give this sandwich extra zip.
—Lisa Huff, Clive, Iowa

- 1/3 **cup mayonnaise**
- 1/4 **cup crumbled blue cheese**
- 2 **teaspoons prepared horseradish**
- 1/8 **teaspoon pepper**
- 1 **large sweet onion, thinly sliced**
- 1 **tablespoon olive oil**
- 8 **slices white bread**
- 8 **slices provolone cheese**
- 8 **slices deli roast beef**
- 2 **tablespoons butter, softened**

In a small bowl, combine the mayonnaise, blue cheese, horseradish and pepper; set aside. In a large skillet, saute onion in oil until tender.

Spread mayonnaise mixture over one side of each slice of bread. On four slices, layer one piece of cheese,

cheese. Broil 3-4 in. from the heat for 2-3 minutes or until cheese is melted. **Yield:** 4 servings.

Nutrition Facts: 1 sandwich equals 344 calories, 12 g fat (4 g saturated fat), 10 mg cholesterol, 681 mg sodium, 47 g carbohydrate, 4 g fiber, 17 g protein.

Chipotle Cheeseburgers

(Pictured below)

PREP/TOTAL TIME: 25 min.

Heat up a casual meal with these zesty mozzarella burgers. If you like, use ground turkey instead of beef...or try a different cheese.
—*Crystal Jo Bruns, Iliff, Colorado*

- **1 small onion, finely chopped**
- **2 tablespoons minced fresh cilantro**
- **1 chipotle pepper in adobo sauce, finely chopped**
- **1 teaspoon onion powder**
- **1 teaspoon garlic powder**
- **1 teaspoon seasoned salt**
- **1/4 teaspoon pepper**
- **1 pound ground beef**
- **4 slices part-skim mozzarella cheese**
- **4 hamburger buns, split and toasted**

Lettuce leaves and tomato slices, optional

In a small bowl, combine the first seven ingredients. Crumble beef over mixture and mix well. Shape into four patties.

Grill, covered, over medium heat or broil 4 in. from the heat for 5-7 minutes on each side or until a meat thermometer reads 160° and juices run clear. Top with mozzarella cheese. Cover and cook 1-2 minutes longer or until cheese is melted. Serve on buns with lettuce and tomato if desired. **Yield:** 4 servings.

two slices of roast beef, sauteed onion and another piece of cheese; top with remaining bread.

Spread the butter over both sides of the sandwiches. Cook on a panini maker or indoor grill for 2-3 minutes or until the bread is browned and cheese is melted. **Yield:** 4 servings.

Philly Cheese Fakes

(Pictured above)

PREP: 30 min. **BROIL:** 5 min.

Shiitake mushrooms are the key to this twist on popular Philly steak sandwiches—a nice meatless option that's tangy and tasty.
—*Veronica Vadakan, Portland, Oregon*

☑ This recipe includes Nutrition Facts.

- **1/4 cup lemon juice**
- **3 garlic cloves, minced**
- **1 tablespoon olive oil**
- **1/2 teaspoon smoked paprika**
- **1/4 teaspoon salt**
- **1/4 teaspoon pepper**
- **1 pound sliced fresh shiitake mushrooms**
- **2 medium green peppers, sliced**
- **1 small onion, thinly sliced**
- **4 hoagie buns, split**
- **4 slices reduced-fat provolone cheese**

In a small bowl, whisk the first six ingredients. In a large bowl, combine the shiitake mushrooms, green peppers and onion. Pour the prepared dressing over vegetables; toss to coat.

Transfer to two 15-in. x 10-in. x 1-in. baking pans coated with cooking spray. Bake at 450° for 15-20 minutes or until crisp-tender, stirring once.

Divide mushroom mixture among buns and top with

broth. Bring to a boil; cook and stir for 1-2 minutes or until thickened. Cool slightly.

Transfer to a blender; add roasted pepper. Cover and puree until smooth.

Return to the pan. Stir in the milk, seafood seasoning, Liquid Smoke if desired and salmon; heat soup through. **Yield:** 4 servings.

Nutrition Facts: 1 cup equals 239 calories, 12 g fat (3 g saturated fat), 43 mg cholesterol, 674 mg sodium, 14 g carbohydrate, 1 g fiber, 17 g protein. **Diabetic Exchanges:** 2 lean meat, 1 starch, 1 fat.

Turkey White Bean Soup

PREP: 35 min. **COOK:** 5 hours

This no-fuss meal-in-a-bowl will stick to your ribs on a cool autumn night. Using leftover turkey will save even more time in the kitchen. —*Amy Martell, Canton, Pennsylvania*

- 1 **pound bulk pork sausage**
- 4 **cups cubed cooked turkey**
- 2 **cans (14-1/2 ounces *each*) beef broth**
- 1 **can (15 ounces) white kidney *or* cannellini beans, rinsed and drained**
- 1 **can (14-1/2 ounces) diced tomatoes, undrained**
- 4 **medium carrots, chopped**
- 1 **medium onion, chopped**
- 1 **medium green pepper, chopped**
- 1 **celery rib, chopped**
- 2 **teaspoons Italian seasoning**
- 1/4 **teaspoon cayenne pepper**

Crumble the sausage into a large skillet; cook and stir until no longer pink. Drain. Transfer to a 5- or 6-qt. slow cooker. Stir in the remaining ingredients. Cover and cook on low for 5-6 hours or until vegetables are tender. **Yield:** 8 servings (3 quarts).

Turkey Dijon Melts

PREP/TOTAL TIME: 25 min.

I make these when I'm craving comfort food but don't have the time or energy for a big meal. The toasted sandwiches always hit the spot. —*Sarah Marshall, Creedmoor, North Carolina*

- 4 **slices whole wheat bread**
- 4 **teaspoons mayonnaise**
- 1/4 **pound thinly sliced cooked turkey**
- 4 **slices Monterey Jack cheese**
- 1/4 **cup thinly sliced onion**

Dash salt and pepper
- 1 **tablespoon honey Dijon salad dressing**
- 1 **tablespoon butter, softened**

Spread two slices of bread with mayonnaise. Layer with turkey, cheese and onion; sprinkle with salt and pepper. Spread remaining slices of bread with salad dressing;

Salmon Bisque

(Pictured above)

PREP: 35 min. **COOK:** 15 min.

Most bisque recipes call for half-and-half or even whipping cream. Even though this recipe uses 2% milk instead, it still has a rich, creamy taste. —*Barbara Parks, Renton, Washington*

☑ **This recipe includes Nutrition Facts and Diabetic Exchanges.**

- 1 **small sweet red pepper**
- 1 **salmon fillet (8 ounces)**
- 1/2 **cup finely chopped carrot**
- 1 **tablespoon chopped shallot**
- 1 **tablespoon canola oil**
- 2 **garlic cloves, minced**
- 3 **tablespoons all-purpose flour**
- 1 **can (14-1/2 ounces) chicken broth**
- 2 **cups 2% milk**
- 1 **teaspoon seafood seasoning**
- 1/4 **teaspoon Liquid Smoke, optional**

Broil red pepper 4 in. from the heat until skin blisters, about 5 minutes. With tongs, rotate pepper a quarter turn. Broil and rotate pepper until all sides are blistered and blackened.

Immediately place pepper in a bowl; cover and let stand for 15-20 minutes. Peel off and discard charred skin. Remove stems and seeds. Set pepper aside.

Broil salmon 4 in. from the heat for 7-10 minutes on each side or until fish flakes easily with a fork. Break salmon into small pieces; set aside.

In a large saucepan, saute the carrot and shallot in oil until tender. Add the garlic; saute 1 minute longer. Stir in the flour until blended. Gradually add the chicken place over onion. Butter the outsides of sandwiches.

In a small skillet over medium heat, toast sandwiches for 4-5 minutes on each side or until the bread is lightly browned and cheese is melted. **Yield:** 2 servings.

Cranburgers with Sweet Potato Fries

PREP/TOTAL TIME: 30 min.

Extra cranberry sauce and stuffing mix from the holidays are put to delicious use in these hearty burgers. Dress up some packaged fries, and dinner is done! —Nancy Bourget, Fort Hood, Texas

1 package (16 ounces) frozen French-fried sweet potatoes
Olive oil-flavored cooking spray
1 teaspoon pesto sauce mix
1/4 teaspoon celery seed
1/4 teaspoon ground thyme
BURGERS:
1 cup whole-berry cranberry sauce
1 cup turkey-flavored stuffing mix
1/4 teaspoon ground thyme
1-1/2 pounds ground turkey
1 tablespoon canola oil
6 lettuce leaves
6 sesame seed hamburger buns, split
1/3 cup turkey gravy, warmed
6 slices jellied cranberry sauce

Place fries in a greased 15-in. x 10-in. x 1-in. baking pan; spritz with cooking spray. Combine the pesto mix, celery seed and thyme; sprinkle over fries. Bake at 400° for 20 minutes.

Meanwhile, in a large bowl, combine whole-berry cranberry sauce, stuffing mix and thyme. Crumble turkey over mixture and mix well. Shape into six patties.

In a large skillet, cook the burgers in oil over medium heat for 6-8 minutes on each side or until a meat thermometer reads 165° and juices run clear.

Place the burgers on lettuce-lined buns; top with a spoonful of gravy and a slice of cranberry sauce. Serve with fries. **Yield:** 6 servings.

Editor's Note: This recipe was tested with McCormick pesto sauce mix.

LIVELY LEFTOVERS. Cranburgers with Sweet Potato Fries (recipe above) is a great solution for Thanksgiving leftovers. Keep in mind:
• Leftover meat combined with gravy and gravy by itself should be used within 1 to 2 days.
• Cranberry sauce and relish can be stored in the refrigerator for 5 to 7 days.

Moroccan Vegetarian Stew

PREP: 20 min. **COOK:** 30 min.

This fragrant stew can also be served over couscous or with warm pita bread. A dollop of yogurt or sour cream on top will cool the spiciness down. —Sonya Labbe, Santa Monica, California

☑ **This recipe includes Nutrition Facts and Diabetic Exchanges.**

1 large onion, chopped
1 tablespoon olive oil
2 teaspoons ground cinnamon
2 teaspoons ground cumin
1 teaspoon ground coriander
1/2 teaspoon cayenne pepper
1/2 teaspoon ground allspice
1/4 teaspoon salt
3 cups water
1 small butternut squash, peeled and cubed
2 medium potatoes, peeled and cubed
4 medium carrots, sliced
3 plum tomatoes, chopped
2 small zucchini, cut into 1-inch pieces
1 can (15 ounces) garbanzo beans *or* chickpeas, rinsed and drained

In a Dutch oven, saute onion in oil until tender. Add spices and salt; cook 1 minute longer.

Stir in the water, squash, potatoes, carrots and tomatoes. Bring to a boil. Reduce heat; simmer, uncovered, for 15-20 minutes or until potatoes and squash are almost tender.

Add zucchini and beans; return to a boil. Reduce heat; simmer, uncovered, for 5-8 minutes or until vegetables are tender. **Yield:** 8 servings (3 quarts).

Nutrition Facts: 1-1/2 cups equals 172 calories, 3 g fat (trace saturated fat), 0 cholesterol, 174 mg sodium, 34 g carbohydrate, 8 g fiber, 5 g protein. **Diabetic Exchanges:** 2 starch, 1 vegetable.

Side Dishes & Condiments

Complement your main dish deliciously with any of the on-the-side sensations here. From Basil Buttered Beans to Poblano Pesto, you can't go wrong!

Peach Chutney 42
Homemade Croutons 42
Basil Buttered Beans 42
Spiced Pickled Beets 43
Strawberry Relish 43
Celestial Cherry Conserve 44
Coffee Barbecue Sauce 44
Pomegranate Jelly 44
Mom's Fried Rice 45
Zucchini Pickles 45
Classic Pesto 46
Cilantro Pesto 46
Black & Green Olive Pesto 47
Poblano Pesto 47
Artichoke Hearts Romano 48
New England Baked Beans 48
Almond Rice Pilaf 49
Orange-Berry Jam 49
Sesame Green Beans 49
Creamy Pumpkin Polenta 50
Strawberry-Kiwi Jam 50
Luscious Blueberry Jam 50
Pear Marmalade 51
Foolproof Gravy 51
Baked Broccolini 51

APPEALING ACCENTS. Clockwise from upper left: Celestial Cherry Conserve (p. 44), Strawberry Relish (p. 43), Peach Chutney (p. 42), Pear Marmalade (p. 51), Luscious Blueberry Jam (p. 50), Strawberry-Kiwi Jam (p. 50) and Orange-Berry Jam (p. 49).

In a Dutch oven, bring the vinegar, brown sugar and sugar to a boil. Add the red pepper, onion, banana pepper, raisins, ginger and salt. Place cloves and cinnamon stick on a double thickness of cheesecloth; bring up corners of cloth and tie with string to form a bag. Add to the pan. Return to a boil. Reduce heat; simmer, uncovered, for 10 minutes.

Add the peaches and return to a boil. Reduce the heat; simmer, uncovered, for 25-30 minutes or until thickened. Discard the spice bag. Carefully ladle the hot chutney into hot half-pint jars, leaving 1/2-in. headspace. Remove air bubbles; wipe rims and adjust lids. Process for 15 minutes in a boiling-water canner. **Yield:** 7 half-pints.

Editor's Note: The processing time listed is for altitudes of 1,000 feet or less. For altitudes up to 3,000 feet, add 5 minutes; 6,000 feet, add 10 minutes; 8,000 feet, add 15 minutes; 10,000 feet, add 20 minutes.

Nutrition Facts: 1/4 cup equals 83 calories, trace fat (trace saturated fat), 0 cholesterol, 88 mg sodium, 21 g carbohydrate, 1 g fiber, 1 g protein.

Homemade Croutons
PREP/TOTAL TIME: 20 min.

You can change up this basic recipe from our Test Kitchen cooks by substituting your favorite herbs and spices. It's so easy, you'll never want to use store-bought croutons again.

> 1 loaf (8 ounces) French bread, cubed
> 1 tablespoon butter, melted
> 1 tablespoon olive oil
> 1/2 teaspoon garlic salt
> 1/2 teaspoon lemon-pepper seasoning
> 1/8 teaspoon ground mustard

Place the bread in a large bowl. Combine the remaining ingredients; drizzle over bread and toss to coat.

Place in a single layer in an ungreased 15-in. x 10-in. x 1-in. baking pan. Bake at 400° for 15-20 minutes or until golden brown, stirring occasionally. Cool. Store in an airtight container. **Yield:** 2-2/3 cups.

Peach Chutney
(Pictured above and on page 41)

PREP: 1 hour **PROCESS:** 15 min.

This is my take on several chutney recipes. The sweet-and-spicy marmalade pairs well with just about any meat or poultry. Or, mix it with some mayonnaise for a delicious sandwich spread.
—Joanne Surfus, Sturgeon Bay, Wisconsin

☑ This recipe includes Nutrition Facts.

> 2-1/2 cups white vinegar
> 1 cup packed brown sugar
> 3/4 cup sugar
> 1 medium sweet red pepper, finely chopped
> 1 small onion, finely chopped
> 1 banana pepper, seeded and finely chopped
> 2/3 cup golden raisins
> 1 tablespoon minced fresh gingerroot
> 1 teaspoon canning salt
> 6 whole cloves
> 1 cinnamon stick (3 inches), cut in half
> 3 pounds fresh peaches, peeled and chopped

Basil Buttered Beans
PREP/TOTAL TIME: 15 min.

I grow green beans and basil, and I thought I'd try combining the two. The results were great, especially because the beans remain crisp and fresh-tasting.   —Bernadette Bennett, Waco, Texas

> 4 cups water
> 1 teaspoon chicken bouillon granules
> 1-1/2 pounds fresh green beans, trimmed
> 1 to 2 tablespoons butter, melted
> 3/4 teaspoon dried basil

In a large saucepan, bring water and bouillon to a boil. Add beans. Cook for 3-4 minutes or until crisp-tender; drain. Stir in butter and basil. **Yield:** 6 servings.

Spiced Pickled Beets

(Pictured below)

PREP: 1-1/4 hours **PROCESS:** 35 min.

Say you don't like beets? With their robust flavor from allspice, cinnamon and cloves, these are good enough to convert you!
—Edna Hoffman, Hebron, Indiana

☑ This recipe includes Nutrition Facts and Diabetic Exchanges.

- **3 pounds small fresh beets**
- **2 cups sugar**
- **2 cups water**
- **2 cups cider vinegar**
- **2 cinnamon sticks (3 inches)**
- **1 teaspoon whole cloves**
- **1 teaspoon whole allspice**

Scrub beets and trim tops to 1 in. Place in a Dutch oven and cover with water. Bring to a boil. Reduce heat; cover and simmer for 25-35 minutes or until tender. Remove from the water; cool. Peel beets and cut into fourths.

Place the beets in a Dutch oven. Add the sugar, water and vinegar. Place the spices on a double thickness of cheesecloth; bring up corners of cloth and tie with string to form a bag. Add to the beet mixture. Bring to a boil. Reduce heat; cover and simmer for 10 minutes. Discard spice bag.

Carefully pack beets into hot pint jars to within 1/2 in. of the top. Carefully ladle hot liquid over beets, leaving 1/2-in. headspace. Remove air bubbles; wipe rims and adjust lids. Process for 35 minutes in a boiling-water canner. **Yield:** 4 pints.

Editor's Note: The processing time listed is for altitudes of 1,000 feet or less. For altitudes up to 3,000 feet, add 5 minutes; 6,000 feet, add 10 minutes; 8,000 feet, add 15 minutes; 10,000 feet, add 20 minutes.

Nutrition Facts: 1/4 cup equals 53 calories, trace fat (trace saturated fat), 0 cholesterol, 44 mg sodium, 12 g carbohydrate, 1 g fiber, 1 g protein. **Diabetic Exchanges:** 1 vegetable, 1/2 starch.

Strawberry Relish

(Pictured above and on page 41)

PREP/TOTAL TIME: 30 min.

Whenever my husband grills chicken, we put a few tablespoons of this relish over the top. We've served it for company and always get recipe requests. —Pat Gardetta, Osage Beach, Missouri

☑ This recipe includes Nutrition Facts.

- **1/2 cup packed brown sugar**
- **1 tablespoon water**
- **1/2 cup raspberry vinegar**
- **1 medium tart apple, finely chopped**
- **1 tablespoon finely chopped jalapeno pepper**
- **1 teaspoon minced fresh gingerroot**
- **1 garlic clove, minced**
- **1/4 teaspoon minced fresh cilantro**
- **1/8 teaspoon salt**
- **1/8 teaspoon ground cinnamon**
- **1/8 teaspoon ground cloves**
- **1/8 teaspoon pepper**
- **2 cups fresh strawberries, *divided***

In a large saucepan over medium heat, cook and stir brown sugar and water for 5 minutes. Add vinegar and apple; bring to a boil. Reduce heat; add the jalapeno, ginger, garlic, cilantro, salt, cinnamon, cloves and pepper. Simmer, uncovered, for 10-15 minutes or until apple is tender. Cool slightly.

Transfer to a blender; add 1 cup strawberries. Cover and process until blended. Chop the remaining strawberries; stir into relish. Serve with your favorite grilled meats. **Yield:** 2 cups.

Editor's Note: When cutting hot peppers, disposable gloves are recommended. Avoid touching your face.

Nutrition Facts: 1/4 cup equals 79 calories, trace fat (trace saturated fat), 0 cholesterol, 43 mg sodium, 20 g carbohydrate, 1 g fiber, trace protein, 1 starch.

Celestial Cherry Conserve

(Pictured below and on page 40)

PREP: 40 min. **PROCESS:** 5 min.

This conserve's concentrated cherry flavor is wonderful on toast, ice cream or cheesecake. I've also had great results using mango, strawberries and blueberries, as well as different fruit–flavored herbal teas. —Maureen Delves, Kamloops, British Columbia

☑ This recipe includes Nutrition Facts and Diabetic Exchange.

    2 **medium oranges**
    6 **cups fresh dark sweet cherries, pitted**
3-1/2 **cups sugar**
    6 **tablespoons lemon juice**
    4 **individual black cherry** *or* **wild berry herbal tea bags**
    1 **cup boiling water**
    1 **pouch (3 ounces) liquid fruit pectin**

Grate zest from the oranges; set zest aside. Peel oranges and discard peel; chop the oranges. In a large saucepan, combine the cherries, sugar, lemon juice and chopped oranges. Bring to a boil. Reduce the heat and simmer, uncovered, for 6-8 minutes or until slightly thickened.

Meanwhile, place tea bags in a small bowl. Add boiling water. Cover and steep for 5-6 minutes. Discard tea bags; add liquid to cherry mixture. Bring to a full rolling boil over high heat, stirring constantly. Stir in pectin. Boil for 1 minute, stirring constantly.

Remove from the heat; skim off foam. Ladle the hot

mixture into hot sterilized half-pint jars, leaving 1/4-in. headspace. Remove air bubbles; wipe rims and adjust lids. Process for 5 minutes in a boiling-water canner. **Yield:** 6 half-pints.

Editor's Note: The processing time listed in the recipe is for altitudes of 1,000 feet or less. Add 1 minute to the processing time for each 1,000 feet of additional altitude.

Nutrition Facts: 2 tablespoons equals 72 calories, trace fat (trace saturated fat), 0 cholesterol, trace sodium, 18 g carbohydrate, trace fiber, trace protein. **Diabetic Exchange:** 1 starch.

Coffee Barbecue Sauce

PREP: 15 min. **COOK:** 50 min.

Strong brewed coffee and instant coffee granules add rich color and depth to this robust, sweet–and–sour barbecue sauce. We especially like it spooned over grilled chicken or pork chops. —Julia Bushree, Georgetown, Texas

    1 **medium onion, finely chopped**
    2 **tablespoons olive oil**
    8 **garlic cloves, minced**
    2 **cups ketchup**
    1 **cup cider vinegar**
    1 **cup honey**
1/2 **cup reduced-sodium soy sauce**
1/2 **cup strong brewed coffee**
    2 **teaspoons instant coffee granules**
1/4 **teaspoon salt**
1/4 **teaspoon pepper**

In a large saucepan, saute onion in oil until tender. Add garlic; cook 2 minutes longer. Stir in the remaining ingredients and bring to a boil. Reduce heat; simmer, uncovered, for 35-45 minutes or until the desired consistency, stirring occasionally. **Yield:** 4-1/2 cups.

Pomegranate Jelly

PREP: 15 min. **PROCESS:** 5 min.

For as long as I can remember, my mother has been making this pomegranate jelly and sending all of us home with a few jars. If you can't find pomegranate juice, use cranberry instead. —Tatiana Kushnir, Montara, California

3-1/2 **cups pomegranate juice**
    1 **package (1-3/4 ounces) powdered fruit pectin**
    5 **cups sugar**

In a Dutch oven, combine the pomegranate juice and pectin. Bring to a full rolling boil over high heat, stirring constantly. Stir in sugar; return to a full rolling boil. Boil for 2 minutes, stirring constantly.

Remove from the heat; skim off foam. Pour the hot liquid into hot sterilized half-pint jars, leaving 1/4-in. headspace. Wipe the rims and adjust lids. Process for

5 minutes in a boiling-water canner. **Yield:** 6 half-pints.

Editor's Note: The processing time listed in this recipe is for altitudes of 1,000 feet or less. Add 1 minute to the processing time for each 1,000 feet of additional altitude.

Mom's Fried Rice

(Pictured above)

PREP/TOTAL TIME: 25 min.

Bacon adds a savory smokiness to this classic fried rice recipe, and frozen peas add a splash of color. Feel free to toss in a little cubed chicken or steak. —*Carey Hunt, Portland, Oregon*

- 1 teaspoon canola oil
- 1 egg, beaten
- 8 bacon strips, chopped
- 1 cup chopped fresh mushrooms
- 8 green onions, thinly sliced
- 3 cups leftover cooked rice
- 1 cup bean sprouts
- 1 cup frozen peas, thawed
- 1/4 cup reduced-sodium soy sauce

In a large skillet, heat the oil over medium-high heat. Pour egg into the pan. As egg sets, lift the edges, letting the uncooked portion flow underneath. When the egg is completely cooked, remove to a plate. Set aside.

In the same skillet, cook the bacon over medium heat until crisp. Using a slotted spoon, remove to the paper towels; drain, reserving 2 tablespoons drippings. Saute mushrooms and onions in the drippings. Stir in the rice, bean sprouts, peas, soy sauce and bacon. Chop egg into small pieces; stir into the pan and heat through. **Yield:** 4 servings.

Zucchini Pickles

(Pictured below)

PREP: 35 min. + standing **PROCESS:** 10 min.

Is your vegetable garden overrun with zucchini each summer? Put your bounty to good use by making these crunchy, flavorful burger toppings. —*Romaine Wetzel, Ronks, Pennsylvania*

☑ This recipe includes Nutrition Facts and Diabetic Exchange.

- 8 cups sliced zucchini
- 4 large onions, sliced
- 1 large green pepper, sliced
- 3 tablespoons canning salt
- 1 quart white vinegar
- 2 cups sugar
- 2 teaspoons celery salt
- 2 teaspoons ground turmeric
- 1 teaspoon ground mustard

In a large bowl, combine zucchini, onions and pepper; sprinkle with canning salt and cover with cold water. Let stand for 2 hours; rinse and drain.

In a large saucepan, bring the remaining ingredients to a boil. Pour over zucchini mixture; cover and let stand for 2 hours.

Transfer to a stockpot. Bring to a boil. Reduce heat; simmer, uncovered, for 5 minutes. Carefully ladle hot mixture into hot pint jars, leaving 1/2-in. headspace. Remove air bubbles; wipe rims and adjust lids. Process for 10 minutes in a boiling-water canner. **Yield:** 5 pints.

Editor's Note: The processing time listed is for altitudes of 1,000 feet or less. For altitudes up to 3,000 feet, add 5 minutes; 6,000 feet, add 10 minutes; 8,000 feet, add 15 minutes; 10,000 feet, add 20 minutes.

Nutrition Facts: 1/4 cup equals 31 calories, trace fat (trace saturated fat), 0 cholesterol, 237 mg sodium, 7 g carbohydrate, 1 g fiber, 1 g protein. **Diabetic Exchange:** 1/2 starch.

Presto, Pesto!

YOU WON'T BELIEVE how easy it is to make authentic Italian pesto right in your own kitchen. All you have to do is gather some everyday ingredients and follow the easy recipes we've featured here.

Enjoy the traditional taste of Classic Pesto...or try a twist by accenting the recipe with cilantro, green olives, peppers or other ingredients. You're sure to find a favorite variety you'll want to make again and again for your family.

Want to know how pesto can enhance everyday menus? Just check out the tip box at bottom right for some creative and mouthwatering ideas.

Classic Pesto

(Pictured at right)

PREP/TOTAL TIME: 10 min.

With garlic and basil, this versatile pesto is simple yet boasts a wonderful herb flavor. For a terrific Italian meal, pair it with your favorite pasta and round out the menu with a tossed green salad and breadsticks. Go all out with Italian ice for dessert!
—Iola Egle, Bella Vista, Arizona

- **4 cups loosely packed basil leaves**
- **1/2 cup grated Parmesan cheese**
- **2 garlic cloves, halved**
- **1/4 teaspoon salt**
- **1/2 cup pine nuts, toasted**
- **1/2 cup olive oil**

Place the basil, Parmesan cheese, garlic and salt in a food processor; cover and pulse until chopped. Add the pine nuts; cover and process until blended. While processing, gradually add the oil in a steady stream. **Yield:** 1 cup.

Cilantro Pesto

(Pictured at top far right)

PREP/TOTAL TIME: 10 min.

This brightly colored pesto is so fresh-tasting and great with shrimp. Feel free to make this simple variety ahead of time and freeze it. —Karen Deaver, Babylon Village, New York

- **1 cup fresh cilantro leaves**
- **1/4 cup grated Parmesan cheese**
- **1/4 cup chopped walnuts**
- **2 tablespoons lime juice**
- **1/2 cup olive oil**
Cooked jumbo shrimp, peeled and deveined

Place cilantro and Parmesan cheese in a food processor; cover and pulse until chopped. Add nuts and lime juice; cover and process until blended. While processing, gradually add the oil in a steady stream. Serve with shrimp. **Yield:** 1 cup.

Black & Green Olive Pesto

(Pictured at center right)

PREP/TOTAL TIME: 10 min.

Basic yet flavor-packed, this recipe is perfect for an impromptu gathering. —GaleLynn Peterson, Long Beach, California

- **1 cup pimiento-stuffed olives**
- **1 cup pitted ripe olives**
- **1/2 cup grated Parmesan cheese**
- **2 garlic cloves, halved**
- **2 tablespoons plus 1 teaspoon olive oil**

Assorted crackers

In a food processor, combine the first four ingredients; cover and pulse until finely chopped. While processing, gradually add the oil in a steady stream. Serve with crackers. **Yield:** 2-1/2 cups.

Poblano Pesto

(Pictured at bottom right)

PREP/TOTAL TIME: 25 min.

Blend this spicy pesto with cream and tomatoes, then pour it over your favorite pasta. —Susie Fisher, Watertown, Massachusetts

- **2 large poblano peppers**
- **1 jalapeno pepper**
- **1/4 cup slivered almonds**
- **1/4 cup grated Parmesan cheese**
- **1/2 teaspoon salt**
- **1/4 teaspoon pepper**
- **1/2 cup olive oil**

Cut the peppers in half; remove the stems, seeds and membranes. In a large skillet, bring 1 in. of water to a boil. Add poblanos and jalapeno; cover and cook for 5-6 minutes or until tender. Drain; cool slightly and pat dry.

Place the peppers in food processor; cover and pulse until blended. Add almonds, cheese, salt and pepper; cover and process until blended. While processing, gradually add oil in a steady stream. **Yield:** 1-1/4 cups.

PESTO POSSIBILITIES. Wondering what you can do with pesto? Here are delicious options:
- Toss pesto with pasta or roasted vegetables for a great side dish or light entree.
- For a simple yet delicious appetizer, spread it on toasted baguette slices.
- Blend pesto with mayonnaise for a flavorful sandwich spread.
- Mix it into ordinary mashed potatoes, salads, meat loaves or casseroles.

Artichoke Hearts Romano

(Pictured above)

PREP: 1-1/2 hours **COOK:** 5 min./batch

I've enjoyed cooking all my life, and most of my endeavors are Italian. With a homemade dipping sauce, these golden, breaded artichoke quarters make a unique but zippy side or appetizer.
—Anthony Greco, Saylorsburg, Pennsylvania

> **6 large artichokes**
> **SAUCE:**
>   **1/4 cup chopped onion**
>   **2 tablespoons olive oil**
>   **1 garlic clove, minced**
>   **1 can (16 ounces) crushed tomatoes**
>   **1/4 cup water**
>   **2 tablespoons dry red wine**
>   **1/2 teaspoon sugar**
>   **1/4 teaspoon dried oregano**
>   **1/4 teaspoon dried basil**
>   **1/4 teaspoon crushed red pepper flakes**
> **FOR COOKING:**
>   **1 egg**
>   **1 tablespoon milk**
>   **1 cup seasoned bread crumbs**
>   **1 tablespoon grated Romano cheese**
>   **1 tablespoon minced fresh parsley**
> **Dash pepper**
>   **1/4 cup canola oil**

Using a sharp knife, level the bottom of each artichoke and cut 1 in. from the tops. Using kitchen scissors, snip off tips of outer leaves. Place artichokes in a large saucepan; add 1 in. of water. Bring to a boil. Reduce heat; cover and simmer for 30-35 minutes or until leaves near the center pull out easily.

Invert the artichokes to drain for 10 minutes. With a spoon, carefully remove the fuzzy centers and discard. Cut artichoke hearts into fourths.

In a large saucepan, saute onion in oil until tender. Add garlic; cook 1 minute longer. Add the remaining sauce ingredients; bring to a boil. Reduce heat; simmer, uncovered, for 15-20 minutes or until slightly thickened.

In a shallow bowl, whisk egg and milk. Combine the bread crumbs, cheese, parsley and pepper in another shallow bowl. Dip the artichoke pieces in egg mixture, then coat with crumbs.

In a large skillet, cook artichokes in oil for 1-2 minutes on each side or until golden brown. Serve immediately with the sauce. **Yield:** 2 dozen (2 cups sauce).

New England Baked Beans

PREP: 1-1/2 hours + soaking **BAKE:** 2-1/2 hours

For a potluck or picnic, you can't beat this classic side that starts with a pound of dried beans. Molasses and maple syrup give it a slight sweetness. —Pat Medeiros, Tiverton, Rhode Island

> **1 pound dried great northern beans**
> **1/2 pound thick-sliced bacon strips, chopped**
>   **2 large onions, chopped**
>   **3 garlic cloves, minced**
>   **2 cups ketchup**
> **1-1/2 cups packed dark brown sugar**
>   **1/3 cup molasses**
>   **1/3 cup maple syrup**
>   **1/4 cup Worcestershire sauce**
>   **1/2 teaspoon salt**
>   **1/4 teaspoon coarsely ground pepper**

Sort beans and rinse with cold water. Place beans in a Dutch oven; add enough water to cover by 2 in. Bring to a boil; boil for 2 minutes. Remove from the heat; cover and let stand for 1 hour or until beans are softened.

Drain and rinse beans, discarding liquid. Return beans to Dutch oven; add 6 cups water. Bring to a boil. Reduce heat; cover and simmer for 1 hour or until beans are almost tender.

In a large skillet, cook bacon over medium heat until crisp. Remove to paper towels with a slotted spoon; drain, reserving 2 tablespoons drippings. Saute onions in drippings until tender. Add garlic; cook 1 minute longer. Stir in the remaining ingredients.

Drain the beans, reserving the cooking liquid; place in an ungreased 3-qt. baking dish. Stir in the onion mixture and bacon.

Cover and bake at 300° for 2-1/2 hours or until beans are tender and reach desired consistency, stirring every 30 minutes. Add the reserved cooking liquid as needed. **Yield:** 12 servings (2/3 cup each).

Almond Rice Pilaf

PREP/TOTAL TIME: 15 min.

With quick–cooking rice, this pilaf is a speedy side dish...but the almonds make it special enough for company. It goes well with all kinds of meats. —Sharon Adamczyk, Wind Lake, Wisconsin

- 3/4 cup chopped onion
- 1/2 cup slivered almonds
- 1 tablespoon butter
- 2 cups chicken broth
- 2 cups uncooked instant rice

In a saucepan, saute the onion and almonds in butter until the onion is tender and the almonds are lightly browned. Add broth; bring to a boil. Stir in rice and cover. Remove from the heat. Let stand for 5-8 minutes or until the liquid is absorbed. **Yield:** 6 servings.

Orange-Berry Jam

(Pictured below and on page 40)

PREP: 30 min. **PROCESS:** 5 min.

This jam is a beautiful color—and tastes just as good as it looks! Expect a refreshing tang from the orange segments and peel.
—Earlene Ertelt, Woodburn, Oregon

- 3 cups fresh raspberries
- 2 cups fresh blueberries
- 6-1/2 cups sugar
- 1/2 cup finely chopped orange segments
- 2 tablespoons lemon juice
- 4 teaspoons grated orange peel
- 1 pouch (3 ounces) liquid fruit pectin

Place raspberries and blueberries in a food processor; cover and process until blended. Transfer to a Dutch oven. Stir in the sugar, orange segments, lemon juice and orange peel. Bring to a full rolling boil over high heat, stirring constantly. Stir in pectin. Boil for 1 minute, stirring constantly.

Remove from the heat; skim off foam. Ladle hot mixture into hot sterilized half-pint jars, leaving 1/4-in. headspace. Remove air bubbles; wipe rims and adjust lids. Process for 5 minutes in a boiling-water canner. **Yield:** 6 half-pints.

Editor's Note: The processing time listed in this recipe is for altitudes of 1,000 feet or less. Add 1 minute to the processing time for each 1,000 feet of additional altitude.

Sesame Green Beans

(Pictured above)

PREP: 25 min. **COOK:** 10 min.

My love for Chinese cooking inspired this easy side dish, which is great with grilled chicken or pork. I like to use just–picked beans from our garden. —Debra Broeker, Rocky Mount, Missouri

- 2 pounds fresh green beans, trimmed
- 2/3 cup finely chopped sweet onion
- 3 tablespoons canola oil
- 3 garlic cloves, minced
- 1/4 cup reduced-sodium soy sauce
- 1 teaspoon pepper
- 1 tablespoon sesame seeds, toasted

Place beans in a large saucepan and cover with water. Bring to a boil. Cover and cook for 4-7 minutes or until crisp-tender. Drain and immediately place beans in ice water. Drain and pat dry.

In a large skillet, saute beans and onion in oil until onion is tender. Add garlic; cook 1 minute longer. Stir in the soy sauce and pepper. Transfer to a serving dish; sprinkle with sesame seeds. **Yield:** 8 servings.

Creamy Pumpkin Polenta

(Pictured below)

PREP/TOTAL TIME: 25 min.

Sometimes I hollow out a small pumpkin to serve this creamy, golden polenta. The pepitas, or Mexican pumpkin seeds, make a fitting topping. —Debi George, Mansfield, Texas

☑ **This recipe includes Nutrition Facts and Diabetic Exchanges.**

- 5-1/3 **cups water**
- 1 **teaspoon salt**
- 1-1/3 **cups yellow cornmeal**
- 1/2 **teaspoon ground nutmeg**
- 3/4 **cup canned pumpkin**
- 1/2 **cup cream cheese, cubed**

Salted pumpkin seeds *or* **pepitas, optional**

In a large heavy saucepan, bring water and salt to a boil.

Reduce heat to a gentle boil; slowly whisk in cornmeal and nutmeg. Cook and stir with a wooden spoon for 15-20 minutes or until polenta is thickened and pulls away cleanly from the sides of the pan. Stir in pumpkin and cream cheese until smooth. Sprinkle each serving with pumpkin seeds if desired. **Yield:** 6 servings.

Nutrition Facts: 3/4 cup equals 191 calories, 7 g fat (4 g saturated fat), 21 mg cholesterol, 453 mg sodium, 27 g carbohydrate, 4 g fiber, 5 g protein. **Diabetic Exchanges:** 2 starch, 1 fat.

Strawberry-Kiwi Jam

(Pictured at far right and on page 40)

PREP: 20 min. **COOK:** 15 min. + standing

The bright strawberries and kiwi in this recipe make a wonderful combination. —Kathy Kittell, Lenexa, Kansas

- 6 **cups fresh strawberries**
- 3 **medium kiwifruit, peeled and finely chopped**
- 1 **tablespoon lemon juice**
- 1 **tablespoon chopped crystallized ginger**
- 1 **package (1-3/4 ounces) powdered fruit pectin**
- 5 **cups sugar**

In a large bowl, mash berries; transfer to a Dutch oven. Add the kiwi, lemon juice and ginger. Stir in pectin. Bring to a full rolling boil over high heat, stirring constantly.

Stir in the sugar; return to a full rolling boil. Boil for 1 minute, stirring constantly. Remove from the heat; skim off foam. Ladle into jars or freezer containers and cool to room temperature, about 1 hour.

Cover and let stand overnight or until set, but not longer than 24 hours. Refrigerate for up to 3 weeks or freeze for up to 12 months. **Yield:** 5-3/4 cups.

Luscious Blueberry Jam

(Pictured at far right and on page 40)

PREP: 20 min. **COOK:** 20 min. + standing

This perfectly spreadable jam boasts a gorgeous dark color and sweet, seasonal flavor. —Karen Haen, Sturgeon Bay, Wisconsin

- 8 **cups fresh blueberries**
- 2 **tablespoons lemon juice**
- 1 **package (1-3/4 ounces) powdered fruit pectin**
- 7 **cups sugar**

Mash blueberries; transfer to a Dutch oven. Add lemon juice; stir in pectin. Bring to a full rolling boil over high heat, stirring constantly.

Stir in the sugar; return to a full rolling boil. Boil for 1 minute, stirring constantly. Remove from the heat; skim off foam. Ladle into jars or freezer containers and cool to room temperature, about 1 hour.

Cover and let stand overnight or until set, but not longer than 24 hours. Refrigerate for up to 3 weeks or freeze for up to 12 months. **Yield:** 8 cups.

PECTIN POINTER. Always use the type of pectin called for in the recipe. Usually, powdered pectin is stirred into the fruit and brought to a boil before the sugar is added. Liquid pectin, on the other hand, is added to the mixture after all other ingredients have been brought to a boil.

Pear Marmalade

(Pictured at right and on page 40)

PREP: 15 min. **COOK:** 10 min. + standing

I didn't care for pear preserves until I tried this recipe I received from my husband's Aunt Helen. One taste, and I was a fan! The marmalade is always a favorite at my dinner table.
—*Patty Schreck, Davenport, Washington*

- **4 to 5 medium ripe pears, peeled and quartered**
- **1 can (8 ounces) unsweetened crushed pineapple, undrained**
- **1/2 cup orange juice**
- **2 tablespoons lemon juice**
- **1 tablespoon grated orange peel**
- **1 package (1-3/4 ounces) powdered fruit pectin**
- **5-1/2 cups sugar**

In a food processor, cover and process the pears in batches until pureed. Measure out enough pears to make 2-1/2 cups.

In a Dutch oven, combine the pineapple, orange juice, lemon juice, orange peel and pureed pears. Stir in fruit pectin. Bring to a full rolling boil over high heat, stirring constantly.

Stir in the sugar; return to a full rolling boil. Boil for 1 minute, stirring constantly. Remove from the heat; skim off foam. Ladle into jars or freezer containers and cool to room temperature, about 1 hour.

Cover and let stand overnight or until set, but not longer than 24 hours. Refrigerate for up to 3 weeks or freeze for up to 12 months. **Yield:** 6 cups.

Foolproof Gravy

PREP/TOTAL TIME: 20 min.

Make your Thanksgiving or other special-occasion dinner easy with this can't-miss recipe. Use the drippings from your roasted turkey, and the gravy is done in just 20 minutes.
—*Edie DeSpain, West Logan, Utah*

- **Drippings from 1 roasted turkey**
- **1/2 to 1 cup turkey *or* chicken broth**
- **1/4 cup plus 1 tablespoon all-purpose flour**
- **1/2 cup fat-free milk**
- **1 teaspoon chicken bouillon granules**
- **1/4 teaspoon poultry seasoning**
- **1/8 teaspoon white pepper**

Pour drippings into a 2-cup measuring cup. Skim and discard fat. Add enough broth to the drippings to measure 2 cups; transfer to a small saucepan and bring to a boil.

In a small bowl, combine flour and milk until smooth. Gradually stir into the drippings mixture. Stir in the bouillon granules, poultry seasoning and white pepper. Bring to a boil; cook and stir for 2 minutes or until thickened. **Yield:** 2-1/3 cups.

Baked Broccolini

PREP/TOTAL TIME: 15 min.

Broccoli is my favorite vegetable, but I heard about Broccolini and wanted to try it out. This is really tasty and I think other people will love it. —*Katie Helliwell, San Diego, California*

☑ This recipe includes Nutrition Facts and Diabetic Exchanges.

- **3/4 pound Broccolini *or* broccoli spears**
- **2 tablespoons lemon juice**
- **2 tablespoons olive oil**
- **1/2 teaspoon salt**
- **1/8 teaspoon pepper**

Place Broccolini in a greased 15-in. x 10-in. x 1-in. baking pan. Combine the lemon juice, oil, salt and pepper; drizzle over Broccolini and toss to coat.

Bake, uncovered, at 425° for 10-15 minutes or until tender, stirring occasionally. **Yield:** 4 servings.

Nutrition Facts: 1 serving equals 97 calories, 7 g fat (1 g saturated fat), 0 cholesterol, 320 mg sodium, 7 g carbohydrate, 1 g fiber, 3 g protein. **Diabetic Exchanges:** 1 vegetable, 1 fat.

Main Dishes

From a slow-cooked meal-in-one such as Texas Pork Burritos to fancier fare like Mascarpone-Pesto Chicken Rolls, the recipes in this extra-big chapter will give you family-pleasing entree choices for every occasion.

Southern Fried Chicken Strips 54
Italian Shepherd's Pies......................................54
Roadside Diner Cheeseburger Quiche 54
Fire Island Ziti 55
Mascarpone-Pesto Chicken Rolls.......................55
Ginger Chicken 56
Apple-Brined Chicken Thighs............................56
Kielbasa Chicken Kabobs 57
Tacoritos...57
Curried Chicken Shepherd's Pie.........................58
Chicken Dijon & Couscous 58
Ham with Orange-Apricot Sauce 59
Bacon Potato Waffles 59
Hearty Macaroni Casserole 59
Spiced Cran-Apple Brisket.................................60
Chicken Mole Ole 60
Bacon Cheeseburger Pizza 61
Jamaica-Me-Crazy Chicken Tropicale..................61
Slow Cooker Beef Stroganoff............................62
Grilled Tomatillo Chicken 62
BBQ Chicken Baked Potatoes............................62
Texas Pork Burritos 63
Sweet and Spicy Jerk Ribs 63
Ranch Mac & Cheese...64
Baked Mac & Cheese...65
Bistro Mac & Cheese...65

Meatball Sub Casserole......................................66
Sesame-Pepper Flank Steak 66
Genrose's Stuffed Beef Tenderloin 66
Fish with Fennel 67
Caprese Chicken with Bacon 67
Sloppy Jose Supper 68
Herbed Standing Rib Roast 68
Chicken Continental...68
Mushroom Turkey Tetrazzini 69
Herbed Roast Chicken 69
Hot Tamale Casserole 70
Sunday's Best Chicken.......................................70
Slow Cooker Beef with Red Sauce 70
Beef & Bacon Stroganoff 71
One-Skillet Pasta 71
Beef Roast Au Poivre
    with Caramelized Onions..............................72
Pistachio-Crusted Chicken
    with Garden Spinach 72
Pumpkin Pancakes with
    Cinnamon Brown Butter................................73
Fish Tacos with Avocado Sauce 73
Cream Cheese and Swiss Lasagna 74
Baked Fish with Cheese Sauce 74
Maui-Inspired Turkey Breast Roll........................74
Shrimp & Shiitake Stir-Fry
    with Crispy Noodles 75

MAIN EVENT. Clockwise from top left: Hot Tamale Casserole (p. 70), Roadside Diner Cheeseburger Quiche (p. 54), Mascarpone-Pesto Chicken Rolls (p. 55), Herbed Roast Chicken (p. 69) and Bacon Cheeseburger Pizza (p. 61).

Southern Fried Chicken Strips

(Pictured above)

PREP: 30 min. **COOK:** 5 min./batch

Your family and friends are sure to enjoy this crowd-pleasing chicken that has a hint of garlic. Coleslaw makes the perfect side.
—Genise Krause, Sturgeon Bay, Wisconsin

- 1 egg
- 1/2 cup buttermilk
- 1 cup all-purpose flour
- 1-1/2 teaspoons garlic powder
- 1-1/2 teaspoons pepper
- 1/2 teaspoon salt
- 1/2 teaspoon paprika
- 2 pounds chicken tenderloins
- Oil for deep-fat frying
- 2 tablespoons grated Parmesan cheese

In a shallow bowl, whisk the egg and buttermilk. In a separate shallow bowl, combine flour, garlic powder, pepper, salt and paprika. Dip chicken in egg mixture, then flour mixture.

In an electric skillet, heat oil to 375°. Fry the chicken, a few pieces at a time, for 2-3 minutes on each side or until no longer pink. Drain on paper towels. Sprinkle with cheese. **Yield:** 6 servings.

Italian Shepherd's Pies

PREP: 20 min. **BAKE:** 15 min.

Baked in four single-serving dishes, these hearty little pies have biscuit-like tops and a saucy filling with plenty of beef. You can also prepare this recipe using a 1-1/2-quart casserole dish.
—Sonya Labbe, Santa Monica, California

- 1 pound ground beef
- 1 medium onion, finely chopped
- 2 cups marinara sauce
- 1/8 teaspoon salt
- 1/8 teaspoon pepper
- **TOPPING:**
- 1 cup all-purpose flour
- 1/4 cup grated Parmesan cheese
- 1-1/2 teaspoons baking powder
- 1/2 teaspoon salt
- 1/4 teaspoon Italian seasoning
- 1/2 cup 2% milk
- 1/4 cup butter, melted

In a large skillet, cook beef and onion over medium heat until meat is no longer pink; drain. Add marinara sauce, salt and pepper; cook and stir for 8-10 minutes or until thickened. Spoon into four 8-oz. ramekins or custard cups; set aside.

In a small bowl, combine the flour, Parmesan cheese, baking powder, salt and Italian seasoning. Stir in the milk and butter just until moistened. Spoon dough over meat mixture; place ramekins on a baking sheet.

Bake at 450° for 12-15 minutes or until golden brown. **Yield:** 4 servings.

Roadside Diner Cheeseburger Quiche

(Pictured below and on page 52)

PREP: 20 min. **BAKE:** 50 min. + standing

Love cheeseburgers? Why not enjoy that same all-American flavor for breakfast? This delicious quiche lets you do just that.
—Barbie Miller, Oakdale, Minnesota

- 1 sheet refrigerated pie pastry
- 3/4 pound ground beef
- 2 plum tomatoes, seeded and chopped
- 1 medium onion, chopped
- 1/2 cup dill pickle relish

1/2 cup crumbled cooked bacon
5 eggs
1 cup heavy whipping cream
1/2 cup 2% milk
2 teaspoons prepared mustard
1 teaspoon hot pepper sauce
1/2 teaspoon salt
1/4 teaspoon pepper
1-1/2 cups (6 ounces) shredded cheddar cheese
1/2 cup shredded Parmesan cheese
OPTIONAL GARNISHES:
Mayonnaise, additional pickle relish, crumbled
  cooked bacon, and chopped onion and tomato

Unroll pastry into a 9-in. deep-dish pie plate; flute edges and set aside. In a large skillet, cook beef over medium heat until no longer pink; drain. Stir in the tomatoes, onion, relish and bacon. Transfer to prepared pastry.

In a large bowl, whisk the eggs, cream, milk, mustard, pepper sauce, salt and pepper. Pour over beef mixture. Sprinkle with cheeses.

Bake at 375° for 50-60 minutes or until a knife inserted near the center comes out clean. Cover the edges with foil during the last 15 minutes to prevent overbrowning if necessary. Let stand for 10 minutes before cutting. Garnish with the optional ingredients if desired. **Yield:** 8 servings.

Fire Island Ziti

PREP: 30 min. COOK: 20 min.

I've always been fascinated by Fire Island, New York, a small car-free island and popular vacation destination. I thought the name perfectly fit this slightly spicy sausage–and–pasta dish.
—Candace Reed, De Soto, Texas

2 pounds plum tomatoes, halved lengthwise
3 tablespoons olive oil, *divided*
2 garlic cloves, minced
1 teaspoon salt
8 ounces uncooked ziti
2 cups fresh broccoli florets
1 pound Italian sausage links, cut into 1/2-inch slices
1/2 teaspoon crushed red pepper flakes
1/3 cup grated Romano *or* Parmesan cheese

Toss the tomatoes with 2 tablespoons oil, garlic and salt. Place cut side down in a 15-in. x 10-in. x 1-in. baking pan. Bake at 450° for 20-25 minutes or until tender. Chop when cool enough to handle.

Cook ziti according to the package directions, adding broccoli during the last 4 minutes. Meanwhile, in a large skillet over medium heat, cook sausage in remaining oil until no longer pink. Add pepper flakes; cook 1 minute longer. Stir in tomatoes and heat through.

Drain ziti mixture; toss with sausage mixture. Sprinkle with cheese. **Yield:** 5 servings.

Mascarpone-Pesto Chicken Rolls

(Pictured above and on page 52)

PREP: 20 min. BAKE: 35 min.

Who could resist these golden–brown roll–ups spiraled with rich Mascarpone cheese and pesto? They're great dinner-party fare and easy to fix, too. —Sheryl Little, Sherwood, Arizona

4 boneless skinless chicken breast halves
  (6 ounces *each*)
3/4 teaspoon garlic salt
1/2 cup Mascarpone cheese
1/4 cup prepared pesto
1 egg
2 teaspoons water
1 cup seasoned bread crumbs
8 teaspoons butter, melted, *divided*
8 ounces uncooked fettuccine
Fresh basil leaves, optional

Flatten the chicken to 1/4-in. thickness; sprinkle with garlic salt. Combine the cheese and pesto; spread over the chicken. Roll up each from a short side and secure with toothpicks.

In a shallow bowl, whisk the egg and water. Place the bread crumbs in a separate shallow bowl. Dip the chicken in egg mixture, then coat with crumbs. Place seam side down in a greased 11-in. x 7-in. baking dish. Drizzle with 4 teaspoons butter. Bake, uncovered, at 350° for 35-40 minutes or until a meat thermometer reads 170°. Discard toothpicks.

Meanwhile, cook the fettuccine according to package directions. Drain fettuccine; toss with remaining butter. Serve with chicken. Garnish with basil if desired. **Yield:** 4 servings.

Ginger Chicken

(Pictured below)

PREP: 20 min. + chilling **COOK:** 15 min.

Fresh ginger and soy sauce lend an Asian flair to this stir–fried main dish. Serve it over rice for a complete and satisfying dinner.
—Ben Haen, Baldwin, Wisconsin

☑ This recipe includes Nutrition Facts and Diabetic Exchanges.

  1 **egg white, beaten**
  1 **tablespoon soy sauce**
  1 **teaspoon cornstarch**
1/8 **teaspoon white pepper**
  1 **pound boneless skinless chicken breasts, cut into 1-inch pieces**
SAUCE:
1/2 **teaspoon cornstarch**
  2 **tablespoons rice vinegar**
  2 **tablespoons soy sauce**
  1 **teaspoon sugar**
STIR-FRY:
  1 **tablespoon plus 2 teaspoons peanut oil, *divided***
  1 **medium green pepper, julienned**
  3 **green onions, cut into 1-inch lengths**
1/2 **cup canned bamboo shoots, finely chopped**
  2 **to 3 teaspoons minced fresh gingerroot**
1/4 **cup slivered almonds, toasted**
Hot cooked rice, optional

In a large resealable plastic bag, combine the egg white, soy sauce, cornstarch and pepper. Add chicken; seal bag and turn to coat. Refrigerate for 30 minutes. For sauce, combine the cornstarch, vinegar, soy sauce and sugar until smooth; set aside.

  Drain the chicken and discard the marinade. In a large skillet or wok, stir-fry chicken in 1 tablespoon oil until no longer pink. Remove and keep warm.

  Stir-fry green pepper and green onions in remaining oil for 2 minutes. Add the bamboo shoots and ginger; stir-fry 3-4 minutes longer or until the vegetables are crisp-tender.

  Stir sauce mixture and add to the pan. Bring to a boil; cook and stir for 2 minutes or until thickened. Add chicken and heat through. Sprinkle with almonds. Serve with rice if desired. **Yield:** 4 servings.

  Nutrition Facts: 1 cup stir-fry (calculated without rice) equals 248 calories, 12 g fat (2 g saturated fat), 63 mg cholesterol, 748 mg sodium, 7 g carbohydrate, 2 g fiber, 28 g protein. **Diabetic Exchanges:** 3 lean meat, 1-1/2 fat, 1/2 starch.

Apple-Brined Chicken Thighs

PREP: 30 min. + chilling **BAKE:** 55 min.

I love chicken baked with apples. When I had a bumper crop of green beans, I wanted to include them, too. This recipe is the tasty result. *—Kathy Rairigh, Milford, Indiana*

  3 **cups apple cider *or* juice**
  1 **medium onion, sliced**
  1 **medium lemon, sliced**
  4 **fresh rosemary sprigs**
1/3 **cup kosher salt**
1/2 **cup packed brown sugar, *divided***
  4 **garlic cloves, minced**
  1 **bay leaf**
  1 **teaspoon whole peppercorns**
  2 **cups cold water**
10 **bone-in chicken thighs (about 3-3/4 pounds)**
One 2-gallon resealable plastic bag
  1 **pound fresh green beans, trimmed**
  3 **medium tart apples, cut into wedges**
  1 **tablespoon minced fresh rosemary *or* 1 teaspoon dried rosemary, crushed**
  1 **tablespoon olive oil**
1/4 **teaspoon pepper**

In a Dutch oven, combine cider, onion, lemon, rosemary sprigs, salt, 1/4 cup brown sugar, garlic, bay leaf and peppercorns. Bring to a boil. Cook and stir until salt and brown sugar are dissolved. Remove from the heat; stir in water. Cool brine to room temperature.

  Place the chicken in the 2-gallon resealable plastic bag. Carefully pour the cooled brine into bag. Squeeze out as much air as possible; seal bag and turn to coat. Place in a roasting pan. Refrigerate for 2 hours, turning occasionally.

  Place beans and apples in a greased roasting pan. Drain chicken; place in prepared pan. Bake, uncovered, at 400° for 40 minutes.

  Combine minced rosemary, oil, pepper and remaining brown sugar; sprinkle over chicken. Bake 15-25 minutes longer or until a meat thermometer reads 180° and the beans are tender. **Yield:** 5 servings.

Kielbasa Chicken Kabobs

(Pictured above)

PREP: 20 min. + marinating **GRILL:** 20 min.

Just about any veggies, especially mushrooms, work well for these marinated kabobs. You could also substitute orange juice for the pineapple juice...or use chunks of beef instead of chicken.
—Cristi Smay, Clearfield, Pennsylvania

- 3/4 cup unsweetened pineapple juice
- 1/4 cup cider vinegar
- 1/4 cup canola oil
- 2 tablespoons sugar
- 2 tablespoons soy sauce
- 1/2 teaspoon garlic powder
- 1/4 teaspoon lemon-pepper seasoning
- 2 pounds boneless skinless chicken breasts, cut into 1-inch cubes
- 1 pound smoked kielbasa *or* Polish sausage, thickly sliced
- 1 can (20 ounces) unsweetened pineapple chunks, drained
- 2 medium green peppers, quartered
- 2 cups grape tomatoes
- 2 medium red onions, quartered

In a small bowl, combine the first seven ingredients. Remove 1/2 cup for basting; cover and refrigerate. Divide the remaining marinade between two large resealable plastic bags. Add chicken to one bag; add the kielbasa, pineapple and vegetables to the other bag. Seal bags and turn to coat; refrigerate for at least 2 hours.

On 16 metal or soaked wooden skewers, alternately thread the chicken, kielbasa, pineapple and vegetables.

Using long-handled tongs, dip a paper towel in cooking oil and lightly coat the grill rack. Grill kabobs, covered, over medium heat or broil 4 in. from the heat for 10-15 minutes or until the chicken is no longer pink, turning frequently and basting with reserved marinade. **Yield:** 16 kabobs.

Tacoritos

(Pictured below)

PREP: 40 min. **BAKE:** 20 min.

This mild and meaty Southwestern supper combines the popular flavor of tacos with the heartiness of burritos. Your family's going to love them! —Monica Flatford, Knoxville, Tennessee

- 1/4 cup butter, cubed
- 1/4 cup all-purpose flour
- 4 cups water
- 3 tablespoons chili powder
- 1 teaspoon garlic salt
- 1 pound ground beef
- 1 pound bulk pork sausage
- 1/4 cup chopped onion
- 1 cup refried beans
- 8 flour tortillas (8 inches), warmed
- 3 cups (12 ounces) shredded Monterey Jack cheese

OPTIONAL TOPPINGS:
Shredded lettuce, chopped tomatoes, sliced ripe olives and sour cream

In a large saucepan, melt the butter. Stir in flour until smooth; gradually add water. Bring to a boil; cook and stir for 1 minute or until thickened. Stir in chili powder and garlic salt. Bring to a boil. Reduce heat; simmer, uncovered, for 10 minutes.

In a large skillet over medium heat, cook the beef, sausage and onion until meat is no longer pink; drain. Stir in refried beans; heat through.

Spread 1/4 cup sauce in a greased 13-in. x 9-in. baking dish. Spread 1 tablespoon sauce over each tortilla; place 2/3 cup meat mixture down the center of each. Top each with 1/4 cup cheese. Roll up and place seam side down in prepared dish. Pour the remaining sauce over the top; sprinkle with remaining cheese.

Bake, uncovered, at 350° for 18-22 minutes or until bubbly and the cheese is melted. Serve with optional toppings if desired. **Yield:** 8 servings.

Curried Chicken Shepherd's Pie

(Pictured above)

PREP: 25 min. **BAKE:** 25 min.

Using leftover mashed potatoes to top this comforting casserole is a great time-saver. The creamy chicken-and-vegetable mixture is mildly seasoned with curry to please almost any palate.
—*Lori Lockrey, Scarborough, Ontario*

- 1 large onion, chopped
- 2 celery ribs, chopped
- 3 tablespoons butter, *divided*
- 1 cup frozen peas and carrots
- 3 tablespoons all-purpose flour
- 1 teaspoon curry powder
- 1-1/2 cups reduced-sodium chicken broth
- 1/2 cup 2% milk
- 2 cups cubed cooked chicken
- 2 tablespoons dried parsley flakes
- 1/2 teaspoon salt
- 1/2 teaspoon pepper
- 2 cups mashed potatoes (with added milk and butter)
- 1/4 teaspoon paprika

In a large skillet, saute onion and celery in 1 tablespoon butter until tender. Add the frozen vegetables and the remaining butter; cook 2 minutes longer.

Stir in flour and curry powder until blended; gradually add chicken broth and milk. Bring to a boil; cook and stir for 1 minute or until thickened. Add chicken, parsley, salt and pepper.

Transfer to a greased 2-qt. baking dish. Top with the potatoes; sprinkle with paprika. Bake, uncovered, at 350° for 25-30 minutes or until heated through. **Yield:** 4 servings.

Chicken Dijon & Couscous

(Pictured below)

PREP: 20 min. **BAKE:** 20 min.

When I created this chicken entree, it was a hit with my family. Serve it over couscous...or use another pasta or rice instead.
—*Susan Marshall, Colorado Springs, Colorado*

- 4 boneless skinless chicken breast halves (6 ounces *each*)
- 1/2 cup white wine *or* chicken broth
- 2 teaspoons minced fresh tarragon *or* 1/2 teaspoon dried tarragon
- 1/8 teaspoon pepper

COUSCOUS:
- 1-1/2 cups water
- 1 cup uncooked couscous
- 1 tablespoon butter
- 1 teaspoon chicken bouillon granules
- 1 teaspoon minced fresh tarragon *or* 1/4 teaspoon dried tarragon

SAUCE:
- 1 tablespoon butter
- 3 tablespoons all-purpose flour
- 1/2 teaspoon salt
- 3/4 cup 2% milk
- 1/3 cup reduced-fat sour cream
- 2 tablespoons Dijon mustard

Place chicken in an ungreased 11-in. x 7-in. baking dish. Pour wine over chicken; sprinkle with tarragon and pepper. Cover and bake at 400° for 15 minutes. Uncover; bake 5-10 minutes longer or until a meat thermometer reads 170°. Remove chicken and keep warm, reserving the pan juices.

For couscous, in a small saucepan, bring water to a boil. Stir in the couscous, butter, bouillon and tarragon. Remove from the heat; cover and let stand for 5-10 minutes or until liquid is absorbed. Fluff with a fork.

For sauce, in a small saucepan, melt butter. Stir in flour and salt until smooth; gradually add milk and pan

juices. Bring to a boil; cook and stir for 2 minutes or until thickened. Remove from the heat; stir in the sour cream and mustard. Serve with chicken and couscous. **Yield:** 4 servings.

Ham with Orange-Apricot Sauce

PREP: 10 min. **BAKE:** 1-1/2 hours

I'm always taking dishes to buffets. When I wanted to bring ham, I came up with this recipe featuring a tangy fruit sauce.
—*Shirley Hewitt, Milwaukie, Oregon*

- 1 **fully cooked spiral-sliced ham (6 to 7 pounds)**
- 1 **cup thawed orange juice concentrate**
- 1 **cup sugar**
- 1 **cup dried apricots, chopped**
- 1/2 **cup water**
- 1/2 **cup dried cranberries**
- 3 **tablespoons dried currants**

Place the ham on a rack in a shallow roasting pan. Cover and bake at 325° for 1-1/2 to 2 hours or until a meat thermometer reads 140°.

In a large saucepan, combine the concentrate, sugar, apricots, water, cranberries and currants. Bring to a boil. Reduce heat; simmer, uncovered, for 3-5 minutes or until slightly thickened. Serve with ham. **Yield:** 15 servings (2-1/4 cups sauce).

Bacon Potato Waffles

PREP: 20 min. **COOK:** 5 min./batch

I like to garnish these homemade waffles with sour cream and chives, or even a simple cheese sauce. My mother used to sprinkle them with a little sugar.   —*Laura Fall–Sutton, Buhl, Idaho*

- 1 **cup all-purpose flour**
- 2 **tablespoons sugar**
- 2 **teaspoons baking powder**
- 1/2 **teaspoon salt**
- 2 **eggs**
- 1-1/2 **cups mashed potatoes (with added milk and butter)**
- 1 **cup 2% milk**
- 5 **tablespoons canola oil**
- 1/4 **cup finely chopped onion**
- 3 **bacon strips, cooked and crumbled**

Maple syrup *or* chunky applesauce
Additional crumbled cooked bacon, optional

In a large bowl, combine the flour, sugar, baking powder and salt. In another bowl, whisk eggs, potatoes, milk and oil. Stir into dry ingredients just until moistened. Fold in onion and bacon.

Bake in a preheated waffle iron according to the manufacturer's directions until golden brown. Serve

waffles with maple syrup or applesauce. Sprinkle with additional bacon if desired. **Yield:** 12 waffles.

Hearty Macaroni Casserole

(Pictured above)

PREP: 20 min. **BAKE:** 30 min.

This easy, family–pleasing recipe is twice as nice because it makes two casseroles. Enjoy one now and freeze the other for later.
—*Joy Sauers, Sioux Falls, South Dakota*

- 1 **package (7-1/4 ounces) macaroni and cheese dinner mix**
- 1 **pound ground beef**
- 1 **cup chopped green pepper**
- 1/2 **cup chopped onion**
- 1 **can (14-1/2 ounces) Italian diced tomatoes, drained**
- 2 **cups (8 ounces) shredded cheddar cheese, *divided***
- 1 **cup French-fried onions**

Prepare macaroni and cheese according to package directions. Meanwhile, in a large skillet, cook the beef, green pepper and onion over medium heat until meat is no longer pink; drain. Add to the prepared macaroni. Stir in tomatoes.

Divide half of mixture between two greased 1-1/2-qt. baking dishes; sprinkle each with 1/2 cup cheese. Top with remaining mixture.

Sprinkle remaining cheese over one casserole. Cover and freeze for up to 3 months. Sprinkle the second casserole with French-fried onions. Bake, uncovered, at 350° for 30 minutes or until heated through.

To use frozen casserole: Completely thaw in the refrigerator. Remove from the refrigerator 30 minutes before baking. Bake as directed. **Yield:** 2 casseroles (4 servings each).

Spiced Cran-Apple Brisket
(Pictured below)

PREP: 20 min. **COOK:** 8 hours

It seems everyone who samples this tender beef brisket becomes an instant fan. The apples and cranberries are perfect for fall.
—*Aysha Schurman, Ammon, Idaho*

☑ This recipe includes Nutrition Facts and Diabetic Exchanges

- 1 fresh beef brisket (4 pounds)
- 1/2 cup apple butter
- 1/4 cup ruby port wine
- 2 tablespoons cider vinegar
- 1 teaspoon coarsely ground pepper
- 1/2 teaspoon salt
- 1 medium tart apple, peeled and cubed
- 1 celery rib, chopped
- 1 small red onion, chopped
- 1/3 cup dried apples, chopped
- 1/3 cup dried cranberries
- 2 garlic cloves, minced
- 1 tablespoon cornstarch
- 3 tablespoons cold water

Cut brisket in half; place in a 5-qt. slow cooker. In a large bowl, combine apple butter, wine, vinegar, pepper and salt. Stir in tart apple, celery, red onion, dried apples, cranberries and garlic. Pour over brisket. Cover and cook on low for 8-10 hours or until the meat is tender.

Remove meat to a serving platter; keep warm. Skim fat from cooking juices; transfer to a small saucepan. Bring liquid to a boil. Combine cornstarch and water until smooth. Gradually stir into the pan. Bring to a boil; cook and stir for 2 minutes or until thickened. Serve with meat. **Yield:** 9 servings.

Editor's Note: This is a fresh beef brisket, not corned beef. This recipe was tested with commercially prepared apple butter.

Nutrition Facts: 4 ounces cooked beef with 1/3 cup cooking juices equals 334 calories, 9 g fat (3 g saturated fat), 86 mg cholesterol, 208 mg sodium, 18 g carbohydrate, 1 g fiber, 42 g protein. **Diabetic Exchanges:** 6 lean meat, 1 starch.

Chicken Mole Ole

PREP: 40 min. **COOK:** 4 hours

You're sure to get a kick out of this slow-cooked Southwestern favorite. It requires a bit of preparation time but is well worth it.
—*Johnna Johnson, Scottsdale, Arizona*

- 2 dried ancho chilies
- 1-1/2 pounds tomatillos, husks removed, halved
- 2 medium onions, sliced, *divided*
- 1 serrano pepper, halved and seeded
- 3 garlic cloves, peeled
- 3 pounds bone-in chicken breast halves, skin removed
- 1 tablespoon canola oil
- 2 teaspoons ground cumin, *divided*
- 1-1/2 teaspoons chili powder
- 1 teaspoon pepper
- 1/4 teaspoon ground cinnamon
- 2 whole cloves
- 1/2 cup almonds
- 1 ounce unsweetened chocolate, chopped
- 1 tablespoon lime juice
- 1 teaspoon salt
- 1-1/2 cups (6 ounces) shredded cheddar-Monterey Jack cheese
- 1/2 cup minced fresh cilantro

Place ancho chilies in a small bowl. Cover with boiling water; let stand for 20 minutes. Drain. Remove stems and seeds. Coarsely chop; set aside.

Place the tomatillos, 1 onion, serrano pepper and garlic in a greased 15-in. x 10-in. x 1-in. baking pan. Bake, uncovered, at 400° for 10-15 minutes or until tender, stirring once.

In a large skillet, brown the chicken in oil. Transfer to a 4-qt. slow cooker. In same skillet, saute remaining onion until tender. Add 1 teaspoon cumin, chili powder, pepper, cinnamon, cloves and hydrated chilies; cook 1 minute longer. Discard cloves.

Place almonds in a food processor; cover and process until ground. Add spiced onion mixture and chocolate; cover and process until blended. Transfer to a bowl.

Place the tomatillo mixture, lime juice, salt and remaining cumin in food processor; cover and process until chopped. Stir into the almond mixture. Pour over the chicken.

Cover and cook on low for 4-5 hours or until chicken is tender. Sprinkle each serving with cheese and cilantro. **Yield:** 6 servings.

Editor's Note: When cutting hot peppers, disposable gloves are recommended. Avoid touching your face.

Bacon Cheeseburger Pizza

(Pictured above and on page 52)

PREP: 30 min. + standing **BAKE:** 15 min.

Why order out for pizza when you can enjoy this mouthwatering, homemade pie fresh from the oven? The burger ingredients are a fun and tasty twist. —Vivian Taylor, Middleburg, Florida

- 3 **cups bread flour**
- 2 **tablespoons sugar**
- 1 **package (1/4 ounce) quick-rise yeast**
- 1-1/2 **teaspoons salt**
- 3/4 **cup warm water (120° to 130°)**
- 2 **tablespoons olive oil**
- 1 **pound lean ground beef (90% lean)**
- 3 **garlic cloves, minced**
- 1/8 **teaspoon pepper**
- 1 **cup grated Parmesan cheese**
- 1 **jar (10 ounces) sun-dried tomato pesto**
- 1 **large red onion, chopped**
- 1/4 **cup bacon bits**
- 1 **cup (4 ounces) shredded part-skim mozzarella cheese**
- 1 **cup (4 ounces) sharp shredded cheddar cheese**

In a large bowl, combine 2 cups flour, sugar, yeast and salt. Add water and oil; mix until smooth. Stir in enough remaining flour to form a firm dough.

Turn the dough onto a lightly floured surface; knead until smooth and elastic, about 6-8 minutes. Cover and let rest for 10 minutes.

Meanwhile, in a large skillet over medium heat, cook the beef, garlic and pepper until the meat is no longer pink; drain.

On a floured surface, roll the dough into a 15-in. circle. Transfer to a greased 14-in. pizza pan. Build up edges slightly. Prick the dough thoroughly with a fork. Bake at 450° for 5-8 minutes or until lightly browned.

Sprinkle crust with Parmesan cheese. Top with pesto, meat mixture, onion, bacon bits, and mozzarella and cheddar cheeses. Bake for 15-20 minutes or until cheese is melted. **Yield:** 6 slices.

Jamaica-Me-Crazy Chicken Tropicale

(Pictured below)

PREP: 25 min. **COOK:** 5 hours

I try the sauce about 30 minutes before taking this flavorful chicken out of the slow cooker, and then I adjust the seasonings as needed. If you like, thicken it with a tablespoon of cornstarch. —Mary Louise Lever, Rome, Georgia

- 3 **medium sweet potatoes, peeled and cut into 2-inch pieces**
- 1 **can (8 ounces) sliced water chestnuts, drained**
- 1 **cup dried cranberries**
- 1 **can (20 ounces) unsweetened pineapple tidbits**
- 2 **pounds bone-in chicken breast halves, skin removed**
- 2 **tablespoons Caribbean jerk seasoning**
- 1/4 **cup dried minced onion**
- 3 **tablespoons minced fresh gingerroot**
- 2 **tablespoons Worcestershire sauce**
- 1 **tablespoon grated lime peel**
- 1 **teaspoon cumin seeds, crushed**
- 3 **fresh thyme sprigs**

Hot cooked rice

Place potatoes in a 4- or 5-qt. slow cooker. Add the water chestnuts and cranberries. Drain pineapple, reserving juice; add pineapple to slow cooker. Top with chicken. Sprinkle jerk seasoning over chicken.

Combine onion, ginger, Worcestershire sauce, lime peel, cumin seeds and reserved juice. Pour over chicken. Top with thyme sprigs.

Cover; cook on low for 5-6 hours or until chicken and vegetables are tender. Serve with rice. **Yield:** 4 servings.

Slow Cooker Beef Stroganoff

(Pictured above)

PREP: 20 min. **COOK:** 6 hours

Tired of standing and stirring at the stove? This rich Stroganoff preps in a skillet, then cooks during the day while you're away.
—Sarah Vasques, Milford, New Hampshire

- **2 pounds beef top sirloin steak, cut into thin strips**
- **3 tablespoons olive oil**
- **1 cup water**
- **1 envelope (1-1/2 ounces) beef stroganoff seasoning for the slow cooker**
- **1 pound sliced baby portobello mushrooms**
- **1 small onion, chopped**
- **3 tablespoons butter**
- **1/4 cup port wine *or* beef broth**
- **2 teaspoons ground mustard**
- **1 teaspoon sugar**
- **1-1/2 cups (12 ounces) sour cream**
- **Hot cooked egg noodles**
- **Minced fresh parsley, optional**

In a large skillet, brown the meat in oil. Add the water and stroganoff seasoning mix, stirring to loosen the browned bits from pan. Transfer meat and drippings to a 3-qt. slow cooker.

In the same skillet, saute mushrooms and onion in butter until tender. Combine the wine, mustard and sugar; stir into the mushroom mixture. Add to slow cooker; stir to combine.

Cover and cook on low for 6-8 hours or until meat is tender. Stir in sour cream. Serve with noodles. Sprinkle with parsley if desired. **Yield:** 7 servings.

Grilled Tomatillo Chicken

PREP: 25 min. **GRILL:** 10 min.

This winning dish gets its kick from a tomatillo mixture jazzed up with lime juice, cilantro and jalapeno pepper. Serve it with rice and sour cream for a complete and memorable meal.
—Audrey Kinne, Elkhart, Indiana

- **4 boneless skinless chicken breast halves (6 ounces *each*)**
- **4 slices provolone cheese**
- **1 medium onion, chopped**
- **1 tablespoon olive oil**
- **6 tomatillos, husks removed, chopped**
- **1/4 cup lime juice**
- **6 pickled jalapeno slices, chopped**
- **1 garlic clove, minced**
- **1/4 cup minced fresh cilantro**
- **1 teaspoon ground cumin**
- **1/2 teaspoon salt**
- **1/4 teaspoon pepper**
- **Hot cooked rice**
- **Sour cream, optional**

Using long-handled tongs, dip a paper towel in cooking oil and lightly coat grill rack. Grill chicken, covered, over medium heat or broil 4 in. from the heat for 4-7 minutes on each side or until a meat thermometer reads 170°. Top with the cheese; cook 1 minute longer or until the cheese is melted.

In a large skillet, saute onion in oil until tender. Add the tomatillos, lime juice and jalapenos; cook 3 minutes longer. Add garlic; cook 1 minute longer.

Stir in the cilantro, cumin, salt and pepper. Serve the tomatillo mixture and chicken with rice; dollop with sour cream if desired. **Yield:** 4 servings.

BBQ Chicken Baked Potatoes

PREP: 15 min. **COOK:** 6 hours

The smoky barbecue flavor of these chicken-topped potatoes will make your mouth water. I like to garnish them with blue cheese and green onions.
—Amber Massey, Coppell, Texas

- **4-1/2 pounds bone-in chicken breast halves, skin removed**
- **2 tablespoons garlic powder**
- **1 large red onion, sliced into thick rings**
- **1 bottle (18 ounces) honey barbecue sauce**
- **1 cup Italian salad dressing**
- **1/2 cup packed brown sugar**
- **1/2 cup cider vinegar**
- **1/4 cup Worcestershire sauce**
- **2 tablespoons Liquid Smoke, optional**
- **10 medium potatoes, baked**
- **Crumbled blue cheese and chopped green onions, optional**

Place the chicken in a greased 5- or 6-qt. slow cooker; sprinkle with the garlic powder and top with the onion. Combine the barbecue sauce, salad dressing, brown sugar, vinegar, Worcestershire sauce and Liquid Smoke if desired; pour over chicken.

Cover and cook on low for 6-8 hours or until chicken is tender. When cool enough to handle, remove chicken from the bones; discard bones and onion. Skim fat from cooking juices. Shred meat and return to slow cooker; heat through. Serve over potatoes with blue cheese and green onions if desired. **Yield:** 10 servings.

Texas Pork Burritos

(Pictured below)

PREP: 40 min. **COOK:** 6-1/2 hours

I've been experimenting lately with green enchilada sauce, and it really lights up the pork filling in these crowd–pleasing burritos.
—*Sally Sibthorpe, Shelby Township, Michigan*

- 1 **boneless pork shoulder roast (3 to 4 pounds), cubed**
- 1 **teaspoon salt**
- 1/2 **teaspoon pepper**
- 2 **tablespoons canola oil**
- 2 **cans (10 ounces *each*) green enchilada sauce**
- 1 **large onion, thinly sliced**
- 2 **medium carrots, thinly sliced**
- 2 **cans (2-1/4 ounces *each*) sliced ripe olives, drained**
- 1/2 **cup chicken broth**
- 2 **tablespoons ground cumin**
- 3 **garlic cloves, minced**
- 2 **teaspoons dried oregano**
- 2 **tablespoons all-purpose flour**
- 1 **cup (8 ounces) sour cream**
- 1/2 **cup minced fresh cilantro**
- 10 **flour tortillas (8 inches), warmed**
- 2 **cups (8 ounces) shredded Mexican cheese blend**

Sprinkle pork with salt and pepper. In a large skillet, brown the meat in oil in batches. Transfer to a 3-qt. slow cooker. Combine the enchilada sauce, onion, carrots, ripe olives, chicken broth, cumin, garlic and oregano; pour over meat. Cover and cook on low for 6-8 hours or until meat is tender.

Combine flour and sour cream; stir into meat mixture. Cover; cook on high for 30 minutes or until thickened. Stir in cilantro.

Spoon 2/3 cup pork mixture onto each tortilla; top with about 3 tablespoons cheese. Roll up tightly. **Yield:** 10 servings.

Sweet and Spicy Jerk Ribs

(Pictured above)

PREP: 10 min. **COOK:** 6 hours

With a sweet and fruity sauce, these ribs are sure to become a family favorite. You'll need just 10 minutes to get them into the slow cooker. —*Geri Lesch, New Port Richey, Florida*

- 2 **racks pork baby back ribs (about 4-1/2 pounds)**
- 3 **tablespoons olive oil**
- 1/3 **cup Caribbean jerk seasoning**
- 3 **cups honey barbecue sauce**
- 3 **tablespoons apricot preserves**
- 2 **tablespoons honey**

Cut the ribs into serving-size pieces; brush with oil and rub with the jerk seasoning. Place in a 5- or 6-qt. slow cooker. Combine the remaining ingredients; pour over the ribs.

Cover and cook on low for 6-8 hours or until the meat is tender. Skim the fat from sauce before serving. **Yield:** 5 servings.

Mac 'n' Cheese, Please!

IT'S THE ULTIMATE comfort food—tender macaroni smothered in a rich and creamy cheese sauce. No wonder it's a perennial favorite of kids and adults alike.

Here, you'll find tasty ways to dress up this classic dish...and you won't believe how easily they come together. These recipes are so simple, you can treat your family to homemade mac 'n' cheese in a snap and please everyone at the table.

Remember that macaroni and cheese is versatile, too. For example, it's a great way to use up ends of various blocks of cheese. Shred and combine three or more types for wonderful flavor and texture.

Trying to give your family a nutrition boost? You could also use whole wheat pasta for extra fiber.

Check out the tip box below left for more ideas...or try enhancing your mac with any of these add-ins:
• **Meats.** Cooked turkey, tuna, chicken, diced ham, sliced smoked sausage links, sliced turkey sausage, sliced hot dogs or bacon.
• **Vegetables.** Green beans, onion, roasted red pepper or chopped pimiento.
• **Spices/herbs.** Dash hot pepper sauce, dash cayenne, nutmeg, chili powder, dried parsley flakes, sage or chives.
• **Toppings.** Wheat germ, shredded cheese, buttered and crushed saltines, chopped nuts (almonds, walnuts or cashews) or buttered soft bread crumbs.

A TWIST ON TRADITION

WITHOUT A DOUBT, macaroni and cheese is as all-American as apple pie. Why not take your mac to a new, deliciously different level with some international flair? Just choose a variation below, then add the listed ingredients...and get ready to take a trip with your taste buds!

ASIAN

Cabbage, 1-1/2 teaspoons Thai chili garlic sauce, water chestnuts, sugar snap peas, carrots and green onions. Top with chow mein noodles and sesame seeds.

MEXICAN

Cooked seasoned ground beef, onion, tomatoes, olives, Mexicorn, pepper jack cheese, salsa, green chilies and 1-2 tablespoons taco seasoning. Top with crushed tortilla chips.

ITALIAN

Pepperoni, diced tomatoes, pesto, fresh oregano and basil, mushrooms, chopped artichoke hearts, olives, Italian seasoning and shredded mozzarella. Sprinkle with Italian-flavored bread crumbs.

MEDITERRANEAN

Kalamata olives, cooked shrimp or crabmeat, bell peppers, diced tomato, capers, chopped broccoli, spinach, roasted eggplant, garbanzo beans, feta cheese, rosemary or thyme. Top with chopped pine nuts, almonds or walnuts.

Ranch Mac & Cheese

(Pictured below)

PREP/TOTAL TIME: 30 min.

I dreamed up the recipe for this creamy macaroni and cheese that features popular ranch flavor. My husband requests it often.
—Michelle Rotunno, Independence, Missouri

- 1 **package (16 ounces) elbow macaroni**
- 1 **cup 2% milk**
- 1/4 **cup butter, cubed**
- 1 **envelope ranch salad dressing mix**
- 1 **teaspoon garlic salt**
- 1 **teaspoon garlic pepper blend**
- 1 **teaspoon lemon-pepper seasoning**
- 1 **cup (4 ounces) shredded Monterey Jack cheese**
- 1 **cup (4 ounces) shredded Colby cheese**
- 1 **cup (8 ounces) sour cream**
- 1/2 **cup crushed saltines**
- 1/3 **cup grated Parmesan cheese**

Cook the macaroni according to package directions. Meanwhile, in a Dutch oven, combine the milk, butter, dressing mix and seasonings; heat through. Stir in the Monterey Jack and Colby cheeses until melted. Stir in the sour cream.

Drain the macaroni; stir into the cheese sauce with the saltines. Sprinkle with Parmesan cheese. **Yield:** 8 servings.

Baked Mac & Cheese

(Pictured below)

PREP: 20 min. **BAKE:** 20 min.

Everyone comes running when I pull this hot and bubbly dish from the oven. When I want a heartier version to serve as an all-in-one meal, I'll toss in some cauliflower, broccoli or turkey.
—Denise Hash, Billings, Montana

- 4 cups uncooked spiral pasta
- 1/4 cup butter, cubed
- 1/4 cup all-purpose flour
- 4 cups 2% milk
- 1/2 teaspoon salt
- 1/4 teaspoon pepper
- 1/4 teaspoon ground mustard
- 1/4 teaspoon Worcestershire sauce
- Dash ground nutmeg
- 2 cups (8 ounces) shredded cheddar cheese
- 1 cup cubed process cheese (Velveeta)

Cook the spiral pasta according to package directions. In a large saucepan, melt the butter; stir in the flour until smooth.

Gradually add milk; stir in the salt, pepper, mustard, Worcestershire sauce and nutmeg. Bring to a boil; cook and stir for 1-2 minutes or until thickened. Stir in the cheeses until melted.

Drain the spiral pasta; stir in the prepared cheese sauce. Transfer to an ungreased 2-qt. baking dish. Bake, uncovered, at 350° for 20-25 minutes or until bubbly. **Yield:** 8 servings.

Bistro Mac & Cheese

(Pictured below)

PREP/TOTAL TIME: 30 min.

With four varieties of cheese—mozzarella, cheddar, Gorgonzola and cream cheese—this satisfying creation feels upscale but will fit just about any budget. Sour cream adds even more richness. See the Editor's Note at the end of the recipe for a fun baked variation that's finished off with a buttery bread-crumb topping.
—Charlotte Giltner, Mesa, Arizona

- 1 package (16 ounces) uncooked elbow macaroni
- 3 tablespoons butter
- 3 tablespoons all-purpose flour
- 2-1/2 cups 2% milk
- 1 teaspoon salt
- 1/2 teaspoon onion powder
- 1/2 teaspoon pepper
- 1/4 teaspoon garlic powder
- 1 cup (4 ounces) shredded part-skim mozzarella cheese
- 1 cup (4 ounces) shredded cheddar cheese
- 1 package (3 ounces) cream cheese, softened
- 1/2 cup crumbled Gorgonzola cheese
- 1/2 cup sour cream

Cook the elbow macaroni according to the package directions.

Meanwhile, in a Dutch oven, melt the butter. Stir in the flour until smooth. Gradually stir in the milk and seasonings. Bring to a boil; cook and stir for 2 minutes or until thickened.

Reduce the heat; add cheeses and stir until melted. Stir in sour cream. Drain macaroni; stir into sauce. **Yield:** 8 servings.

Editor's Note: This recipe can also be baked with a crumb topping. Place the macaroni in a greased 3-qt. baking dish. Combine 1/3 cup seasoned bread crumbs and 2 tablespoons melted butter; sprinkle over the macaroni. Bake, uncovered, at 350° for 20-25 minutes or until bubbly.

Meatball Sub Casserole

(Pictured above)

PREP: 40 min. **BAKE:** 30 min.

This oven–baked dish has all of the flavor of popular meatball sandwiches. The only thing that's missing? The mess!
—*Gina Harris, Seneca, South Carolina*

1/3 cup chopped green onions
1/4 cup seasoned bread crumbs
  3 tablespoons grated Parmesan cheese
  1 pound ground beef
  1 loaf (1 pound) Italian bread, cut into 1-inch slices
  1 package (8 ounces) cream cheese, softened
1/2 cup mayonnaise
  1 teaspoon Italian seasoning
1/4 teaspoon pepper
  2 cups (8 ounces) shredded part-skim mozzarella cheese, *divided*
  1 jar (28 ounces) spaghetti sauce
  1 cup water
  2 garlic cloves, minced

In a bowl, combine the onions, crumbs and Parmesan cheese. Add the beef and mix well. Shape into 1-in. balls; place on a greased rack in a shallow baking pan. Bake at 400° for 15-20 minutes or until no longer pink.

Meanwhile, arrange the bread in a single layer in an ungreased 13-in. x 9-in. baking dish (all of the bread might not be used).

Combine the cream cheese, mayonnaise, Italian seasoning and pepper; spread over the bread. Sprinkle with 1/2 cup mozzarella.

Combine the sauce, water and garlic; add meatballs. Pour over cheese mixture; sprinkle with the remaining mozzarella. Bake, uncovered, at 350° for 30 minutes or until heated through. **Yield:** 6 servings.

Sesame-Pepper Flank Steak

PREP: 10 min. + marinating **GRILL:** 15 min.

Peppery yet pleasingly sweet, this tender beef flank steak makes a hearty, satisfying ending to a busy day at school or the office.
—*Vera Reid, Laramie, Wyoming*

1/4 cup sugar
1/4 cup reduced-sodium soy sauce
  4 green onions, sliced
  4 garlic cloves, minced
  1 tablespoon sesame seeds
  1 tablespoon minced fresh gingerroot
  1 tablespoon sesame oil
  2 teaspoons pepper
  1 beef flank steak (2 pounds)

In a large resealable plastic bag, combine the first eight ingredients. Score the surface of the beef with shallow diagonal cuts, making diamond shapes; place in the bag. Seal bag and turn to coat; refrigerate for 8 hours or overnight.

Drain and discard the marinade. Using long-handled tongs, dip a paper towel in cooking oil and lightly coat the grill rack. Grill beef, covered, over medium heat or broil 4 in. from heat for 6-8 minutes on each side or until the meat reaches desired doneness (for medium-rare, a meat thermometer should read 145°; medium, 160°; well-done, 170°).

Let stand for 5 minutes; thinly slice across the grain. **Yield:** 8 servings.

Genrose's Stuffed Beef Tenderloin

(Pictured below)

PREP: 30 min. **BAKE:** 50 min. + standing

This wonderful recipe is from the supper club my husband, I and four other couples have belonged to for more than 45 years.
—*Katie Whitworth, Lexington, Kentucky*

  5 bacon strips
1/2 pound sliced fresh mushrooms

1 medium onion, chopped
1 tablespoon butter
2 cups seasoned stuffing cubes
1/4 cup chicken broth
1/4 teaspoon salt
1/4 teaspoon garlic salt
1/4 teaspoon pepper
1 beef tenderloin (5 pounds)

In a large skillet, cook the bacon over medium heat until partially cooked but not crisp. Remove to paper towels to drain; keep warm.

In the same skillet, saute the mushrooms and onion in butter until tender. Stir in stuffing cubes, chicken broth, salt, garlic salt and pepper.

Make a lengthwise slit down the center of tenderloin to within 1/2 in. of bottom. Open the meat so it lies flat. Mound stuffing over the center. Bring up the sides of the tenderloin; tie at 2-in. intervals with kitchen string. Place on a rack in a shallow roasting pan. Arrange the bacon over the top.

Bake, uncovered, at 425° for 50-80 minutes or until the meat reaches the desired doneness (for medium-rare, a meat thermometer should read 145°; medium, 160°; well-done, 170°). Cover loosely with foil if top browns too quickly.

Remove the meat to a serving platter. Cover and let stand for 10 minutes before slicing. **Yield:** 16 servings.

Fish with Fennel

PREP: 30 min. **COOK:** 10 min.

Like cooking with fennel? This well-seasoned fish entree is a fantastic showcase for it. You'll use the seeds, bulb and fronds.
—Barbara Stelluto, Devon, Pennsylvania

1 medium lime
1 teaspoon fennel seeds
1 large fennel bulb, sliced
1/4 teaspoon salt
4 teaspoons olive oil, *divided*
2 garlic cloves, minced
4 striped bass *or* barramundi fillets (8 ounces *each*)
1 tablespoon chopped fennel fronds

Cut the lime in half; cut four slices from one half for garnish. Finely grate enough peel from remaining half to measure 3/4 teaspoon; squeeze juice from lime half. Set aside.

In a small dry skillet over medium heat, toast fennel seeds until aromatic, about 1-2 minutes. Cool. Crush seeds in a spice grinder or with a mortar and pestle.

In a large saucepan, bring 1 in. of water to a boil. Add sliced fennel and salt; cover and boil for 6-10 minutes or until crisp-tender. Drain and pat dry.

In a large nonstick skillet, saute fennel in 2 teaspoons oil for 3 minutes. Add garlic; cook 1-2 minutes longer or

until fennel is lightly browned. Remove from the pan and set aside.

In the same skillet over medium-high heat, cook fillets in remaining oil for 3-4 minutes on each side or until fish flakes easily with a fork. Drizzle with lime juice; sprinkle with lime peel and crushed fennel seeds. Serve with sauteed fennel. Garnish with fennel fronds and lime slices. **Yield:** 4 servings.

Caprese Chicken with Bacon

(Pictured above)

PREP: 20 min. **BAKE:** 20 min.

Smoky bacon, fresh basil, ripe tomatoes and gooey mozzarella top these chicken breasts. The aroma as they bake is irresistible!
—Tammy Hayden, Quincy, Michigan

8 bacon strips
4 boneless skinless chicken breast halves (6 ounces *each*)
1 tablespoon olive oil
1/2 teaspoon salt
1/4 teaspoon pepper
2 plum tomatoes, sliced
6 fresh basil leaves, thinly sliced
4 slices part-skim mozzarella cheese

Place bacon in an ungreased 15-in. x 10-in. x 1-in. baking pan. Bake at 400° for 8-10 minutes or until partially cooked but not crisp. Remove to paper towels to drain.

Place chicken in an ungreased 13-in. x 9-in. baking pan; brush with oil and sprinkle with salt and pepper. Top with tomatoes and basil. Wrap each in two bacon strips, arranging bacon in a crisscross.

Bake, uncovered, at 400° for 20-25 minutes or until a meat thermometer reads 170°. Top with cheese; bake 1 minute longer or until melted. **Yield:** 4 servings.

Sloppy Jose Supper

PREP: 15 min. **COOK:** 20 min.

This fun, south-of-the-border take on sloppy Joes starts with a corn bread mix. —Bethany Creaser, Derby Line, Vermont

- 1 package (8-1/2 ounces) corn bread/muffin mix
- 1 pound lean ground beef (90% lean)
- 1/2 cup chopped sweet red pepper
- 1/3 cup chopped onion
- 1 celery rib, chopped
- 2 garlic cloves, minced
- 1 chipotle pepper in adobo sauce, chopped
- 1 teaspoon chili powder
- 1 teaspoon ground cumin
- 1-1/4 cups salsa
- 2 tablespoons chili sauce
- 2/3 cup shredded Mexican cheese blend

Sour cream

Prepare and bake the corn bread according to the package directions.

Meanwhile, in a large skillet, cook the beef, red pepper, onion and celery over medium heat until meat is no longer pink; drain. Add the garlic, chipotle pepper, chili powder and cumin; cook 1 minute longer.

Stir in salsa and chili sauce; simmer for 3-5 minutes or until slightly thickened.

Cut corn bread into nine squares; save four pieces for another use. Top each square of remaining bread with 2/3 cup beef mixture and 2 tablespoons cheese. Dollop with sour cream. **Yield:** 5 servings plus leftover bread.

Herbed Standing Rib Roast

(Pictured below)

PREP: 10 min. **BAKE:** 2-1/4 hours + standing

We're a meat-and-potatoes family, so this succulent beef rib roast is right up our alley. —Carol Stevens, Basye, Virginia

- 3 tablespoons grated onion
- 2 tablespoons olive oil
- 4 garlic cloves, minced
- 2 teaspoons celery seed
- 1 teaspoon coarsely ground pepper
- 1 teaspoon paprika
- 1/4 teaspoon dried thyme
- 1 bone-in beef rib roast (6 to 7 pounds)
- 2 large onions, cut into wedges
- 2 large carrots, cut into 2-inch pieces
- 2 celery ribs, cut into 2-inch pieces
- 1/4 cup red wine *or beef broth*

Assorted herbs and fruit, optional

In a bowl, combine the first seven ingredients; rub over roast. Place the onions, carrots and celery in a large roasting pan; place roast over vegetables.

Bake, uncovered, at 325° for 1-3/4 to 2-1/2 hours or until meat reaches desired doneness (for medium-rare, a meat thermometer should read 145°; medium, 160°; well-done, 170°). Remove the roast to a serving platter and keep warm; let stand for 15 minutes before slicing.

Meanwhile, for the au jus, strain and discard the vegetables. Pour drippings into a measuring cup; skim the fat. Add wine or broth to the roasting pan, stirring to remove any browned bits. Stir in the drippings; heat through. Serve au jus with roast. Garnish serving platter with herbs and fruit if desired. **Yield:** 10-12 servings.

Chicken Continental

PREP: 30 min. **COOK:** 40 min.

Mushroom lovers rejoice! This moist, mouthwatering chicken entree combines garlic and mushrooms for a dinnertime delight. —Rebecca Baird, Salt Lake City, Utah

☑ This recipe includes Nutrition Facts and Diabetic Exchanges.

- 2/3 cup uncooked brown rice
- 2 tablespoons plus 2 teaspoons cornstarch, *divided*
- 1/4 teaspoon garlic-herb seasoning blend
- 4 boneless skinless chicken breast halves (5 ounces *each*)
- 1 tablespoon olive oil
- 3/4 pound sliced fresh mushrooms
- 6 green onions, thinly sliced
- 1/4 cup balsamic vinegar
- 2 garlic cloves, minced
- 1 tablespoon capers, drained
- 3/4 cup reduced-sodium chicken broth
- 1 bay leaf
- 1 teaspoon minced fresh thyme *or 1/4 teaspoon dried thyme*
- 2 teaspoons cold water

Cook the rice according to the package directions. In a small bowl, combine 2 tablespoons cornstarch and the garlic-herb seasoning blend; sprinkle over the chicken on both sides.

In a large skillet over medium heat, brown chicken in oil. Remove and keep warm. Add mushrooms and onions to the pan; cook and stir for 3 minutes. Add the vinegar, garlic and capers; cook and stir 2 minutes longer.

Return the chicken to the pan; carefully add broth, bay leaf and thyme. Bring to a boil. Reduce heat; cover and simmer for 10 minutes or until a meat thermometer reads 170°.

Combine remaining cornstarch with the water until smooth; stir into the pan. Bring to a boil; cook and stir for 2 minutes or until thickened. Discard bay leaf. Serve chicken and mushrooms with rice. **Yield:** 4 servings.

Nutrition Facts: 1 chicken breast half with 3/4 cup mushroom mixture and 1/2 cup rice equals 354 calories, 8 g fat (2 g saturated fat), 78 mg cholesterol, 265 mg sodium, 35 g carbohydrate, 4 g fiber, 35 g protein. **Diabetic Exchanges:** 4 very lean meat, 2 starch, 1 vegetable, 1/2 fat.

Mushroom Turkey Tetrazzini

PREP: 35 min. **BAKE:** 25 min.

Use up that leftover Thanksgiving or Christmas turkey with this creamy, comforting casserole. —Linda Howe, Lisle, Illinois

- 12 **ounces uncooked spaghetti, broken into 2-inch pieces**
- 2 **teaspoons chicken bouillon granules**
- 1/2 **pound sliced fresh mushrooms**
- 2 **tablespoons butter**
- 2 **tablespoons all-purpose flour**
- 1/4 **cup sherry *or* reduced-sodium chicken broth**
- 3/4 **teaspoon salt-free lemon-pepper seasoning**
- 1/2 **teaspoon salt**
- 1/8 **teaspoon ground nutmeg**
- 1 **cup fat-free evaporated milk**
- 2/3 **cup grated Parmesan cheese, *divided***
- 4 **cups cubed cooked turkey breast**
- 1/4 **teaspoon paprika**

Cook spaghetti according to package directions. Drain, reserving 2-1/2 cups cooking liquid. Stir bouillon into cooking liquid and set aside. Place spaghetti in a 13-in. x 9-in. baking dish coated with cooking spray; set aside.

In a large nonstick skillet, saute mushrooms in butter until tender. Stir in flour until blended. Gradually stir in sherry or broth and reserved cooking liquid. Add the lemon-pepper, salt and nutmeg. Bring to a boil; cook and stir for 2 minutes or until thickened.

Reduce heat to low; stir in milk and 1/3 cup Parmesan cheese until blended. Add turkey; cook and stir until heated through. Pour turkey mixture over spaghetti and toss to combine. Sprinkle with paprika and remaining Parmesan cheese.

Cover and bake at 375° for 25-30 minutes or until bubbly. **Yield:** 8 servings.

Herbed Roast Chicken

(Pictured above and on page 52)

PREP: 15 min. + marinating **BAKE:** 2-1/4 hours + standing

Marinating this chicken before roasting gives it a mild citrus tang and attractive look. —Samuel Onizuk, Elkton, Maryland

✓ This recipe includes Nutrition Facts.

One 2-gallon resealable plastic bag
- 1/2 **cup orange juice**
- 1/3 **cup olive oil**
- 2 **tablespoons butter, melted**
- 1 **tablespoon balsamic vinegar**
- 1 **tablespoon Worcestershire sauce**
- 6 **garlic cloves, minced**
- 1 **tablespoon minced chives**
- 1 **tablespoon dried parsley flakes**
- 1 **tablespoon dried basil**
- 1 **teaspoon salt**
- 1 **teaspoon pepper**
- 1/2 **teaspoon dried marjoram**
- 1/2 **teaspoon dried rosemary, crushed**
- 1/4 **teaspoon dried tarragon**
- 1 **roasting chicken (6 to 7 pounds)**

In the 2-gallon resealable plastic bag, combine juice, oil, butter, vinegar, Worcestershire sauce, garlic, chives and seasonings. Add the chicken; seal bag and turn to coat. Refrigerate for 8 hours or overnight, turning occasionally.

Drain and discard the marinade. Place chicken on a rack in a shallow roasting pan. Bake, uncovered, at 350° for 2-1/4 to 2-3/4 hours or until a meat thermometer reads 180°. Cover loosely with foil if the chicken browns too quickly. Cover and let stand for 15 minutes before carving. **Yield:** 8 servings.

Nutrition Facts: 6 ounces cooked chicken equals 433 calories, 28 g fat (8 g saturated fat), 136 mg cholesterol, 241 mg sodium, 1 g carbohydrate, trace fiber, 42 g protein.

Hot Tamale Casserole

(Pictured above and on page 52)

PREP: 35 min. **BAKE:** 30 min.

If you like tamales, you're going to love this appetizing layered dish. It's ooey-gooey good with just the right amount of heat.
—Sharon Delaney-Chronis, South Milwaukee, Wisconsin

> 2 **cups water**
> 1/4 **teaspoon salt**
> 1/8 **teaspoon cayenne pepper**
> 1/2 **cup cornmeal**
> 1-1/2 **pounds lean ground beef (90% lean)**
> 1 **large onion, chopped**
> 1 **medium green pepper, chopped**
> 2 **garlic cloves, minced**
> 1 **can (16 ounces) kidney beans, rinsed and drained**
> 1 **can (10 ounces) enchilada sauce**
> 1 **can (4 ounces) chopped green chilies**
> 1 **can (2-1/4 ounces) sliced ripe olives, drained**
> 2 **teaspoons chili powder**
> 2 **teaspoons minced fresh cilantro**
> 3/4 **cup shredded cheddar cheese**

In a small heavy saucepan, bring the water, salt and cayenne to a boil. Reduce heat to a gentle boil; slowly whisk in cornmeal. Cook and stir with a wooden spoon for 15-20 minutes or until polenta is thickened and pulls away cleanly from the sides of the pan.

Meanwhile, in a large skillet, cook beef, onion, green pepper and garlic over medium heat until meat is no longer pink. Stir in the beans, enchilada sauce, chilies, olives, chili powder and cilantro; heat through.

Spread the polenta into a greased 8-in. square baking dish. Top with meat mixture. Cover and bake at 350° for 25 minutes. Sprinkle with cheese. Bake, uncovered, for 2-5 minutes or until the filling is bubbly and the cheese is melted. **Yield:** 6 servings.

Sunday's Best Chicken

PREP: 40 min. **BAKE:** 2-1/4 hours + standing

In our family, Sunday dinners are especially important...and everyone's happy when I make this old-fashioned chicken recipe.
—Amy Jenkins, Mesa, Arizona

> 2 **to 3 medium lemons**
> 2 **fresh rosemary sprigs**
> 1 **roasting chicken (6 to 7 pounds)**
> 1 **tablespoon olive oil**
> 2 **tablespoons minced fresh rosemary**
> 1 **tablespoon coarsely ground pepper**
> 1-1/2 **teaspoons salt**

Finely grate the peel from the lemons to measure 2 tablespoons; set aside. Coarsely chop 2 lemons; place the chopped lemons and rosemary sprigs in the chicken cavity. Save remaining lemon for another use.

Place the chicken on a rack in a shallow roasting pan; brush with oil. Combine the minced rosemary, pepper, salt and lemon peel; rub over chicken.

Bake, uncovered, at 350° for 2-1/4 to 2-3/4 hours or until a meat thermometer reads 180°, basting occasionally with drippings. (Cover loosely with foil if chicken browns too quickly.) Let stand for 15 minutes before carving. Discard lemons and rosemary sprigs. **Yield:** 6 servings.

Slow Cooker Beef With Red Sauce

PREP: 25 min. **COOK:** 8 hours

A homemade rub spices up this tender beef while tomatoes and gingersnaps add an interesting taste combination to the sauce.
—Laurie Tietze, Longview, Texas

> 2 **tablespoons canola oil**
> 2 **tablespoons baking cocoa**
> 1 **tablespoon chili powder**
> 2 **teaspoons dried oregano**
> 1 **teaspoon salt**
> 1 **teaspoon pepper**
> 1 **teaspoon ground cumin**
> 1/2 **teaspoon ground cloves**
> 1/2 **teaspoon ground cinnamon**
> 1 **beef rump roast *or* bottom round roast (3 pounds), cut into 1-1/2-inch cubes**
> 1 **large onion, chopped**
> 1 **can (28 ounces) whole tomatoes, undrained**
> 3 **tablespoons cider vinegar**
> 1-1/2 **cups crushed gingersnap cookies (about 30 cookies)**
> 9 **garlic cloves, peeled**
> 1 **tablespoon sugar**
> **Hot cooked noodles, rice *or* mashed potatoes**

In a small bowl, combine the first nine ingredients; set the mixture aside.

Place the beef and onion in a 4-qt. slow cooker; rub beef with the spice mixture. Pour tomatoes over the top; sprinkle with vinegar, gingersnaps and garlic. Cover and cook on low for 8-10 hours or until meat is tender. Stir in sugar. Serve with noodles. **Yield:** 8 servings.

Beef & Bacon Stroganoff

(Pictured below)

PREP: 20 min. **COOK:** 20 min.

Warm and saucy, this stovetop beef Stroganoff is true comfort food. It gets an unexpected kick from prepared horseradish.
—*Melissa Millwood, Lyman, South Carolina*

- 1 **pound lean ground beef (90% lean)**
- 5 **thick-sliced bacon strips, chopped**
- 1 **cup sliced fresh mushrooms**
- 1 **medium onion, chopped**
- 2 **garlic cloves, minced**
- 2 **tablespoons all-purpose flour**
- 1 **can (14-1/2 ounces) beef broth**
- 1 **can (10-3/4 ounces) condensed cream of mushroom with roasted garlic soup, undiluted**
- 2 **tablespoons Worcestershire sauce**
- 1 **teaspoon pepper**
- 1/4 **teaspoon salt**
- 1/4 **teaspoon paprika**
- 6 **cups uncooked egg noodles**
- 1 **cup (8 ounces) sour cream**
- 2 **teaspoons prepared horseradish**
- 1/2 **cup shredded white cheddar cheese**

Minced fresh parsley, optional

In a large skillet over medium heat, cook beef, bacon, mushrooms, onion and garlic until the beef is no longer pink; drain. Stir in the flour until blended. Add broth, soup, Worcestershire sauce, pepper, salt and paprika. Bring to a boil. Reduce heat; simmer, uncovered, for 10-15 minutes, stirring occasionally.

Meanwhile, cook the noodles according to package directions; drain.

Stir sour cream and horseradish into beef mixture; heat through (do not boil). Serve with noodles. Sprinkle with the cheese. Garnish with parsley if desired. **Yield:** 6 servings.

One-Skillet Pasta

(Pictured above)

PREP: 20 min. **COOK:** 1-1/4 hours

This simple family–pleaser is a twist on traditional spaghetti. Cooking everything in one pot saves time on prep and cleanup.
—*Susan Spence, Lawrenceville, Virginia*

- 1-1/2 **pounds ground turkey**
- 1 **medium onion, finely chopped**
- 1 **medium sweet red pepper, finely chopped**
- 1 **can (28 ounces) diced tomatoes, undrained**
- 1 **can (14-1/2 ounces) fire-roasted diced tomatoes, undrained**
- 1 **can (14-1/2 ounces) reduced-sodium beef broth**
- 1 **can (4 ounces) sliced mushrooms**
- 1 **tablespoon packed brown sugar**
- 1 **tablespoon chili powder**
- 8 **ounces uncooked angel hair pasta**
- 1 **cup (4 ounces) shredded cheddar cheese**

In a large skillet, cook the turkey, onion and pepper over medium heat until meat is no longer pink; drain.

Add the tomatoes, broth, mushrooms, brown sugar and chili powder. Bring to a boil. Reduce heat; simmer, uncovered, for 30 minutes. Add pasta; return to a boil. Reduce heat; cover and simmer for 30-35 minutes or until pasta is tender. Sprinkle with cheese. Cover and cook 2-3 minutes longer or until cheese is melted. **Yield:** 5 servings.

cover and refrigerate for 8 hours or overnight.

Place the roast on a rack in a shallow roasting pan. Bake, uncovered, at 425° for 1 to 1-1/2 hours or until the meat reaches desired doneness (for medium-rare, a meat thermometer should read 145°; medium, 160°; well-done, 170°).

Meanwhile, in a large skillet, cook the onions in oil over low heat for 30-35 minutes or until golden brown, stirring frequently. Stir in the wine and bring to a boil. Reduce heat; cook and stir for 1-2 minutes or until liquid is evaporated. Stir in the thyme, pepper and salt.

Transfer meat to a warm serving platter. Let stand for 10 minutes before slicing. Sprinkle with parsley. Serve with onions. **Yield:** 6 servings.

Pistachio-Crusted Chicken With Garden Spinach

PREP: 1-1/4 hours **BAKE:** 35 min.

For a summery entree, try this moist chicken filled with creamy goat cheese. It's lovely draped with roasted red pepper sauce and served on baby spinach.   —Nancy Baumel, Park Ridge, Illinois

      1 large sweet red pepper
  1-1/4 cups pistachios
    3/4 cup panko (Japanese) bread crumbs
      1 cup buttermilk
      4 boneless skinless chicken breast halves
        (6 ounces *each*)
    1/2 cup crumbled goat cheese
    1/4 cup minced fresh basil
      2 tablespoons butter, melted
    1/4 teaspoon salt
    1/4 teaspoon pepper
      1 shallot, chopped
  1-1/2 teaspoons olive oil
      2 garlic cloves, minced
    1/2 cup reduced-sodium chicken broth
SALAD:
      1 tablespoon balsamic vinegar
      1 teaspoon olive oil
      3 cups fresh baby spinach
    1/2 cup minced fresh basil

Broil the pepper 4 in. from heat until blistered. Rotate pepper a quarter turn. Broil and rotate until all sides are blistered and blackened. Place in a small bowl; cover and let stand 20 minutes. Process pistachios in a food processor until ground. Transfer to a shallow bowl; add bread crumbs. Place buttermilk in another bowl.

Flatten chicken to 1/4-in. thickness; dip in buttermilk, then coat with the pistachio mixture. Place on a work surface; top with goat cheese and basil. Fold chicken in half; secure with toothpicks if necessary.

Place the chicken in a greased 11-in. x 7-in. baking dish. Drizzle with butter; sprinkle with salt and pepper. Bake, uncovered, at 350° for 35-40 minutes or until a

Beef Roast Au Poivre With Caramelized Onions

(Pictured above)

PREP: 30 min. + chilling **BAKE:** 1 hour + standing

Ground chilies and peppercorns really spice up this robust beef roast. The aroma is out of this world—and so is the taste!
—Elaine Sweet, Dallas, Texas

      2 tablespoons *each* whole black and pink
        peppercorns *and/or* 1/4 cup whole black
        peppercorns
      3 dried chipotle chilies, stems removed
      1 tablespoon coriander seeds
      1 tablespoon dried minced onion
      1 tablespoon dried thyme
  1-1/2 teaspoons salt
      1 teaspoon dried orange peel
      3 tablespoons steak sauce
      1 beef tri-tip roast (2 to 3 pounds)
ONIONS:
      4 large onions, thinly sliced
      3 tablespoons olive oil
    1/2 cup chardonnay *and/or* other white wine
      2 teaspoons dried thyme
    1/2 teaspoon pepper
    1/8 teaspoon salt
      2 tablespoons minced fresh parsley

Place peppercorns, chilies and coriander in a blender. Cover and process until coarsely ground. Stir in onion, thyme, salt and orange peel.

Rub steak sauce and seasoning mixture over roast;

meat thermometer reads 170°. Discard toothpicks.

Discard charred skin from pepper; discard seeds and membranes. Place pepper in a food processor. In a small skillet, saute shallot in oil until tender. Add garlic; cook 1 minute longer. Add broth; heat through. Add mixture to the food processor; process until blended.

Whisk vinegar and oil. Add spinach and basil; toss to coat. Divide salad among four plates; top with chicken and pepper sauce. **Yield:** 4 servings.

Pumpkin Pancakes with Cinnamon Brown Butter

PREP: 20 min. **COOK:** 10 min./batch

Good morning, indeed! Everyone will have a great one when these rich pumpkin pancakes are on the breakfast table. They're even better topped with the homemade maple–cinnamon butter.
—Courtney Shay, Gaithersburg, Maryland

- 1/2 **cup butter, cubed**
- 1/4 **cup maple syrup**
- 1/2 **teaspoon ground cinnamon**
- 1/4 **teaspoon ground nutmeg**
- 1/2 **cup chopped pecans, toasted**
- 1-1/2 **cups all-purpose flour**
-   2 **tablespoons packed brown sugar**
-   2 **teaspoons baking powder**
-   1 **teaspoon salt**
-   2 **eggs**
- 1-1/3 **cups 2% milk**
- 3/4 **cup canned pumpkin**
- 1/2 **cup ricotta cheese**

In a small heavy saucepan, cook butter over medium heat for 8-10 minutes or until golden brown, stirring occasionally. Add maple syrup, cinnamon and nutmeg. Remove from the heat; stir in pecans.

In a small bowl, combine flour, brown sugar, baking powder and salt. In another bowl, whisk the eggs, milk, pumpkin and cheese. Stir into the dry ingredients just until moistened.

Drop the batter by 1/4 cupfuls onto a greased hot griddle; turn when bubbles form on top. Cook until the second side is golden brown. Serve with brown butter. **Yield:** 14 pancakes (1 cup brown butter).

Fish Tacos with Avocado Sauce

(Pictured at right)

PREP: 30 min. + marinating **BROIL:** 10 min.

I grew up in Alaska, where halibut was readily available. One of my good friends, who normally doesn't care for fish, went back for fourth helpings of these flavorful, refreshing tacos.
—Cortney Claeson, Spokane, Washington

- 1/4 **cup lemon juice**
-   1 **tablespoon olive oil**
-   3 **garlic cloves, minced**
-   1 **pound halibut** *or tilapia fillets*
SAUCE:
-   2 **medium ripe avocados,** *divided*
- 1/4 **cup fat-free sour cream**
- 1/4 **cup reduced-fat mayonnaise**
-   1 **tablespoon lime juice**
-   1 **garlic clove, minced**
-   1 **teaspoon dill weed**
- 1/4 **teaspoon ground cumin**
- 1/4 **teaspoon dried oregano**
- 1/4 **teaspoon dried parsley flakes**
Dash cayenne pepper
SALSA:
-   1 **medium tomato, seeded and chopped**
-   1 **small red onion, chopped**
- 4-1/2 **teaspoons chopped seeded jalapeno pepper**
-   1 **tablespoon minced fresh cilantro**
- 1-1/2 **teaspoons lime juice**
-   1 **garlic clove, minced**
- 1/8 **teaspoon salt**
TACOS:
-   8 **flour tortillas (6 inches)**
-   2 **cups shredded cabbage**

In a large resealable plastic bag, combine lemon juice, oil and garlic. Add the halibut; seal bag and turn to coat. Refrigerate for 30 minutes.

For the sauce and salsa, peel and cube avocados. In a small bowl, mash 1/4 cup avocado. Stir in the remaining sauce ingredients. Place remaining avocado in a small bowl; stir in remaining salsa ingredients. Refrigerate sauce and salsa until serving.

Drain fish and discard marinade. Broil halibut 4-6 in. from the heat for 8-10 minutes or until fish flakes easily with a fork. Place fish on the center of each tortilla. Top each with 1/4 cup cabbage, about 1 tablespoon sauce and 1/4 cup salsa. **Yield:** 4 servings.

Editor's Note: When cutting hot peppers, wear disposable gloves. Avoid touching your face or eyes.

Cream Cheese and Swiss Lasagna

(Pictured below)

PREP: 40 min. + simmering **BAKE:** 55 min. + standing

I fix the meat sauce for this a day ahead so the flavors can blend. It serves 12, unless you have big eaters—who will definitely want seconds!
—Betty Lou Pearson, Edgewater, Maryland

- 1-1/2 **pounds lean ground beef (90% lean)**
- 1 **pound bulk Italian sausage**
- 1 **medium onion, finely chopped**
- 3 **garlic cloves, minced**
- 2 **cans (15 ounces *each*) tomato sauce**
- 1 **can (14-1/2 ounces) Italian diced tomatoes, undrained**
- 1 **can (6 ounces) tomato paste**
- 2 **teaspoons dried oregano**
- 1 **teaspoon dried basil**
- 1 **teaspoon Italian seasoning**
- 1/2 **teaspoon sugar**
- 1/2 **teaspoon salt**
- 1/4 **teaspoon pepper**
- 9 **no-cook lasagna noodles**
- 12 **ounces cream cheese, softened**
- 2 **cups shredded part-skim mozzarella cheese, *divided***
- 2 **cups shredded Parmesan cheese**
- 2 **cups shredded Swiss cheese**

In a Dutch oven over medium heat, cook beef, sausage, onion and garlic until meat is no longer pink; drain. Stir in the tomato sauce, tomatoes, tomato paste, oregano, basil, Italian seasoning, sugar, salt and pepper. Bring to a boil. Reduce heat; simmer, uncovered, for 30 minutes.

Spread 1 cup sauce in a greased 13-in. x 9-in. baking dish. Top with three noodles. Drop a third of the cream cheese by teaspoonfuls over the top. Sprinkle with 1/2 cup mozzarella and 2/3 cup each of Parmesan and Swiss; spoon a third of the remaining sauce over the top. Repeat layers of noodles, cheeses and sauce twice (dish will be full). Place dish on a baking sheet.

Cover and bake at 350° for 45 minutes. Sprinkle with remaining mozzarella cheese. Bake, uncovered, 10-15 minutes longer or until bubbly and cheese is melted. Let stand for 15 minutes before cutting. **Yield:** 12 servings.

Baked Fish with Cheese Sauce

(Pictured above)

PREP/TOTAL TIME: 20 min.

The tangy mustard–cheese sauce in this recipe transforms flaky orange roughy into a special entree that's ready in minutes.
—Kristin Reynolds, Van Buren, Arkansas

✓ This recipe includes Nutrition Facts and Diabetic Exchanges.

- 4 **orange roughy fillets (4 ounces *each*)**
- 1 **tablespoon butter, melted**
- 2 **tablespoons dry bread crumbs**
- 1 **tablespoon all-purpose flour**
- 3/4 **cup 2% milk**
- 1/2 **cup shredded cheddar cheese**
- 1-1/2 **teaspoons Dijon mustard**

Place fish in a greased 11-in. x 7-in. baking dish. Brush with butter; sprinkle with bread crumbs. Bake at 400° for 15-20 minutes or until fish flakes easily with a fork.

Meanwhile, in a small saucepan, combine flour and milk until smooth. Bring to a boil; cook and stir for 2 minutes or until thickened. Stir in cheese and mustard until cheese is melted. Serve with fish. **Yield:** 4 servings.

Nutrition Facts: 1 fillet with 3 tablespoons sauce equals 206 calories, 9 g fat (5 g saturated fat), 94 mg cholesterol, 279 mg sodium, 7 g carbohydrate, trace fiber, 24 g protein. **Diabetic Exchanges:** 3 lean meat, 1 fat, 1/2 starch.

Maui-Inspired Turkey Breast Roll

PREP: 40 min. **BAKE:** 2-1/4 hours

I came up with this recipe because my family likes macadamia nuts—and not having to deal with turkey bones on Thanksgiving. It was a success! —Leimomi Lear, Wakefield, New Hampshire

2 boneless turkey breast halves (2 to 2-1/2 pounds *each*)
3/4 cup butter, softened, *divided*
4 garlic cloves, minced
1 tablespoon fresh sage *or* 1 teaspoon dried sage leaves
2 celery ribs, chopped
1 small onion, chopped
3 cups reduced-sodium chicken broth
1/2 cup chopped macadamia nuts, toasted
2 teaspoons poultry seasoning
1/4 teaspoon salt
1/4 teaspoon pepper
1 package (12 ounces) unseasoned stuffing cubes
1/2 cup unsweetened pineapple juice
1 tablespoon olive oil

GRAVY:
1-3/4 cups reduced-sodium chicken broth
2 tablespoons cornstarch
2 tablespoons unsweetened pineapple juice

Remove skin from the turkey breasts; set aside. Flatten turkey breasts to 3/8-in. thickness. Place breasts side by side so that they are overlapping slightly. Combine 1/2 cup butter, garlic and sage; rub over turkey.

In a large skillet, melt remaining butter. Add celery and onion; saute until tender. Add the broth, nuts and seasonings. Bring to a boil. Reduce the heat; simmer, uncovered, for 2 minutes. Stir in stuffing cubes.

Spread stuffing mixture over turkey to within 1 in. of edges. Roll up jelly-roll style, rolling turkey away from you; arrange skin over top of roll. Tie with kitchen string at 2-in. intervals.

Place on a rack in a large roasting pan. Combine the pineapple juice and olive oil; set aside.

Bake the turkey at 325° for 2-1/4 to 2-3/4 hours or until a meat thermometer reads 170°, basting occasionally with pineapple juice mixture.

Remove meat to a serving platter and keep warm. For gravy, add chicken broth to the pan, scraping to loosen browned bits. Pour into a small saucepan and bring to a boil. Combine the cornstarch and pineapple juice until smooth; gradually stir into the pan. Bring to a boil; cook and stir for 2 minutes or until thickened. Serve with the turkey. **Yield:** 12 servings.

Shrimp & Shiitake Stir-Fry With Crispy Noodles

(Pictured at right)

PREP: 20 min. **COOK:** 15 min.

We love the crispy noodles that top off this time-saving Asian dish. The roasted cashews are a wonderful complement as well.
—Wolfgang Hanau, West Palm Beach, Florida

☑ This recipe includes Nutrition Facts and Diabetic Exchanges.

1-1/2 teaspoons cornstarch
1/2 cup chicken broth
2 tablespoons reduced-sodium soy sauce
1 small head bok choy
1 pound uncooked medium shrimp, peeled and deveined
2 tablespoons canola oil, *divided*
2 tablespoons minced fresh gingerroot
1 garlic clove, thinly sliced
1/2 teaspoon crushed red pepper flakes
1 large onion, halved and thinly sliced
2 cups sliced fresh shiitake mushrooms
Hot cooked brown rice, optional
1/4 cup chow mein noodles

In a small bowl, combine the cornstarch, broth and soy sauce until smooth; set aside. Cut off and discard root end of bok choy, leaving stalks with leaves. Cut leaves from stalks. Slice leaves; set aside. Slice stalks.

In a large skillet or wok, stir-fry shrimp in 1 tablespoon oil until shrimp turn pink. Remove and keep warm.

Stir-fry ginger, garlic and pepper flakes in remaining oil for 1 minute. Add the onion, mushrooms and bok choy stalks; stir-fry for 4 minutes. Add bok choy leaves; stir-fry 2-4 minutes longer or until vegetables are crisp-tender.

Stir cornstarch mixture and add to the pan. Bring to a boil; cook and stir for 2 minutes or until thickened. Add shrimp; heat through. Serve with rice if desired. Sprinkle with chow mein noodles. **Yield:** 4 servings.

Nutrition Facts: 1 cup stir-fry with 1 tablespoon chow mein noodles (calculated without rice) equals 238 calories, 10 g fat (1 g saturated fat), 139 mg cholesterol, 710 mg sodium, 15 g carbohydrate, 3 g fiber, 24 g protein.
Diabetic Exchanges: 3 lean meat, 2 vegetable, 1 fat.

Breads, Rolls & Muffins

Turn your kitchen into a specialty bakery filled with golden-brown goodies for family and friends. It's as easy as the tempting recipes here!

Overnight Cherry Danish.................................78
Monterey Ranch Bread..................................78
Spanish Fritters...78
Kids' Favorite Blueberry Muffins 79
Homemade Tortillas 79
Nut and Poppy Seed Rolls 80
Chive Biscuits..80
Pumpkin Banana Bread.................................80
Bacon Scones 81
Crisscross Apple Crowns................................81
Sour Cream Coffee Cake 82
First-Prize Doughnuts.....................................82
Apricot Sunshine Coffee Cake 83
French Loaves 83
Chocolate Biscuit Puffs..................................83
Toasted Sunflower Bread 84
Braided Wreath Bread 84
Apple Cinnamon Rolls....................................85
Chocolate Cinnamon Rolls 86
Herbed Bread Slices..86
Italian Drop Biscuits..86
Old-Time Cake Doughnuts 87
Little Snail Rolls 87
Christmas Wreath Bread 88
Almond-Filled Butterhorns............................88
White Chocolate Berry Muffins 89
Caramel-Pecan Monkey Bread 89

FRESH FROM THE OVEN. Clockwise from top left: Chocolate Cinnamon Rolls (p. 86), Overnight Cherry Danish (p. 78), Christmas Wreath Bread (p. 88), Nut and Poppy Seed Rolls (p. 80) and Crisscross Apple Crowns (p. 81).

Overnight Cherry Danish

(Pictured above and on page 77)

PREP: 1-1/2 hours + rising **BAKE:** 15 min.

These flaky treats absolutely melt in your mouth! The ruby-red cherries put a touch of festive color on a Christmas table, too.
—*Leann Sauder, Tremont, Illinois*

> **2 packages (1/4 ounce *each*) active dry yeast**
> **1/2 cup warm 2% milk (110° to 115°)**
> **6 cups all-purpose flour**
> **1/3 cup sugar**
> **2 teaspoons salt**
> **1 cup cold butter**
> **1-1/2 cups warm half-and-half cream (110° to 115°)**
> **6 egg yolks, beaten**
> **1 can (21 ounces) cherry pie filling**
> **ICING:**
> **2 tablespoons butter, softened**
> **3 cups confectioners' sugar**
> **1/4 teaspoon vanilla extract**
> **Dash salt**
> **4 to 5 tablespoons half-and-half cream**

In a small bowl, dissolve yeast in warm milk. In a large bowl, combine the flour, sugar and salt. Cut in butter until crumbly. Add the yeast mixture, cream and egg yolks; stir until mixture forms a soft dough (dough will be sticky). Cover and refrigerate overnight.

Punch down dough; divide into quarters. Roll each portion into an 18-in. x 4-in. rectangle; cut into 1-in. x 4-in. strips.

Place two strips side by side; twist together. Shape into a ring; pinch ends together. Repeat with remaining strips. Place 2 in. apart on greased baking sheets. Cover and let rise in a warm place until doubled, about 45 minutes.

Using the end of a wooden spoon handle, make a 1/2-in.-deep indentation in the center of each roll. Fill each with about 1 tablespoon pie filling.

Bake at 350° for 14-16 minutes or until lightly browned. Remove from pans to wire racks to cool.

For icing, in a large bowl, beat butter until fluffy. Gradually beat in the confectioners' sugar, vanilla, salt and enough cream to achieve a drizzling consistency. Drizzle over rolls. **Yield:** 3 dozen.

Monterey Ranch Bread

PREP/TOTAL TIME: 25 min.

This rich, cheesy loaf is a quick-and-easy addition to any meal. Or, serve it as an appealing appetizer for a casual get-together.
—*Shirley Privratsky, Dickinson, North Dakota*

> **2 cups (8 ounces) shredded Monterey Jack cheese**
> **3/4 cup ranch salad dressing with bacon**
> **1 loaf (1 pound) unsliced French bread**
> **2 tablespoons butter, melted**
> **Minced fresh parsley**

In a bowl, combine the cheese and salad dressing; set aside. Cut bread in half lengthwise; brush with butter. Place on baking sheets. Broil 4 in. from the heat until golden brown.

Spread with cheese mixture. Bake at 350° for 10-15 minutes or until cheese is melted. Sprinkle with parsley. **Yield:** 8 servings.

Spanish Fritters

PREP: 15 min. + cooling **COOK:** 20 min.

These fried cinnamon-sugar goodies from our Test Kitchen staff are best when fresh and hot from the skillet. Try them with cups of coffee or hot chocolate...and don't be surprised if people start dunking, then go back for more fritters!

> **1/2 cup water**
> **1/2 cup milk**
> **1 tablespoon vegetable oil**
> **1/4 teaspoon salt**
> **1 cup all-purpose flour**
> **1 egg**
> **1/4 teaspoon grated lemon peel**
> **Additional oil for frying**
> **1/2 cup sugar**
> **1/4 teaspoon ground cinnamon**

In a large saucepan, combine the water, milk, oil and salt. Bring to a boil over medium-high heat. Add flour all at once. Reduce heat to low; beat vigorously with a wooden spoon until mixture forms a stiff ball. Transfer to a large mixing bowl; let stand for 5 minutes.

Beat the dough on medium-high speed for 1 minute or until the dough softens. Add the egg and lemon peel;

beat for 1-2 minutes. Set aside to cool.

In a deep skillet, heat 1 in. of oil to 375°. Insert a large star tip in a pastry bag; fill with dough. Holding the bag perpendicular to a baking sheet, pipe dough into 4-in. strips. Transfer strips to skillet and fry until golden brown on both sides. Drain on paper towels. Combine the sugar and cinnamon; sprinkle over fritters. Serve warm. **Yield:** about 1 dozen.

Kids' Favorite Blueberry Muffins

(Pictured below)

PREP/TOTAL TIME: 30 min.

My daughter had just gotten out of bed when we threw together these muffins dotted with blueberries. The results were great!
—Lisa Allen, Joppa, Alabama

☑ **This recipe includes Nutrition Facts and Diabetic Exchanges.**

- **2-1/2 cups pancake mix**
- **1/2 cup sugar**
- **1 egg**
- **2/3 cup water**
- **1/4 cup canola oil**
- **1-1/2 cups fresh *or* frozen blueberries**

In a large bowl, combine pancake mix and sugar. In another bowl, whisk the egg, water and oil. Stir into dry ingredients just until moistened. Fold in blueberries.

Fill paper-lined muffin cups two-thirds full. Bake at 400° for 14-16 minutes or until a toothpick comes out clean. Cool the muffins for 5 minutes before removing

from the pan to a wire rack. **Yield:** 1 dozen.

Editor's Note: If using frozen blueberries, use without thawing to avoid discoloring the batter.

Nutrition Facts: 1 muffin equals 173 calories, 6 g fat (1 g saturated fat), 18 mg cholesterol, 312 mg sodium, 28 g carbohydrate, 2 g fiber, 3 g protein. **Diabetic Exchanges:** 2 starch, 1 fat.

Homemade Tortillas

(Pictured above)

PREP/TOTAL TIME: 30 min.

These tortillas are so tender, chewy and simple to make, you'll be amazed—and inclined to bypass store-bought versions in the future. I usually double this recipe because we go through them so quickly.   —Kristen Van Dyken, West Richland, Washington

☑ **This recipe includes Nutrition Facts and Diabetic Exchanges.**

- **2 cups all-purpose flour**
- **1/2 teaspoon salt**
- **3/4 cup water**
- **3 tablespoons olive oil**

In a large bowl, combine flour and salt. Stir in water and oil. Turn onto a floured surface; knead 10-12 times, adding a little flour or water if needed to achieve a smooth dough. Divide dough into 8 portions. On a lightly floured surface, roll each portion into a 7-in. circle.

In a large nonstick skillet coated with cooking spray, cook the tortillas over medium heat for 1 minute on each side or until lightly browned. Keep warm. **Yield:** 8 tortillas.

Nutrition Facts: 1 tortilla equals 159 calories, 5 g fat (1 g saturated fat), 0 cholesterol, 148 mg sodium, 24 g carbohydrate, 1 g fiber, 3 g protein. **Diabetic Exchanges:** 1-1/2 starch, 1 fat.

Nut and Poppy Seed Rolls

(Pictured below and on page 76)

PREP: 40 min. + chilling **BAKE:** 35 min. + cooling

This Hungarian family favorite is a real holiday treat. I love it with a cup of coffee on Christmas morning as I sit by the tree.
—Carrie Gamble, Doylestown, Pennsylvania

- **2 packages (1/4 ounce *each*) active dry yeast**
- **1/2 cup warm water (110° to 115°)**
- **1 cup warm 2% milk (110° to 115°)**
- **1 cup sour cream**
- **1/2 cup sugar**
- **1/2 cup butter, melted**
- **2 eggs**
- **1 teaspoon salt**
- **6 cups all-purpose flour**

NUT FILLING:
- **1 cup ground pecans**
- **1/2 cup sugar**
- **1/2 cup chopped dates**
- **1/2 cup 2% milk**
- **1 teaspoon salt**
- **1 egg white**

POPPY SEED FILLING:
- **1 can (12-1/2 ounces) poppy seed cake and pastry filling**
- **1/4 cup chopped raisins**
- **1/4 cup chopped walnuts**

ICING:
- **2 cups confectioners' sugar**
- **2 to 3 tablespoons water**

In a large bowl, dissolve yeast in warm water. Add milk, sour cream, sugar, butter, eggs, salt and 3 cups flour. Beat until smooth. Beat in remaining flour until mixture forms a soft dough. Transfer to a greased bowl, turning once to grease the top; cover and refrigerate overnight.

Divide the dough in half. Roll each portion into a 14-in. x 12-in. rectangle. For the nut filling, in a small bowl, combine the pecans, sugar, dates, milk and salt. In another bowl, beat the egg white until stiff peaks form; fold into the pecan mixture. Spread over one portion. Spread the poppy seed cake and pastry filling over remaining dough; sprinkle with raisins and walnuts.

Roll up each jelly-roll style, starting with a long side; pinch seams to seal and tuck ends under. Place seam side down on parchment paper-lined baking sheets. Let rise in a warm place until doubled, about 30 minutes.

Bake at 350° for 35-40 minutes or until golden brown. Cool on a wire rack. Combine confectioners' sugar and enough water to achieve desired consistency; drizzle over breads. **Yield:** 2 loaves (14 slices each).

Editor's Note: This recipe was tested with Solo brand cake and pastry filling. Look for it in the baking aisle.

Chive Biscuits

PREP/TOTAL TIME: 25 min.

I like to serve these moist biscuits with my soups, stews and roasts during fall and winter. Sometimes I substitute different herbs for a change of pace.   —Norma Erne, Albuquerque, New Mexico

- **2 cups all-purpose flour**
- **3 teaspoons baking powder**
- **1/2 teaspoon salt**
- **1/4 teaspoon baking soda**
- **1/3 cup butter-flavored shortening**
- **1 cup buttermilk**
- **2 tablespoons snipped chives**

In a small bowl, combine the flour, baking powder, salt and baking soda. Cut in the shortening until mixture resembles coarse crumbs. Stir in buttermilk and chives just until moistened.

Drop by tablespoonfuls 2 in. apart onto a greased baking sheet. Bake at 450° for 10-12 minutes or until lightly browned. Serve warm. **Yield:** 1 dozen.

Pumpkin Banana Bread

PREP: 15 min. **BAKE:** 35 min. + cooling

This recipe conveniently yields a quartet of mini loaves, ideal for holiday gift-giving. The bananas and pumpkin make a different but yummy combination.   —Linda Wood, Roanoke, Virginia

- **1/2 cup shortening**
- **1-1/2 cups sugar**
- **2 eggs**
- **1 cup mashed ripe bananas (about 2 medium)**
- **3/4 cup canned pumpkin**
- **1 teaspoon vanilla extract**
- **1-3/4 cups all-purpose flour**
- **1-1/2 teaspoons baking powder**
- **3/4 teaspoon baking soda**

separate. Sprinkle with the remaining bacon. Bake at 400° for 15-20 minutes or until golden brown. Serve warm. **Yield:** 8 scones.

Crisscross Apple Crowns

(Pictured below and on page 76)

PREP: 30 min. **COOK:** 20 min.

Wake up your family on chilly mornings with the tempting aroma of apples and cinnamon. Chances are, they'll come running!
—Teresa Morris, Laurel, Delaware

  1-1/3 cups chopped peeled tart apples
  1/3 cup chopped walnuts
  1/3 cup raisins
  1/2 cup sugar, *divided*
  2 tablespoons all-purpose flour
  2 teaspoons ground cinnamon, *divided*
Dash salt
  1 package (17.3 ounces) large refrigerated flaky biscuits
  2 teaspoons butter, melted

In a large microwave-safe bowl, combine the apples, walnuts, raisins, 3 tablespoons sugar, flour, 3/4 teaspoon cinnamon and salt. Microwave 2-3 minutes or until almost tender.

Flatten each biscuit into a 5-in. circle. Combine the remaining sugar and cinnamon; sprinkle a rounded teaspoonful of sugar mixture over each. Top each with 1/4 cup apple mixture. Bring up edges to enclose mixture; pinch edges to seal.

Place seam side down in ungreased muffin cups. Brush tops with butter; sprinkle with remaining sugar mixture. With a sharp knife, cut an "X" in the top of each.

Bake at 350° for 18-22 minutes or until golden brown. Cool for 5 minutes before removing from pan to a wire rack. **Yield:** 8 servings.

1/2 teaspoon salt
1/2 cup chopped walnuts *or* pecans

In a large mixing bowl, cream shortening and sugar. Add the eggs, one at a time, beating well after each addition. Beat in the bananas, pumpkin and vanilla. Combine the flour, baking powder, baking soda and salt; gradually add to creamed mixture. Fold in nuts.

Pour into four greased 5-3/4-in. x 3-in. x 2-in. loaf pans. Bake at 350° for 35-40 minutes or until a toothpick inserted near the center comes out clean. Cool for 10 minutes before removing from pans to wire racks. **Yield:** 4 mini loaves.

Bacon Scones

(Pictured above)

PREP: 20 min. **BAKE:** 15 min.

I grew up with this popular recipe in Scotland. Featuring bacon bits and cheese, the buttery scones are great with salad or eggs.
—Teresa Royston, Seabeck, Washington

  1-3/4 cups all-purpose flour
  2-1/4 teaspoons baking powder
  1 teaspoon ground mustard
  1/2 teaspoon salt
  1/4 teaspoon pepper
  6 tablespoons cold butter
  2 eggs
  1/3 cup 2% milk
  1/2 cup chopped onion
  1/4 cup shredded cheddar cheese
  6 bacon strips, cooked and crumbled, *divided*

In a large bowl, combine the first five ingredients. Cut in butter until mixture resembles coarse crumbs. In a small bowl, whisk the eggs and milk. Stir into dry ingredients just until moistened. Fold in the onion, cheese and two-thirds of the bacon.

Transfer the dough to a greased baking sheet. Pat into a 7-1/2-in. circle. Cut into eight wedges, but do not

Sour Cream Coffee Cake

(Pictured above)

PREP: 40 min. **BAKE:** 45 min. + cooling

This scrumptious cake is so moist, you won't even need a cup of coffee! Serve it the next time you have guests—they're sure to thank you.
— *Kathleen Larimer, Dayton, Ohio*

  2/3 cup chopped pecans
    2 tablespoons brown sugar
1-1/2 teaspoons ground cinnamon
BATTER:
    1 cup butter, softened
    2 cups sugar
    2 eggs
  1/2 teaspoon vanilla extract
    2 cups all-purpose flour
    1 teaspoon baking powder
  1/4 teaspoon baking soda
  1/4 teaspoon salt
    1 cup (8 ounces) sour cream
Confectioners' sugar

In a small bowl, combine the pecans, brown sugar and cinnamon; set aside. In a large bowl, cream butter and sugar until light and fluffy. Add eggs, one at a time, beating well after each addition. Beat in vanilla. Combine the flour, baking powder, baking soda and salt; add to creamed mixture alternately with sour cream.

Pour half of the batter into a greased and floured 10-in. fluted tube pan; sprinkle with half of the pecan mixture. Gently top with remaining batter and pecan mixture.

Bake at 350° for 45-50 minutes or until a toothpick inserted near the center comes out clean. Cool for 10 minutes before removing from pan to a wire rack to cool completely. Sprinkle with confectioners' sugar.
Yield: 16 servings.

First-Prize Doughnuts

(Pictured below)

PREP: 25 min. + rising **COOK:** 5 min./batch

I've been making doughnuts since I was a young bride. This is my favorite recipe, a blue–ribbon winner at the county fair. It's fun to decorate the glazed goodies with colored sprinkles or cereals.
— *Betty Claycomb, Alverton, Pennsylvania*

    2 packages (1/4 ounce *each*) active dry yeast
  1/2 cup warm water (110° to 115°)
  1/2 cup warm 2% milk (110° to 115°)
  1/2 cup sugar
  1/2 cup shortening
    2 eggs
    1 teaspoon salt
4-1/2 to 5 cups all-purpose flour
Oil for deep-fat frying
TOPPINGS:
1-1/4 cups confectioners' sugar
    4 to 6 tablespoons water
Colored sprinkles *and/or* assorted breakfast cereals

In a large bowl, dissolve yeast in warm water. Add the milk, sugar, shortening, eggs, salt and 2 cups flour; beat until smooth. Stir in enough remaining flour to form a soft dough.

Turn onto a floured surface; knead until smooth and elastic, about 6-8 minutes. Place in a greased bowl, turning once to grease the top. Cover and let rise in a warm place until doubled, about 1 hour.

Punch dough down. Turn onto a floured surface; roll out to 1/2-in. thickness. Cut with a floured 2-1/2-in. doughnut cutter. Place on greased baking sheets. Cover and let rise until doubled, about 1 hour.

In an electric skillet or deep-fat fryer, heat oil to 375°. Fry doughnuts, a few at a time, until golden brown on

both sides. Drain on paper towels.

In a shallow bowl, combine the confectioners' sugar and water until smooth. Dip the warm doughnuts in the glaze; decorate as desired with colored sprinkles and/or breakfast cereals. **Yield:** 20 doughnuts.

Apricot Sunshine Coffee Cake

PREP: 20 min. **BAKE:** 30 min. + cooling

What a great way to start a weekend morning! With sunny apricots, pecans and cinnamon, this treat is sure to brighten up anyone's day. —*Joyce Stewart, Vernon, British Columbia*

- **2 tablespoons butter, melted**
- **1/4 cup packed brown sugar**
- **1 teaspoon ground cinnamon**
- **8 to 12 fresh apricots, halved** *or* **2 cans (15-1/4 ounces** *each***) apricot halves, drained**
- **1/4 cup shortening**
- **3/4 cup sugar**
- **1 egg**
- **1-1/2 cups all-purpose flour**
- **2 teaspoons baking powder**
- **1/2 teaspoon salt**
- **1/2 cup milk**
- **16 to 24 pecan** *or* **walnut halves**

Pour butter into a greased 8-in. square baking dish; sprinkle with brown sugar and cinnamon. Arrange apricot halves, cut side down, in a single layer over top; set aside.

In a small mixing bowl, beat the shortening and sugar for 2 minutes or until crumbly. Beat in the egg. Combine the flour, baking powder and salt; add to the crumb mixture alternately with milk until combined. Spread over the apricots.

Bake at 375° for 30-40 minutes or until a toothpick inserted near the center comes out clean. Cool for 10 minutes before inverting onto a serving plate. Place a pecan half in the center of each apricot half. Serve warm. **Yield:** 9-12 servings.

French Loaves

PREP: 30 min. + rising **BAKE:** 15 min.

My children help me make these easy, delicious loaves, and we have them with many different menus. The kids love that they can be eating fresh homemade bread in less than 2 hours.
—*Denise Boutin, Grand Isle, Vermont*

☑ This recipe includes Nutrition Facts and Diabetic Exchange.

- **2 tablespoons active dry yeast**
- **2 cups warm water (110° to 115°)**
- **2 teaspoons salt**
- **1 teaspoon sugar**
- **4-1/2 to 5 cups bread flour**
- **1 teaspoon cornmeal**

In a large bowl, dissolve yeast in warm water. Add the salt, sugar and 2 cups flour. Beat until smooth. Stir in enough remaining flour to form a soft dough.

Turn onto a floured surface; knead until smooth and elastic, about 6-8 minutes. Place in a greased bowl, turning once to grease the top. Cover and let rise in a warm place until doubled, about 1 hour.

Punch dough down. Turn onto a lightly floured surface; divide in half. Shape into 12-in.-long loaves.

Place seam side down on a greased baking sheet. Cover and let rise until doubled, about 30 minutes. Sprinkle with cornmeal. With a sharp knife, make four shallow slashes across the top of each loaf. Bake at 450° for 15-20 minutes or until golden brown. **Yield:** 2 loaves (12 slices each).

Nutrition Facts: 1 slice equals 79 calories, trace fat (trace saturated fat), 0 cholesterol, 197 mg sodium, 17 g carbohydrate, 1 g fiber, 3 g protein. **Diabetic Exchange:** 1 starch.

Chocolate Biscuit Puffs

(Pictured above)

PREP/TOTAL TIME: 20 min.

I created these when I was 9 years old, and I'm still baking them today. The three-ingredient recipe features a candy bar tucked inside refrigerated dough. —*Joy Clark, Seabeck, Washington*

- **1 package (7-1/2 ounces) refrigerated flaky buttermilk biscuits**
- **1 milk chocolate candy bar (1.55 ounces)**
- **2 teaspoons cinnamon-sugar**

Flatten each biscuit into a 3-in. circle. Break candy bar into 10 pieces; place a piece on each biscuit. Bring up edges to enclose candy and pinch to seal.

Place on an ungreased baking sheet. Sprinkle with cinnamon-sugar. Bake at 450° for 8-10 minutes or until golden brown. **Yield:** 10 servings.

Toasted Sunflower Bread

(Pictured below)

PREP: 45 min. + rising **BAKE:** 40 min. + cooling

Although I discovered this recipe while looking through an old cookbook, I've found that the hearty flavor appeals to all ages. Accented with soy sauce and sprinkled with sunflower seeds, this loaf is a nice alternative to ordinary whole wheat bread.
—*Caroline Kunkel, St. Joseph, Missouri*

- 1-1/4 **cups sunflower kernels,** *divided*
- 1 **tablespoon soy sauce**
- 1 **tablespoon active dry yeast**
- 3 **cups warm water (110° to 115°)**
- 4 **cups whole wheat flour**
- 1 **tablespoon brown sugar**
- 1 **tablespoon vegetable oil**
- 2 **teaspoons salt**
- 2 to 2-1/2 **cups all-purpose flour**
- 1 **egg**
- 1 **tablespoon cold water**

In a small skillet over medium heat, cook and stir 1 cup of sunflower kernels until lightly browned, about 6 minutes; remove from the heat. Stir in the soy sauce until kernels are evenly coated. Cool, stirring several times. Transfer to a blender or food processor; cover and process until ground.

In a large mixing bowl, dissolve the yeast in warm water. Add the wheat flour, brown sugar, oil, salt and ground sunflower kernels; beat until smooth. Stir in enough all-purpose flour to form a firm dough.

Turn onto a floured surface; knead until smooth and elastic, about 5-7 minutes. Place in a greased bowl, turning once to grease top. Cover and let rise in a warm place until doubled, about 1 hour.

Punch dough down. Turn onto a floured surface; knead 10 times. Divide in half; let rest for 5 minutes.

Sprinkle 3 tablespoons of sunflower kernels over the bottom and sides of two greased 8-in. x 4-in. loaf pans. Shape the dough into loaves; place in the prepared pans. Press the remaining sunflower kernels into the top of the dough. Cover and let rise until doubled, about 45 minutes.

Beat egg and cold water; brush over dough. Bake at 375° for 40-45 minutes or until golden brown. Remove from pans to wire racks to cool. **Yield:** 2 loaves.

Braided Wreath Bread

(Pictured at right)

PREP: 30 min. + rising **BAKE:** 30 min. + cooling

I love to make this attractive, citrusy braided bread to celebrate Santa Lucia Day on December 13. This Swedish custom is the symbolic start of Christmas in Scandinavia, a festival of lights that brightens the short, dark days of the winter season.
—*Janet Uram, Willowick, Ohio*

- 1 **package (1/4 ounce) active dry yeast**
- 1/4 **cup warm water (110° to 115°)**
- 1/3 **cup warm milk (110° to 115°)**
- 1/4 **cup sugar**
- 1/4 **cup butter, cubed**
- 2 **eggs**
- 1 **teaspoon grated orange peel**
- 1/2 **teaspoon salt**
- 1/2 **teaspoon orange extract**
- 2-1/2 to 3 **cups all-purpose flour**

In a large mixing bowl, dissolve yeast in warm water. Add the milk, sugar, butter, 1 egg, orange peel, salt, extract and 1 cup flour; beat until smooth. Stir in enough remaining flour to form a soft dough.

Turn onto a floured surface; knead until smooth and elastic, about 6-8 minutes. Place in a greased bowl, turning once to grease top. Cover and let rise in a warm place until doubled, about 1 hour.

Punch dough down; divide into thirds. Roll each portion into a 20-in. rope. Braid the ropes; shape into a wreath and pinch ends to seal. Place on a greased baking sheet. Cover and let rise in a warm place until doubled, about 45 minutes.

Beat the remaining egg; lightly brush over dough. Bake at 350° for 30-35 minutes or until golden brown. Cool for 10 minutes before removing from pan to a wire rack. **Yield:** 12 servings.

Apple Cinnamon Rolls

(Pictured above)

PREP: 30 min. + chilling **BAKE:** 30 min.

*One word sums up these from–scratch breakfast treats—yum!
They boast a filling of grated apple, pecans, brown sugar and
cinnamon, plus a sweet glaze drizzled on top. Whip up a batch
for a holiday brunch, for overnight guests or any time at all.*
—Lynn Thomas, Lakewood, New York

4-1/2 to 5 cups all-purpose flour
1/3 cup sugar
1 package (1/4 ounce) active dry yeast
1/2 teaspoon salt
1 cup milk
1/3 cup butter, cubed
3 eggs
FILLING:
3/4 cup packed brown sugar
1/4 cup all-purpose flour
1 tablespoon ground cinnamon
1/2 cup cold butter
1 cup grated peeled apple
1/2 cup chopped pecans

GLAZE:
1 cup confectioners' sugar
2 tablespoons milk

In a large mixing bowl, combine 2-1/4 cups flour, sugar, yeast and salt. In a saucepan, heat milk and butter to 120°-130°. Add to the dry ingredients; beat just until moistened. Add eggs; beat until smooth. Stir in enough remaining flour to form a soft dough.

Turn onto a floured surface; knead until smooth and elastic, about 6-8 minutes. Place in a greased bowl, turning once to grease top. Cover and let rise in a warm place until doubled, about 1 hour.

In a bowl, combine brown sugar, flour and cinnamon. Cut in butter until crumbly; set aside. Punch dough down. Turn onto a floured surface; let rest for 10 minutes. Roll into a 12-in. square. Sprinkle crumb mixture to within 1/2 in. of edges; top with apple and pecans.

Roll up jelly-roll style, starting with a long side; pinch seams to seal. Cut into 1-1/2-in. slices. Place cut side up in a greased 13-in. x 9-in. baking dish. Cover and refrigerate for 2 to 24 hours.

Uncover rolls and let stand at room temperature for 30 minutes before baking. Bake at 350° for 30-35 minutes or until golden brown. Combine the glaze ingredients; drizzle over rolls. Serve warm. **Yield:** 9 rolls.

turning once to grease top. Cover and let rise in a warm place until doubled, about 1 hour.

Turn onto a lightly floured surface; divide in half. Roll each portion into a 12-in. x 10-in. rectangle; brush with melted butter. Combine the sugar, cinnamon, chocolate chips and nuts if desired; sprinkle over each rectangle to within 1/2 in. of edges.

Roll up each rectangle jelly-roll style, starting with a long side; pinch seams to seal. Cut each into 10 slices. Place cut side down in a greased 15-in. x 10-in. x 1-in. baking pan. Cover and let rise until doubled, about 45 minutes.

Bake at 375° for 25-30 minutes or until lightly browned. In a small bowl, combine confectioners' sugar, milk and vanilla. Spread over rolls while slightly warm; sprinkle with additional chips if desired. **Yield:** 20 rolls.

Chocolate Cinnamon Rolls

(Pictured above and on page 76)

PREP: 30 min. + rising **BAKE:** 25 min.

These tempting rolls dotted with miniature chocolate chips are oh-so-good. When I take them to a potluck, they get snatched up in a flash. —*Myrna Sippel, Thomson, Illinois*

- **2 packages (1/4 ounce *each*) active dry yeast**
- **1-1/2 cups warm water (110° to 115°), *divided***
- **1/2 cup butter, softened**
- **1/2 cup sugar**
- **1 teaspoon salt**
- **4-1/2 to 4-3/4 cups all-purpose flour**
- **2/3 cup baking cocoa**

FILLING:
- **2 tablespoons butter, melted**
- **1/3 cup sugar**
- **1/2 teaspoon ground cinnamon**
- **1 cup miniature semisweet chocolate chips**
- **2/3 cup finely chopped nuts, optional**

ICING:
- **2 cups confectioners' sugar**
- **2 to 3 tablespoons milk**
- **1/2 teaspoon vanilla extract**
- **Additional miniature semisweet chocolate chips, optional**

In a large mixing bowl, dissolve yeast in 1/2 cup warm water. Add the butter, sugar, salt and remaining water. Stir in 2-1/2 cups flour and cocoa. Beat on medium speed for 3 minutes or until smooth. Stir in enough remaining flour to form a soft dough.

Turn onto a lightly floured surface; knead until smooth and elastic, about 6-8 minutes. Place in a greased bowl,

Herbed Bread Slices

PREP/TOTAL TIME: 10 min.

In this recipe, herbs add flavor and color to turn ordinary French bread into everyone's favorite addition to an Italian dinner. —*Margie Wampler, Butler, Pennsylvania*

- **3 tablespoons prepared Italian salad dressing**
- **1 loaf (8 ounces) French bread, halved lengthwise**
- **1 teaspoon dried rosemary, crushed**
- **1/2 teaspoon dried oregano**

Brush salad dressing over cut sides of bread. Sprinkle with rosemary and oregano. Place on an ungreased baking sheet. Broil 6 in. from the heat for 2-3 minutes or until lightly browned. Cut into 2-in. slices. **Yield:** 8 servings.

Italian Drop Biscuits

PREP/TOTAL TIME: 20 min.

I'd been whipping up garlic cheese biscuits for years before I tried spicing them up with some green chilies. I loved the results! —*LaDonna Reed, Ponca City, Oklahoma*

- **2 cups biscuit/baking mix**
- **1 cup (4 ounces) shredded cheddar cheese**
- **1/2 cup cold water**
- **2 tablespoons chopped green chilies**
- **1/4 cup butter, melted**
- **1 teaspoon dried parsley flakes**
- **1/2 teaspoon Italian seasoning**
- **1/4 teaspoon garlic powder**

In a bowl, combine biscuit mix, cheese, water and chilies just until moistened. Drop by heaping tablespoonfuls onto a greased baking sheet. Bake at 450° for 8-10 minutes or until golden brown. In a small bowl, combine butter, parsley, Italian seasoning and garlic powder; brush over warm biscuits. **Yield:** 1-1/2 dozen.

Old-Time Cake Doughnuts

(Pictured below)

PREP: 30 min. + chilling **COOK:** 5 min./batch

This tender cake doughnut is a little piece of heaven at breakfast. Sometimes I add a tablespoon of dark rum for a richer flavor.
—*Alissa Stehr, Gau–Odernheim, Germany*

☑ This recipe includes Nutrition Facts.

    2 tablespoons unsalted butter, softened
1-1/2 cups sugar, *divided*
    3 eggs
    4 cups all-purpose flour
    1 tablespoon baking powder
    3 teaspoons ground cinnamon, *divided*
  1/2 teaspoon salt
  1/8 teaspoon ground nutmeg
  3/4 cup 2% milk
Oil for deep-fat frying

In a large bowl, beat butter and 1 cup sugar until crumbly, about 2 minutes. Add the eggs, one at a time, beating well after each addition.

Combine flour, baking powder, 1 teaspoon cinnamon, salt and nutmeg; add to the butter mixture alternately with milk, beating well after each addition. Cover and refrigerate for 2 hours.

Turn onto a heavily floured surface; pat dough to 1/4-in. thickness. Cut with a floured 2-1/2-in. doughnut cutter. In an electric skillet or deep-fat fryer, heat oil to 375°.

Fry doughnuts, a few at a time, until golden brown on both sides. Drain on paper towels. Combine remaining sugar and cinnamon; roll warm doughnuts in mixture. **Yield:** about 2 dozen.

Nutrition Facts: 1 doughnut equals 198 calories, 8 g fat (1 g saturated fat), 30 mg cholesterol, 112 mg sodium, 29 g carbohydrate, 1 g fiber, 3 g protein.

Little Snail Rolls

(Pictured above)

PREP/TOTAL TIME: 30 min.

Snails aren't always slow—as this recipe proves. My daughter and I made these fun rolls together in only half an hour. Later, when we served them at a party, they disappeared even faster!
—*Christine Panzarella, Buena Park, California*

    2 cans (11 ounces *each*) refrigerated breadsticks
  12 pretzel sticks, broken into fourths
    1 egg yolk
    1 tablespoon water
Poppy seeds *or* sesame seeds, optional

Separate the breadstick dough into 24 pieces. For each snail, gently roll one piece into an 8-in. rope. Place on an ungreased baking sheet; coil 6-1/2 in. of the rope for the snail's shell.

Slightly separate remaining portion of dough from the coil and curl upward; add two pretzel pieces for the antennae.

In a small bowl, beat egg yolk and water. Brush over dough. Sprinkle with poppy or sesame seeds if desired. Bake at 375° for 10-13 minutes or until golden brown. Serve warm. **Yield:** 2 dozen.

DOUGHNUT DO'S. Doughnuts are best eaten the day they are made, preferably while they are still warm…or no more than an hour or two out of the fryer. Plan to make Old-Time Cake Doughnuts (recipe above left)? For a different sugar topping, sift confectioners' sugar with baking cocoa.

Punch dough down. On a lightly floured surface, roll dough into an 18-in. x 12-in. rectangle. Brush with melted butter. Sprinkle with chopped almonds and cinnamon to within 1/2 in. of edges. Roll up jelly-roll style, starting with a long side; pinch seam to seal.

Place seam side down on a greased baking sheet; pinch ends together to form a ring. With scissors, cut from outside edge to two-thirds of the way toward center of ring at 1-in. intervals. Separate strips slightly; twist to allow filling to show. Cover and let rise until doubled, about 45 minutes.

Bake at 375° for 20-25 minutes or until golden brown. Combine confectioners' sugar, water and extract; drizzle over warm bread. **Yield:** 1 wreath (16 slices).

Almond-Filled Butterhorns

(Pictured below)

PREP: 30 min. + rising **BAKE:** 10 min./batch

I add mashed potato flakes to make my butterhorn rolls moist and tender. With just the right amount of sweetness, they're a coffee–hour favorite and complement almost any meal.
—Loraine Meyer, Bend, Oregon

3-1/4 teaspoons active dry yeast
  2 cups warm milk (110° to 115°)
  4 eggs
  1 cup mashed potato flakes
  1 cup butter, softened
1/2 cup sugar
1-1/8 teaspoons salt
  7 to 8 cups all-purpose flour
  1 can (12-1/2 ounces) almond cake and pastry filling

In a large mixing bowl, dissolve yeast in milk. Add the eggs, potato flakes, butter, sugar, salt and 4 cups flour. Beat on medium speed for 3 minutes. Beat until smooth. Stir in enough remaining flour to form a soft dough (dough will be sticky).

Turn onto a floured surface; knead until smooth and

Christmas Wreath Bread

(Pictured above and on page 77)

PREP: 30 min. + rising **BAKE:** 20 min. + cooling

I love this wreath–shaped bread because it looks so festive for the holiday season. I make extras for bazaars and to give as gifts.
—Agnes Ward, Stratford, Ontario

  2 packages (1/4 ounce *each*) active dry yeast
1-1/2 cups warm water (110° to 115°)
  6 tablespoons butter
1/3 cup nonfat dry milk powder
1/4 cup sugar
  1 egg
3/4 teaspoon salt
4-1/2 to 5-1/2 cups all-purpose flour
  2 tablespoons butter, melted
1/2 cup chopped almonds
1-1/2 teaspoons ground cinnamon
  1 cup confectioners' sugar
  1 tablespoon water
1/4 teaspoon almond extract

In a large bowl, dissolve the yeast in warm water. Add the butter, milk powder, sugar, egg, salt and 3 cups flour. Beat on medium speed for 3 minutes. Stir in enough remaining flour to form a soft dough (dough will be sticky).

Turn onto a floured surface; knead until smooth and elastic, about 6-8 minutes. Place in a greased bowl, turning once to grease the top. Cover and let rise in a warm place until doubled, about 1 hour.

elastic, about 6-8 minutes. Place in a greased bowl, turning once to grease top. Cover and let rise in a warm place until doubled, about 1 hour.

Punch the dough down. Turn onto a lightly floured surface; divide into thirds. Roll each portion into a 12-in. circle; spread each with filling. Cut each circle into 12 wedges. Roll up wedges from the wide end and place point side down 2 in. apart on greased baking sheets. Curve ends to form a crescent. Cover and let rise until doubled, about 30 minutes.

Bake at 375° for 10-12 minutes or until lightly browned. Remove from the pans to wire racks. Serve warm. **Yield:** 3 dozen.

Editor's Note: This recipe was tested with Solo cake and pastry filling. Look for it in the baking aisle of your grocery store.

White Chocolate Berry Muffins

PREP: 15 min. **BAKE:** 20 min.

These rich muffins give you white chocolate chips and juicy fresh raspberries in every bite. It's a heavenly combination!
—Mary Lou Wayman, Salt Lake City, Utah

- 1 **package (8 ounces) cream cheese, softened**
- 1 **cup sugar**
- 2 **eggs**
- 1 **teaspoon vanilla extract**
- 1-1/2 **cups all-purpose flour**
- 2 **teaspoons baking powder**
- 1/2 **teaspoon salt**
- 1 **cup fresh raspberries**
- 1/2 **cup vanilla *or* white chips**

In a large bowl, beat the cream cheese and sugar until smooth. Add eggs, beating well after each addition. Stir in vanilla. Combine the flour, baking powder and salt; add to cream cheese mixture just until blended. Fold in raspberries and chips.

Fill greased or paper-lined muffin cups two-thirds full. Bake at 375° for 20-25 minutes or until a toothpick comes out clean. Cool for 5 minutes before removing from pan to a wire rack. **Yield:** 1 dozen.

Caramel-Pecan Monkey Bread

(Pictured above right)

PREP: 20 min. + rising **BAKE:** 30 min. + cooling

Our Test Kitchen staff created this irresistible bread. Cut it into slices...or let everyone pick off the ooey–gooey pieces themselves, just like the monkeys it's named for!

- 1 **package (1/4 ounce) active dry yeast**
- 1/4 **cup water (110° to 115°)**
- 1-1/4 **cups warm 2% milk (110° to 115°)**
- 1/3 **cup butter, melted**
- 1/4 **cup sugar**
- 2 **eggs**
- 1 **teaspoon salt**
- 5 **cups all-purpose flour**

CARAMEL:
- 2/3 **cup packed brown sugar**
- 1/4 **cup butter, cubed**
- 1/4 **cup heavy whipping cream**

ASSEMBLY:
- 3/4 **cup chopped pecans**
- 1 **cup sugar**
- 1 **teaspoon ground cinnamon**
- 1/2 **cup butter, melted**

In a large bowl, dissolve yeast in warm water. Add the milk, butter, sugar, eggs, salt and 3 cups flour. Beat on medium speed for 3 minutes. Stir in enough remaining flour to form a firm dough.

Turn onto a floured surface; knead until smooth and elastic, about 6-8 minutes. Place in a greased bowl, turning once to grease the top. Cover and let rise in a warm place until doubled, about 1 hour.

For caramel, in a small saucepan, bring the brown sugar, butter and cream to a boil. Cook and stir for 3 minutes. Pour half into a greased 10-in. fluted tube pan; sprinkle with half of the pecans.

Punch the dough down; shape into 40 balls (about 1-1/4-in. diameter). In a shallow bowl, combine sugar and cinnamon. Place melted butter in another bowl. Dip balls in butter, then roll in sugar mixture.

Place 20 balls in the tube pan; top with remaining caramel and pecans. Top with remaining balls. Cover and let rise until doubled, about 45 minutes.

Bake at 350° for 30-35 minutes or until golden brown. (Cover loosely with foil if top browns too quickly.) Cool for 10 minutes before inverting onto a serving plate. Serve warm. **Yield:** 1 loaf (20 servings).

Cookies, Bars & Candies

Whether you want to make Coconut Macaroons, Mocha Logs or another one of these scrumptious recipes, consider making extra. They won't last long!

Extra-Special Cashew Crescents............................92
Coconut Almond Bombs 92
Mocha Logs 93
Brazil Nut Cookies 93
German Chocolate Thumbprints........................94
Holiday Spritz..94
No-Bake Cookie Balls..95
Pinwheel Mints..95
Chocolate-Dipped Orange Cookies 95
Molasses Cookies with a Kick..............................96
Soft Lemon-Ginger Cookies 96
Ginger Cranberry Bars 97
Mini Cinnamon Roll Cookies 97
Chocolate Toffee Delights....................................98
Cranberry-Port Fudge Brownies 98
Green Mint Bark 98
Cheesecake Brownies 99
Go Nuts! Coconut Caramels.................................99
White Chocolate-Almond Dipped Cookies 100
Daria's Best-Ever Sugar Cookies 100
White Chocolate Raspberry Truffles 101
Cuccidati 101
Crispy Peanut Butter Balls...................................102
Coconut Macaroons...102
Chunky Orange Marmalade Cookies 102
Dried Cherry Biscotti 103
Raspberry Walnut Bars 103

GOODIES TO GRAB. Clockwise from top left: Brazil Nut Cookies (p. 93), Holiday Spritz (p. 94), Molasses Cookies with a Kick (p. 96) and Extra-Special Cashew Crescents (p. 92).

Extra-Special Cashew Crescents

(Pictured below and on page 90)

PREP: 15 min. + chilling **BAKE:** 10 min./batch + cooling

These nutty shortbread crescents are simply scrumptious, no matter if they're plain, glazed or dusted with confectioners' sugar.
—Paula Marchesi, Lenhartsville, Pennsylvania

☑ This recipe includes Nutrition Facts and Diabetic Exchange.

- 1-2/3 cups lightly salted cashews
- 1 cup butter, softened
- 3/4 cup packed brown sugar
- 1/2 cup sugar
- 2 teaspoons vanilla extract, *divided*
- 1-2/3 cups all-purpose flour
- 1/4 teaspoon salt
- 2 cups confectioners' sugar
- 3 tablespoons 2% milk

Chopped lightly salted cashews and additional confectioners' sugar, optional

Place cashews in a food processor; cover and process until finely ground.

In a large bowl, cream butter and sugars until light and fluffy. Beat in 1 teaspoon vanilla. Combine the flour, salt and ground cashews; gradually add to the creamed mixture and mix well.

Divide the dough in half; shape each into a ball, then flatten into a disk. Wrap in plastic wrap and refrigerate for 30 minutes.

On a lightly floured surface, roll the dough to 1/4-in. thickness. Using a floured scalloped round 3-in. cookie cutter, cut a semicircle from one corner of the dough, forming the inside of a crescent shape. Reposition the cutter 1-1/4 in. from the inside of crescent; cut cookie, forming a crescent 1-1/4 in. wide at its widest point. Repeat. Chill and reroll scraps if desired.

Place 1 in. apart on ungreased baking sheets. Bake at 375° for 6-7 minutes or until edges begin to brown. Cool for 1 minute before removing from pans to wire racks to cool completely.

Combine the confectioners' sugar, milk and remaining vanilla; spread or drizzle over cookies as desired. Sprinkle with chopped cashews if desired. Leave some cookies plain or sprinkle them with additional confectioners' sugar. Let iced cookies stand until set. Store in an airtight container. **Yield:** 10 dozen.

Nutrition Facts: 1 cookie (calculated without optional cashews) equals 48 calories, 2 g fat (1 g saturated fat), 4 mg cholesterol, 20 mg sodium, 6 g carbohydrate, trace fiber, 1 g protein. **Diabetic Exchange:** 1/2 starch.

Coconut Almond Bombs

(Pictured above)

PREP: 50 min. + chilling **BAKE:** 15 min./batch

I've made these special-looking cookies for both holiday parties and weddings. Guests always get a big "bang" out of them!
—Deb Holbrook, Abington, Massachusetts

- 1 package (7 ounces) almond paste
- 2 cups confectioners' sugar
- 1 package (14 ounces) flaked coconut
- 3 egg whites
- 1 teaspoon vanilla extract
- 1 carton (8 ounces) Mascarpone cheese
- 2 pounds white candy coating, chopped
- 2/3 cup sliced almonds

Gold pearl dust

Place the almond paste in a food processor; cover and process until finely chopped. Transfer to a large bowl; add the confectioners' sugar and coconut. Beat until mixture resembles coarse crumbs. In a small bowl, beat egg whites and vanilla until stiff peaks form; fold into coconut mixture.

Drop by tablespoonfuls 2 in. apart onto parchment paper-lined baking sheets. Bake at 325° for 14-18 minutes or until lightly browned. Remove to wire racks to cool.

Spread about 1 teaspoon of cheese over each cookie; refrigerate for 20 minutes or until cheese is firm.

In a microwave, melt candy coating; stir until smooth. Dip cookies in coating; allow excess to drip off. Place on waxed paper; sprinkle with almonds. Let stand until set. Brush pearl dust over the almonds. Store in an airtight container in the refrigerator. **Yield:** 3-1/2 dozen.

Editor's Note: Pearl dust is available from Wilton Industries. Call 1-800/794-5866 or visit *www.wilton.com*.

Mocha Logs

PREP: 50 min. **BAKE:** 10 min./batch + cooling

My mother has baked these fancy coffee logs since I was a child. Now, I make my own to give to friends at Christmastime.
—Gayle Tarkowski, Traverse City, Michigan

   1 **cup butter, softened**
   2 **tablespoons instant coffee granules**
3/4 **cup sugar**
   1 **egg**
   1 **teaspoon vanilla extract**
2-1/4 **cups all-purpose flour**
1/2 **teaspoon salt**
1/4 **teaspoon baking powder**
   1 **cup (6 ounces) semisweet chocolate chips**
1-1/2 **teaspoons shortening**
   1 **cup chopped walnuts**

In a small mixing bowl, beat the butter and coffee granules for 1 minute. Add the sugar; beat until light and fluffy. Beat in the egg and vanilla. Combine the flour, salt and baking powder; gradually add to the creamed mixture and mix well.

Roll dough into 1/2-in.-thick logs; cut into 2-in. pieces. Place on ungreased baking sheets. Or use a cookie press fitted with a star-shaped disk to press the dough into 2-in. logs 1 in. apart on baking sheets.

Bake at 375° for 8-12 minutes or until lightly browned.

PACKAGING POINTER. At Christmas or anytime, a tin of cookies makes a great gift. When packaging cookies or other food gifts, place waxed paper between the layers to avoid a gooey-sticky mess and to keep treats looking their best.

Cool for 2 minutes before removing to the wire racks to cool completely.

In a small microwave-safe bowl, melt the chocolate chips and shortening; stir until smooth. Dip one end of each cookie in the chocolate; allow the excess to drip off. Sprinkle with the walnuts. Place cookies on waxed paper; let stand until set. Store in an airtight container. **Yield:** 12-1/2 dozen.

Brazil Nut Cookies

(Pictured below and on page 90)

PREP: 15 min. **BAKE:** 10 min./batch

Brazil nuts may be an unusual ingredient for cookies, but the flavor they add is outstanding. Just try these and see for yourself!
—Charlotte Mains, Cuyahoga Falls, Ohio

   1 **cup butter, softened**
   1 **cup sugar**
   2 **eggs**
1-1/2 **teaspoons vanilla extract**
2-1/4 **cups all-purpose flour**
1/2 **teaspoon baking soda**
1/4 **teaspoon salt**
   2 **cups chopped Brazil nuts**
1/2 **cup flaked coconut**

In a large mixing bowl, cream the butter and sugar. Add the eggs, one at a time, beating well after each addition. Beat in the vanilla. Combine the flour, baking soda and salt; gradually add to the creamed mixture. Stir in the nuts and coconut.

Drop by tablespoonfuls 3 in. apart onto ungreased baking sheets. Bake at 350° for 10-12 minutes or until bottom of cookies are lightly browned. Remove to wire racks. **Yield:** about 4-1/2 dozen.

Roll into 1-in. balls. Place 2 in. apart on greased baking sheets. Using the end of a wooden spoon handle, make an indentation in the center of each ball. Bake at 350° for 6-8 minutes or until firm. Remove to wire racks to cool completely.

Meanwhile, for filling, in a small bowl, combine the coconut, pecans and vanilla. Stir in enough milk to form a stiff mixture. Fill the cookies with filling, a rounded teaspoonful in each. Melt the chocolate chips with the shortening; stir until smooth. Drizzle over cookies. Store in an airtight container. **Yield:** 4 dozen.

Holiday Spritz

(Pictured below and on page 91)

PREP: 30 min. **BAKE:** 10 min./batch

I substituted rum extract for vanilla in this classic recipe, and the end result was a cookie that tastes a lot like eggnog. Delicious!
—Lisa Varner, Charleston, South Carolina

    1 **cup butter, softened**
    1 **cup confectioners' sugar**
    1 **egg**
 1-1/2 **teaspoons rum extract**
 2-1/2 **cups all-purpose flour**
   1/4 **teaspoon salt**
Colored sugar

In a small bowl, cream butter and confectioners' sugar until light and fluffy. Beat in egg and extract. Combine flour and salt; gradually add to creamed mixture and mix well.

Using a cookie press fitted with the disk of your choice, press cookies 1 in. apart onto ungreased baking sheets. Sprinkle with colored sugar.

Bake at 375° for 6-9 minutes or until lightly browned. Cool for 2 minutes before removing from pans to wire racks. **Yield:** 7 dozen.

German Chocolate Thumbprints

(Pictured above)

PREP: 45 min. **BAKE:** 10 min./batch + cooling

For a festive presentation, place these fancy drizzled cookies in silver or gold foil candy cups or on a silver or gold foil doily.
—Donna-Marie Ryan, Topsfield, Massachusetts

   1/2 **cup semisweet chocolate chips**
    1 **tablespoon shortening**
   1/2 **cup butter, softened**
   3/4 **cup sugar**
    1 **egg**
    1 **tablespoon strong brewed coffee**
    1 **teaspoon vanilla extract**
    2 **cups all-purpose flour**
    1 **tablespoon baking cocoa**
    1 **teaspoon baking powder**
   1/4 **teaspoon salt**
FILLING:
   3/4 **cup flaked coconut, toasted**
   3/4 **cup chopped pecans, toasted**
    1 **teaspoon vanilla extract**
    4 **to 6 tablespoons sweetened condensed milk**
DRIZZLE:
   1/2 **cup semisweet chocolate chips**
    1 **tablespoon shortening**

In a microwave, melt chocolate chips and shortening; stir until smooth. Set aside. In a large bowl, cream the butter and sugar until light and fluffy. Beat in the egg, coffee, vanilla and melted chocolate mixture. Combine the flour, cocoa, baking powder and salt; gradually add to creamed mixture and mix well.

No-Bake Cookie Balls

PREP/TOTAL TIME: 20 min.

These quick bites are a great choice when you're short on time or don't want to turn on the oven. I make them a day or two ahead because I think they're even better when the flavors blend.
—Carmeletta Dailey, Winfield, Texas

- 1 cup (6 ounces) semisweet chocolate chips
- 3 cups confectioners' sugar
- 1-3/4 cups crushed vanilla wafers (about 50 wafers)
- 1 cup chopped walnuts, toasted
- 1/3 cup orange juice
- 3 tablespoons light corn syrup

Additional confectioners' sugar

In a large microwave-safe bowl, melt chocolate chips; stir until smooth.

Stir in confectioners' sugar, vanilla wafers, walnuts, orange juice and corn syrup. Roll into 1-in. balls; roll in additional confectioners' sugar. Store in an airtight container. **Yield:** 5 dozen.

Pinwheel Mints

PREP: 45 min. + chilling

Both my grandmother and mom used to make these eye-catching confections as a replacement for ordinary mints at Christmas. My guests always ask how I created the swirl pattern.
—Marilou Roth, Milford, Nebraska

- 1 package (8 ounces) cream cheese, softened
- 1/2 to 1 teaspoon mint extract
- 7-1/2 to 8-1/2 cups confectioners' sugar

Red and green food coloring
Additional confectioners' sugar

In a large mixing bowl, combine the cream cheese and mint extract. Gradually beat in as much confectioners' sugar as possible; knead in remaining confectioners' sugar until a firm mixture is achieved. Divide mixture in half; with food coloring, tint half pink and the other light green.

On waxed paper, lightly sprinkle the additional confectioners' sugar into a 12-in. x 5-in. rectangle. Divide pink portion in half; shape each portion into a 10-in. log. Place one log on sugared waxed paper; flatten slightly. Cover with waxed paper and roll into a 12-in. x 5-in. rectangle. Repeat with the remaining pink portion; set aside. Repeat with light green portion.

Remove top piece of waxed paper from one pink and one green rectangle. Place one over the other. Remove bottom piece of waxed paper from top rectangle. Roll up jelly-roll style, starting with a long side. Wrap in waxed paper; twist the ends. Repeat. Chill overnight.

To serve, cut into 1/2-in. slices. Store the mints in an airtight container in the refrigerator for up to 1 week. **Yield:** about 3 dozen.

Chocolate-Dipped Orange Cookies

(Pictured above)

PREP: 20 min. BAKE: 20 min./batch + cooling

These tender treats are so pretty, and the combination of cream cheese, orange, chocolate and almonds makes them irresistible.
—Linda Call, Falun, Kansas

- 1 cup butter, softened
- 1 package (8 ounces) cream cheese, softened
- 1 cup sugar
- 1/2 teaspoon vanilla extract
- 2 tablespoons grated orange peel
- 2-1/2 cups all-purpose flour
- 1/2 teaspoon salt
- 1 cup finely chopped blanched almonds

GLAZE:
- 5 squares (1 ounce *each*) semisweet chocolate
- 3 tablespoons butter
- 1/4 cup finely chopped blanched almonds

In a large mixing bowl, cream the butter, cream cheese and sugar. Beat in the vanilla and orange peel. Combine the flour and salt; gradually add to creamed mixture. Stir in almonds.

Roll the dough into 1-in. balls. Place 2 in. apart on ungreased baking sheets. Flatten with a glass dipped in sugar. Bake at 325° for 20-25 minutes or until firm. Remove to wire racks to cool.

For glaze, in a microwave-safe bowl, melt chocolate and butter; stir until smooth. Dip each cookie halfway into chocolate; shake off excess. Immediately sprinkle with almonds. Place cookies on waxed paper to harden. **Yield:** 6 dozen.

Sugar 'n' Spice

A DASH of cinnamon, a teaspoon of ginger, a pinch of nutmeg…a little bit of spice from your kitchen cupboard can make cookies and bars even yummier. The recipes here prove it!

From Molasses Cookies with a Kick and Mini Cinnamon Roll Cookies to Soft Lemon-Ginger Cookies and nut-topped Ginger Cranberry Bars, these fresh-baked treats are guaranteed to tingle taste buds with their sweet-and-spicy combination.

Whether you need special goodies for a holiday gift tin, a church potluck dinner or just the cookie jar, you won't want to pass up these flavorful favorites.

Molasses Cookies with a Kick

(Pictured below and on page 91)

PREP: 40 min. + chilling **BAKE:** 10 min./batch

I've used this combination of spices for a long time. My mom's a big fan—I get requests from her to bake these treats year-round.
—Tamara Rau, Medina, North Dakota

☑ **This recipe includes Nutrition Facts and Diabetic Exchange.**

    3/4 cup butter, softened
    1/2 cup sugar
    1/2 cup packed brown sugar
    1/4 cup molasses
      1 egg
  1-1/2 teaspoons minced fresh gingerroot
  2-1/4 cups all-purpose flour
      1 teaspoon ground cinnamon
    3/4 teaspoon baking soda
    1/2 teaspoon ground cloves
    1/4 to 1/2 teaspoon cayenne pepper
    1/4 teaspoon salt
    1/4 teaspoon ground nutmeg
    1/8 teaspoon *each* ground white pepper, cardamom and coriander
    3/4 cup turbinado (washed raw) sugar

In a large bowl, cream the butter and sugars until light and fluffy. Beat in molasses, egg and ginger.

Combine the flour, cinnamon, baking soda, cloves, cayenne, salt, nutmeg, white pepper, cardamom and coriander; gradually add to the creamed mixture and mix well. Cover and refrigerate dough for 1-1/2 hours or until easy to handle.

Roll into 1/2-in. balls; roll in turbinado sugar. Place 3 in. apart on lightly greased baking sheets. Bake at 350° for 8-10 minutes or until set. Cool for 2 minutes before removing from pans to wire racks. Store in an airtight container. **Yield:** 8 dozen.

Nutrition Facts: 1 cookie equals 41 calories, 2 g fat (1 g saturated fat), 6 mg cholesterol, 28 mg sodium, 7 g carbohydrate, trace fiber, trace protein. **Diabetic Exchange:** 1/2 starch.

Soft Lemon-Ginger Cookies

PREP/TOTAL TIME: 30 min.

This recipe of my mother's is one of the first cookies I learned to make. My family loves these soft goodies warm from the oven.
—Sharon Bretz, Havre de Grace, Maryland

    1/2 cup butter, softened
      1 cup packed brown sugar
      1 egg
      3 tablespoons sour cream
    1/2 teaspoon lemon extract
    1/2 teaspoon vanilla extract
  1-3/4 cups all-purpose flour
      1 teaspoon baking soda
      1 teaspoon cream of tartar
      1 teaspoon ground ginger
    1/4 teaspoon salt

In a small mixing bowl, cream the butter and brown sugar. Beat in egg, sour cream and extracts. Combine the flour, baking soda, cream of tartar, ginger and salt; gradually beat into the creamed mixture.

Drop dough by rounded teaspoonfuls 2 in. apart onto ungreased baking sheets. Bake at 350° for 10-12 minutes or until lightly browned. Immediately remove from pans to wire racks. **Yield:** 2 dozen.

Ginger Cranberry Bars

(Pictured above)

PREP: 15 min. **BAKE:** 40 min. + cooling

These ruby-red squares were among the winners of a cranberry festival bake-off. —*Lynn Newman, Gainesville, Florida*

- 1 cup butter, softened
- 1/2 cup sugar
- 2 teaspoons almond extract, *divided*
- 2 cups all-purpose flour
- 2 cans (16 ounces *each*) whole-berry cranberry sauce
- 2 tablespoons candied *or* crystallized ginger, chopped
- 3 egg whites
- 1/2 cup confectioners' sugar
- 1/2 cup sliced almonds

In a large mixing bowl, cream the butter and sugar until light and fluffy. Stir in 1-1/2 teaspoons almond extract. Beat in flour until crumbly.

Press into a greased 13-in. x 9-in. baking dish. Bake at 350° for 25-28 minutes or until golden brown.

Meanwhile, in a small saucepan, heat cranberry sauce and ginger. In a small mixing bowl, beat egg whites on medium speed until soft peaks form. Gradually beat in confectioners' sugar and remaining extract on high until stiff glossy peaks form. Spread cranberry mixture over crust. Spread meringue over the cranberry layer; sprinkle with almonds.

Increase heat to 400°. Bake for 14-15 minutes or until lightly browned. Cool completely before cutting into bars. Refrigerate leftovers. **Yield:** 2 dozen.

Mini Cinnamon Roll Cookies

(Pictured at right)

PREP: 1 hour **BAKE:** 10 min./batch + cooling

Intense cinnamon flavor fills these cookies, which are a yummy cross between a snickerdoodle and a cinnamon roll. Some people say they taste like Christmas! —*Mary Gauntt, Denton, Texas*

✓ This recipe includes Nutrition Facts and Diabetic Exchanges.

- 1 cup butter, softened
- 1-3/4 cups sugar, *divided*
- 3 egg yolks
- 1 tablespoon plus 1 teaspoon honey, *divided*
- 1 teaspoon vanilla extract
- 2-1/2 cups all-purpose flour
- 1 teaspoon baking powder
- 1/2 teaspoon salt
- 1/2 teaspoon cream of tartar
- 1 tablespoon ground cinnamon
- 8 ounces white baking chocolate, chopped

In a large bowl, cream butter and 1-1/4 cups sugar until light and fluffy. Beat in egg yolks, 1 tablespoon honey and vanilla. Combine the flour, baking powder, salt and cream of tartar; gradually add to the creamed mixture and mix well.

Shape a heaping tablespoonful of the dough into a 6-in. log. In a shallow bowl, combine the cinnamon and remaining sugar; roll log in cinnamon-sugar. Loosely coil log into a spiral shape; place on a greased baking sheet. Repeat, placing cookies 1 in. apart. Sprinkle with remaining cinnamon-sugar.

Bake at 350° for 8-10 minutes or until set. Remove to wire racks to cool completely. In a small bowl, melt the baking chocolate with the remaining honey; stir until smooth. Drizzle over cookies. Let stand until set. Store in an airtight container. **Yield:** about 2-1/2 dozen.

Nutrition Facts: 1 cookie equals 189 calories, 9 g fat (6 g saturated fat), 38 mg cholesterol, 105 mg sodium, 25 g carbohydrate, trace fiber, 2 g protein. **Diabetic Exchanges:** 1-1/2 starch, 1-1/2 fat.

smooth. Drizzle over caramel mixture. Let stand until the chocolate is set. Cut into bars. Store in an airtight container. **Yield:** 3 dozen.

   Nutrition Facts: 1 bar equals 149 calories, 8 g fat (5 g saturated fat), 13 mg cholesterol, 92 mg sodium, 19 g carbohydrate, trace fiber, 2 g protein. **Diabetic Exchanges:** 1-1/2 fat, 1 starch.

Cranberry-Port Fudge Brownies

PREP: 25 min. **BAKE:** 30 min. + cooling

My friend Krysta loves these fudgy, cranberry-dotted brownies. The port wine adds a splash of sophistication to these treats.
—*Kelly Heft, Somersville, Massachusetts*

   4 ounces unsweetened chocolate, chopped
   1/2 cup butter, cubed
   1-1/2 cups sugar
   1/2 teaspoon vanilla extract
   2 eggs
   3/4 cup all-purpose flour
   1/4 teaspoon salt
   1/2 cup dried cranberries
   1/2 cup tawny port wine

In a small saucepan, melt chocolate and butter; stir until smooth. Remove from heat; stir in sugar and vanilla. Add eggs, one at a time, stirring well after each addition. Stir in flour and salt just until blended.

   In a small saucepan, combine cranberries and wine. Bring to a boil over medium heat; cook until the liquid is reduced to a thin syrupy consistency (about 3 minutes). Stir into batter.

   Transfer to a greased 9-in. square baking pan. Bake at 325° for 30-35 minutes or until a toothpick inserted near the center comes out clean (do not overbake). Cool on a wire rack. **Yield:** 16 servings.

Green Mint Bark

PREP: 20 min. + chilling

I started making this easy bark a few years ago. The green candy coating gives it an extra-festive look for the Christmas season.
—*Hillary Templin, Kennewick, Washington*

☑ This recipe includes Nutrition Facts and Diabetic Exchanges.

   1 package (10 to 12 ounces) white baking chips
   12 ounces green candy coating disks
   1 teaspoon peppermint extract
   2 to 3 candy canes, crushed

Line a baking sheet with foil; set aside. In a microwave, melt chips; stir until smooth. Spread into a 13-in. x 9-in. rectangle on prepared baking sheet.

   In a microwave, melt the green candy coating; stir until smooth. Stir in the peppermint extract. Spread

Chocolate Toffee Delights

(Pictured above)

PREP: 15 min. **BAKE:** 30 min. + cooling

I combined my best shortbread recipe with some ingredients I had on hand and created these bars. They remind me of my favorite Girl Scout cookies.   —*Shannon Koene, Blacksburg, Virginia*

☑ This recipe includes Nutrition Facts and Diabetic Exchanges.

   1 cup butter, softened
   1/2 cup plus 2 tablespoons sugar, *divided*
   3/4 teaspoon almond extract
   1/2 teaspoon coconut extract
   2 cups all-purpose flour
   1/4 teaspoon salt
   1/4 teaspoon baking powder
   1/2 cup flaked coconut
   1/2 cup sliced almonds, toasted and cooled
   1 jar (12-1/4 ounces) caramel ice cream topping
   3/4 cup dark chocolate chips

In a small bowl, cream butter and 1/2 cup sugar until light and fluffy. Beat in extracts. Combine the flour, salt and baking powder; gradually add to creamed mixture and mix well.

   Press into a greased 13-in. x 9-in. baking pan. Bake at 350° for 10 minutes. Prick crust with a fork; sprinkle with remaining sugar. Bake 15 minutes longer or until set.

   Meanwhile, place the coconut and almonds in a food processor; cover and process until finely chopped. Transfer to a small bowl; stir in the ice cream topping. Spread over crust. Bake for 5-10 minutes or until edges are bubbly. Cool on a wire rack.

   In a microwave, melt the chocolate chips; stir until

over the white layer; sprinkle with candy.

Chill for 10 minutes or until firm. Break into pieces. Store in an airtight container. **Yield:** 1-1/2 pounds.

Nutrition Facts: 1 ounce equals 171 calories, 9 g fat (7 g saturated fat), 3 mg cholesterol, 32 mg sodium, 21 g carbohydrate, 0 fiber, 1 g protein. **Diabetic Exchanges:** 2 fat, 1 starch.

Cheesecake Brownies

(Pictured below)

PREP: 30 min. **BAKE:** 30 min. + cooling

My grandson likes this brownie recipe because he can help by pouring in the mix, cracking the eggs and stirring the batter.
—*Barbara Banzhof, Muncy, Pennsylvania*

  1 **package fudge brownie mix (13-inch x 9-inch pan size)**
  2 **packages (3 ounces *each*) cream cheese, softened**
  6 **tablespoons butter, softened**
1/2 **cup sugar**
  2 **tablespoons all-purpose flour**
  1 **teaspoon vanilla extract**
  2 **eggs, lightly beaten**
  1 **can (16 ounces) chocolate frosting**

Prepare the brownie mix batter according to package directions. Spread 2 cups into a greased 13-in. x 9-in. baking dish; set aside.

In a small bowl, beat the cream cheese, butter, sugar, flour and vanilla until smooth. Add eggs; beat on low speed just until combined. Spread evenly over brownie batter. Top with remaining brownie batter. Cut through batter with a knife to swirl.

Bake at 350° for 28-32 minutes or until a toothpick inserted near the center comes out with moist crumbs (the brownies may appear moist). Cool completely on a wire rack. Spread chocolate frosting over the brownies. **Yield:** 3 dozen.

Go Nuts! Coconut Caramels

(Pictured above)

PREP: 10 min. **COOK:** 5 min. + cooling

I got this recipe from a cooking show on TV but altered it to suit our tastes. The sweet–salty combination is simply heavenly!
—*Deanna Polito-Laughinghouse, Raleigh, North Carolina*

☑ **This recipe includes Nutrition Facts and Diabetic Exchanges.**

  1 **teaspoon butter**
 24 **caramels**
3/4 **cup plus 2 tablespoons flaked coconut, *divided***
1/2 **cup white baking chips**
1/2 **cup salted peanuts**

Line an 8-in. x 4-in. loaf pan with foil and grease the foil with butter; set aside.

In a microwave-safe bowl, combine the caramels, 3/4 cup coconut, baking chips and peanuts. Microwave on high, uncovered, for 1 minute; stir. Cook, uncovered, 30-60 seconds longer or until caramels are melted; stir to combine. Press into prepared pan. Sprinkle with the remaining coconut. Cool.

Using foil, lift candy out of pan. Discard foil; cut candy into 1-in. squares. **Yield:** about 3/4 pound.

Editor's Note: This recipe was tested in a 1,100-watt microwave.

Nutrition Facts: 1 piece equals 70 calories, 4 g fat (2 g saturated fat), 1 mg cholesterol, 38 mg sodium, 9 g carbohydrate, trace fiber, 1 g protein. **Diabetic Exchanges:** 1/2 starch, 1/2 fat.

White Chocolate-Almond Dipped Cookies

(Pictured below)

PREP: 35 min. **BAKE:** 10 min./batch + cooling

These easy-to-make cookies are always popular. I've dipped them in dark chocolate instead of white candy coating and also used walnuts instead of almonds. —Trisha Kruse, Eagle, Idaho

☑ This recipe includes Nutrition Facts and Diabetic Exchanges.

        1 cup butter, softened
    1/2 cup confectioners' sugar
    1/2 teaspoon almond extract
        2 cups all-purpose flour
        1 cup finely chopped dried apricots
        8 ounces white candy coating, chopped
        1 cup finely chopped almonds, toasted

In a large bowl, cream butter and confectioners' sugar until light and fluffy. Beat in extract. Gradually add flour and mix well. Stir in apricots.

Roll 1 tablespoonful of dough into a 2-1/2-in. log; shape into a crescent. Repeat. Place 2 in. apart on greased baking sheets. Bake at 350° for 10-14 minutes or until set. Remove to wire racks to cool completely.

In a microwave, melt candy coating; stir until smooth. Dip half of each cookie in coating; allow excess to drip off. Press into almonds; place on waxed paper. Let stand until set. Store in an airtight container. **Yield:** 3 dozen.

Nutrition Facts: 1 cookie equals 138 calories, 9 g fat (5 g saturated fat), 13 mg cholesterol, 39 mg sodium, 13 g carbohydrate, 1 g fiber, 2 g protein. **Diabetic Exchanges:** 1 starch, 1 fat.

Daria's Best-Ever Sugar Cookies

(Pictured above)

PREP: 2 hours + chilling **BAKE:** 10 min./batch + cooling

After years of searching for the best sugar cookie recipe, I can now say that this recipe is it! Almond paste brings an extra-rich flavor to these moist cookies that have a subtle crunch.
—Daria Burcar, Rochester, Michigan

☑ This recipe includes Nutrition Facts and Diabetic Exchange.

    1/2 cup almond paste
        4 egg yolks
        2 cups butter, softened
    1-3/4 cups sugar
    1/2 teaspoon salt
    3-3/4 cups all-purpose flour
FROSTING:
    3-3/4 cups confectioners' sugar
        3 tablespoons meringue powder
    1/3 cup water
Food coloring, coarse sugar and assorted sprinkles, optional

In a large bowl, beat almond paste and egg yolks until crumbly. Add the butter, sugar and salt; beat until light and fluffy. Gradually add flour and mix well. Divide into four portions; shape each into a ball, then flatten into a disk. Wrap in plastic wrap and refrigerate for 1-2 hours or until easy to handle.

On a lightly floured surface, roll one portion of dough to 1/4-in. thickness. Cut with a floured 2-1/2-in. cookie cutter. Place 2 in. apart on ungreased baking sheets. Repeat with remaining dough.

Bake at 375° for 6-8 minutes or until edges begin to brown. Cool for 2 minutes before removing from pans to wire racks to cool completely.

For frosting, beat the confectioners' sugar, meringue powder and water until fluffy, about 5 minutes. Color frosting if desired.

Frost the cookies; decorate with coarse sugar and sprinkles if desired. Let cookies stand until set. Store in an airtight container. **Yield:** about 13-1/2 dozen.

Editor's Note: Meringue powder is available from Wilton Industries. Call 1-800/794-5866 or visit *www.wilton.com*.

Nutrition Facts: 1 cookie equals 55 calories, 3 g fat (1 g saturated fat), 11 mg cholesterol, 25 mg sodium, 7 g carbohydrate, trace fiber, 1 g protein. **Diabetic Exchange:** 1/2 starch.

White Chocolate Raspberry Truffles

PREP: 20 min. + chilling

These no-bake confections couldn't be much simpler to create. The mouthwatering truffles require just five everyday ingredients. For the finishing touch, I roll the balls in toasted almonds.
—Molly Seidel, Edgewood, New Mexico

- 1 package (8 ounces) cream cheese, softened
- 1 cup vanilla *or* white chips, melted
- 3/4 cup crushed vanilla wafers (about 25 wafers)
- 1/4 cup seedless raspberry preserves
- 2/3 cup finely chopped almonds, toasted

In a small mixing bowl, beat the cream cheese until smooth. Beat in the melted vanilla chips, vanilla wafer crumbs and raspberry preserves. Cover and refrigerate for 2 hours or until easy to handle.

Shape mixture into 1-in. balls; roll each in chopped almonds. Store in an airtight container in refrigerator. **Yield:** about 3-1/2 dozen.

Cuccidati

(Pictured at right)

PREP: 30 min. + chilling **BAKE:** 10 min./batch + cooling

A wedding favorite, these classic Italian goodies are well worth the time it takes to prepare them. The combination of raisins, dates and figs makes them perfect for Christmastime, too.
—Carolyn Fafinski, Dunkirk, New York

✓ This recipe includes Nutrition Facts and Diabetic Exchanges.

- 2 cups raisins
- 3/4 pound pitted dates
- 3/4 cup sugar
- 2 small navel oranges, peeled and quartered
- 1/3 pound dried figs
- 1/3 cup chopped walnuts
- 1/4 cup water
DOUGH:
- 1 cup shortening

- 1 cup sugar
- 2 eggs
- 1/4 cup 2% milk
- 2 teaspoons vanilla extract
- 3-1/2 cups all-purpose flour
- 1 teaspoon salt
- 1 teaspoon baking powder
- 1 teaspoon baking soda
GLAZE:
- 2 cups confectioners' sugar
- 2 to 3 tablespoons 2% milk

Place the first seven ingredients in a food processor; cover and process until finely chopped. Set aside.

In a large bowl, cream the shortening and sugar until light and fluffy. Beat in eggs, milk and vanilla. Combine flour, salt, baking powder and baking soda; gradually add to the creamed mixture and mix well. Divide dough into four portions; cover and refrigerate for 1 hour.

Roll out each portion between two sheets of waxed paper into a 16-in. x 6-in. rectangle. Spread 1 cup filling lengthwise down the center of each. Starting at a long side, fold dough over filling; fold the other side over the top. Pinch the seams and edges to seal. Cut each rectangle diagonally into 1-in strips. Place seam side down on parchment paper-lined baking sheets.

Bake at 400° for 10-14 minutes or until the edges are golden brown. Cool for 10 minutes before removing from pans to wire racks to cool completely.

Combine confectioners' sugar and enough milk to achieve desired consistency; drizzle over cookies. Store in an airtight container. **Yield:** about 5 dozen.

Nutrition Facts: 1 cookie equals 132 calories, 4 g fat (1 g saturated fat), 7 mg cholesterol, 67 mg sodium, 24 g carbohydrate, 1 g fiber, 1 g protein. **Diabetic Exchanges:** 1 starch, 1/2 fruit, 1/2 fat.

Coconut Macaroons

PREP/TOTAL TIME: 25 min.

Simple, chewy and oh-so-good, these five-ingredient goodies are perfect for bake sales or as a quick snack for your family.
—Sabrina Shafer, Minooka, Illinois

☑ This recipe includes Nutrition Facts and Diabetic Exchanges.

2-1/2 cups flaked coconut
1/3 cup all-purpose flour
1/8 teaspoon salt
2/3 cup sweetened condensed milk
1 teaspoon vanilla extract

In a small bowl, combine the coconut, flour and salt. Add the milk and vanilla; mix well (batter will be stiff).
Drop by tablespoonfuls 1 inch apart onto a greased baking sheet. Bake at 350° for 15-20 minutes or until golden brown. Remove to wire racks. **Yield:** 1-1/2 dozen.
Nutrition Facts: 1 cookie equals 110 calories, 6 g fat (5 g saturated fat), 4 mg cholesterol, 65 mg sodium, 14 g carbohydrate, 1 g fiber, 2 g protein. **Diabetic Exchanges:** 1 starch, 1 fat.

Crispy Peanut Butter Balls

(Pictured above)

PREP: 40 min. + chilling

After sampling this drizzled, dipped candy at a buffet at work, I requested the recipe for my files immediately! If you like the combination of chocolate and peanut butter as much as I do, you'll love these, too. The crisp rice cereal adds a fun crunch.
—Liz David, St. Catharines, Ontario

2 cups creamy peanut butter
1/2 cup butter, softened
3-3/4 cups confectioners' sugar
3 cups crisp rice cereal
4 cups (24 ounces) semisweet chocolate chips
1/4 cup plus 1 teaspoon shortening, *divided*
1/3 cup vanilla *or* white chips

In a large mixing bowl, beat the peanut butter and butter until blended; gradually beat in confectioners' sugar. Stir in cereal. Shape into 1-in. balls. Refrigerate until chilled.
In a large microwave-safe bowl, combine chocolate chips and 1/4 cup shortening. Microwave on high until the chips are melted; stir until smooth. Dip balls into chocolate; place on a waxed paper-lined pan.
In a small microwave-safe bowl, combine vanilla chips and remaining shortening. Microwave at 70% power until melted; stir until smooth. Drizzle over the candies. Refrigerate until set. **Yield:** 6 dozen.
Editor's Note: Reduced-fat or generic brands of peanut butter are not recommended for this recipe.

Chunky Orange Marmalade Cookies

PREP: 10 min. **BAKE:** 15 min./batch

This recipe doesn't use sugar. Instead, the sweetness comes from chocolate and marmalade. —Mary Small, Monmouth, Maine

1/4 cup shortening
1 egg yolk
1/2 cup orange marmalade
1/2 teaspoon vanilla extract
1 cup all-purpose flour
1/2 teaspoon salt
1/2 teaspoon baking powder
1/2 teaspoon baking soda
1/2 teaspoon ground cinnamon
1/2 teaspoon ground nutmeg
1/2 cup semisweet chocolate chips
1/2 teaspoon chopped pecans

In a small mixing bowl, cream the shortening, egg yolk and marmalade until light and fluffy. Beat in the vanilla.

CANDY CREATIVITY. Feel free to change the recipe for Crispy Peanut Butter Balls (at left) to suit the occasion. For example, for a baby shower, drizzle them with blue or pink candy coating instead of the melted vanilla-chip mixture.

Combine the flour, salt, baking powder, baking soda, cinnamon and nutmeg; add to the creamed mixture and mix well. Stir in chocolate chips and pecans.

Drop by tablespoonfuls 2 in. apart onto greased baking sheets. Bake at 350° for 12-15 minutes or until lightly browned. Remove to wire racks. **Yield:** 2 dozen.

Editor's Note: This recipe uses orange marmalade for sweetener and does not need additional sugar.

Dried Cherry Biscotti

(Pictured below)

PREP: 25 min. **BAKE:** 25 min. + cooling

Need a treat that's not overly sweet? Consider these traditional twice-baked Italian cookies. The cherries and almonds add color and texture while a dusting of powdered sugar dresses them up.
—*Sharon Martin, Manistee, Michigan*

✓ This recipe includes Nutrition Facts and Diabetic Exchanges.

   2 tablespoons butter, softened
1/2 cup sugar
   4 egg whites
   2 teaspoons almond extract
   2 cups all-purpose flour
   2 teaspoons baking powder
1/4 teaspoon salt
1/2 cup dried cherries
1/4 cup chopped almonds, toasted
   2 teaspoons confectioners' sugar

In a small mixing bowl, beat the butter and sugar for 2 minutes or until crumbly. Beat in the egg whites and almond extract. Combine the flour, baking powder and salt; gradually add to sugar mixture. Stir in cherries and almonds (dough will be stiff).

Press the cookie dough into an 8-in. square baking dish coated with nonstick cooking spray. Bake at 375°

for 15-20 minutes or until lightly browned.

Cool for 5 minutes. Remove from the pan to a cutting board; cut biscotti in half with a serrated knife. Cut each half into 1/2-in. slices.

Place slices cut side down on baking sheets coated with nonstick cooking spray. Bake for 8-10 minutes or until light golden brown, turning once. Remove to wire racks to cool. Sprinkle with confectioners' sugar. **Yield:** 2-1/2 dozen.

Nutrition Facts: 2 cookies equals 135 calories, 3 g fat (1 g saturated fat), 4 mg cholesterol, 123 mg sodium, 24 g carbohydrate, 1 g fiber, 3 g protein. **Diabetic Exchanges:** 1-1/2 starch, 1/2 fat.

Raspberry Walnut Bars

(Pictured above)

PREP: 10 min. **BAKE:** 35 min. + cooling

Many of my treasured recipes have come from a group of moms I used to meet with for tea and coffee when our kids were small. I adapted this recipe from a friend who made it with strawberry jam. Instead, I use raspberry jam made with the crop from my big raspberry patch. —*Marilyn Forsell, Hydesville, California*

   1 cup butter, softened
   1 cup sugar
   2 egg yolks
   2 cups all-purpose flour
   1 cup finely chopped walnuts
1/2 cup seedless raspberry jam

In a large mixing bowl, cream butter and sugar. Beat in yolks. Gradually add flour and nuts. Pat half of mixture into a greased 8-in. square baking pan. Spread with jam. Crumble the remaining crust mixture over jam.

Bake at 350° for 35-40 minutes or until lightly browned. Cool on a wire rack. **Yield:** 16 bars.

Cakes & Pies

Give everyone at the table a little slice of heaven with these home-style recipes, from luscious Raspberry Chocolate Torte to rich Pumpkin Cheesecake Pie.

Apple & Blackberry Pie 106
Candy Explosion Cake 106
Creative Cake 106
Pumpkin Cheesecake Pie 107
Chocolate-Strawberry Celebration Cake 107
Chocolate Truffle Cake...108
Apricot Almond Torte 108
Five-Fruit Pie 109
Raspberry Chocolate Torte...109
Brittle Torte 110
Rhubarb Cake with Lemon Sauce...............................110
Truffle Cake with Candy Cane Cream...............111
Chocolate Banana Cream Cake...............................111
Streusel Peach Pie...112
Chocolate Raspberry Tunnel Cake 112
Lemon-Rosemary Layer Cake 113
"Give Me S'more" Cake 113
Blueberry Dream Pie 114
Strawberries & Cream Pie 114
Chocolate Toffee Cake...115
Chocolate Lover's Delight Cake...............................115
White Chocolate Raspberry Torte 116
Can't Miss Coconut Custard Pie...............................116
Cherry-Berry Streusel Pie 116
Box-of-Chocolates Cupcakes 117

DELECTABLE DELIGHTS. Clockwise from top left: "Give Me S'more" Cake (p. 113), Apple & Blackberry Pie (p. 106), Chocolate Banana Cream Cake (p. 111), Chocolate Truffle Cake (p. 108) and Raspberry Chocolate Torte (p. 109).

Apple & Blackberry Pie

(Pictured above and on page 105)

PREP: 25 min. **BAKE:** 55 min. + cooling

With a pretty sugar topping, this home-style pie is chock-full of juicy fruit that's spiced just right with cinnamon and nutmeg.
—*Frances Tompkins, Bealeton, Virginia*

Pastry for double-crust pie (9 inches)
   3 pounds tart apples, peeled and sliced
   2 cups fresh blackberries
1/4 cup butter, melted
   1 tablespoon lemon juice
   1 cup sugar
   3 tablespoons cornstarch
   1 teaspoon ground cinnamon
1/8 teaspoon ground nutmeg
   2 tablespoons half-and-half cream
   2 tablespoons coarse sugar

Divide dough in half so that one portion is slightly larger than the other; wrap each in plastic wrap. Refrigerate for 30 minutes or until easy to handle.

On a lightly floured surface, roll out larger portion of dough to fit a 9-in. deep-dish pie plate.

In a large bowl, combine the apples, blackberries, butter and lemon juice. Combine the sugar, cornstarch, cinnamon and nutmeg; add to fruit mixture and toss to coat. Place in crust.

Roll out remaining pastry to fit top of pie; place over filling. Trim, seal and flute the edges. Cut slits in pastry. Brush with cream; sprinkle with coarse sugar.

Bake at 375° for 55-65 minutes or until golden brown and filling is bubbly. Cover edges with foil during the last 30 minutes to prevent overbrowning if necessary. Cool on a wire rack. **Yield:** 8 servings.

Candy Explosion Cake

PREP: 1-1/2 hours

I made this cake for a friend's birthday party using chocolate buttercream frosting and dark chocolate candies. It was a hit!
—*Heidi Axelrod, Flower Mound, Texas*

Two-layer cake of your choice (9 inch)
Chocolate frosting of your choice
Assorted chocolate candies: chocolate kisses, white baking chips, chocolate chips, milk and dark chocolate candies, Sno-Caps, chocolate-covered nougats, miniature peanut butter cups and fun-size Twix and Kit Kat bars

Place cake on a serving platter; spread frosting between layers and over the top and sides of cake. Top with the chocolate candies of your choice. **Yield:** 12 servings.

Creative Cake

(Pictured below)

PREP: 2 hours

Whether you use fondant that's homemade or store-bought, this artistic cake will get raves. It's fun for just about any occasion.
—*Katie Molitor, Cedar, Minnesota*

Two-layer cake of your choice (9 inch)
Frosting of your choice (in a pale color)
White and dark brown ready-to-use rolled fondant
New paintbrush
   1 tablespoon clear vanilla extract *or* water
White pearl dragees
Fresh strawberries

Place cake on a serving platter; spread frosting between layers and over top and sides of cake (save 2 teaspoons frosting for decorating cake).

Roll out white fondant into a 16-in. circle; place over cake. Smooth top and sides of cake; trim excess. (Keep

unused fondant wrapped in plastic wrap to prevent it from drying out.)

Roll brown fondant into 16-in. x 4-in. rectangle; cut with a 3-in. x 2-in. diamond-shaped cookie cutter. Dip the paintbrush in vanilla; lightly brush over a diamond. Secure diamond to the side of cake. Repeat. Decorate with dragees, securing with reserved frosting. Top with strawberries. **Yield:** 12 servings.

Pumpkin Cheesecake Pie

PREP: 45 min. **BAKE:** 40 min. + chilling

Good, old-fashioned pumpkin flavor combines with cream cheese and a pecan cookie crust for this creamy holiday dessert.
—Kim Wallace, Dennison, Ohio

- 2 cups finely crushed pecan shortbread cookies
- 1 tablespoon all-purpose flour
- 3 tablespoons butter, melted

FILLING:
- 2 packages (one 8 ounce, one 3 ounce) cream cheese, softened
- 1 cup sugar
- 1 can (15 ounces) solid-pack pumpkin
- 3 tablespoons all-purpose flour
- 1 tablespoon milk
- 1 teaspoon ground cinnamon
- 1/4 teaspoon *each* ground ginger, nutmeg and cloves
- 3 eggs, lightly beaten

In a small bowl, combine the cookie crumbs, flour and butter; press into an ungreased 9-in. deep-dish pie plate. Bake at 350° for 9-11 minutes or until lightly browned. Cool on a wire rack.

For filling, in a large bowl, beat the cream cheese and sugar until smooth. Beat in the pumpkin, flour, milk and spices. Add eggs; beat on low speed just until combined. Pour into crust.

Bake at 350° for 40-50 minutes or until center is almost set. Cover edges with foil during the last 15 minutes to prevent overbrowning if necessary. Cool on a wire rack for 1 hour. Refrigerate for at least 4 hours before serving. **Yield:** 8 servings.

Chocolate-Strawberry Celebration Cake

(Pictured above right)

PREP: 30 min. **BAKE:** 30 min. + cooling

This recipe really dresses up an ordinary boxed mix. Made as a groom's cake, it gets more attention than the wedding cake!
—Nora Fitzgerald, Sevierville, Tennnessee

- 1 package (18-1/4 ounces) chocolate cake mix
- 1 package (3.9 ounces) instant chocolate pudding mix
- 4 eggs
- 1 cup (8 ounces) sour cream
- 3/4 cup water
- 1/4 cup canola oil
- 4 ounces semisweet chocolate, melted

FROSTING:
- 2 cups butter, softened
- 4 cups confectioners' sugar
- 3/4 cup baking cocoa
- 1/2 cup 2% milk

GARNISHES:
- 2 ounces semisweet chocolate, melted
- 1 pound fresh strawberries, hulled

GANACHE:
- 4 ounces semisweet chocolate, chopped
- 1/2 cup heavy whipping cream

Combine the first seven ingredients; beat on low speed for 30 seconds. Beat on medium for 2 minutes. Transfer to two greased and floured 9-in. round baking pans.

Bake at 350° for 28-32 minutes or until a toothpick comes out clean. Cool for 10 minutes before removing from pans to wire racks to cool completely. Beat the butter, confectioners' sugar and cocoa until blended; add the milk and beat until smooth. Spread frosting between layers and over top and sides of cake.

Pipe or spoon the melted chocolate onto waxed paper in decorative designs; let stand until set. Arrange the strawberries on top of cake. For the ganache, place the chocolate in a small bowl. Heat the cream just to a boil; pour over chocolate; whisk until smooth. Drizzle over top of cake, allowing ganache to drape down the sides. Top with chocolate garnishes. **Yield:** 12 servings.

clean. Cool for 10 minutes before removing from pans to wire racks to cool completely.

For the filling, in a small saucepan, melt butter and chocolate. Stir in the confectioners' sugar and cream until smooth.

For ganache, place chocolate in a small bowl. In a small saucepan, bring cream just to a boil. Pour over chocolate; whisk until smooth. Cool, stirring occasionally, until the ganache reaches a spreading consistency.

Set aside 1/2 cup filling for the garnish. Place one cake layer on a serving plate; spread with half of the remaining filling. Repeat layers. Top with remaining cake layer. Spread ganache over top and sides of cake. Decorate with reserved filling. Store in refrigerator. **Yield:** 16 servings.

Chocolate Truffle Cake

(Pictured above and on page 104)

PREP: 35 min. + chilling **BAKE:** 25 min. + cooling

Love chocolate? Then this luxurious layer cake is the one for you! With a ganache glaze and fabulous bittersweet filling, it's a true indulgence. —Jo Ann Koerkenmeier, Damiansville, Illinois

- 2-1/2 cups 2% milk
- 1 cup butter, cubed
- 8 ounces semisweet chocolate, chopped
- 3 eggs
- 2 teaspoons vanilla extract
- 2-2/3 cups all-purpose flour
- 2 cups sugar
- 1 teaspoon baking soda
- 1/2 teaspoon salt
FILLING:
- 6 tablespoons butter, cubed
- 4 ounces bittersweet chocolate, chopped
- 2-1/2 cups confectioners' sugar
- 1/2 cup heavy whipping cream
GANACHE:
- 10 ounces semisweet chocolate, chopped
- 2/3 cup heavy whipping cream

In a large saucepan, cook the milk, butter and chocolate over low heat until melted. Remove from the heat; let stand for 10 minutes.

In a large bowl, beat eggs and vanilla; stir in chocolate mixture until smooth. Combine the flour, sugar, baking soda and salt; gradually beat into mixture (the batter will be thin). Transfer to three greased and floured 9-in. round baking pans. Bake at 325° for 25-30 minutes or until a toothpick inserted near the center comes out

Apricot Almond Torte

PREP: 45 min. **BAKE:** 25 min. + cooling

This beautiful cake takes a bit of time, so I like to make the layers in advance and assemble it the day of serving, making it an easier option for entertaining. —Trisha Kruse, Eagle, Idaho

- 3 eggs
- 1-1/2 cups sugar
- 1 teaspoon vanilla extract
- 1-3/4 cups all-purpose flour
- 1 cup ground almonds, toasted
- 2 teaspoons baking powder
- 1/2 teaspoon salt
- 1-1/2 cups heavy whipping cream, whipped
FROSTING:
- 1 package (8 ounces) cream cheese, softened
- 1 cup sugar
- 1/8 teaspoon salt
- 1 teaspoon almond extract
- 1-1/2 cups heavy whipping cream, whipped
- 1 jar (10 to 12 ounces) apricot preserves
- 1/2 cup slivered almonds, toasted

In a large bowl, beat the eggs, sugar and vanilla on high speed until thick and lemon-colored. Combine the flour, almonds, baking powder and salt; gradually fold into egg mixture alternately with whipped cream.

Transfer to two greased and floured 9-in. round baking pans. Bake at 350° for 22-28 minutes or until a toothpick inserted near the center comes out clean. Cool for 10 minutes before removing from pans to wire racks to cool completely.

In a large bowl, beat the cream cheese, sugar and salt until smooth. Beat in extract. Fold in whipped cream.

Cut each cake horizontally into two layers. Place the bottom layer on serving plate; spread with 1 cup frosting. Top with another cake layer; spread with half of the preserves. Repeat layers. Frost the sides of cake; decorate top edge with remaining frosting. Sprinkle with almonds. **Yield:** 12 servings.

Five-Fruit Pie

PREP: 40 min. **BAKE:** 45 min. + cooling

I've given this sweet, fruit-filled pie to new neighbors or anyone who needed a pick-me-up. It always gets compliments galore.
—Jean Ross, Oil City, Pennsylvania

- 1-1/2 cups sugar
- 3 tablespoons cornstarch
- 2 tablespoons quick-cooking tapioca
- 1 cup chopped peeled tart apples
- 1 cup chopped fresh *or* frozen rhubarb
- 1 cup *each* fresh *or* frozen raspberries, blueberries and sliced strawberries

CRUST:
- 2 cups all-purpose flour
- 1/2 teaspoon salt
- 1/2 cup shortening
- 1 egg
- 1/4 cup cold water
- 2 teaspoons white vinegar
- 2 tablespoons half-and-half cream
- 2 tablespoons coarse sugar

In a large bowl, combine the sugar, cornstarch, tapioca and fruit; let stand for 15 minutes. In another bowl, combine flour and salt; cut in shortening until mixture resembles coarse crumbs. Combine the egg, water and vinegar; stir into flour mixture just until moistened.

Divide dough in half so that one portion is slightly larger than the other. On a lightly floured surface, roll out larger portion to fit a 9-inch pie plate. Transfer the pastry to pie plate; trim pastry even with edge. Spoon fruit mixture into crust.

Roll out the remaining pastry to fit top of pie; make a lattice crust. Trim, seal and flute the edges. Brush with cream; sprinkle with coarse sugar.

Bake at 375° for 45-55 minutes or until crust is golden brown and filling is bubbly. Cool completely on a wire rack. **Yield:** 8 servings.

Editor's Note: If using frozen fruit, measure fruit while still frozen, then thaw completely. Drain in a colander, but do not press liquid out.

Raspberry Chocolate Torte

(Pictured at right and on page 104)

PREP: 40 min. **BAKE:** 20 min. + cooling

Wow your guests on holidays or anytime by serving this striking layer cake. With fresh raspberries and fluffy chocolate mounds on top, it looks fancy but is actually easy to decorate.
—Amy Helbig, Mesa, Arizona

- 1 cup butter, softened
- 2 cups sugar
- 4 eggs
- 1 teaspoon vanilla extract
- 1-1/2 cups all-purpose flour
- 1/3 cup baking cocoa

GLAZE:
- 1/4 cup boiling water
- 4 teaspoons raspberry gelatin
- 2 tablespoons seedless raspberry jam

TOPPING:
- 2 cups (12 ounces) semisweet chocolate chips
- 2 cartons (8 ounces *each*) frozen whipped topping, thawed
- 2 cups fresh raspberries

Line a greased 15-in. x 10-in. x 1-in. baking pan with waxed paper; grease paper. In a large bowl, cream the butter and sugar until light and fluffy. Add eggs, one at a time, beating well after each addition. Beat in vanilla. Combine flour and cocoa; gradually beat into creamed mixture. Transfer to prepared pan.

Bake at 350° for 20-25 minutes or until a toothpick inserted near center comes out clean. Cool for 5 minutes before inverting onto a wire rack to cool completely. Carefully remove waxed paper.

For glaze, stir water and gelatin until dissolved. Stir in jam. Brush evenly over bottom of cake. Trim edges; cut cake widthwise into thirds.

For the topping, in a microwave, melt the chips; stir until smooth. Fold in half of the whipped topping until blended; fold in remaining whipped topping (mixture will be thick).

Place one cake layer on a serving platter; spread with 3/4 cup topping. Repeat layers; top with remaining cake. Frost and decorate with the raspberries and remaining topping. **Yield:** 12 servings.

Brittle Torte

(Pictured below)

PREP: 50 min. **BAKE:** 50 min. + cooling

This was my mother's favorite cake for special occasions. When I was in high school, she often asked me to make it for her. The homemade brittle sprinkled on top gives it a nice crunch.
—Phyllis Murphey, Lower Lake, California

    8 eggs, *separated*
1-1/2 cups all-purpose flour
1-1/2 cups sugar
    1 teaspoon salt
  1/4 cup water
    1 teaspoon lemon juice
    1 teaspoon vanilla extract
    1 teaspoon cream of tartar
TOPPING:
1-1/2 cups sugar
  1/4 cup light corn syrup
  1/4 cup water
  1/4 teaspoon instant coffee granules
    1 teaspoon baking soda
WHIPPED CREAM:
    2 cups heavy whipping cream
    2 tablespoons sugar
    2 teaspoons vanilla extract

Let the eggs stand at room temperature 30 minutes. Combine the flour, sugar and salt. Whisk the egg yolks, water, lemon juice and vanilla; add to flour mixture. Beat until blended.

Beat the egg whites and cream of tartar until soft peaks form; fold into batter. Spoon into an ungreased 10-in. tube pan. Cut through the batter with a knife to remove air pockets. Bake on lowest oven rack at 325° for 50-60 minutes or until top springs back when touched. Immediately invert pan; cool completely.

For topping, grease a 15-in. x 10-in. x 1-in. pan. In a heavy saucepan, combine sugar, corn syrup, water and coffee granules. Bring to a boil, stirring constantly. Cook, without stirring, to 300° (hard-crack stage). Remove from heat; stir in the baking soda. Immediately pour into the prepared pan. Stretch the brittle in pan with two forks; cool. Break into pieces.

Beat whipping cream until it begins to thicken. Add sugar and vanilla; beat until stiff peaks form.

Unmold cake; cut into four layers. Place bottom layer on a plate; top with 1/2 cup whipped cream. Repeat the layers twice; top with the remaining layer. Frost the top and sides of cake with remaining cream. Sprinkle with brittle. **Yield:** 12 servings.

Rhubarb Cake With Lemon Sauce

PREP: 20 min. **BAKE:** 35 min.

Here is our all-time favorite rhubarb recipe. I think it tastes best when both the cake and sauce are warm, but it's still yummy if just the sauce is warm.
—Karen Graham, Star, Idaho

  1/2 cup butter, softened
  1/2 cup sugar
  1/2 cup packed brown sugar
    1 egg
    2 teaspoons vanilla extract
    3 cups all-purpose flour
    1 teaspoon baking powder
    1 teaspoon ground cinnamon
  1/2 teaspoon salt
  1/2 teaspoon baking soda
    1 cup buttermilk
    2 cups chopped fresh *or* frozen rhubarb
    1 tablespoon cinnamon-sugar
LEMON SAUCE:
    1 cup sugar
  1/2 cup butter, cubed
  1/3 cup water
    3 tablespoons lemon juice
    1 egg, beaten
    1 teaspoon grated lemon peel
    1 teaspoon ground nutmeg

In a large bowl, cream the butter and sugars until light and fluffy. Beat in egg and vanilla. Combine the flour, baking powder, cinnamon, salt and baking soda; add to the creamed mixture alternately with the buttermilk. Fold in rhubarb.

Transfer to a greased 13-in. x 9-in. baking dish. Sprinkle with cinnamon-sugar. Bake at 350° for 35-40 minutes or until a toothpick inserted near the center comes out clean. Place on a wire rack.

For sauce, in a small saucepan, combine sugar, butter, water and lemon juice. Bring to a boil over medium heat, stirring constantly. Whisk a small amount of the hot mixture into the egg; return all to the pan, stirring constantly. Cook and stir until the mixture is thickened

and coats the back of a spoon. Stir in lemon peel and nutmeg. Serve sauce warm with cake. **Yield:** 12 servings (1-1/2 cups sauce).

Editor's Note: If using frozen rhubarb, measure rhubarb while still frozen, then thaw completely. Drain in a colander, but do not press liquid out.

Truffle Cake With Candy Cane Cream

PREP: 35 min. **BAKE:** 40 min. + chilling

You can't help but catch the Christmas spirit when you taste this chocolate delight, accented with a dollop of peppermint topping.
—Cristi Kirkham, West Jordan, Utah

- 1 cup graham cracker crumbs
- 1 cup chopped pecans, toasted and coarsely ground
- 2 tablespoons plus 3/4 cup sugar, *divided*
- 1/4 cup butter, melted
- 16 ounces semisweet chocolate, coarsely chopped
- 1 cup heavy whipping cream
- 6 eggs
- 1/3 cup all-purpose flour

CREAM:
- 1 cup heavy whipping cream
- 2 tablespoons sugar
- 4 candy canes, finely ground
- 1/4 to 1/2 teaspoon peppermint extract, optional

Combine the cracker crumbs, pecans, 2 tablespoons sugar and butter; press onto the bottom and 1-1/2 in. up the sides of a greased 9-in. springform pan. Place pan on a baking sheet.

In a large saucepan, cook the chocolate and cream over low heat until chocolate is melted. Cool. In a large bowl, beat the eggs, flour and remaining sugar on high speed until thick and lemon-colored, about 5 minutes. Gradually beat in chocolate mixture.

Pour the batter into prepared crust. Bake at 325° for 40-45 minutes or until the center is almost set. Cool on wire rack for 10 minutes. Carefully run a knife around edge of pan to loosen; cool 1 hour longer. Refrigerate for 4 hours or overnight.

Beat cream and sugar until stiff peaks form; fold in ground candy and extract if desired. Serve with cake. **Yield:** 16 servings.

Chocolate Banana Cream Cake

(Pictured above right and on page 105)

PREP: 30 min. **BAKE:** 20 min. + cooling

My inspiration for this recipe came from my desire to combine three things—my dad's love of cake, my mom's love of chocolate and my love of bananas. This dessert does just that!
—Susie Schueller, Grandview Heights, Ohio

- 1/2 cup butter, softened
- 1-1/4 cups sugar
- 2 eggs, *separated*
- 1-1/2 cups mashed ripe bananas (about 3 medium)
- 1/4 cup sour cream
- 2 teaspoons vanilla extract
- 1-1/2 cups all-purpose flour
- 1 teaspoon baking soda
- 1/4 teaspoon salt

FILLING/FROSTING:
- 1-1/2 cups cold whole milk
- 1 package (3.4 ounces) instant banana cream pudding mix
- 1 can (16 ounces) chocolate frosting
- 2 medium firm bananas, sliced
- 3 tablespoons lemon juice

In a large bowl, cream butter and sugar until light and fluffy. Add egg yolks; mix well. Beat in the bananas, sour cream and vanilla. Combine the flour, baking soda and salt; add to the creamed mixture and beat well.

In a small bowl, beat the egg whites until stiff peaks form. Fold into the batter. Transfer to two greased and floured 9-in. round baking pans. Bake at 350° for 20-25 minutes or until a toothpick comes out clean. Cool for 10 minutes before removing from pans to wire racks to cool completely.

For the filling, in a small bowl, whisk the milk and pudding mix for 2 minutes. Let stand for 2 minutes or until soft-set. Cover and refrigerate until chilled.

In a small bowl, beat the frosting until light and fluffy. Place bananas in a small bowl; toss with lemon juice.

Place one cake layer on a serving plate; spread with 3 tablespoons frosting. Stir pudding; spread half over frosting. Top with half of bananas and remaining cake layer. Repeat frosting, filling and banana layers. Frost sides and decorate top edge of cake with remaining frosting. Store in refrigerator. **Yield:** 12 servings.

Streusel Peach Pie

(Pictured above)

PREP: 20 min. **BAKE:** 50 min. + cooling

With a dollop of whipped cream, this delectable streusel-topped pie is a wonderful way to enjoy summer's fresh peaches.
—*Marie Rizzio, Interlochen, Michigan*

Pastry for single-crust pie (9 inches)
    5 cups sliced peeled fresh *or* frozen peaches, thawed
    1/2 cup sugar
    1/4 cup all-purpose flour
Dash ground nutmeg
    1 egg
    2 tablespoons heavy whipping cream
TOPPING:
    1/2 cup all-purpose flour
    1/2 cup packed brown sugar
    1 teaspoon ground cinnamon
    3 tablespoons cold butter
Whipped cream, optional

Line a 9-in. pie plate with pastry; trim pastry to 1/2 inch beyond edge of plate and flute edges.

In a large bowl, combine the peaches, sugar, flour and nutmeg. In a small bowl, whisk the egg and cream. Pour over peaches; toss to combine. Place in crust. Bake at 375° for 35 minutes.

For the topping, in a small bowl, combine the flour, brown sugar and cinnamon. Cut in butter until crumbly. Sprinkle the topping over the outer edges of the pie, leaving the center uncovered.

Bake for 15-20 minutes or until golden brown, covering edges with foil to prevent overbrowning if necessary. Cool pie on a wire rack. Serve with whipped cream if desired. **Yield:** 8 servings.

Chocolate Raspberry Tunnel Cake

PREP: 50 min. **BAKE:** 45 min. + cooling

Get ready for a delightful surprise! The fluffy raspberry filling in the "tunnel" gives this chocolate cake its tantalizing twist.
—*Ed Leland, Van Wert, Ohio*

    2/3 cup butter, softened
1-2/3 cups sugar
    3 eggs
    1/2 teaspoon vanilla extract
    2 cups all-purpose flour
    2/3 cup baking cocoa
1-1/4 teaspoons baking powder
    1/4 teaspoon baking soda
1-1/3 cups 2% milk
FILLING:
    2 packages (3 ounces *each*) cream cheese, softened
    1 can (14 ounces) sweetened condensed milk
    1/3 cup lemon juice
    1/2 teaspoon almond extract
    2 drops red food coloring, optional
    1 carton (12 ounces) frozen whipped topping, thawed, *divided*
    1 cup fresh raspberries
Lemon peel strips and additional fresh raspberries, optional

Cream butter and sugar until fluffy. Add eggs, one at a time, beating after each addition. Beat in vanilla. Combine flour, cocoa, baking powder and soda; add to creamed mixture alternately with milk, beating well after each addition. Transfer to a greased and floured 10-in. tube pan. Bake at 350° for 45-55 minutes or until a toothpick comes out clean.

Cool 10 minutes before removing from pan to a wire rack to cool completely. Cut a 1-in. slice off the top of cake; set aside. Hollow out the bottom portion of cake, leaving a 1-in. shell. Cube the removed cake to measure 1 cup; set aside. (Save remaining cake for another use.)

Beat cream cheese until fluffy. Gradually beat in milk, lemon juice, extract and food coloring if desired. Fold in 1 cup whipped topping. Set aside 1 cup cream cheese mixture; fold the berries and reserved cake cubes into remaining mixture. Fill tunnel with cake cube mixture; replace top.

Spread the reserved cream cheese mixture over the top of cake to within 1 in. of edge. Frost top edge and sides of cake with remaining whipped topping. Garnish with lemon peel and additional berries if desired. Chill. **Yield:** 12 servings.

Lemon-Rosemary Layer Cake

PREP: 20 min. **BAKE:** 25 min. + cooling

With lemon peel, fresh rosemary and a homemade cream cheese frosting, this out-of-the-ordinary dessert is sure to impress.
—Mary Fraser, Surprise, Arizona

- 1 cup plus 2 tablespoons butter, softened
- 2-1/2 cups sugar
- 4 eggs
- 1 egg yolk
- 4 cups all-purpose flour
- 3 teaspoons baking powder
- 1-1/2 teaspoons salt
- 1/4 teaspoon plus 1/8 teaspoon baking soda
- 1-1/2 cups (12 ounces) sour cream
- 6 tablespoons lemon juice
- 3 teaspoons grated lemon peel
- 3 teaspoons minced fresh rosemary

FROSTING:
- 2 packages (8 ounces *each*) cream cheese, softened
- 8-1/4 cups confectioners' sugar
- 3 teaspoons grated lemon peel
- 2-1/4 teaspoons lemon juice

In a large bowl, cream butter and sugar until light and fluffy. Add the eggs and yolk, one at a time, beating well after each addition. Combine flour, baking powder, salt and baking soda; add to creamed mixture alternately with sour cream, beating well after each addition. Beat in the lemon juice, peel and rosemary.

Transfer to three greased and floured 9-in. round baking pans. Bake at 350° for 25-30 minutes or until the edges begin to brown. Cool for 10 minutes before removing from pans to wire racks to cool completely.

For frosting, in a large bowl, beat cream cheese until fluffy. Add the confectioners' sugar, lemon peel and juice; beat until smooth.

Spread frosting between layers and over top and sides of cake. Refrigerate leftovers. **Yield:** 16 servings.

"Give Me S'more" Cake

(Pictured at right and on page 104)

PREP: 50 min. **BAKE:** 20 min. + cooling

Bring some summer fun to your table with a yummy campfire favorite—minus the sticky marshmallow fingers! Both kids and kids-at-heart will love this new take on the popular treat.
—Katie Lemery, Cuddebackville, New York

- 1/2 cup shortening
- 1/4 cup butter, softened
- 1 cup sugar
- 3 eggs
- 1 teaspoon vanilla extract
- 2-3/4 cups graham cracker crumbs
- 3 teaspoons baking powder
- 1 can (12 ounces) evaporated milk

MARSHMALLOW FROSTING:
- 4 egg whites
- 1 cup sugar
- 1/2 teaspoon cream of tartar
- 1-1/2 teaspoons vanilla extract
- 1-1/2 cups miniature semisweet chocolate chips, *divided*

Line two 9-in. round baking pans with waxed paper and grease the paper; set aside. In a large bowl, cream the shortening, butter and sugar until light and fluffy. Add the eggs, one at a time, beating well after each addition. Beat in vanilla. Combine the cracker crumbs and baking powder; add to the creamed mixture alternately with milk, beating well after each addition.

Transfer to the prepared pans. Bake at 350° for 18-22 minutes or until a toothpick inserted near center comes out clean. Cool for 10 minutes before removing from pans to wire racks to cool completely.

In a large heavy saucepan, combine the egg whites, sugar and cream of tartar over low heat. With a hand mixer, beat on low speed for 1 minute. Continue beating on low over low heat until frosting reaches 160°, about 8-10 minutes. Pour into a large bowl; add vanilla. Beat on high until stiff peaks form, about 7 minutes.

Place a cake layer on a serving plate; spread with 2/3 cup frosting and sprinkle with half of chips. Top with remaining cake layer. Frost top and sides of cake; sprinkle with remaining chips. **Yield:** 12 servings.

Blueberry Dream Pie

(Pictured below)

PREP: 40 min. **BAKE:** 35 min. + cooling

This showstopping pie can be decorated with pastry cutouts to fit any season or occasion. I like to make stars for Independence Day and hearts for Valentine's Day. Have fun with it!
—*Kerry Nakayama, New York, New York*

Pastry for double-crust pie (9 inches)
CHEESE FILLING:
  4 ounces reduced-fat cream cheese
1/2 cup confectioners' sugar
  1 tablespoon lemon juice
  1 egg yolk
BLUEBERRY FILLING:
1/2 cup plus 1 tablespoon sugar, *divided*
  2 tablespoons all-purpose flour
  1 tablespoon cornstarch
1/4 cup cold water
  6 cups fresh *or* frozen blueberries, *divided*
  2 tablespoons lemon juice
  1 tablespoon minced fresh mint *or* 1 teaspoon dried mint
  1 egg white, beaten

Line a 9-inch deep-dish pie plate with the bottom crust. Trim the pastry to 1/2 inch beyond edge of plate; flute the edges. Line unpricked pastry shell with a double thickness of heavy-duty foil. Bake at 450° for 8 minutes. Remove foil; bake 5 minutes longer. Cool on a wire rack. Reduce heat to 375°.

In a small bowl, beat the cream cheese, confectioners' sugar and lemon juice until light and fluffy. Beat in egg yolk until blended. Spread into crust.

In a large saucepan, combine 1/2 cup sugar, flour and cornstarch; stir in the water until smooth. Stir in 2 cups berries. Bring to a boil; cook and stir for 1-2 minutes or until thickened. Cool slightly. Gently stir in lemon juice, mint and remaining berries. Pour over cheese filling.

Cut decorative cutouts in remaining pastry; arrange over filling, leaving center uncovered. Brush pastry with egg white; sprinkle with remaining sugar.

Bake at 375° for 35-40 minutes or until crust is golden brown and filling is bubbly. Cover the edges with foil during the last 15 minutes to prevent overbrowning if necessary. Cool on a wire rack. Refrigerate leftovers. **Yield:** 8 servings.

Strawberries & Cream Pie

(Pictured above)

PREP: 20 min. + chilling

Every time I bring this chocolate-drizzled dessert to a family dinner, church gathering or other event, it disappears quickly.
—*Angela Moore, Tollesboro, Kentucky*

  1 cup (6 ounces) semisweet chocolate chips, *divided*
  3 teaspoons shortening, *divided*
  1 graham cracker crust (10 inches)
  1 package (8 ounces) cream cheese, softened
1/2 cup sugar
1/2 cup sour cream
  1 teaspoon vanilla extract
  1 carton (8 ounces) frozen whipped topping, thawed
  2 cups fresh strawberries, halved
1/2 cup seedless strawberry jam

In a microwave, melt 3/4 cup chocolate chips and 2 teaspoons shortening; stir until smooth. Brush over crust. Refrigerate until firm.

In a small bowl, beat the cream cheese, sugar, sour cream and vanilla until smooth. Fold in the whipped topping. Spoon into crust. Refrigerate for 1 hour.

Arrange the strawberries over pie. In a microwave, heat the jam until melted; brush over the top. Melt the remaining chocolate chips and shortening; stir until smooth. Drizzle over the pie. Refrigerate until chilled. **Yield:** 8 servings.

Chocolate Toffee Cake

PREP: 25 min. **BAKE:** 55 min. + cooling

This is my most-requested cake for coffee get-togethers. Now that I have two grandsons, I serve it for birthday parties, too!
—Penny McNeill, Kitchener, Ontario

- 1 package (8 ounces) milk chocolate English toffee bits
- 1 cup (6 ounces) semisweet chocolate chips
- 2 tablespoons brown sugar

CAKE:
- 1 cup butter, softened
- 1-1/4 cups packed brown sugar
- 4 eggs
- 1 teaspoon vanilla extract
- 3 cups all-purpose flour
- 1-1/2 teaspoons baking powder
- 1/2 teaspoon salt
- 1/2 teaspoon baking soda
- 1-1/4 cups buttermilk

CARAMEL ICING:
- 1/4 cup butter, cubed
- 2 teaspoons all-purpose flour
- 1 can (5 ounces) evaporated milk
- 1 cup packed brown sugar

Combine the toffee bits, chocolate chips and brown sugar; set aside.

In a large bowl, cream butter and brown sugar until light and fluffy. Add eggs, one at a time, beating well after each addition (mixture will appear curdled). Beat in vanilla. Combine the flour, baking powder, salt and baking soda; add to the creamed mixture alternately with buttermilk, beating well after each addition.

Pour a third of the batter into a greased and floured 10-in. fluted tube pan. Sprinkle with a third of the toffee mixture. Repeat the layers twice. Bake at 350° for 55-65 minutes or until a toothpick inserted near the center comes out clean.

Cool for 10 minutes before removing from pan to wire rack to cool completely. For icing, in a small saucepan, melt butter. Stir in the flour until smooth; gradually add evaporated milk and brown sugar. Bring to a boil; cook and stir for 4-5 minutes or until thickened. Cool. Drizzle over cake. **Yield:** 12 servings.

Chocolate Lover's Delight Cake

(Pictured at right)

PREP: 50 min. **BAKE:** 20 min. + cooling

For years, my husband and I belonged to a supper club, and I always made the desserts. This luscious recipe was given to me by one of the members. —Sandra Hackney, Tuscaloosa, Alabama

- 1-1/2 cups sugar, *divided*
- 1 cup buttermilk
- 1/2 cup canola oil
- 2 eggs, *separated*
- 2 ounces German sweet chocolate, melted
- 1-3/4 cups all-purpose flour
- 1/4 teaspoon plus 1/8 teaspoon salt, *divided*
- 1/4 teaspoon baking soda
- 2 cups heavy whipping cream
- 1 cup confectioners' sugar
- 1/3 cup baking cocoa
- 1/4 teaspoon almond extract
- 1/4 cup creme de cacao
- 1/2 cup ground almonds

Grease and flour two 9-in. round baking pans; set aside. In a large bowl, beat 1 cup sugar, buttermilk, oil, egg yolks and melted chocolate until well blended. Combine the flour, 1/4 teaspoon salt and baking soda; gradually beat into sugar mixture until blended.

In a large bowl with clean beaters, beat egg whites until soft peaks form. Gradually beat in the remaining sugar, 1 tablespoon at a time, on high until stiff peaks form. Fold into the batter.

Transfer to the prepared pans. Bake at 350° for 18-22 minutes or until a toothpick inserted near the center comes out clean. Cool for 10 minutes before removing from pans to wire racks to cool completely.

For the frosting, in a large bowl, beat whipping cream, confectioners' sugar, cocoa, extract and the remaining salt until stiff peaks form.

Cut each cake horizontally into two layers; brush the layers with cream de cacao. Place the bottom layer on a serving plate; top with 1/2 cup frosting and sprinkle with 2 tablespoons almonds. Repeat layers twice. Top with remaining cake layer. Spread remaining frosting over top and sides of cake; sprinkle remaining almonds over the top. **Yield:** 12 servings.

White Chocolate Raspberry Torte

(Pictured above)

PREP: I hour **BAKE:** 30 min. + cooling

We grow raspberries, and this luscious torte is one of my favorite ways to use them. —Martha Schwartz, Sarasota, Florida

    3/4 cup butter
      2 cups sugar
      4 eggs
      1 cup white baking chips, melted and cooled
      1 teaspoon vanilla extract
      3 cups cake flour
      1 teaspoon baking powder
    1/2 teaspoon baking soda
      1 cup buttermilk
FILLING:
      2 cups fresh *and/or* frozen raspberries
    3/4 cup water
    1/2 cup sugar
      3 tablespoons cornstarch
FROSTING:
      1 package (8 ounces) cream cheese, softened
      1 cup vanilla *and/or* white chips, melted and cooled
      1 carton (12 ounces) frozen whipped topping, thawed
Fresh raspberries, optional

Cream butter and sugar until fluffy. Add eggs, one at a time, beating well after each addition. Beat in melted chips and vanilla. Combine flour, baking powder and soda; add to the creamed mixture alternately with the buttermilk, beating well after each addition.

Transfer to two greased and floured 9-in. round baking pans. Bake at 350° for 28-32 minutes or until a toothpick comes out clean. Cool 10 minutes before removing from pans to wire racks to cool completely.

In a small saucepan, bring raspberries and water to a boil. Reduce heat; simmer 5 minutes. Strain raspberry mixture; discard seeds. Cool. In the same pan, combine the sugar and cornstarch; stir in raspberry puree until smooth. Bring to a boil; cook and stir for 2 minutes or until thickened. Cool. Spread between cake layers.

In a large bowl, beat the cream cheese until fluffy. Beat in the melted chips; fold in the whipped topping. Spread over top and sides of cake. Pipe frosting over top edge of cake and garnish with berries if desired. Store in refrigerator. **Yield:** 12 servings.

Can't Miss Coconut Custard Pie

PREP: 20 min. **BAKE:** 45 min. + cooling

This soft custard pie has a mild coconut flavor. Top it off with a dollop of whipped cream. —Betty Swain, Bear, Delaware

Pastry for single-crust pie (9 inches)
      1 cup flaked coconut, chopped
      3 eggs, beaten
  2-2/3 cups 2% milk
    2/3 cup sugar
      3 tablespoons all-purpose flour
      1 teaspoon vanilla extract
    1/2 teaspoon salt
    1/4 teaspoon ground nutmeg

Line a 9-in. deep-dish pie plate with pastry; trim and flute edges. Line unpricked pastry with a double thickness of heavy-duty foil. Bake at 450° for 8 minutes. Remove foil; bake 5 minutes longer. Sprinkle coconut over crust; set aside.

In a large bowl, combine the eggs, milk, sugar, flour, vanilla and salt. Pour over the coconut; sprinkle with the nutmeg.

Bake, uncovered, at 350° for 45-50 minutes or until a knife inserted near the center comes out clean. Cool on a wire rack. Refrigerate leftovers. **Yield:** 8 servings.

Cherry-Berry Streusel Pie

PREP: I hour + chilling **BAKE:** 55 min. + cooling

Pretty and scrumptious, this fruit–filled pie won a ribbon at the Oklahoma State Fair. —Rosalie Seebeck, Bethany, Oklahoma

  2-1/2 cups all-purpose flour
      1 tablespoon sugar
      1 teaspoon salt
      1 cup cold butter
      7 to 8 tablespoons cold water
FILLING:
      2 cans (21 ounces *each*) cherry pie filling
      1 cup fresh *or* frozen raspberries
    1/4 cup packed brown sugar

1/4 teaspoon ground cinnamon

TOPPING:
1 cup yellow cake mix
1/2 cup chopped pecans, toasted
1/2 cup flaked coconut
1/4 cup butter, melted
2 tablespoons 2% milk
2 tablespoons sugar

Place flour, sugar and salt in a food processor; cover and pulse until blended. Add butter; cover and pulse until mixture resembles coarse crumbs. While processing, gradually add water until dough forms a ball.

Divide dough in half so that one portion is slightly larger than the other; wrap each in plastic wrap. Refrigerate for 30 minutes or until easy to handle.

On a lightly floured surface, roll out the larger portion of dough to fit a 9-inch deep-dish pie plate. Transfer the pastry to pie plate; trim the pastry to 1/2 inch beyond the edge of the plate. Combine the filling ingredients; spoon into the crust. Sprinkle with dry yellow cake mix, pecans and coconut. Drizzle with butter.

Roll out remaining pastry to a 13-inch circle; cut into strips for lattice top. While creating lattice, twist pastry strips for a decorative effect. Seal and flute edges of pie.

Brush the lattice top with milk; sprinkle with sugar. Cover the edges loosely with foil. Bake at 375° for 55-65 minutes or until the crust is golden brown and the filling is bubbly. **Yield:** 8 servings.

Box-of-Chocolates Cupcakes

(Pictured below right)

PREP: 1 hour + chilling **BAKE:** 20 min. + cooling

Surprise someone special with a box of these irresistible treats, featuring three different fillings, from our Test Kitchen staff.

1 package (18-1/4 ounces) devil's food cake mix
1-1/3 cups strong brewed coffee
3 eggs
1/2 cup canola oil

FILLINGS:
8 ounces bittersweet chocolate, chopped
3 tablespoons sugar
4 tablespoons strong brewed coffee, *divided*
3 egg yolks, beaten
2 tablespoons thawed orange juice concentrate
2 tablespoons chocolate hazelnut spread
1 tablespoon heavy whipping cream
1-1/2 cups whipped topping

GANACHE:
4 ounces bittersweet chocolate, chopped
2 ounces white baking chocolate, chopped
3/4 cup heavy whipping cream, *divided*
2-1/2 teaspoons corn syrup, *divided*
Paste food coloring of your choice

In a large bowl, combine cake mix, coffee, eggs and oil; beat on low speed for 30 seconds. Beat on medium for 2 minutes. Fill paper lined muffin cups two-thirds full.

Bake at 350° for 18-22 minutes or until a toothpick inserted near the center comes out clean. Cool for 10 minutes before removing from pans to wire racks to cool.

Meanwhile, in a double boiler or metal bowl over simmering water, constantly stir chocolate, sugar and 3 tablespoons coffee until smooth. Remove from heat (mixture will be thick). Stir a small amount of hot mixture into yolks; return all to bowl, stirring constantly. Cook and stir for 4-5 minutes or until mixture reaches 160°.

Divide the mixture among three small bowls. Into one bowl, stir the orange juice concentrate. Stir hazelnut spread and cream into another; stir remaining coffee into the third bowl. Fold 1/2 cup of whipped topping into each. Chill for 10 minutes.

Cut a small hole in the corner of a pastry or plastic bag; insert a very small tip. Fill with one filling flavor. Push the tip through the bottoms of the paper liners to fill eight cupcakes. Repeat with remaining fillings and cupcakes.

For ganache, place the chocolates in separate small bowls. In a small saucepan, bring cream just to a boil. Pour 1/2 cup cream over bittersweet chocolate; pour the remaining cream over white chocolate. Whisk the chocolate mixtures until smooth.

Stir 2 teaspoons corn syrup into bittersweet ganache and 1/2 teaspoon corn syrup into white ganache. Cool, stirring occasionally, to room temperature or until ganache thickens slightly, about 10 minutes.

Dip the tops of cupcakes in bittersweet ganache. Tint the white ganache as desired; pipe desired designs over the tops of cupcakes. Refrigerate until set. Store in an airtight container in the refrigerator. **Yield:** 2 dozen.

Just Desserts

Save room for sweet treats such as Ricotta Cheesecake, Lemon Sorbet Torte and Strawberry Malted Mousse Cups. They're worth waiting for!

Lemon-Basil Frozen Yogurt 120
Banana Pineapple Sundaes...................................120
Toffee-Crunch Coffee Sundaes 120
Sweet Spiced Caramel Apples 120
Bacon Baklava 121
Mexican Ice Cream..121
Blueberry Cream Dessert 122
Grilled Pineapple Butterscotch Sundaes 122
Ricotta Cheesecake 123
Hot Cherry Sauce..123
Tuxedo Cream Dessert 124
Citrus Tartlets 124
Summertime Fruit Cones......................................125
Cocoa Meringues with Berries.............................125
Peanut Ice Cream Delight 126
French Cream with Sugared Grapes....................126
Strawberry Malted Mousse Cups.........................127
Watermelon Sorbet 127
Strawberry Crumble Parfaits................................127
Pear Sorbet 128
Pomegranate Poached Pears...............................128
Roasted Pears in Pecan Sauce............................129
Sweet Riesling Pears 129
Lemon Sorbet Torte..130
Chocolate Mousse with Cranberry Sauce 130
Lavender Brownie Cheesecake............................131
Slow-Cooked Stuffed Apples................................131
Candy Bar Ice Cream 132
Pumpkin Cranberry Bread Pudding....................132
Chocolate Mint Apple Fondue 133
Praline Crunch Ice Cream.....................................133

SIMPLY IRRESISTIBLE. Clockwise from top left: Peanut Ice Cream Delight (p. 126), Tuxedo Cream Dessert (p. 124), Chocolate Mousse with Cranberry Sauce (p. 130) and Cocoa Meringues with Berries (p. 125).

Lemon-Basil Frozen Yogurt

(Pictured above)

PREP: 20 min. + chilling **PROCESS:** 20 min. + freezing

The unique flavor of this frozen yogurt will tickle your taste buds as it cools you down.   —Bryan Kennedy, Kaneohe, Hawaii

> **6 cups (48 ounces) plain yogurt**
> **1 cup fresh basil leaves, thinly sliced**
> **1/2 cup sugar**
> **1/2 cup chopped walnuts, toasted**
> **4 teaspoons grated lemon peel**

Line a strainer with four layers of cheesecloth or one coffee filter and place over a bowl. Place yogurt in the prepared strainer; cover yogurt with the edges of the cheesecloth. Refrigerate for 8 hours or overnight.

Discard liquid from bowl. Place yogurt in a large bowl; stir in basil, sugar, walnuts and lemon peel. Fill cylinder of ice cream freezer; freeze according to manufacturer's directions. Transfer to a freezer container; freeze for 2-4 hours before serving. **Yield:** 3 cups.

Banana Pineapple Sundaes

PREP/TOTAL TIME: 15 min.

I served these fruity sundaes at a shower. No sooner did I pass out the spoons than the room was filled with oohs and aahs.
                    —Ruth Lee, Troy, Ontario

> **6 tablespoons brown sugar**
> **1/4 cup orange juice**
> **1-1/2 teaspoons butter**
> **1/8 teaspoon ground cinnamon**
> **2 small firm bananas, sliced**
> **1 cup cubed fresh pineapple**

> **1/2 teaspoon rum extract**
> **2 cups vanilla ice cream**

In a large saucepan, combine brown sugar, juice, butter and cinnamon. Bring to a boil. Reduce heat to medium; cook and stir for 2 minutes. Add the fruit; cook and stir 1-2 minutes longer. Remove from the heat; stir in the extract. Serve over ice cream. **Yield:** 4 servings.

Toffee-Crunch Coffee Sundaes

PREP/TOTAL TIME: 15 min.

This recipe has a secret ingredient: coffee ice cream. I created it one day when I was out of heavy cream and wanted to make hot fudge sauce for company.   —Beth Royals, Richmond, Virginia

> **1 cup (6 ounces) semisweet chocolate chips**
> **1 quart coffee ice cream,** *divided*
> **1 tablespoon light corn syrup**
> **1/2 cup chopped Heath candy bars (about 1-1/2 bars)**
> **Whipped cream**
> **Additional chopped Heath candy bars, optional**

In a microwave-safe bowl, combine the chocolate chips, 1/2 cup ice cream and corn syrup. Microwave on high for 45 seconds or until smooth.

Spoon 1/3 cup of ice cream into each of four parfait glasses. Top each with 2 tablespoons chocolate sauce and 1 tablespoon chopped candy bars. Repeat layers. Top with remaining ice cream. Garnish with whipped cream and additional candy if desired. **Yield:** 4 servings.

Sweet Spiced Caramel Apples

PREP: 20 min. **COOK:** 1 hour + standing

I love caramel apples, and this is the best variation I've ever had. The sweetness of white chocolate and the spice of cinnamon add a yummy new dimension to these traditional treats. They make delicious gifts for loved ones during autumn or any time of year.
                    —Anna Ogden, Logan, Utah

> **10 medium tart apples**
> **10 Popsicle sticks**
> **2-1/4 cups packed brown sugar**
> **2 cups half-and-half cream**
> **1 cup light corn syrup**
> **1 cup butter, cubed**
> **1 teaspoon vanilla extract**
> **2 tablespoons sugar**
> **1 tablespoon ground cinnamon**
> **2-3/4 cups white baking chips**
> **3 tablespoons shortening**

Wash and dry apples; remove stems. Insert Popsicle sticks into the bottoms of apples. Place on a buttered baking sheet; refrigerate until ready to use.

In a large heavy saucepan, combine the brown sugar,

cream, corn syrup and butter. Bring to a boil over medium-high heat. Cook and stir until a candy thermometer reads 248° (firm-ball stage), about 50 minutes. Remove from the heat; stir in vanilla. Dip apples into the hot caramel to completely coat. Place on prepared pan; let stand until set.

In a small bowl, combine the sugar and cinnamon; set aside. In a microwave, melt white chips and shortening; stir until smooth. Dip one caramel apple into the warm white chip mixture and immediately sprinkle with the cinnamon-sugar. Place on a waxed paper-lined baking sheet. Repeat. **Yield:** 10 servings.

Editor's Note: We recommend that you test your candy thermometer before each use by bringing water to a boil; the thermometer should read 212°. Adjust your recipe temperature up or down based on your test.

Bacon Baklava

(Pictured below)

PREP: 50 min. **BAKE:** 35 min. + chilling

Who says bacon can't be a dessert ingredient? One bite of this surprisingly scrumptious baklava will convert any naysayers.
—*Preci D'Silva, Dubai, United Arab Emerates*

- 1-1/2 **pounds bacon strips**
- 1 **cup toasted chopped almonds**
- 3/4 **cup chopped dates**
- 10 **tablespoons butter, melted**
- 20 **sheets phyllo dough (14 inch x 9 inch)**
- 1-1/2 **cups sugar**
- 1 **cup maple syrup**
- 1/2 **cup water**
- 2 **tablespoons bourbon**
- 2 **teaspoons grated orange peel**

In a large skillet, cook bacon over medium heat until crisp. Remove to paper towels to drain.

Crumble bacon into a food processor; add almonds

and dates. Cover and process until finely chopped. Brush a 13-in. x 9-in. baking pan with some of the butter. Unroll phyllo dough; trim to fit into pan.

Layer five sheets of phyllo dough in the prepared pan, brushing each with butter. (Keep the remaining dough covered with plastic wrap and a damp towel to prevent it from drying out.) Sprinkle with a third of the bacon mixture. Repeat layers twice. Top with remaining phyllo dough, brushing each sheet with butter.

Using a sharp knife, cut into 1-1/2-in. diamond shapes. Bake at 350° for 30-35 minutes or until golden brown.

Meanwhile, in a small saucepan, combine remaining ingredients; bring to a boil. Reduce the heat; simmer, uncovered, for 10 minutes. Pour over warm baklava. Cool completely on a wire rack. Cover and refrigerate overnight. **Yield:** about 3 dozen.

Mexican Ice Cream

(Pictured above)

PREP: 20 min. + freezing

I made this fun ice cream for my grandma and her friends, and they loved it. It's a simple recipe that kids can help with.
—*Ben Phipps, Lima, Ohio*

- 2 **cups vanilla ice cream**
- 1/2 **cup frosted cornflakes, crushed**
- 1/4 **cup sugar**
- 1 **teaspoon ground cinnamon**
- 1/4 **cup honey**

Place four 1/2-cup scoops of ice cream on a waxed paper-lined baking sheet. Freeze for 1 hour or until firm.

In a shallow bowl, combine cornflake crumbs, sugar and cinnamon. Roll the ice cream in the crumb mixture to coat. Freeze until serving. Drizzle each serving with 1 tablespoon honey. **Yield:** 4 servings.

Blueberry Cream Dessert

(Pictured above)

PREP: 20 min. + chilling

Here's a cool treat I like serving for spring or summer luncheons or as a light finish to dinner. You can vary the flavor to match in-season fruit. —*Susan Kruspe, Shortsville, New York*

    1 cup (8 ounces) sour cream
    1 carton (6 ounces) blueberry yogurt
    1 envelope unflavored gelatin
  3/4 cup cold water
  3/4 cup sugar, *divided*
  1/2 teaspoon vanilla extract
1-1/4 cups graham cracker crumbs
    6 tablespoons butter, melted
    1 cup fresh blueberries
  1/2 cup heavy whipping cream, whipped

In a small bowl, combine the sour cream and blueberry yogurt; set aside. In a small saucepan, sprinkle gelatin over the cold water; let stand for 1 minute. Add 1/2 cup sugar. Cook and stir over low heat until the gelatin is completely dissolved.

Remove from the heat; stir in vanilla and sour cream mixture until blended. Transfer to a large bowl. Chill until partially set.

Meanwhile, in a small bowl, combine the graham cracker crumbs, butter and remaining sugar; set aside 1/4 cup for topping. Press the remaining crumb mixture into an ungreased 8-in. square dish; set aside.

Stir blueberries into gelatin mixture; fold in whipped cream. Spoon into the crust. Sprinkle with the reserved crumb mixture. Chill until set. Refrigerate leftovers.
Yield: 9 servings.

Grilled Pineapple Butterscotch Sundaes

(Pictured below)

PREP/TOTAL TIME: 30 min.

This is a great dessert for a cookout. Sometimes I use bananas in place of pineapple. Just be careful when grilling them—don't let the bananas get too soft. —*Arla Boss, Temperance, Michigan*

    2 fresh pineapples
    6 tablespoons plus 1/2 cup butter, *divided*
    2 tablespoons sugar
  1/4 teaspoon ground nutmeg
    1 cup packed brown sugar
  1/2 cup heavy whipping cream
  1/2 teaspoon vanilla extract
Dash salt
    3 cups vanilla ice cream

Peel, core and cut each pineapple into six spears. In a small saucepan, melt 6 tablespoons butter with sugar and nutmeg. Brush over the pineapple. Grill, covered, over medium heat or broil 4 in. from the heat for 7-10 minutes or until lightly browned, turning occasionally.

For sauce, in a small saucepan, melt remaining butter. Stir in the brown sugar and whipping cream. Bring to a boil, stirring constantly. Remove from the heat; stir in the vanilla and salt. Serve the sauce with ice cream and grilled pineapple. **Yield:** 6 servings.

Ricotta Cheesecake

(Pictured above)

PREP: 30 min. **BAKE:** 50 min. + chilling

When I was a nurse, my coworkers and I regularly swapped recipes during lunch breaks. This creamy cheesecake was one of the best I received. —Georgiann Franklin, Canfield, Ohio

- 1-1/4 cups graham cracker crumbs
- 3 tablespoons sugar
- 1/3 cup butter, melted

FILLING:

- 2 cartons (15 ounces *each*) ricotta cheese
- 1 cup sugar
- 3 eggs, lightly beaten
- 2 tablespoons all-purpose flour
- 1 teaspoon vanilla extract

In a bowl, combine the graham cracker crumbs and sugar; stir in butter. Press onto the bottom and 1 in. up the sides of a greased 9-in. springform pan. Place on a baking sheet. Bake at 400° for 6-8 minutes or until crust is lightly browned around the edges. Cool on a wire rack.

In a large mixing bowl, beat ricotta cheese on medium speed for 1 minute. Add sugar; beat for 1 minute. Add eggs; beat just until combined. Beat in flour and vanilla. Pour into crust.

Place pan on a baking sheet. Bake at 350° for 50-60 minutes or until center is almost set. Cool on a wire rack for 10 minutes. Carefully run a knife around the edge of pan to loosen; cool 1 hour longer. Refrigerate overnight. Remove sides of pan. Refrigerate the leftovers. **Yield:** 12 servings.

Hot Cherry Sauce

(Pictured above)

PREP/TOTAL TIME: 15 min.

This ruby–red, sweet–tart sauce makes a delightful topping for cheesecakes and other desserts, but I've also used it with ham. —Noreen Martinac, Stevensville, Montana

- 2 cans (14-1/2 ounces *each*) pitted tart cherries
- 1 cup sugar
- 1/4 cup cornstarch
- 1/4 to 1/2 teaspoon ground cloves
- 1 to 2 drops red food coloring, optional

Drain cherries, reserving juice; set cherries aside. In a large saucepan, combine the sugar, cornstarch and cloves; whisk in reserved cherry juice. Bring to a boil; cook and stir for 2 minutes or until thickened. Remove from the heat; stir in the cherries and food coloring if desired. **Yield:** about 3-1/2 cups.

Transfer to an 8-in. x 4-in. loaf pan coated with cooking spray. Cover and refrigerate for 30 minutes or until firm.

For vanilla layer, in a small bowl, sprinkle gelatin over cold water; let stand for 1 minute. In a small saucepan, bring 1 cup cream and sugar to a simmer. Stir in the gelatin mixture until gelatin is completely dissolved. Stir in the vanilla and remaining cream. Carefully spoon over chocolate layer. Cover and refrigerate for at least 2 hours or until firm.

For the sauce, in a blender or food processor, puree strawberries and sugar. Transfer to a bowl; cover and refrigerate until serving.

Just before serving, unmold dessert and cut into slices. Serve with strawberry sauce. **Yield:** 6-8 servings.

Citrus Tartlets

(Pictured below)

PREP: 15 min. + chilling

Made in individual tart shells, these treats are always popular at church bake sales and get–togethers. The men in my family are sometimes hard to please, but they really enjoy these.
—Sandra Kea, Nashville, North Carolina

 1 **package (3 ounces) cream cheese, softened**
 1 **can (14 ounces) sweetened condensed milk**
1/4 **cup orange juice concentrate**
 3 **tablespoons lemon juice**
 3 **drops yellow food coloring, optional**
 1 **cup heavy whipping cream, whipped**
 2 **packages (6 count *each*) individual graham cracker tart shells**
Additional whipped cream
 2 **teaspoons grated orange peel**
 2 **teaspoons grated lemon peel**

In a large bowl, beat the cream cheese until smooth. Gradually add the milk, beating until smooth. Stir in the orange juice concentrate, lemon juice and food coloring if desired. Fold in whipped cream.

Spoon the filling into the tart shells; chill for several hours or overnight. Garnish with a dollop of whipped cream; sprinkle with the orange peel and lemon peel. **Yield:** 12 tarts.

Tuxedo Cream Dessert

(Pictured above and on page 119)

PREP: 40 min. + chilling

This is my adaptation of my grandmother's signature dessert. The name says it all—this rich creation is fancy enough to be served at a formal event. Gran and I have both used the recipe often for entertaining. —Camilla Saulsbury, Nacogdoches, Texas

1-3/4 **teaspoons unflavored gelatin**
 2 **tablespoons cold water**
1-1/2 **cups heavy whipping cream, *divided***
3/4 **cup semisweet chocolate chips**
VANILLA LAYER:
1-3/4 **teaspoons unflavored gelatin**
 2 **tablespoons cold water**
1-2/3 **cups heavy whipping cream, *divided***
1/4 **cup sugar**
 2 **teaspoons vanilla extract**
STRAWBERRY SAUCE:
 2 **cups sliced fresh strawberries**
 2 **to 3 tablespoons sugar**

In a small bowl, sprinkle the gelatin over the cold water; let stand for 1 minute. In a small saucepan, bring 1 cup cream to a simmer. Stir 1/2 cup into the gelatin mixture until gelatin is completely dissolved. Stir the chocolate chips into the remaining warm cream until melted. Stir in the gelatin mixture and remaining cream.

Summertime Fruit Cones

(Pictured above)

PREP/TOTAL TIME: 20 min.

This simple summer dessert from our Test Kitchen staff appeals to both kids and adults. You could also assemble the fruity, creamy filling in parfait glasses instead of ice cream cones.

☑ This recipe includes Nutrition Facts and Diabetic Exchanges.

- 2 **medium nectarines, chopped**
- 1 **cup whole small fresh strawberries**
- 1 **cup fresh blueberries**
- 2 **tablespoons mashed fresh strawberries**
- 1 **teaspoon crystallized ginger**
- 1/4 **teaspoon ground cinnamon**
- 1 **cup reduced-fat whipped topping**
- 4 **ice cream waffle cones**

In a small bowl, combine nectarines, whole strawberries and blueberries.

In another bowl, combine the mashed strawberries, ginger and cinnamon. Fold in whipped topping.

Fill each waffle cone with 1/4 cup fruit mixture; top with 2 tablespoons whipped topping mixture. Repeat layers. Serve immediately. **Yield:** 4 servings.

Nutrition Facts: 1 serving equals 162 calories, 4 g fat (2 g saturated fat), 1 mg cholesterol, 18 mg sodium, 31 g carbohydrate, 3 g fiber, 2 g protein. **Diabetic Exchanges:** 1 starch, 1 fruit, 1/2 fat.

Cocoa Meringues with Berries

(Pictured below and on page 118)

PREP: 20 min. **BAKE:** 50 min. + standing

Meringues can be challenging on a humid day, but if you're really craving some, pick them up at a bakery and just add the berry sauce. —Raymonde Bourgeois, Swastika, Ontario

- 1 **egg white**
- 1/8 **teaspoon cream of tartar**

Dash salt

- 3 **tablespoons sugar,** *divided*
- 1 **tablespoon baking cocoa**
- 1/4 **teaspoon vanilla extract**
- 2 **tablespoons finely chopped bittersweet chocolate**

BERRY SAUCE:

- 2 **tablespoons sugar**
- 1 **teaspoon cornstarch**
- 2 **tablespoons orange juice**
- 1 **tablespoon water**
- 1/2 **cup fresh** *or* **frozen blueberries, thawed**
- 1/2 **cup fresh** *or* **frozen raspberries, thawed**

Place the egg white in a small bowl; let stand at room temperature for 30 minutes. Add the cream of tartar and salt; beat on medium speed until soft peaks form. Gradually beat in 2 tablespoons sugar. Combine cocoa and remaining sugar; add to meringue with vanilla. Beat on high until stiff glossy peaks form and the sugar is dissolved. Fold in the chopped chocolate.

Drop two mounds onto a parchment paper-lined baking sheet. Shape into 3-in. cups with the back of a spoon. Bake at 275° for 50-60 minutes or until set and dry. Turn oven off; leave meringues in oven for 1 hour.

In a small saucepan, combine the sugar, cornstarch, orange juice and water. Bring to a boil; cook and stir for 1 minute or until thickened. Remove from the heat; stir in berries. Cool to room temperature. Spoon into meringues. **Yield:** 2 servings.

Peanut Ice Cream Delight

(Pictured above and on page 118)

PREP: 50 min. + freezing

*A cookie crust, ice cream, peanuts and homemade toppings...
it's no wonder this was such a hit at my future daughter-in-law's
bridal shower!* —*Barb Rader, Brock, Nebraska*

- **1** **package (14 ounces) cream-filled chocolate
sandwich cookies, crushed**
- **1/3** **cup butter, melted**
- **1/2** **gallon vanilla ice cream, softened**
- **1-1/2** **cups salted peanuts**
- **CARAMEL SAUCE:**
- **1** **cup packed brown sugar**
- **1** **cup heavy whipping cream**
- **1/2** **cup butter, cubed**
- **1** **teaspoon vanilla extract**
- **CHOCOLATE SAUCE:**
- **1** **can (12 ounces) evaporated milk**
- **1** **cup (6 ounces) semisweet chocolate chips**
- **1/2** **cup butter, cubed**
- **2** **cups confectioners' sugar**
- **1** **teaspoon vanilla extract**

In a bowl, combine cookie crumbs and butter; press
onto the bottom and up the sides of an ungreased 13-in.
x 9-in. dish. Spread ice cream over crust; sprinkle with
peanuts. Cover and freeze for at least 1 hour.

For caramel sauce, in a small saucepan, combine the
brown sugar, cream and butter. Bring to a boil; cook and
stir for 1 minute. Remove from the heat; stir in vanilla.
Cool. Drizzle over the peanuts. Cover and freeze for at
least 1 hour.

For chocolate sauce, in a large saucepan, combine the

milk, chocolate chips and butter. Cook and stir over low
heat until melted and smooth. Stir in the confectioners'
sugar. Bring to a boil. Reduce heat; simmer, uncovered,
for 8-10 minutes or until thickened, stirring frequently.
Remove from the heat; stir in vanilla. Cool.

Drizzle over dessert. Cover and freeze for 2 hours or
until firm. **Yield:** 12-15 servings.

French Cream with Sugared Grapes

(Pictured below)

PREP: 20 min. + chilling

*Looking for a truly elegant finale? This dessert looks so regal
surrounded by fancy sugared fruit, and every bite is divine.*
—*June Bridges, Franklin, Indiana*

- **1** **cup (8 ounces) sour cream**
- **1** **cup heavy whipping cream**
- **3/4** **cup sugar**
- **1** **envelope unflavored gelatin**
- **1/4** **cup cold water**
- **1** **package (8 ounces) cream cheese, softened**
- **1** **teaspoon vanilla extract**
- **Seedless green and red grapes**
- **Additional sugar**

In a saucepan, combine sour cream and cream until well
blended. Gradually stir in the sugar. Cook and stir over
medium heat just until mixture is warm and sugar is
dissolved. Remove from the heat.

In a small microwave-safe bowl, sprinkle the gelatin
over the cold water; let stand for 1 minute. Microwave,
uncovered, on high for 40 seconds. Stir; let stand for
1 minute or until gelatin is completely dissolved. Stir
into sour cream mixture.

In a small mixing bowl, beat cream cheese until light
and fluffy. Gradually add gelatin cream mixture and
vanilla, beating on low speed until combined. Pour into
a 4-cup mold coated with cooking spray. Chill for at
least 4 hours or until set.

Dip grapes into water and shake off excess moisture;

dip into sugar, turning to coat. Unmold the dessert onto a serving platter; surround with the sugared grapes. **Yield:** 6 servings.

Editor's Note: Reduced-fat or fat-free sour cream and cream cheese are not recommended for this recipe.

Strawberry Malted Mousse Cups

PREP: 20 min. + chilling

Eyes light up whenever I bring these lovely cups to the table. They're nice not only for ladies' luncheons but also for holidays.
—*Anna Ginsberg, Austin, Texas*

- 1 **package (3 ounces) strawberry gelatin**
- 1 **tablespoon cornstarch**
- 1 **cup water**
- 1/4 **cup malted milk powder**
- 1 **cup refrigerated French vanilla nondairy creamer**
- 1 **carton (8 ounces) frozen whipped topping, thawed, *divided***

Fresh strawberries and mint, optional

In a small saucepan, combine the gelatin, cornstarch and water until smooth. Bring to a boil; cook and stir for 3-5 minutes or until mixture becomes clear. Remove from the heat; cool for 5 minutes.

In a small bowl, combine the malted milk powder and creamer; whisk into the gelatin mixture. Stir in 2 cups whipped topping. Spoon into six dessert dishes; chill until set.

Just before serving, dollop with remaining whipped topping. Garnish with berries and mint if desired. **Yield:** 6 servings.

Watermelon Sorbet

(Pictured above right)

PREP: 35 min. + freezing

No ice cream maker is needed to make this easy, four–ingredient sorbet. We had only one problem, however—we couldn't keep enough watermelon in the house to keep up with the demand!
—*Kory Figura, Waverly, Iowa*

- 1 **cup sugar**
- 1 **cup water**
- 8 **cups cubed seedless watermelon**
- 2 **tablespoons lemon juice**

In a small saucepan, bring the sugar and water to a boil. Cook and stir until sugar is dissolved; set aside.

In a blender or food processor, process watermelon in batches until pureed. Transfer to a large bowl; stir in the sugar syrup and lemon juice. Pour into a 13-in. x 9-in. dish; cover and freeze for 8 hours or until firm.

Just before serving, puree the watermelon mixture in batches until smooth. **Yield:** 1-1/2 quarts.

Strawberry Crumble Parfaits

(Pictured above)

PREP: 30 min. + freezing

Whether they're served in parfait glasses or bowls, these pretty but effortless layered treats are simply perfect for entertaining on a warm summer evening. You'll love the contrast between the smooth, creamy berry mixture and the buttery, crunchy topping.
—*Carol Anderson, Salt Lake City, Utah*

- 1 **cup all-purpose flour**
- 1/4 **cup packed brown sugar**
- 1/2 **cup chopped pecans**
- 1/2 **cup cold butter**
- 1 **can (14 ounces) sweetened condensed milk**
- 3 **tablespoons lemon juice**
- 3 **tablespoons orange juice**
- 2 **cups chopped fresh strawberries**
- 1 **cup heavy whipping cream, whipped**

In a bowl, combine the flour, brown sugar and pecans; cut in the cold butter until the mixture resembles coarse crumbs. Spread into an ungreased 15-in. x 10-in. x 1-in. baking pan. Bake at 350° for 15-18 minutes or until golden brown.

In a large bowl, combine the sweetened condensed milk, lemon juice and orange juice. Add strawberries; mix well. Fold in whipped cream.

Spoon 1 tablespoon of the crumb mixture into each parfait glass; top with a scant 3 tablespoonfuls of berry mixture. Repeat layers. Sprinkle with remaining crumb mixture. Freeze until firm.

Remove parfaits from freezer 20-30 minutes before serving. **Yield:** 10 servings.

Pears with Flair

WHEN ORCHARDS are bursting with fresh pears ripe for the picking, why not take advantage of that bounty in your kitchen? The delectable dessert recipes here will let you do just that.

You'll be amazed at the tempting treats you can fix with this versatile fruit. For example, use pears and just three other basic ingredients—wine, sugar and lemon juice—to make an elegant sorbet.

Or, pop pear wedges in the oven and drizzle them with a creamy pecan sauce...create an elegant show-stopper with pomegranate juice and Mascarpone cheese...or top ice cream with a flavorful fruit sauce.

Pear Sorbet

(Pictured below)

PREP: 20 min. + freezing

Touches of sweet white wine and citrus make this lovely pear sorbet simply refreshing. Serve it as a light finale to a big, hearty holiday meal...or treat friends and family to a scoop on a hot summer's day. You can use canned pears when fresh ones aren't available, and lime juice is a good substitute for lemon.
—*Deirdre Dee Cox, Milwaukee, Wisconsin*

   5 small pears, peeled and sliced
3/4 cup sweet white wine *or* apple juice
1/3 cup sugar
4-1/2 teaspoons lemon juice

In a large saucepan, combine all ingredients. Bring to a boil. Reduce heat; simmer, uncovered, for 8-10 minutes or until pears are tender. Cool slightly.

Pour into a food processor; cover and process for 1-2 minutes or until smooth. Transfer to a 13-in. x 9-in. dish. Cover and freeze for 4 hours or until firm.

Just before serving, process again in a food processor for 1-2 minutes or until smooth. Spoon into dessert dishes. **Yield:** 4 servings.

Pomegranate Poached Pears

(Pictured above)

PREP: 20 min. **COOK:** 1 hour 25 min.

The poaching liquid lets these extra-fancy pears pick up flavor and ruby-red color from the pomegranate juice, orange juice, wine, rosemary and cinnamon. You'll enjoy the subtle tastes in the reduction sauce and the Mascarpone cheese, too.
—*Bev Jones, Brunswick, Missouri*

   3 cups dry red wine *or* red grape juice
   1 bottle (16 ounces) pomegranate juice
   1 cup water
1/2 cup sugar
1/4 cup orange juice
   2 tablespoons grated orange peel
   3 fresh rosemary sprigs (4 inches)
   1 cinnamon stick (3 inches)
   6 medium pears
   6 orange slices
   6 tablespoons Mascarpone cheese

In a Dutch oven, combine the first eight ingredients. Core pears from the bottom, leaving stems intact. Peel pears; place on their sides in the pan.

Bring to a boil. Reduce the heat; cover and simmer for 25-30 minutes or until pears are almost tender. Remove with a slotted spoon; cool.

Strain the poaching liquid and return to the Dutch oven. Bring poaching liquid to a boil; cook until reduced to 1 cup, about 45 minutes. Discard the rosemary sprigs and cinnamon stick.

Place an orange slice on each serving plate; top with 1 tablespoon cheese and a pear. Drizzle with poaching liquid. **Yield:** 6 servings.

Roasted Pears in Pecan Sauce

(Pictured below)

PREP: 20 min. **BAKE:** 30 min.

Whenever I bring pears home, my family begs me to make this comforting, home-style dessert. They love the roasted wedges of fruit smothered in a luscious pecan sauce. Serve it over scoops of vanilla ice cream or even slices of store-bought pound cake.
—*Darlene King, Estevan, Saskatchewan*

- **4 medium pears, peeled and cut into wedges**
- **3 tablespoons brown sugar**
- **3 tablespoons unsweetened apple juice**
- **3 tablespoons butter, melted**
- **1/4 cup chopped pecans**
- **3 tablespoons heavy whipping cream**
- **Vanilla ice cream, optional**

Place pears in an ungreased 13-in. x 9-in. baking dish. In a small bowl, combine the brown sugar, apple juice and butter; pour over pears. Bake, uncovered, at 400° for 20 minutes, basting occasionally.

Sprinkle with the pecans. Bake 10-15 minutes longer or until the pears are tender. Transfer the pears to serving dishes.

Pour cooking juices into a small bowl; whisk in cream until blended. Drizzle over pears. Serve with ice cream if desired. **Yield:** 4 servings.

Sweet Riesling Pears

(Pictured above)

PREP: 10 min. **CAKE:** 50 min.

With these aromatic poached pears simmering on the stovetop and filling the house with a mouthwatering scent, you don't need potpourri! This simple, sumptuous dessert tastes just as good and is sure to please guests, especially on a cool fall or winter day.
—*Sunny McDaniel, Cary, North Carolina*

- **4 cups Riesling *or* other sweet white wine**
- **1/2 cup sugar**
- **3 fresh rosemary sprigs**
- **5 cups chopped peeled ripe pears**
- **Vanilla ice cream, optional**

In a large saucepan, bring wine, sugar and rosemary to a boil. Reduce heat; simmer, uncovered, for 20-30 minutes or until flavors are blended.

Discard rosemary sprigs. Add the pears to saucepan. Bring to a boil. Reduce the heat; simmer, uncovered, for 4-6 minutes or until tender. Remove pears with a slotted spoon; keep warm.

Bring liquid to a boil; cook and stir for 15-20 minutes or until reduced and amber-colored. Remove from the heat; stir in pears. Serve over vanilla ice cream if desired. **Yield:** 4 cups.

Lemon Sorbet Torte

(Pictured above)

PREP: 30 min. + freezing

With the tangy flavors of lemon, rhubarb and strawberries, this gorgeous torte is a wonderful choice for a springtime party.
—*Sarah Bradley, Athens, Texas*

    3 cups slivered almonds, toasted
  1/2 cup sugar
  1/4 teaspoon ground cinnamon
    5 tablespoons butter, melted
  1/3 cup seedless strawberry jam
    3 pints lemon sorbet, softened
STRAWBERRY-RHUBARB SAUCE:
  1/2 cup sugar
  1/4 cup water
2-1/2 cups sliced fresh *or* frozen rhubarb
2-1/2 cups frozen unsweetened strawberries, partially thawed and sliced
  3/4 teaspoon vanilla extract
    1 pint fresh strawberries, sliced

Place the almonds, sugar and cinnamon in a food processor; cover and process until finely chopped. Stir in the butter. Press onto the bottom and 2 in. up the sides of an ungreased 9-in. springform pan. Place pan on a baking sheet. Bake at 350° for 15-20 minutes or until lightly browned. Cool completely on a wire rack.

In a small saucepan over low heat, melt jam; spread over bottom of crust. Top with sorbet. Freeze until firm.

Meanwhile, for sauce, combine sugar and water in a large saucepan. Bring to a boil. Add rhubarb; return to a boil. Reduce heat; cover and simmer for 5-8 minutes or until rhubarb is tender. Add thawed strawberries; bring to a boil. Remove from heat; cool to room temperature. Stir in vanilla. Cover and refrigerate.

Just before serving, remove the sides of springform pan. Spoon 1/2 cup sauce onto the center of torte; top with fresh strawberries. Serve with remaining sauce. **Yield:** 12 servings.

Chocolate Mousse With Cranberry Sauce

(Pictured below and on page 119)

PREP: 45 min. + chilling

This unique dessert features slices of firm mousse drizzled with cranberry sauce. The sweet–tart combination tingles your taste buds. —*Barbara Nowakowski, North Tonawanda, New York*

    2 cups (12 ounces) semisweet chocolate chips
  1/4 cup butter, cubed
    1 egg yolk, lightly beaten
1-1/2 cups heavy whipping cream, *divided*
  1/3 cup light corn syrup
    1 teaspoon vanilla extract
SAUCE:
  1/3 cup cranberry juice
    1 teaspoon lime juice
    1 cup jellied cranberry sauce

In a large microwave-safe bowl, melt chips and butter; stir until smooth. In a small heavy saucepan, combine yolk, 1/4 cup cream and corn syrup. Cook and stir over low heat until mixture reaches 160°, about 2 minutes.

Remove from the heat; stir into chocolate mixture. Refrigerate for 20 minutes or until cooled and slightly thickened, stirring occasionally. Line a 1-qt. bowl with plastic wrap; set aside.

In a large mixing bowl, beat remaining cream until it begins to thicken. Add vanilla; beat until soft peaks form. Fold into chocolate mixture. Spoon into prepared bowl. Cover and refrigerate overnight.

Place the sauce ingredients in a blender; cover and process until smooth. Transfer to a small bowl; cover and refrigerate until serving.

Just before serving, invert mousse onto a platter; remove plastic wrap. Cut into wedges; serve with the cranberry sauce. **Yield:** 10 servings (about 1 cup sauce).

Lavender Brownie Cheesecake

PREP: 45 min. **BAKE:** 1 hour + chilling

When you want to impress guests, this is the recipe for you! The chocolaty cheesecake is so luscious and pretty, especially when garnished with more lavender. —*Peggy Armstrong, Buhl, Idaho*

- 4 **squares (1 ounce** *each***) semisweet chocolate**
- 1/2 **cup butter**
- 1 **cup sugar**
- 2 **eggs**
- 1 **teaspoon vanilla extract**
- 3/4 **cup all-purpose flour**
- 1/2 **teaspoon salt**

FILLING:
- 3 **packages (8 ounces** *each***) cream cheese, softened**
- 3/4 **cup sugar**
- 3 **eggs, lightly beaten**
- 1/2 **cup sour cream**
- 1 **teaspoon vanilla extract**
- 1 **to 2 teaspoons lavender buds, ground**

TOPPING:
- 1/2 **cup sour cream**
- 2 **teaspoons sugar**
- 1 **teaspoon lavender buds, optional**

In a microwave, melt the chocolate and butter; stir until smooth. Cool slightly. In a large mixing bowl, combine the sugar, eggs, vanilla and cooled chocolate mixture. Combine the flour and salt; stir into chocolate mixture. Spread into a greased 9-in. springform pan. Place on a baking sheet. Bake at 325° for 25-30 minutes or until set. Cool on a wire rack for 10 minutes.

In a large mixing bowl, beat cream cheese and sugar until smooth. Add the eggs; beat on low speed just until combined. Beat in sour cream, vanilla and lavender just until blended. Pour over brownie crust.

Place the pan on a double thickness of heavy-duty foil (about 16 in. square). Securely wrap the foil around the pan. Place in a larger baking pan; add 1 in. of hot water to the larger pan. Bake for 60-70 minutes or until center is just set.

Remove springform pan from water bath. Remove foil. Cool on a wire rack for 10 minutes. Carefully run a knife around the edge of pan to loosen; cool 1 hour longer.

LOCATING LAVENDER. The recipe for Lavender Brownie Cheesecake (above) calls for lavender in the filling and also as an optional topping. Look for dried lavender flowers in spice shops. If you're using lavender from the garden, make sure it has not been treated with chemicals.

Chill for 3-4 hours or overnight. Remove the sides of the pan. Combine sour cream and sugar; spread evenly over the top of cheesecake. Garnish with lavender if desired. Refrigerate leftovers. **Yield:** 12 servings.

Slow-Cooked Stuffed Apples

(Pictured above)

PREP: 20 min. **COOK:** 3 hours

This irresistible dessert is slow-cooker easy and perfect for a chilly autumn or winter day. Warm and comforting, the tender apples are filled with chewy pecans and yummy caramel topping.
—*Pam Kaiser, Mansfield, Missouri*

- 6 **large tart apples**
- 2 **teaspoons lemon juice**
- 1/3 **cup chopped pecans**
- 1/4 **cup chopped dried apricots**
- 1/4 **cup packed brown sugar**
- 3 **tablespoons butter, melted**
- 3/4 **teaspoon ground cinnamon**
- 1/4 **teaspoon ground nutmeg**

Granola and caramel ice cream topping, optional

Core the apples and peel the top third of each; brush the peeled portions with lemon juice. Place in a 6-qt. slow cooker.

Combine the pecans, apricots, brown sugar, butter, cinnamon and nutmeg. Place a heaping tablespoonful of the mixture in each apple. Pour 2 cups water around the apples.

Cover and cook on low for 3-4 hours or until apples are tender. Serve apples with granola and caramel topping if desired. **Yield:** 6 servings.

Candy Bar Ice Cream

(Pictured above)

PREP: 25 min. + chilling
PROCESS: 20 min./batch + freezing

You can count on a bowl of this tempting treat to beat summer's heat. People of all ages line up for the combination of ice cream and Butterfinger candy bars. —Pam West, Centralia, Missouri

    2 quarts half-and-half cream
    1 cup milk
 2-1/4 cups sugar
  1/4 teaspoon salt
    4 eggs, beaten
 4-1/2 teaspoons vanilla extract
    5 Butterfinger candy bars (2.1 ounces *each*)

In a large heavy saucepan, heat the half-and-half and milk to 175°; stir in the sugar and salt until dissolved. Whisk a small amount of the hot mixture into the eggs.

Return all to the pan, whisking constantly. Cook and stir over low heat until mixture reaches at least 160° and coats the back of a metal spoon.

Remove from the heat. Cool quickly by placing pan in a bowl of ice water; stir for 2 minutes. Stir in vanilla. Press plastic wrap onto surface of custard. Refrigerate for several hours or overnight.

Stir in candy bars. Fill cylinder of ice cream freezer two-thirds full; freeze according to manufacturer's instructions. Refrigerate remaining mixture until ready to freeze. Allow to ripen in ice cream freezer or firm up in the refrigerator freezer for 2-4 hours before serving.
Yield: 3 quarts.

Pumpkin Cranberry Bread Pudding

(Pictured below)

PREP: 15 min. **COOK:** 3 hours

Savor two of everyone's favorite autumn flavors—pumpkin and cranberry—with this scrumptious bread pudding. I serve it warm with a homemade vanilla sauce. For an extra–special finish, put a dollop of whipped cream or scoop of ice cream on top.
—Judith Bucciarelli, Johnson, New York

    8 slices cinnamon bread, cut into 1-inch cubes
    4 eggs, beaten
    2 cups 2% milk
    1 cup canned pumpkin
  1/4 cup packed brown sugar
  1/4 cup butter, melted
    1 teaspoon vanilla extract
  1/2 teaspoon ground cinnamon
  1/4 teaspoon ground nutmeg
  1/2 cup dried cranberries
SAUCE:
    1 cup sugar
  2/3 cup water
    1 cup heavy whipping cream
    2 teaspoons vanilla extract

Place bread in a greased 3- or 4-qt. slow cooker. In a large bowl, combine the eggs, milk, pumpkin, brown sugar, butter, vanilla, cinnamon and nutmeg; stir in the cranberries. Pour over bread cubes. Cover and cook on low for 3-4 hours or until a knife inserted near center comes out clean.

For the sauce, in a large saucepan, bring the sugar and water to a boil over medium heat. Cook until the sugar is dissolved and the mixture turns a golden amber color, about 20 minutes.

Gradually stir in cream until smooth. Remove from the heat; stir in vanilla. Serve sauce warm with bread pudding. **Yield:** 8 servings (1-1/3 cups sauce).

Chocolate Mint Apple Fondue

(Pictured above)

PREP/TOTAL TIME: 10 min.

This recipe is so simple to make, and kids love it. You can dip just about any fruit, bread or cookie that tastes good with chocolate.
—Deb Danner, Dayton, Ohio

- **1 can (14 ounces) sweetened condensed milk**
- **1 cup (6 ounces) semisweet chocolate chips**
- **10 chocolate-covered peppermint patties, chopped**

Sliced apples

In a small saucepan, combine the milk, chocolate chips and patties. Cook and stir over medium-low heat until smooth. Serve warm with the apples. **Yield:** 2-1/2 cups.

Praline Crunch Ice Cream

(Pictured at right)

PREP: 30 min. + chilling
PROCESS: 20 min./batch + freezing

If you're a caramel lover, you'll definitely want to try this special ice cream topped with pralines and a rich caramel sauce. Yum!
—Julia Register, Huntersville, North Carolina

- **1-3/4 cups milk**
- **2/3 cup sugar**
- **2 eggs, beaten**
- **2 cups heavy whipping cream**
- **1 teaspoon vanilla extract**

CANDIED PECANS:
- **1 tablespoon butter**
- **1/4 cup packed brown sugar**
- **1/4 teaspoon ground cinnamon**

Dash ground nutmeg
- **1/2 cup chopped pecans**

CARAMEL SAUCE:
- **1 cup butter, cubed**
- **1/2 cup water**
- **1 tablespoon light corn syrup**
- **2 cups sugar**
- **1 cup heavy whipping cream**

In a heavy saucepan, heat milk to 175°; stir in sugar until dissolved. Whisk a small amount of the hot mixture into eggs; return all to the pan, whisking constantly. Cook and stir over low heat until the mixture reaches at least 160° and coats the back of a metal spoon.

Remove from the heat. Cool quickly by placing pan in a bowl of ice water; stir for 2 minutes. Stir in cream and vanilla. Transfer to a bowl. Press the plastic wrap onto surface of custard. Refrigerate for several hours or overnight.

Fill cylinder of ice cream freezer two-thirds full; freeze according to the manufacturer's directions. Refrigerate remaining mixture until ready to freeze. Transfer to a freezer container; freeze for 2-4 hours before serving.

In a heavy skillet, melt the butter over medium heat. Stir in brown sugar, cinnamon and nutmeg; cook and stir until sugar is dissolved. Add pecans; cook and stir for 2-3 minutes or until coated. Spread pecans onto a greased foil-lined baking sheet. Cool completely.

For sauce, combine butter, water and corn syrup in a heavy saucepan. Cook and stir over medium-low heat until the butter is melted. Add sugar; cook and stir until sugar is dissolved. Bring to a boil over medium-high heat without stirring. Boil for 4 minutes. Stir for 6-8 minutes or until mixture is caramel-colored.

Remove from the heat. Carefully stir in cream until smooth. Serve the caramel sauce and candied pecans over the ice cream. **Yield:** about 1-1/2 quarts ice cream (1-1/2 cups sauce).

Potluck Pleasers

Put your best on the buffet table with the large-yield recipes in this chapter. You'll find impressive salads, bars, main dishes, appetizers and more!

Rainbow Pepper Medley 136
Rich Peanut Clusters...136
Pumpkin-Filled Crescent Rolls 136
Grilled Vegetable Sandwiches 137
Crunchy Potato Mounds 137
Pickled Veggie Salad 138
Deli Beef Heroes 138
Layered Taco Salad 139
Layered Lemon Pies 139
Roasted Vegetable Salad..140
Peanut Butter Brownie Trifle 140
Lemon Delight Trifle 140
Tex-Mex Chili 141
Fiesta Tuna Salad Sandwiches................................141
Summer Salad with Lemon Vinaigrette.............142
Pumpkin Dessert Bars 142
Wake Up! Breakfast Casserole 143
Pretty Pumpkin Wontons 143
Hot Wing Dip...143
Bacon-Cheese Stuffed Shells..................................144
Balsamic Pork Scallopine 144
Italian Sausage Grinders...145
The Best Eggplant Parmesan...................................145

WOW THE CROWD. Clockwise from upper left: Tex-Mex Chili (p. 141), Pumpkin Dessert Bars (p. 142), Grilled Vegetable Sandwiches (p. 137) and Hot Wing Dip (p. 143).

Rainbow Pepper Medley

(Pictured above)

PREP: 20 min. + chilling

This colorful, crunchy salad is a great way to enjoy your summer harvest of peppers. —*Margaret Allen, Abingdon, Virginia*

- **2 medium green peppers, julienned**
- **2 medium sweet red peppers, julienned**
- **1 medium sweet yellow pepper, julienned**
- **1 small red onion, chopped**
- **1 jalapeno pepper, seeded, finely chopped**

VINAIGRETTE:

- **1/3 cup canola oil**
- **2 tablespoons tarragon vinegar**
- **1 tablespoon Dijon mustard**
- **2 teaspoons sugar**
- **2 teaspoons caraway seeds**
- **1 teaspoon salt**
- **1 teaspoon grated lime peel**
- **1/4 teaspoon pepper**
- **1/4 teaspoon Louisiana-style hot sauce**

In a large bowl, combine the first five ingredients. In a small bowl, whisk the vinaigrette ingredients. Pour over vegetables and toss to coat. Cover; refrigerate for at least 3 hours before serving. **Yield:** 12 servings (1/2 cup each).

Editor's Note: When cutting hot peppers, disposable gloves are recommended. Avoid touching your face.

Rich Peanut Clusters

PREP: 20 min. + chilling

My husband and sons-in-law can devour these rich homemade candies in minutes! —*Janice Garvert, Plainville, Kansas*

- **2 packages (12 ounces *each*) semisweet chocolate chips**
- **2 packages (10 to 12 ounces *each*) vanilla *or* white chips**
- **1 tablespoon shortening**
- **1 teaspoon vanilla extract**
- **1/2 teaspoon butter, softened**
- **2 cans (12 ounces *each*) salted peanuts**

In a large microwave-safe bowl, heat the semisweet chocolate chips and vanilla chips with the shortening on high until melted, stirring occasionally. Stir until smooth. Stir in the vanilla and butter. Add the peanuts; mix well.

Drop the mixture by teaspoonfuls onto waxed paper-lined pans. Refrigerate until set. Store in an airtight container. **Yield:** about 15 dozen.

Pumpkin-Filled Crescent Rolls

PREP: 40 min. + chilling **BAKE:** 15 min./batch

When my grandmother made these yummy rolls, she didn't use traditional measuring cups. So we measured her handfuls and pinches to come up with this version of her old-world recipe. —*Gary Wanosky, North Ridgeville, Ohio*

- **4 teaspoons active dry yeast**
- **1/4 cup warm 2% milk (110° to 115°)**
- **4 cups all-purpose flour**
- **1/4 cup sugar**
- **1 teaspoon salt**
- **1 cup butter, cubed**
- **1/2 cup shortening**
- **1 cup (8 ounces) sour cream**
- **4 egg yolks**
- **2 teaspoons grated lemon peel**

FILLING:

- **3/4 cup canned pumpkin**
- **1/3 cup sugar**
- **1-1/2 teaspoons pumpkin pie spice**

In a small bowl, dissolve yeast in milk. In a large bowl, combine 3 cups flour, sugar and salt; cut in butter and shortening until crumbly. Add the sour cream, egg yolks, lemon peel and yeast mixture; mix well. Stir in enough remaining flour to form a soft dough.

Turn onto a floured surface; knead until smooth and elastic, about 6-8 minutes. Place in a greased bowl, turning once to grease the top. Cover and refrigerate overnight.

Let dough stand at room temperature for 1 hour. Punch dough down; turn onto a lightly floured surface. Divide into thirds. Roll each into a 12-in. circle; cut each circle into 12 wedges.

Combine the filling ingredients; spread a rounded teaspoonful of filling over each wedge. Roll up wedges from wide ends and place point side down 2 in. apart on greased baking sheets. Curve ends to form crescents.

Cover and let rise in a warm place for 30 minutes.
    Bake at 350° for 13-18 minutes or until golden brown. Remove from pans to wire racks. **Yield:** 3 dozen.

Grilled Vegetable Sandwiches

(Pictured below and on page 135)

PREP: 30 min. **GRILL:** 20 min.

Pick some of your fresh garden bounty to build these hearty and unique subs. The basil–lemon mayo adds terrific flavor.
    —*Kathy Hewitt, Cranston, Rhode Island*

- 3 **large sweet red peppers**
- 3 **medium red onions**
- 3 **large zucchini**
- 1/4 **cup olive oil**
- 3/4 **teaspoon salt**
- 3/4 **teaspoon coarsely ground pepper**
- 3/4 **cup reduced-fat mayonnaise**
- 1/3 **cup minced fresh basil**
- 2 **tablespoons lemon juice**
- 6 **garlic cloves, minced**
- 12 **submarine buns, split**
- 24 **slices cheddar cheese**
- 3 **medium tomatoes, sliced**
- 3/4 **cup hummus**

Cut the red peppers into eighths; cut the onions and zucchini into 1/2-in. slices. Brush the vegetables with oil; sprinkle with salt and pepper. Grill vegetables in batches, covered, over medium heat or broil 4 in. from the heat for 4-5 minutes on each side or until crisp-tender. Cool.
    Combine the mayonnaise, basil, lemon juice and garlic; spread over bun bottoms. Layer with cheese, grilled vegetables and tomatoes. Spread hummus over bun tops; replace tops. **Yield:** 12 servings.

Crunchy Potato Mounds

(Pictured above)

PREP: 30 min. + chilling **BAKE:** 30 min.

Here's a great way to use up leftover mashed potatoes and ham from a holiday meal. The bite–size balls are rolled in crushed cornflakes, baked and served with a honey–mustard sauce.
    —*Mary Relyea, Canastota, New York*

- 1/2 **cup Dijon mustard**
- 1/3 **cup honey**
- 2 **tablespoons plus 1/2 cup mayonnaise,** *divided*
- 3-1/2 **cups crushed cornflakes**
- 2 **cups cold homemade mashed potatoes (without added milk and butter)**
- 2 **cups finely chopped fully cooked ham**
- 1 **cup (4 ounces) shredded Swiss cheese**
- 1/4 **cup finely chopped onion**
- 1/4 **cup milk**
- 1 **egg, beaten**
- 1 **teaspoon yellow mustard**

In a small bowl, combine the Dijon mustard, honey and 2 tablespoons mayonnaise until smooth. Cover and refrigerate until serving.
    Place cornflakes in a shallow bowl. In another bowl, combine the mashed potatoes, ham, cheese, onion, milk, egg, yellow mustard and remaining mayonnaise. Shape into 1-in. balls; roll in cornflakes. Place in three greased 15-in. x 10-in. x 1-in. baking pans. Cover and refrigerate for at least 1 hour.
    Bake at 350° for 30 minutes or until golden brown. Serve warm with the prepared mustard sauce. **Yield:** 5 dozen (1 cup sauce).

Pickled Veggie Salad

(Pictured below)

PREP: 20 min. **COOK:** 10 min. + marinating

I created this tangy side to use up brussels sprouts, and my family loved it.   —Bobbi Ballantine, Grove City, Pennsylvania

☑ **This recipe includes Nutrition Facts and Diabetic Exchanges.**

    1 **pound fresh brussels sprouts**
    1 **cup sugar**
  3/4 **cup white vinegar**
  1/2 **pound sliced fresh mushrooms**
    1 **small onion, chopped**
    2 **garlic cloves, minced**
    1 **tablespoon plus 1/4 cup canola oil,** *divided*
    1 **can (8 ounces) sliced water chestnuts, drained**
    2 **cans (2-1/4 ounces** *each***) sliced ripe olives, drained**
    2 **plum tomatoes, sliced**
    1 **jar (2 ounces) diced pimientos, drained**
    1 **tablespoon lemon juice**

Cut an "X" in the core of each brussels sprout. Place 1/2 in. of water in a large saucepan; add the brussels sprouts. Bring to a boil. Reduce heat; cover and simmer for 8-10 minutes or until tender.

Meanwhile, in a small saucepan, bring the sugar and vinegar to a boil; cook and stir for 1 minute or until the sugar is dissolved. Remove from the heat; cool slightly.

In a large skillet, saute mushrooms, onion and garlic in 1 tablespoon oil until tender. Transfer to a large bowl. Add the water chestnuts, olives, tomatoes, pimientos and lemon juice.

Drain brussels sprouts; cool slightly. Cut into quarters and add to the vegetable mixture. Add sugar mixture and remaining oil; toss to coat. Cover and refrigerate overnight. Serve the salad with a slotted spoon. **Yield:** 14 servings (1/2 cup each).

Nutrition Facts: 1/2 cup equals 114 calories, 5 g fat (trace saturated fat), 0 cholesterol, 90 mg sodium, 17 g carbohydrate, 2 g fiber, 2 g protein. **Diabetic Exchanges:** 1 vegetable, 1 fat, 1/2 starch.

Deli Beef Heroes

(Pictured above)

PREP/TOTAL TIME: 35 min.

Marinated artichokes, caramelized onions and green olives add lots of flavor to these crusty roast beef heroes spread with garlic and cheese. They're also good with corned beef or pastrami.
          —Cameron Byrne, Riverton, Wyoming

    2 **large onions, chopped**
  1/4 **cup olive oil**
    6 **ounces cream cheese, softened**
  3/4 **cup ricotta cheese**
  3/4 **cup pimiento-stuffed olives**
    2 **garlic cloves, peeled**
    2 **French bread baguettes (10-1/2 ounces** *each***), split**
    1 **pound sliced deli roast beef**
    2 **jars (7-1/2 ounces** *each***) roasted sweet red peppers, drained and julienned**
    2 **jars (7-1/2 ounces** *each***) marinated quartered artichoke hearts, drained and chopped**

In a large skillet, cook the onions in oil over low heat for 15-20 minutes or until golden brown, stirring occasionally.

Meanwhile, place the cream cheese, ricotta cheese, olives and garlic in a food processor. Cover and process until blended. Spread over baguettes.

Layer the bread bottoms with the roast beef, peppers, artichokes and caramelized onions; replace tops. Cut each into six slices. **Yield:** 12 servings.

SPEEDY SANDWICHES. Deli Beef Heroes (recipe above) are the perfect sandwiches to serve at a game-day party. To cut down on last-minute preparation, combine the ingredients for the olive spread and caramelize the onions the day before.

Layered Taco Salad

PREP/TOTAL TIME: 30 min.

This is so easy to assemble and a favorite at parties, especially football games. It's loaded with beef, cheese, sour cream—all of the favorites! —Elissa Dougherty, Babylon, New York

      1 pound ground beef
    2/3 cup water
      1 envelope taco seasoning
      2 medium ripe avocados, peeled and pitted
      2 tablespoons finely chopped red onion
      3 garlic cloves, minced
      1 teaspoon lemon juice
      4 cups shredded lettuce
      1 can (2-1/4 ounces) sliced ripe olives, drained
      2 medium tomatoes, chopped
      1 small cucumber, peeled and chopped
      5 green onions, chopped
      2 cups (8 ounces) shredded cheddar cheese
      1 cup salsa
      2 cups (16 ounces) sour cream
  Tortilla chips

In a small skillet, cook beef over medium heat until no longer pink; drain. Stir in water and taco seasoning. Bring to a boil; cook and stir for 2 minutes. Cool slightly.

In a small bowl, mash the avocados with onion, garlic and lemon juice. In a 3-qt. glass bowl, layer the beef, avocado mixture, lettuce, olives, tomatoes, cucumber, onions, cheese, salsa and sour cream. Serve immediately with chips. **Yield:** 12 servings (1 cup each).

Layered Lemon Pies

(Pictured at right)

PREP: 55 min. + chilling

My sister shared this creamy, sweet-tart dessert recipe with me. The key to its tongue-tingling taste is fresh lemon juice.
—Nanette Sorensen, Taylorsville, Utah

  Pastry for two single-crust pies (9 inch)
    1-1/2 cups sugar
        6 tablespoons cornstarch
      1/4 teaspoon salt
        2 cups cold water
        3 egg yolks, beaten
      1/3 cup lemon juice
      1/4 cup butter, cubed
        1 teaspoon grated lemon peel
        1 teaspoon lemon extract
        3 drops yellow food coloring, optional
  SECOND LAYER:
        1 package (8 ounces) cream cheese, softened
        1 cup confectioners' sugar
    1-1/2 cups cold 2% milk

        2 packages (3.4 ounces *each*) instant lemon
          pudding mix
  TOPPING:
        1 package (8 ounces) cream cheese, softened
        1 cup confectioners' sugar
        1 carton (16 ounces) frozen whipped topping,
          thawed

Line two 9-in. pie plates with pastry; trim and flute the edges. Line unpricked pastry with a double thickness of heavy-duty foil. Bake at 450° for 8 minutes. Remove foil; bake 5-7 minutes longer or until golden brown. Cool on wire racks.

In a large saucepan, combine the sugar, cornstarch and salt. Stir in water until smooth. Cook and stir over medium-high heat until thickened and bubbly. Reduce heat; cook and stir 2 minutes longer. Remove from heat.

Stir a small amount of hot filling into egg yolks; return all to the pan, stirring constantly. Bring to a gentle boil; cook and stir 2 minutes longer. Remove from the heat. Gently stir in lemon juice, butter, lemon peel, extract and food coloring if desired. Cool to room temperature without stirring. Spread the lemon mixture into crusts. Refrigerate for 30 minutes or until firm.

In a large bowl, beat cream cheese and confectioners' sugar until smooth. Gradually beat in milk. Add pudding mix; beat 2 minutes longer. Let stand for 2 minutes or until soft-set. Gently spread into the pies. Refrigerate for 30 minutes or until set.

For topping, in a large bowl, beat cream cheese and confectioners' sugar until smooth. Fold in the whipped topping. Spread over tops of pies. Refrigerate until set. **Yield:** 2 pies (10 servings each).

Roasted Vegetable Salad

(Pictured above)

PREP: 30 min. **BAKE:** 20 min.

For even more flavor, mix field greens and crumbled bacon into this appealing veggie salad. Or, whisk a tablespoon of honey into the dressing.   —Laura McAllister, Morganton, North Carolina

    1 pound small red potatoes, quartered
    2 medium ears sweet corn, halved
  1/2 pound baby portobello mushrooms, halved
    1 medium sweet red pepper, cut into strips
    2 medium leeks (white portion only), cut into
      2-inch lengths
  1/4 cup plus 2 tablespoons olive oil, *divided*
  1/2 teaspoon salt
  1/4 teaspoon pepper
  1/2 pound fresh asparagus, cut into 2-inch lengths
    2 garlic cloves, minced
  1/2 teaspoon crushed red pepper flakes
    2 cups cubed French bread
   10 cherry tomatoes, halved
    1 cup (4 ounces) crumbled feta cheese
    1 cup thinly sliced fresh basil leaves
DRESSING:
  1/3 cup olive oil
  1/4 cup red wine vinegar

In a large bowl, combine the first five ingredients. Drizzle with 1/4 cup oil; sprinkle with salt and pepper and toss to coat. Place in two greased 15-in. x 10-in. x 1-in. baking pans. Bake at 425° for 20-25 minutes or until potatoes are tender.

Meanwhile, in a large skillet, saute the asparagus in the remaining oil until tender. Add the garlic and red pepper flakes; cook 1 minute longer.

Cut corn from cobs; place in a large bowl. Stir in the bread, tomatoes, cheese, basil, asparagus and roasted vegetable mixture. Combine oil and vinegar; drizzle over the mixture and toss to coat. Serve immediately. **Yield:** 12 servings (2/3 cup each).

Peanut Butter Brownie Trifle

PREP: 1 hour + chilling

You can't beat the classic combo of chocolate and peanut butter in this crowd-pleaser. —Nancy Foust, Stoneboro, Pennsylvania

    1 fudge brownie mix (13-inch x 9-inch pan size)
    1 package (10 ounces) peanut butter chips
    2 packages (13 ounces *each*) miniature peanut
      butter cups
    4 cups cold 2% milk
    2 packages (5.1 ounces *each*) instant vanilla
      pudding mix
    1 cup creamy peanut butter
    4 teaspoons vanilla extract
    3 cartons (8 ounces *each*) frozen whipped
      topping, thawed

Prepare brownie batter according to package directions; stir in peanut butter chips. Bake in a greased 13-in. x 9-in. baking pan at 350° for 20-25 minutes or until a toothpick inserted near center comes out with moist crumbs (do not overbake). Cool on a wire rack; cut into 3/4-in. pieces.

Cut peanut butter cups in half; set aside 1/3 cup for garnish. In a large bowl, whisk milk and pudding mixes for 2 minutes. Let stand for 2 minutes or until soft-set. Add the peanut butter and vanilla; mix well. Fold in 1-1/2 cartons whipped topping.

Place a third of the brownies in a 5-qt. glass bowl; top with a third of the remaining peanut butter cups. Spoon a third of the pudding mixture over the top. Repeat layers twice. Cover with remaining whipped topping; garnish with reserved peanut butter cups. Refrigerate until chilled. **Yield:** 20 servings (1 cup each).

Lemon Delight Trifle

PREP: 30 min. + chilling

Serve this layered dessert in a trifle bowl, a glass 13-in. x 9-in. pan or any favorite dish.   —Kim Wallace, Dennison, Ohio

3-1/2 cups cold 2% milk
    2 packages (3.4 ounces *each*) instant lemon
      pudding mix
    1 package (8 ounces) cream cheese, softened
  1/2 cup butter, softened
  1/2 cup confectioners' sugar
    1 carton (12 ounces) frozen whipped topping,
      thawed, *divided*
    1 package (12 to 14 ounces) lemon cream-filled
      sandwich cookies, crushed

In a large bowl, whisk milk and pudding mixes for 2 minutes. Let stand for 2 minutes or until soft-set.

In another bowl, beat the cream cheese, butter and confectioners' sugar until smooth. Gradually stir in pudding until blended.

Set aside 1/4 cup each of whipped topping and crushed cookies for garnish. Fold remaining whipped topping into pudding mixture.

Place half of the remaining cookies in a 3-qt. glass bowl; top with half of the pudding mixture. Repeat layers. Garnish with the reserved whipped topping and crushed cookies. Refrigerate until serving. **Yield:** 12 servings (1 cup each).

Tex-Mex Chili

(Pictured below and on page 134)

PREP: 20 min. **COOK:** 6 hours

Meaty and spicy, this chili is for hearty appetites. The recipe calls for slow cooking, but you can also simmer it on the stove—the longer, the better! —Eric Hayes, Antioch, California

    3 pounds beef stew meat
    1 tablespoon canola oil
    3 garlic cloves, minced
    3 cans (16 ounces *each*) kidney beans, rinsed
      and drained
    3 cans (15 ounces *each*) tomato sauce
    1 can (14-1/2 ounces) diced tomatoes, undrained
    1 cup water
    1 can (6 ounces) tomato paste
  3/4 cup salsa verde
    1 envelope chili seasoning
    2 teaspoons dried minced onion
    1 teaspoon chili powder
  1/2 teaspoon crushed red pepper flakes
  1/2 teaspoon ground cumin
  1/2 teaspoon cayenne pepper
Shredded cheddar cheese and minced fresh cilantro

In a large skillet, brown the beef stew meat in oil in batches. Add the garlic to the pan; cook and stir for 1 minute. Transfer to a 6-qt. slow cooker.

Stir in remaining ingredients except cheese and cilantro. Cover and cook on low for 6-8 hours or until meat is tender. Garnish each serving with cheese and cilantro. **Yield:** 12 servings (1-1/3 cups each).

Fiesta Tuna Salad Sandwiches

(Pictured above)

PREP/TOTAL TIME: 20 min.

Sometimes I turn this tuna salad into a melt sandwich or use it as a dip. —Kimberly Stewart, Omaha, Nebraska

    6 cans (5 ounces *each*) white water-packed tuna,
      drained and flaked
    1 large red onion, chopped
    2 medium tomatoes, chopped
  2/3 cup reduced-fat mayonnaise
    2 jalapeno peppers, seeded and finely chopped
  1/4 cup lemon juice
    2 garlic cloves, minced
    1 teaspoon seafood seasoning
    1 teaspoon coarsely ground pepper
    2 loaves (14 ounces *each*) ciabatta bread, split
  3/4 pound sliced pepper Jack cheese
   12 lettuce leaves

In a large bowl, combine the first nine ingredients; spread over the bread bottoms. Layer with cheese and lettuce. Replace bread tops. Cut each loaf into six slices. **Yield:** 12 servings.

Editor's Note: When cutting hot peppers, disposable gloves are recommended. Avoid touching your face.

Summer Salad
With Lemon Vinaigrette

(Pictured above)

PREP/TOTAL TIME: 15 min.

This refreshing recipe goes well with grilled fish or chicken. We enjoy the lemony dressing at room temperature, so I make it first and let it rest on the counter while I toss the salad together.
—*Julie Kirkpatrick, Billings, Montana*

☑ **This recipe includes Nutrition Facts and Diabetic Exchanges.**

- 1/4 **cup lemon juice**
- 1/4 **cup olive oil**
- 2 **tablespoons balsamic vinegar**
- 2 **garlic cloves, minced**
- 1 **teaspoon salt**
- 1 **teaspoon grated lemon peel**
- 1 **teaspoon Dijon mustard**
- 1/2 **teaspoon pepper**
- 2 **packages (5-1/2 ounces *each*) torn mixed salad greens**
- 1 **medium red onion, sliced**
- 2 **cups sliced fresh mushrooms**
- 2 **cups fresh raspberries**
- 1 **cup chopped walnuts**

In a small bowl, whisk first eight ingredients. Refrigerate until serving.

In a salad bowl, combine greens, onion, mushrooms, raspberries and nuts. Drizzle with the dressing; toss to coat. Serve immediately. **Yield:** 16 servings (1 cup each).

Nutrition Facts: 1 cup equals 96 calories, 8 g fat (1 g saturated fat), 0 cholesterol, 161 mg sodium, 5 g carbohydrate, 2 g fiber, 3 g protein. **Diabetic Exchanges:** 1 fat, 1/2 starch.

Pumpkin Dessert Bars

(Pictured below and on page 135)

PREP: 35 min. **BAKE:** 20 min. + chilling

With a buttery crumb crust and smooth cream cheese layer, these dressed-up pumpkin bars are special enough to be the grand finale of your Thanksgiving dinner. A dollop of whipped topping and a sprinkling of nutmeg are the perfect finishing touches.
—*Tena Huckleby, Greenville, Tennessee*

- 1-3/4 **cups graham cracker crumbs**
- 1-1/3 **cups sugar, *divided***
- 1/2 **cup butter, melted**
- 1 **package (8 ounces) cream cheese, softened**
- 5 **eggs**
- 1 **can (15 ounces) solid-pack pumpkin**
- 1/2 **cup packed brown sugar**
- 1/2 **cup milk**
- 1/2 **teaspoon salt**
- 1/2 **teaspoon ground cinnamon**
- 1 **envelope unflavored gelatin**
- 1/4 **cup cold water**

Whipped topping and ground nutmeg, optional

In a small bowl, combine graham cracker crumbs and 1/3 cup sugar; stir in butter. Press into a greased 13-in. x 9-in. baking dish. In a small mixing bowl, beat cream cheese and 2/3 cup sugar until smooth. Beat in 2 eggs just until blended. Pour over crust. Bake at 350° for 20-25 minutes or until set. Cool on a wire rack.

Meanwhile, separate remaining eggs and set whites aside. In a large saucepan, combine the yolks, pumpkin, brown sugar, milk, salt and cinnamon. Cook and stir over low heat for 10-12 minutes or until mixture is thickened and reaches 160°. Remove from the heat.

In a small saucepan, sprinkle the gelatin over the cold water; let stand for 1 minute. Heat over low heat, stirring until the gelatin is completely dissolved. Stir into the pumpkin mixture; set aside.

In a large heavy saucepan, combine the reserved egg whites and the remaining sugar. With a portable mixer, beat on low speed for 1 minute. Continue beating over low heat until mixture reaches 160°, about 12 minutes. Remove from the heat; beat until stiff glossy peaks form and sugar is dissolved.

Fold into the pumpkin mixture; spread evenly over cream cheese layer. Cover and refrigerate for 4 hours or until set. Garnish with whipped topping and nutmeg if desired. **Yield:** 15 servings.

Wake Up! Breakfast Casserole

PREP: 20 min. + chilling **BAKE:** 55 min. + standing

Spiced with chorizo sausage and salsa, this eye–opener gets my day started with a kick. I like that I can assemble the casserole the night before, then pop it in the oven in the morning.
—*Kenna Jo Lambertsen, Nevada, Iowa*

- 1 **pound uncooked chorizo**
- 9 **eggs**
- 2-1/2 **cups 2% milk**
- 1 **tablespooon ground mustard**
- 1 **teaspoon cayenne pepper**
- 1 **package (28 ounces) frozen O'Brien potatoes**
- 2 **cups (8 ounces) shredded Monterey Jack cheese**
- 1 **jar (16 ounces) black bean and corn salsa**

Crumble chorizo into a large skillet; cook over medium heat for 6-8 minutes or until fully cooked. Drain.

In a large bowl, whisk the eggs, milk, mustard and cayenne. Stir in the potatoes, cheese, salsa and cooked chorizo. Transfer to a greased 13-in. x 9-in. baking dish. Cover and refrigerate overnight.

Remove from the refrigerator 30 minutes before baking. Bake, uncovered, at 350° for 55-65 minutes or until a knife inserted near center comes out clean. Let stand 10 minutes before cutting. **Yield:** 12 servings.

Pretty Pumpkin Wontons

PREP: 40 min. **COOK:** 15 min.

After having squash ravioli at a restaurant, I wanted to make my own version. I think this is a sensational recipe that can be served as an appeztizer or dessert. —*Joni Hilton, Rocklin, California*

✓ This recipe includes Nutrition Facts.

- 1 **can (15 ounces) solid-pack pumpkin**
- 1 **cup ricotta cheese**
- 1 **teaspoon salt**
- 40 **wonton wrappers**
- **Oil for deep-fat frying**
- **DIP:**
- 1 **cup confectioners' sugar**
- 1/2 **cup sour cream**
- 1/2 **cup apricot preserves**
- 1 **teaspoon ground cinnamon**

In a small bowl, combine the pumpkin, cheese and salt. Place 1 tablespoonful in the center of a wonton wrapper. (Keep remaining wrappers covered with a damp paper towel until ready to use.) Moisten the edges with water; bring corners to the center over filling and press edges together to seal. Repeat.

In an electric skillet or deep-fat fryer, heat oil to 375°. Fry wontons in batches for 30-60 seconds on each side or until golden brown. Drain on paper towels.

Meanwhile, in a small bowl, combine dip ingredients. Serve with wontons. **Yield:** 40 wontons (1-1/2 cups dip).

Nutrition Facts: 1 wonton with 2 teaspoons dip equals 81 calories, 4 g fat (1 g saturated fat), 5 mg cholesterol, 111 mg sodium, 11 g carbohydrate, 1 g fiber, 2 g protein.

Hot Wing Dip

(Pictured above and on page 134)

PREP: 10 min. **COOK:** 1 hour

This cheesy dip is a great "go–to" snack when unexpected guests drop by. —*Coleen Corner, Grove City, Pennsylvania*

- 2 **cups shredded cooked chicken**
- 1 **package (8 ounces) cream cheese, cubed**
- 2 **cups (8 ounces) shredded cheddar cheese**
- 1 **cup ranch salad dressing**
- 1/2 **cup Louisiana-style hot sauce**
- **Tortilla chips *and/or* celery sticks**
- **Minced fresh parsley, optional**

In a 3-qt. slow cooker, combine chicken, cream cheese, cheddar, ranch salad dressing and hot sauce. Cover and cook on low for 1 hour or until cheese is melted.

Serve with chips and/or celery. Sprinkle with parsley if desired. **Yield:** 4-1/2 cups.

in a greased 13-in. x 9-in. baking dish.

In a large saucepan, melt remaining butter. Stir in the flour until smooth; gradually add the cream, broth and milk. Bring to a boil; cook and stir for 1-2 minutes or until thickened.

Stir in the Romano cheese and the remaining cream cheese, Asiago cheese and parsley. Pour over the shells. Sprinkle with mozzarella cheese. Cover and bake at 350° for 30 minutes. Uncover; bake 10-15 minutes longer or until bubbly. **Yield:** 12 servings.

Balsamic Pork Scallopine

(Pictured below)

PREP: 25 min. **COOK:** 30 min.

When my sister wanted to fix a romantic dinner for her fiance, I created this dish by tweaking my veal scallopine recipe. It was a tasty success.   —Mary Cokenour, Monticello, Utah

      3 **pounds pork sirloin cutlets**
  1-1/2 **cups all-purpose flour**
    1/2 **cup olive oil**
      2 **tablespoons butter**
      1 **medium onion, chopped**
    1/2 **cup chopped roasted sweet red peppers**
      6 **garlic cloves, minced**
      1 **can (14-1/2 ounces) reduced-sodium chicken broth**
    1/2 **cup minced fresh basil** *or* **2 tablespoons dried basil**
    1/2 **cup balsamic vinegar**
    1/2 **teaspoon pepper**
NOODLES:
      1 **package (16 ounces) egg noodles**
    1/2 **cup half-and-half cream**
    1/4 **cup grated Romano cheese**
    1/4 **cup butter, cubed**
    1/2 **teaspoon pepper**
    1/4 **teaspoon garlic powder**

Bacon-Cheese Stuffed Shells

(Pictured above)

PREP: 45 min. **BAKE:** 40 min.

These creamy and cheesy shells will satisfy even the pickiest eater. I make them for parties and when friends drop by for supper.
            —Bekie Anderson, Austin, Texas

     24 **uncooked jumbo pasta shells**
      1 **cup chopped fresh mushrooms**
      1 **cup finely chopped onion**
      1 **tablespoon plus 1/4 cup butter,** *divided*
  1-1/2 **cups ricotta cheese**
      1 **package (8 ounces) cream cheese, softened,** *divided*
  1-1/2 **cups shredded Asiago cheese,** *divided*
      1 **cup shredded Parmesan cheese**
      1 **cup crumbled cooked bacon**
      2 **tablespoons minced fresh parsley,** *divided*
    1/2 **teaspoon garlic salt**
    1/2 **teaspoon ground nutmeg**
    1/4 **teaspoon pepper**
      2 **tablespoons all-purpose flour**
      2 **cups heavy whipping cream**
    1/2 **cup chicken broth**
    1/2 **cup 2% milk**
      2 **cups shredded Romano cheese**
  1-1/2 **cups shredded part-skim mozzarella cheese**

Cook the pasta according to the package directions. Meanwhile, in a large skillet, saute mushrooms and onion in 1 tablespoon butter until tender.

In a large bowl, beat ricotta and 4 oz. cream cheese until blended. Stir in 1/2 cup Asiago cheese, Parmesan cheese, bacon, 1 tablespoon parsley, garlic salt, nutmeg, pepper and mushroom mixture. Spoon into shells; place

Dredge the pork cutlets in flour. Heat oil and butter in a large skillet over medium-high heat; add the pork and brown in batches. Set aside.

Add the onion and red peppers to the pan; saute until onion is tender. Add garlic; cook 1 minute longer. Add the broth, basil, vinegar and pepper. Return pork to the pan, layering if necessary. Cover and cook over low heat for 15-20 minutes or meat is no longer pink.

Meanwhile, in a Dutch oven, cook noodles according to package directions. Drain; stir in the cream, cheese, butter, pepper and garlic powder. Serve with the pork. **Yield:** 12 servings.

Italian Sausage Grinders

PREP: 15 min. **COOK:** 30 min.

These well-seasoned sandwiches have been a part of countless meals in our family. I eliminated the anise seed from the original version, but the grinders are wonderful with or without it.
—*Sally Yeagle, Burlington, Wisconsin*

- 12 **Italian sausage links (4 ounces *each*)**
- 3 **tablespoons olive oil**
- 1-1/2 **cups water**
- 2 **cans (6 ounces *each*) tomato paste**
- 1 **can (8 ounces) tomato sauce**
- 3 **garlic cloves, minced**
- 1 **teaspoon sugar**
- 1 **teaspoon *each* dried basil, oregano and parsley flakes**
- 12 **brat buns, split and toasted**
- 1/4 **cup shredded Parmesan cheese**

In a large skillet, brown sausages in oil; drain. Stir in the water, tomato paste, tomato sauce, garlic, sugar and seasonings; bring to a boil. Reduce heat; cover and simmer for 20 minutes or until meat is no longer pink.

Serve the sausages on buns with sauce; sprinkle with Parmesan cheese. **Yield:** 12 servings.

The Best Eggplant Parmesan

(Pictured above right)

PREP: 1-1/4 hours **BAKE:** 35 min. + standing

I love eggplant and have many recipes for it, but this casserole is my all-time favorite and always makes a standout main course.
—*Dottie Kilpatrick, Wilmington, North Carolina*

- 3 **garlic cloves, minced**
- 1/3 **cup olive oil**
- 2 **cans (28 ounces *each*) crushed tomatoes**
- 1 **cup pitted ripe olives, chopped**
- 1/4 **cup thinly sliced fresh basil leaves *or* 1 tablespoon dried basil**
- 3 **tablespoons capers, drained**
- 1 **teaspoon crushed red pepper flakes**
- 1/4 **teaspoon pepper**

EGGPLANT:
- 1 **cup all-purpose flour**
- 4 **eggs, beaten**
- 3 **cups dry bread crumbs**
- 1 **tablespoon garlic powder**
- 1 **tablespoon minced fresh oregano *or* 1 teaspoon dried oregano**
- 4 **small eggplants (about 1 pound *each*), peeled and cut lengthwise into 1/2-inch slices**
- 1 **cup olive oil**

CHEESE:
- 2 **eggs, beaten**
- 2 **cartons (15 ounces *each*) ricotta cheese**
- 1-1/4 **cups shredded Parmesan cheese, *divided***
- 1/2 **cup thinly sliced fresh basil leaves *or* 2 tablespoons dried basil**
- 1/2 **teaspoon pepper**
- 8 **cups (32 ounces) shredded part-skim mozzarella cheese**

In a Dutch oven over medium heat, cook garlic in oil for 1 minute. Stir in the tomatoes, olives, basil, capers, pepper flakes and pepper. Bring to a boil. Reduce heat; simmer, uncovered, for 45-60 minutes or until thickened.

Meanwhile, for eggplant, place flour and eggs in separate shallow bowls. In another bowl, combine the bread crumbs, garlic powder and oregano. Dip eggplant in the flour, eggs, then bread crumb mixture.

In a large skillet, cook the eggplant in batches in oil for 5 minutes on each side or until tender. Drain on paper towels. In a large bowl, combine the eggs, ricotta, 1/2 cup Parmesan cheese, basil and pepper.

In each of two greased 13-in. x 9-in. baking dishes, layer 1-1/2 cups tomato sauce, four eggplant slices, 1 cup ricotta mixture and 2 cups mozzarella cheese. Repeat layers. Sprinkle each with remaining Parmesan cheese. Bake, uncovered, at 350° for 35-40 minutes or until bubbly. Let stand for 10 minutes before cutting. **Yield:** 2 casseroles (8 servings each).

pork chops to the pan and heat through, spooning the sauce over the top. Cook until slightly thickened. **Yield:** 2 servings.

Nutrition Facts: 1 pork chop with 1/3 cup sauce equals 306 calories, 12 g fat (3 g saturated fat), 68 mg cholesterol, 679 mg sodium, 20 g carbohydrate, 2 g fiber, 29 g protein. **Diabetic Exchanges:** 4 lean meat, 1 starch, 1 fat.

Hawaiian Beef Dish

PREP/TOTAL TIME: 25 min.

This all-in-one meal has been in my family since I was a young girl and gets rave reviews from guests. It was created by my dad, who still enjoys experimenting in the kitchen. Sometimes I make this the day before and warm it up while I'm cooking the rice.
—*Marilyn Taus, Mississauga, Ontario*

- **1/2 pound lean ground beef**
- **1 medium onion, halved and sliced**
- **1/3 cup sliced celery**
- **1/3 cup chopped green pepper**
- **1 garlic clove, minced**
- **2 teaspoons butter**
- **1 can (8 ounces) unsweetened pineapple chunks**
- **1/4 cup packed brown sugar**
- **1 tablespoon all-purpose flour**
- **1 tablespoon white wine vinegar**
- **1/4 teaspoon salt**
- **1 cup hot cooked rice**

In a small skillet, cook the beef over medium heat until no longer pink; drain and set aside. In the same skillet, saute the onion, celery, green pepper and garlic in butter for 5 minutes or until crisp-tender.

Drain the pineapple, reserving the juice; set pineapple aside. Add enough water to pineapple juice to measure 1/2 cup. In a bowl, combine the brown sugar, flour, vinegar, salt and pineapple juice mixture until smooth. Add to skillet.

Bring to a boil. Cook and stir over medium heat for 2 minutes. Stir in beef and pineapple; heat through. Serve with rice. **Yield:** 2 servings.

Curried Apricot Pork Chops

(*Pictured above and on page 147*)

PREP/TOTAL TIME: 30 min.

A fruit glaze that's both sweet and savory enhances these tender pork chops. They're pretty and tasty enough for a special dinner.
—*Trisha Kruse, Eagle, Idaho*

✓ This recipe includes Nutrition Facts and Diabetic Exchanges.

- **2 tablespoons apricot nectar**
- **1 tablespoon plus 1-1/2 teaspoons apricot preserves**
- **1 tablespoon Dijon mustard**
- **1 tablespoon reduced-sodium soy sauce**
- **1 teaspoon curry powder**
- **2 boneless pork loin chops (5 ounces *each*)**
- **1/8 teaspoon salt**
- **1/8 teaspoon pepper**
- **1-1/2 teaspoons canola oil**
- **1/2 cup sliced fresh apricots**
- **2 green onions, sliced**

In a small bowl, combine the first five ingredients; set mixture aside.

Sprinkle the pork chops with salt and pepper. In a small nonstick skillet, cook chops in oil for 5-7 minutes on each side or until a meat thermometer reads 160°. Remove and set aside.

Add the apricots and onions to the pan; cook and stir for 2 minutes. Stir in the nectar mixture. Return the

---

COOKING WITH CURRY. Used in Curried Apricot Pork Chops (recipe at left), curry powder adds exotic flavor to vegetables, meat, chicken, seafood, soups, stews and even fruit. Here are some handy hints for cooking with curry:

• To improve the flavor of store-bought curry powder, saute the spices lightly in a little butter or oil before using.

• To enjoy the flavor of curry in a flash, stir a bit into mayonnaise and spread it on sandwiches.

Hamburger Noodle Bake

(Pictured below and on page 147)

PREP: 35 min. **BAKE:** 20 min.

Cream cheese and cottage cheese balance the saucy ground beef and noodles in this hearty casserole. It's a great "go-to" dinner.
—Charissa Dunn, Bartlesville, Oklahoma

- 2 cups uncooked egg noodles
- 1/2 pound lean ground beef (90% lean)
- 2 tablespoons finely chopped onion
- 1 can (8 ounces) tomato sauce
- 1/4 teaspoon sugar
- 1/8 teaspoon salt
- 1/8 teaspoon garlic salt
- Dash pepper
- 1/4 cup cream-style cottage cheese
- 2 ounces cream cheese, softened
- 1 tablespoon thinly sliced green onion
- 1 tablespoon chopped green pepper
- 1 tablespoon sour cream
- 2 tablespoons grated Parmesan cheese

Cook the noodles according to the package directions. Meanwhile, in a large skillet, cook beef and onion until meat is no longer pink; drain. Remove from the heat; stir in the tomato sauce, sugar, salt, garlic salt and pepper. In a small bowl, combine the cottage cheese, cream cheese, green onion, green pepper and sour cream.

Drain noodles; place half of the noodles in a greased 1-quart baking dish. Spoon half of beef mixture over the top. Layer with cottage cheese mixture and remaining noodles. Top with the remaining beef mixture; sprinkle with Parmesan cheese.

Cover and bake at 350° for 20-25 minutes or until the casserole is heated through. **Yield:** 2 servings.

Cowboy Casserole

(Pictured above)

PREP: 15 min. **BAKE:** 20 min.

This cheesy and creamy Tater Tot bake is comfort food for two. You'll love it, especially on a chilly autumn or winter evening.
—Donna Donhauser, Remsen, New York

- 1/2 pound lean ground beef (90% lean)
- 1 can (8-3/4 ounces) whole kernel corn, drained
- 2/3 cup condensed cream of chicken soup, undiluted
- 1/2 cup shredded cheddar cheese, *divided*
- 1/3 cup 2% milk
- 2 tablespoons sour cream
- 3/4 teaspoon onion powder
- 1/4 teaspoon pepper
- 2 cups frozen Tater Tots

In a large skillet, cook beef over medium heat until no longer pink. Stir in the corn, soup, 1/4 cup cheese, milk, sour cream, onion powder and pepper.

Place 1 cup Tater Tots in a 3-cup baking dish coated with cooking spray. Layer with the beef mixture and remaining Tater Tots; sprinkle with the remaining cheese. Bake, uncovered, at 375° for 20-25 minutes or until bubbly. **Yield:** 2 servings.

Chicken Wrapped in Bacon

(Pictured below)

PREP: 20 min. **BAKE:** 35 min.

My husband and I like both chicken and spicy food. This simple, sized-for-two main dish can be changed to a different degree of heat simply by switching from green chilies to jalapeno peppers. Either way, it's a moist, tender and delicious dinner.
—*LaDonna Reed, Ponca City, Oklahoma*

- **6 bacon strips**
- **2 boneless skinless chicken breast halves (5 ounces *each*)**
- **1 package (3 ounces) cream cheese, softened**
- **2 garlic cloves, minced**
- **1/2 teaspoon salt**
- **1 can (4 ounces) chopped green chilies, drained**

In a large skillet, cook the bacon over medium heat until cooked but not crisp. Remove to paper towels to drain. Flatten the chicken breast halves to 1/8-in. thickness. Spread with cream cheese; sprinkle with garlic and salt. Top with green chilies. Roll up from a long side and tuck the ends in.

Wrap three bacon strips around each piece of chicken; secure with toothpicks. Place in a greased 1-qt. baking dish. Bake, uncovered, at 350° for 35-40 minutes or until chicken juices run clear and bacon is crisp. Discard the toothpicks before serving. **Yield:** 2 servings.

Lemon Scallop Linguine

PREP/TOTAL TIME: 20 min.

I was experimenting in the kitchen with new ways of combining foods I love, and this recipe turned out flavorful and satisfying. When I have guests, I serve it in scallop shells alongside colorful mixed vegetables and dinner rolls to round out the menu.
—*Elizabeth Kudriavetz, Carver, Massachusetts*

- **4 ounces uncooked linguine**
- **1 teaspoon dried minced onion**
- **3 tablespoons butter**
- **3/4 pound bay scallops**
- **1/8 teaspoon lemon-pepper seasoning**
- **Pinch pepper**
- **2 tablespoons lemon juice**
- **Minced fresh parsley**

Cook the linguine according to the package directions. Meanwhile, in a skillet, saute minced onion in butter over medium heat for 2-3 minutes or until golden. Add the scallops, lemon-pepper seasoning and pepper. Cook and stir for 4-5 minutes or until the scallops are firm and opaque.

Add the lemon juice; cook 1 minute longer. Drain the linguine; toss with scallop mixture. Sprinkle with the parsley. **Yield:** 2 servings.

Chicken Dinner Packets

PREP: 15 min. **BAKE:** 25 min.

This tasty chicken is baked in foil packets—which saves both time and dishes! The veggies make it a complete meal-in-one.
—*Jeanne Barney, Saratoga Springs, New York*

- **1/2 pound boneless skinless chicken breasts, cut into strips**
- **2 small red potatoes, thinly sliced**
- **3/4 cup shredded cheddar cheese**
- **1/2 small sweet red pepper, julienned**
- **1/2 small green pepper, julienned**
- **2 tablespoons barbecue sauce**
- **1 green onion, chopped**
- **1/4 teaspoon salt**
- **1/8 teaspoon pepper**

Divide the chicken breast strips between two pieces of heavy-duty foil (about 12 in. square).

In a small bowl, combine the remaining ingredients; spoon over the chicken strips. Fold the foil around the mixture and seal tightly.

Place the packets on a baking sheet. Bake at 375° for 25-30 minutes or until the chicken juices run clear and potatoes are tender. Open foil carefully to allow steam to escape. **Yield:** 2 servings.

Turkey Saltimbocca

(Pictured above)

PREP/TOTAL TIME: 30 min.

Here's an Italian twist on a holiday staple. It combines sage and prosciutto for a tenderloin that's so good, you won't believe it's made in a skillet. —Deirdre Dee Cox, Milwaukee, Wisconsin

- **1 turkey breast tenderloin (8 ounces)**
- **1/8 teaspoon pepper**
- **1/4 cup all-purpose flour**
- **2 tablespoons butter,** *divided*
- **1-1/2 teaspoons olive oil**
- **1 thin slice prosciutto** *or* **deli ham, cut into thin strips**
- **2 tablespoons minced fresh sage**
- **1/4 cup white wine** *or* **chicken broth**

Cut tenderloin in half lengthwise; flatten each half to 1/2-in. thickness. Sprinkle with pepper. Place flour in a large shallow bowl; add turkey, one piece at a time, and turn to coat.

In a large skillet, cook turkey in 1 tablespoon butter and oil over medium heat for 3-4 minutes on each side or until no longer pink. Remove and keep warm.

In the same skillet, saute the prosciutto and sage in 1-1/2 teaspoons butter until slightly crisp. Add the wine, stirring to loosen browned bits from the pan. Bring to a boil; cook until the liquid is slightly reduced. Remove from heat; stir in the remaining butter. Serve with the turkey. **Yield:** 2 servings.

Twice-Baked Sweet Potatoes

(Pictured above)

PREP: 20 min. **BAKE:** 15 min.

Almost everyone loves twice-baked potatoes, but I think they're even better made with sweet potatoes! This microwave recipe turns an ordinary vegetable into a dish fit for a special occasion. —Darlene Brenden, Salem, Oregon

- **2 medium sweet potatoes**
- **2 ounces cream cheese, softened**
- **2 tablespoons sour cream**
- **1 tablespoon butter**
- **1/4 teaspoon salt**
- **2 tablespoons brown sugar**
- **1/2 teaspoon ground cinnamon**

Scrub and pierce potatoes; place on a microwave-safe plate. Microwave, uncovered, on high for 12-14 minutes or until tender, turning once.

When cool enough to handle, cut a thin slice off the top of each potato and discard. Scoop out the pulp, leaving a thin shell. In a large bowl, mash the pulp. Add the cream cheese, sour cream, butter and salt; mix well. Spoon into potato shells.

Place the potatoes on a baking sheet. Sprinkle with brown sugar and cinnamon. Bake, uncovered, at 425° for 12-15 minutes or until heated through and the topping is golden brown. **Yield:** 2 servings.

Editor's Note: This recipe was tested in a 1,100-watt microwave.

Downsized Desserts

WHY BAKE a full-size cake, pie or other dessert when there are only one or two of you at the table? Thanks to the cleverly reduced recipes here, you can indulge your sweet tooth in something extra-special without fixing more food than you need.

Home-style treats aren't out of reach when you want to downsize your cooking. Just consider refreshing Strawberry Cream Pie, Classic Cheesecake, Homemade Chocolate Pudding and luscious Apple Pie Dessert, complete with a from-scratch butter sauce.

Simply choose your favorite, then enjoy an after-dinner delight that's sized right for you!

Classic Cheesecake

(Pictured below and on page 146)

PREP: 30 min. **BAKE:** 35 min. + chilling

My husband and I love desserts, and this two-serving cheesecake is a winner. Because there are no leftovers, there are no extra calories, either! —*Therese Fortier, Grand Rapids, Michigan*

   1/4　cup graham cracker crumbs
     1　teaspoon sugar
4-1/2　teaspoons butter, melted
FILLING:
     1　package (3 ounces) cream cheese, softened
   1/4　cup sugar
     1　egg, lightly beaten
     1　teaspoon lemon juice
   1/2　teaspoon grated lemon peel
TOPPING:
   1/4　cup sour cream
     2　teaspoons sugar
   1/4　teaspoon vanilla extract

In a small bowl, combine the cracker crumbs and sugar; stir in butter. Press onto the bottom of a greased 4-in. springform pan. Place on a baking sheet. Bake at 350° for 5 minutes. Cool on a wire rack.

In a small mixing bowl, beat cream cheese and sugar until smooth. Add the egg; beat on low speed just until combined. Stir in lemon juice and peel.

Pour over the crust. Return pan to baking sheet. Bake at 350° for 25-30 minutes or until the center is almost set. Remove from the oven; let stand for 5 minutes (leave oven on).

Combine the topping ingredients; carefully spread over filling. Bake 5 minutes longer. Cool on a wire rack for 10 minutes.

Carefully run a knife around the edge of the pan to loosen; cool 1 hour longer. Refrigerate the cheesecake overnight. Remove the sides of pan just before serving. **Yield:** 2 servings.

Editor's Note: This recipe may be prepared in a 2-cup baking dish. Prepare as directed. Increase the topping amounts to the following: 3/4 cup sour cream, 2 tablespoons sugar and 3/4 teaspoon vanilla.

Apple Pie Dessert

PREP: 25 min. **BAKE:** 25 min.

My aunt passed along this recipe, a wonderful autumn dessert for two. It has all of the taste of traditional apple pie but isn't as time-consuming to prepare. With the special touch of a warm, homemade butter sauce, it always gets rave reviews.
—*Jeanie Krimm, West Hills, California*

1/4　cup butter, softened
1/3　cup sugar
  1　egg
1/2　cup all-purpose flour
1/4　teaspoon baking soda
1/8　teaspoon salt
1/8　teaspoon ground cinnamon
1/8　teaspoon ground nutmeg
  1　cup chopped tart apple
1/4　cup chopped walnuts
BUTTER SAUCE:
1/4　cup sugar

Stir in the chocolate chips; cook and stir until melted. Remove from the heat. Stir in the vanilla. Spoon the pudding into dessert dishes. Serve warm or chilled. **Yield:** 2 servings.

Strawberry Cream Pie

(Pictured below)

PREP: 25 min. + chilling

My mother treated us to strawberry desserts each spring when there was a fresh harvest of berries, and this pie was the one we looked forward to most. I added the chocolate cookie crust to the recipe, and now I make it that way all the time.
—*Judith Kapcsos, Colorado City, Arizona*

- 1/2 cup plus 2 tablespoons crushed cream-filled chocolate sandwich cookies (7 cookies)
- 2 tablespoons sugar
- 2 tablespoons butter, melted

FILLING:
- 4 ounces cream cheese, softened
- 2 tablespoons sugar
- 1/2 teaspoon vanilla extract
- 1/2 cup mashed fresh strawberries
- 1/2 cup heavy whipping cream
- 2 tablespoons confectioners' sugar

For the crust, combine the chocolate sandwich cookie crumbs, sugar and butter; press into a 6-in. pie plate. Bake at 375° for 8 minutes. Cool the crust completely on a wire rack.

In a small mixing bowl, beat the cream cheese, sugar and vanilla until smooth. Stir in strawberries. In another small mixing bowl, beat whipping cream until it begins to thicken.

Gradually add confectioners' sugar, beating until stiff peaks form. Fold into the cream cheese mixture. Spoon into the crust. Refrigerate for 4 hours or overnight. **Yield:** 3-4 servings.

- 1-1/2 teaspoons cornstarch
- 1/8 teaspoon salt
- 1/2 cup water
- 1 tablespoon butter
- 1/2 teaspoon vanilla extract

In a small mixing bowl, cream the butter and sugar. Add the egg and mix well. Combine the flour, baking soda, salt, cinnamon and nutmeg; add to creamed mixture and mix well. Stir in apple and walnuts.

Transfer to a greased 7-in. pie plate. Bake at 350° for 25-35 minutes or until a toothpick inserted near the center comes out clean.

For the sauce, in a small saucepan, combine the sugar, cornstarch and salt. Gradually stir in the water until smooth. Bring to a boil; cook and stir for 2 minutes or until thickened.

Remove from the heat; stir in butter and vanilla. Serve warm with dessert. **Yield:** 2 servings.

Homemade Chocolate Pudding

(Pictured above)

PREP/TOTAL TIME: 15 min.

Every time I fix this yummy treat, I think of my mom. She used to make it whenever she could. During the Great Depression, it was hard to find chocolate, but when she found some, she saved enough to make this pudding because we loved it so much.
—*Maribeth Janus, Ivoryton, Connecticut*

- 2 tablespoons sugar
- 1 tablespoon cornstarch
- 1 cup milk
- 1/3 cup semisweet chocolate chips
- 1/2 teaspoon vanilla extract

In a small saucepan, combine sugar and cornstarch. Add milk; stir until smooth. Cook and stir over medium heat until mixture comes to a boil. Cook and stir 1-2 minutes longer or until thickened.

Julia's Green Beans & Mushrooms

(Pictured above)

PREP/TOTAL TIME: 30 min.

My mother prepared fresh green beans a number of ways. I've put my own stamp on them with this bean–and–mushroom side.
—Julia Beccari, Lewiston, New York

- 1/3 **pound fresh green beans, trimmed**
- 1 **cup sliced fresh mushrooms**
- 1 **tablespoon olive oil**
- 2-1/2 **teaspoons butter**
- 1/4 **teaspoon dried parsley flakes**
- Dash *each* **seasoned salt, garlic powder and coarsely ground pepper**
- 1 **tablespoon dry bread crumbs**
- 1-1/2 **teaspoons grated Romano cheese**

Place beans in a small saucepan and cover with water. Bring to a boil. Cover and cook for 4-7 minutes or until crisp-tender.

Meanwhile, in a small skillet, saute the mushrooms in oil and butter until tender. Stir in the parsley flakes, seasoned salt, garlic powder and pepper. Add bread crumbs; cook until lightly browned.

Drain beans; toss with mushroom mixture. Sprinkle with the cheese. **Yield:** 2 servings.

Berry-Port Game Hens

(Pictured above)

PREP: 20 min. **BAKE:** 50 min.

This recipe uses only a handful of ingredients to create a simple but elegant entree fit for a holiday or other special occasion.
—Josephine Piro, Easton, Pennsylvania

- 1 **large orange**
- 2 **Cornish game hens (20 to 24 ounces *each*)**
- 1/2 **teaspoon salt**
- 1/2 **teaspoon pepper**
- 1 **cup ruby port wine *and/or* grape juice**
- 1/4 **cup seedless strawberry jam**
- 5 **teaspoons stone-ground mustard**

Finely grate peel from orange to measure 1 teaspoon. Cut orange in half widthwise; cut a thin slice from each half. Quarter slices and set aside. Juice the orange to measure 1/4 cup.

Loosen the skin around hen breasts and thighs; place orange slices under the skin.

Place the hens in greased 13-in. x 9-in. baking dish. Sprinkle with salt and pepper. Bake, uncovered, at 350° for 40 minutes. Meanwhile, in a small saucepan, combine the wine, jam and orange juice. Bring to a boil. Reduce the heat; simmer, uncovered, for 6-8 minutes or until slightly thickened. Stir in the mustard and orange peel.

Set aside 1/2 cup sauce for serving; brush remaining sauce over the hens. Bake hens 10-20 minutes longer or until a meat thermometer reads 180°, basting occasionally with pan juices. Warm reserved sauce; serve with hens. **Yield:** 2 servings.

Broccoli Salad

PREP: 15 min. + chilling

After sampling this salad at a barbecue, I asked for the recipe but didn't get the measurements. I experimented on my own, and now I can toss it together with delicious results every time.
—*Sara Sherlock, Port Alice, British Columbia*

  1-1/2 cups fresh broccoli florets
    3/4 cup shredded cheddar cheese
      4 bacon strips, cooked and crumbled
    1/4 cup finely chopped onion
      3 tablespoons mayonnaise
      2 tablespoons white vinegar
      1 tablespoon sugar

In a bowl, combine the broccoli, cheese, bacon and onion. In another bowl, whisk the mayonnaise, vinegar and sugar. Pour over broccoli mixture and toss to coat. Cover and refrigerate for at least 1 hour before serving. **Yield:** 2 servings.

Quick Pizza Sandwiches

PREP/TOTAL TIME: 20 min.

I came up with this recipe years ago when we needed a super-fast supper after a busy day of activities. The saucy, beefy sandwiches have great pizza flavor and go well with a salad and deli pickles. It's my husband's and grandchildren's favorite meal.
—*Marge Barto, Poquoson, Virginia*

  1/2 pound ground beef
  1/4 teaspoon salt
  1/4 teaspoon onion powder
  1/4 teaspoon garlic powder
  1/4 teaspoon Italian seasoning
  1/4 teaspoon rubbed sage
Dash pepper
  3/4 cup pizza sauce
    1 loaf (8 ounces) French bread, halved lengthwise
  1/4 cup shredded part-skim mozzarella cheese

In a small bowl, mix the beef and seasonings just until combined. Divide into six portions; shape each into a 1-1/2-in. patty.

In a large nonstick skillet, cook the patties for 3-1/2 to 4-1/2 minutes on each side or until the meat is no longer pink; drain. Pour the pizza sauce over patties and heat through. Spoon onto French bread; sprinkle with the cheese. Cut into sandwiches. **Yield:** 2 servings.

Corn Bread Salad

(Pictured below)

PREP/TOTAL TIME: 20 min.

This unusual side is a palate-pleasing combination of texture and taste. Present it in a lettuce-lined bowl for extra appeal.
—*Marge Price, Dothan, Alabama*

  1-1/2 cups coarsely crumbled corn bread
    1/4 cup diced tomato
    1/4 cup diced green pepper
    1/4 cup chopped green onions
    1/4 cup chopped celery
      3 tablespoons mayonnaise
      2 bacon strips, cooked and crumbled

In a small bowl, combine the corn bread, tomato, green pepper, onions and celery. Add the mayonnaise; toss to coat. Sprinkle with the bacon. Serve immediately. **Yield:** 2 servings.

Tuscan Pork Medallions

(Pictured below and on page 146)

PREP/TOTAL TIME: 30 min.

These beautifully browned, Italian-style pork slices are quick enough for weeknights yet are sure to impress a dinner guest. The recipe takes just 30 minutes to prepare from start to finish, but the result is an entree that looks and tastes time-consuming.
—Lorraine Caland, Thunder Bay, Ontario

- 3/4 **pound pork tenderloin, cut into 1-inch slices**
- 1/4 **teaspoon salt**
- 1/8 **teaspoon pepper**
- 1 **tablespoon butter**
- 2 **thin slices prosciutto** *or* **deli ham, chopped**
- 2 **garlic cloves, minced**
- 1-1/2 **teaspoons minced fresh sage** *or* **1/2 teaspoon dried sage leaves**
- 2 **tablespoons balsamic vinegar**
- 1/2 **cup heavy whipping cream**
- 3/4 **cup chopped plum tomatoes**
- 4 **fresh basil leaves, thinly sliced**
- 1 **teaspoon grated Parmesan cheese**

Sprinkle pork with salt and pepper. In a large skillet over medium heat, cook pork in butter until no longer pink. Remove; set aside.

In the same skillet, saute prosciutto in the drippings until browned. Add the garlic and sage; cook 1 minute longer. Add the balsamic vinegar, stirring to loosen browned bits from pan.

Stir in the cream; bring to a boil. Reduce heat; cook and stir for 1-2 minutes or until slightly thickened. Add tomatoes and pork; heat through. Sprinkle each serving with basil and cheese. **Yield:** 2 servings.

Tomato-Basil Baked Fish

PREP/TOTAL TIME: 10 min.

This recipe has it all! It can be used with several different kinds of fish, and the ingredients are ones I usually have on hand. Plus, baking the fillets is so easy...and the flavor is terrific.
—Annie Hicks, Zephyrhills, Florida

- 1 **teaspoon lemon juice**
- 1 **teaspoon olive oil**
- 8 **ounces orange roughy, red snapper, cod** *or* **haddock fillets**
- 1/4 **teaspoon dried basil**
- 1/8 **teaspoon salt**
- 1/8 **teaspoon pepper**
- 2 **plum tomatoes, thinly sliced**
- 2 **teaspoons grated Parmesan cheese**

In a shallow dish, combine the lemon juice and oil. Add the fish fillets; turn to coat. Place in a greased 9-in. square baking dish. Sprinkle with basil, salt and pepper. Arrange the tomato slices on top; sprinkle with the Parmesan cheese.

Cover and bake at 400° for 10-12 minutes or until fish flakes easily with a fork. **Yield:** 2 servings.

Veggie Rice Saute

PREP/TOTAL TIME: 25 min.

I came up with this meatless recipe one day when I had nothing but burgers to go on the grill and not enough of any one veggie. It was delicious!
—Claudia Resac, Holmen, Wisconsin

- 3 **tablespoons vegetable oil,** *divided*
- 1 **egg, lightly beaten**
- 3/4 **cup cut fresh green beans (1/2-inch pieces)**
- 1/4 **cup chopped onion**
- 3/4 **cup thinly sliced quartered zucchini**
- 3/4 **cup thinly sliced fresh mushrooms**
- 1 **garlic clove, minced**
- 1-1/2 **cups cooked long grain rice**
- 2 **tablespoons soy sauce**

In a small skillet, heat 1 tablespoon vegetable oil over medium-high heat. Add egg. As egg sets, lift the edges, letting the uncooked portion flow underneath. Remove egg and chop into small pieces; set aside.

In same skillet, saute beans and onion in remaining oil for 1-2 minutes. Add the zucchini, mushrooms and garlic; saute 1 minute longer.

Add rice; cook and stir for 2-3 minutes or until beans are tender and rice is lightly browned. Stir in soy sauce. Return egg to the pan; heat through. Serve immediately. **Yield:** 2 servings.

Onion & Cheddar Biscuits

(Pictured above)

PREP: 25 min. **BAKE:** 15 min.

These made–from–scratch biscuits are impossible to resist. I like to prepare a batch and freeze them. My husband often pops one in the microwave for breakfast. —Elaine Sweet, Dallas, Texas

- 1/4 **cup finely chopped sweet onion**
- 4 **tablespoons cold butter, *divided***
- 1/4 **cup white balsamic vinegar**
- 1 **cup all-purpose flour**
- 1 **tablespoon sugar**
- 1-1/2 **teaspoons baking powder**
- 1/4 **teaspoon garlic salt**
- 1/4 **teaspoon pepper**
- 1/8 **teaspoon cayenne pepper**
- 1/2 **cup shredded cheddar cheese**
- 2 **green onions, chopped**
- 1/4 **cup buttermilk**

In a small skillet, saute sweet onion in 1 tablespoon butter until tender. Add vinegar; cook and stir until liquid is evaporated. Let cool.

In a small bowl, combine the flour, sugar, baking powder and seasonings. Cut in remaining butter until mixture resembles coarse crumbs. Add the onion mixture, cheese and green onions. Stir in buttermilk just until moistened.

Turn onto a lightly floured surface; knead 6-8 times. Pat or roll out to 1/2-in. thickness; cut with a floured 2-1/2-in. biscuit cutter. Place 2 in. apart on a greased baking sheet. Bake at 400° for 12-15 minutes or until golden brown. Serve warm. **Yield:** 6 biscuits.

Creamy Butternut Squash Soup

(Pictured above)

PREP: 15 min. **COOK:** 20 min.

I used to live in Australia, where pumpkin soup is served often. When I tried this similar, velvety–smooth squash soup, I knew I had to have the recipe. —Tiffany Pope, Draper, Utah

- 1/4 **cup chopped onion**
- 1 **tablespoon butter**
- 3 **cups cubed peeled butternut squash**
- 1 **medium potato, peeled and cubed**
- 1-1/2 **cups water**
- 1-1/2 **teaspoons chicken bouillon granules**
- 1/4 **teaspoon salt**

Dash pepper
- 1/4 **cup evaporated milk**

In a small saucepan, saute onion in butter until tender. Add squash and potato; cook and stir for 2 minutes. Add the water, bouillon, salt and pepper; bring to a boil. Reduce heat; cover and simmer for 15-20 minutes or until vegetables are tender.

Cool slightly. In a blender, cover and process the soup until smooth. Return to the pan; stir in milk and heat through. **Yield:** 2 servings.

Holiday & Seasonal Celebrations

From a fancy Thanksgiving dinner and spooky Halloween treats to picnic fare for July Fourth and merry Christmas cookies, the scrumptious recipes in this chapter will make all of your special events even more festive.

Toast to the New Year 160
  Crab Puffs • Smoked Gouda & Bacon Potatoes •
  Tenderloin with Cremini-Apricot Stuffing •
  Perfect Winter Salad • Onion, Garlic & Brie
  Bruschetta • Magnolia Dream Cheesecake

Feast for Fat Tuesday 164
  Traditional New Orleans King Cake •
  Shrimp Gumbo • Bayou Burgers with Spicy
  Remoulade • Crawfish Beignets with Cajun
  Dipping Sauce • Okra and Butter Bean Stew •
  Big-Batch Jambalaya

Fresh for July Fourth 168
  Bacon-Blue Cheese Stuffed Burgers • Grilled
  Potato & Arugula Salad • Ladyfinger Ice Cream
  Cake • Fruit Salad in a Pineapple Boat • Berry
  Delicious Tart • Easy Garden Tomatoes

Halloween Scene 172
  Eyes on You • Orange You Spiky • Purple
  People-Eater • Apple Nachos • Party Caramel
  Apples • Green-Eyed Monster

Thanksgiving Gathering 176
  Champagne-Basted Turkey • Roasted Harvest
  Vegetables • Turkey Dinner Cupcakes •
  Everything Bread • Gorgonzola-Pear Mesclun
  Salad • Green Beans in Yellow Pepper Butter •
  Honey-Thyme Butternut Squash • Cranberry
  Pecan Stuffing • Cranberry-Apple Chutney •
  Upside-Down Apple Pie

Merry Cookie Creations 182
  Nutty Chocolate Batons • Lemon Angel
  Wings • Holiday Sugar Cookies • Linzer
  Cookies • Pecan Goodie Cups • Walnut Horn
  Cookies • Cinnamon Chocolate Minties •
  Candy Cane Cookies • Touch-of-Gold
  Christmas Trees • Pecan Meltaways

Homemade Gifts for Christmas 188
  Cashew Brittle • Pecan Caramels •
  Triple Chocolate Fudge • Homemade
  Marshmallows • Caramel Corn with Nuts •
  Chocolate-Covered Pretzels

CHEERY CHOICES. Clockwise from top left: Feast for Fat Tuesday (p. 164), Fresh for July Fourth (p. 168), Toast to the New Year (p. 160), Merry Cookie Creations (p. 182) and Thanksgiving Gathering (p. 176).

Toast to the New Year

FIVE...four...three...two...one...long before the clock strikes midnight on December 31, your New Year's Eve party guests will be cheering for the sparkling specialties featured here.

Get the celebration started with some irresistible appetizers that are sure to impress—tasty Onion, Garlic & Brie Bruschetta, stuffed Crab Puffs and Smoked Gouda & Bacon Potatoes.

And everyone will want to save room for dinner when they see Tenderloin with Cremini-Apricot Stuffing, Perfect Winter Salad and luscious Magnolia Dream Cheesecake on the menu. All that's left to do is get out the party hats and noisemakers!

Crab Puffs

(Pictured at left and on page 158)

PREP: 45 min. **BAKE:** 20 min./batch

This recipe came from my grandmother, who told me to have fun being creative and experimenting in the kitchen. I'm sure she had fun with these! I love the oohs and aahs I get when I present the little stuffed puffs. —Jean Bevilacqua, Rhododendron, Oregon

- 1 cup water
- 1/2 cup butter, cubed
- 1/4 teaspoon salt
- 1 cup all-purpose flour
- 4 eggs

FILLING:
- 4 hard-cooked eggs, finely chopped
- 1 can (6 ounces) lump crabmeat, drained
- 4 ounces cream cheese, softened
- 1/4 cup mayonnaise
- 2 tablespoons finely chopped onion
- 2 tablespoons prepared horseradish, drained

Minced fresh parsley, optional

In a large saucepan, bring the water, butter and salt to a boil. Add flour all at once and stir until a smooth ball forms. Remove from the heat; let stand for 5 minutes. Add the eggs, one at a time, beating well after each addition. Continue beating until the mixture is smooth and shiny.

Drop by teaspoonfuls 2 in. apart onto greased baking sheets. Bake at 400° for 18-22 minutes or until golden brown. Remove to a wire rack. Immediately split puffs open; remove tops and set aside. Discard soft dough from inside. Cool puffs.

In a large bowl, combine the filling ingredients. Just before serving, spoon 1 teaspoon filling into each puff; sprinkle with parsley if desired. Replace tops. **Yield:** 8 dozen.

Smoked Gouda & Bacon Potatoes

(Pictured at left and on page 158)

PREP: 50 min. **BAKE:** 10 min.

You may need a fork to eat these hearty Gouda cheese and bacon appetizers. —Cheryl Perry, Hertford, North Carolina

- 2 whole garlic bulbs
- 1 tablespoon olive oil
- 15 small red potatoes, halved
- 15 bacon strips
- 2 cups (8 ounces) shredded smoked Gouda cheese
- 1 teaspoon coarsely ground pepper
- 2 cups creme fraiche *and/or* sour cream
- 1/4 cup fresh cilantro leaves

Remove the papery outer skin from the garlic (do not peel or separate the cloves). Cut the tops off of garlic bulbs. Brush with oil. Wrap each bulb in heavy-duty foil. Bake at 425° for 30-35 minutes or until softened. Cool for 10-15 minutes.

Meanwhile, place the potatoes in a large saucepan; cover with water. Bring to a boil. Reduce heat; cover and simmer for 8-10 minutes or just until tender.

Cut bacon strips in half widthwise. In a large skillet, cook bacon over medium heat until partially cooked but not crisp. Remove to paper towels to drain; keep warm.

Place a tablespoon of cheese on the cut side of a potato half. Wrap with a half-strip of bacon and secure with a toothpick. Place on an ungreased baking sheet. Repeat. Sprinkle appetizers with pepper. Bake at 375° for 10-15 minutes or until bacon is crisp.

For the sauce, squeeze softened garlic into a food processor. Add the creme fraiche and cilantro; cover and process until blended. Serve with potatoes. **Yield:** 2-1/2 dozen (2 cups sauce).

PUFF POINTER. Want to make scrumptious Crab Puffs (recipe at left) for your party but don't think you'll have enough time? Get a jump start on this recipe by baking the puffs well in advance of your event. Unfilled cream puffs can be frozen in an airtight container for up to 2 months.

To thaw the puffs, let them stand at room temperature for 10-15 minutes. Fill them with the crab filling just before serving.

Tenderloin with Cremini-Apricot Stuffing

(Pictured above)

PREP: 35 min. **BAKE:** 35 min. + standing

Simple but special, this flavorful beef will get rave reviews. Just try it and see! —Marie Rizzio, Interlochen, Michigan

- 1 cup sliced baby portobello (cremini) mushrooms
- 1/3 cup chopped onion
- 1/3 cup chopped celery
- 2 tablespoons butter
- 1/2 cup chopped dried apricots
- 1 tablespoon minced fresh rosemary
- 1 beef tenderloin roast (2-1/2 pounds)
- 1 tablespoon olive oil
- 3 garlic cloves, minced
- 1/2 teaspoon salt
- 1/4 teaspoon pepper

In a large skillet, saute mushrooms, onion and celery in butter until tender. Transfer to a small bowl; stir in apricots and rosemary. Cool slightly.

Cut a lengthwise slit down the center of tenderloin to within 1/2 in. of bottom. Open tenderloin so it lies flat. On each half, make another lengthwise slit down center to within 1/2 in. of bottom; open roast and cover with plastic wrap. Flatten to 1/2-in. thickness. Remove plastic.

Spread mushroom mixture over meat. Roll up jelly-roll style, starting with a long side. Tie the roast at 1-1/2-in. to 2-in. intervals with kitchen string.

Combine oil, garlic, salt and pepper; rub over roast. In a large ovenproof skillet, brown roast on all sides. Bake at 425° for 35-50 minutes or until meat reaches desired doneness (for medium-rare, a meat thermometer should read 145°; medium, 160°; well-done, 170°). Let stand for 10 minutes before slicing. Place slices on a platter; spoon pan juices over the top. **Yield:** 10 servings.

Perfect Winter Salad

(Pictured above)

PREP/TOTAL TIME: 25 min.

This fruity salad is nice not only as a side, but also as an entree with grilled chicken breast. The recipe includes a maple-flavored dressing. —DeNae Shewmake, Burnsville, Minnesota

- 1/4 cup reduced-fat mayonnaise
- 1/4 cup maple syrup
- 3 tablespoons white wine vinegar
- 2 tablespoons minced shallot
- 2 teaspoons sugar
- 1/2 cup canola oil
- 2 packages (5 ounces *each*) spring mix salad greens
- 2 medium tart apples, thinly sliced
- 1 cup dried cherries
- 1 cup pecan halves
- 1/4 cup thinly sliced red onion

In a small bowl, combine the first five ingredients; whisk in oil. Chill until serving.

In a salad bowl, combine the salad greens, apples, dried cherries, pecans and onion. Just before serving, drizzle with salad dressing and toss to coat. **Yield:** 12 servings (1 cup each).

Onion, Garlic & Brie Bruschetta

(Pictured on page 158)

PREP: 45 min. **BROIL:** 5 min./batch

With a rich–and–sweet combination of flavors, these irresistible hors d'oeuvres will bring color and great taste to your event. The little toasted breads are topped with roasted garlic, caramelized onion and Brie cheese. —Carole Bess White, Portland, Oregon

- 2 whole garlic bulbs
- 3 tablespoons olive oil, *divided*
- 1 large red onion, halved and thinly sliced
- 4-1/2 teaspoons sugar
- 1 teaspoon balsamic vinegar
- 1/2 teaspoon salt
- 1/2 teaspoon pepper
- 1 French bread baguette (10-1/2 ounces), cut into scant 1/2-inch slices
- 1 pound Brie cheese, rind removed, thinly sliced

Minced fresh thyme, optional

Remove papery outer skin from garlic (do not peel or separate cloves). Cut tops off of garlic bulbs. Brush with 1 tablespoon oil. Wrap each bulb in heavy-duty foil. Bake at 425° for 30-35 minutes or until softened. Cool for 10-15 minutes.

Meanwhile, in a large skillet over medium heat, cook and stir the onion, sugar, vinegar, salt and pepper in the remaining oil for 15-20 minutes or until very tender and browned.

Place bread on ungreased baking sheets. Broil 3-4 in. from the heat for 3-4 minutes or until edges are lightly browned. Squeeze the softened garlic into a bowl; mash with a fork. Spread over toast. Top with Brie cheese and onion. Broil 3-4 in. from the heat for 2-3 minutes or until the cheese is melted. Sprinkle with thyme if desired. **Yield:** 3-1/2 dozen.

Magnolia Dream Cheesecake

(Pictured at right)

PREP: 50 min. **BAKE:** 1-1/2 hours + chilling

This tempting made–from–scratch cheesecake is velvety smooth and rich in both peach and hazelnut flavors. Each serving looks so pretty with fruit slices and nuts arranged on top. —Charlene Chambers, Ormond Beach, Florida

- 1 cup hazelnuts, toasted, *divided*
- 12 whole graham crackers
- 1/4 cup sugar
- 6 tablespoons unsalted butter, melted

FILLING:
- 1-1/2 pounds ricotta cheese
- 2 packages (8 ounces *each*) cream cheese, softened
- 2 cups (16 ounces) sour cream
- 1-1/2 cups sugar
- 6 tablespoons all-purpose flour
- 4 tablespoons hazelnut liqueur, *divided*
- 6 eggs, lightly beaten
- 3 medium peaches, sliced

Place a greased 10-in. springform pan on a double thickness of heavy-duty foil (about 18 in. square). Securely wrap foil around pan.

Place hazelnuts in a food processor; cover and pulse until coarsely chopped. Set aside 1/4 cup for garnish. Add graham crackers and sugar to food processor; cover and process until finely chopped. Add butter; process until blended. Press onto the bottom and 1 in. up the sides of the prepared pan. Place pan on a baking sheet. Bake at 325° for 10 minutes. Cool on a wire rack.

In a large bowl, beat the ricotta, cream cheese, sour cream and sugar until well blended. Beat in flour and 2 tablespoons liqueur. Add eggs; beat on low speed just until combined. Pour into crust. Place springform pan in a large baking pan; add 1 in. of hot water to larger pan.

Bake at 325° for 1-1/2 hours or until center is just set and top appears dull. Remove springform pan from the water bath. Cool on a wire rack for 10 minutes. Carefully run a knife around edge of pan to loosen; cool 1 hour longer. Refrigerate overnight.

Toss peaches with remaining liqueur; arrange over top of cheesecake. Sprinkle reserved hazelnuts in the center. **Yield:** 16 servings.

Feast for Fat Tuesday

MAKE MARDI GRAS a flavorful celebration for your family and friends with the very special menu here. No matter where you live, it'll bring the distinctive Cajun taste of New Orleans right to your home.

Okra and Butter Bean Stew...Bayou Burgers with Spicy Remoulade...Big-Batch Jambalaya...Shrimp Gumbo...any of these hearty dishes is sure to make a mouthwatering main course.

Don't forget a starter of Crawfish Beignets with Cajun Dipping Sauce, plus a dessert of Traditional New Orleans King Cake—and plenty of party beads!

Traditional New Orleans King Cake

(Pictured at left)

PREP: 40 min. + rising **BAKE:** 25 min. + cooling

Legend has it that if you hide a tiny plastic baby in this classic cinnamon–swirl cake, whoever finds it has 1 year of good luck! (Just don't bake the plastic baby in the cake—after the cake has been baked and cooled, cut a small slit in the bottom and then insert the token.) —Rebecca Baird, Salt Lake City, Utah

- 2 packages (1/4 ounce *each*) active dry yeast
- 1/2 cup warm water (110° to 115°)
- 3/4 cup sugar, *divided*
- 1/2 cup butter, softened
- 1/2 cup warm 2% milk (110° to 115°)
- 2 egg yolks
- 1-1/4 teaspoons salt
- 1 teaspoon grated lemon peel
- 1/4 teaspoon ground nutmeg
- 3-1/4 to 3-3/4 cups all-purpose flour
- 1 teaspoon ground cinnamon
- 1 egg, beaten

GLAZE:
- 1-1/2 cups confectioners' sugar
- 2 teaspoons lemon juice
- 2 to 3 tablespoons water

Green, purple and yellow sugars

In a large bowl, dissolve the yeast in warm water. Add 1/2 cup sugar, butter, milk, yolks, salt, peel, nutmeg and 2 cups flour. Beat until smooth. Stir in enough remaining flour to form a soft dough (dough will be sticky).

Turn onto a floured surface; knead until smooth and elastic, about 6-8 minutes. Place in a greased bowl, turning once to grease the top. Cover and let rise in a warm place until doubled, about 1 hour.

Punch the dough down. Turn onto a lightly floured surface. Roll into a 16-in. x 10-in. rectangle. Combine cinnamon and remaining sugar; sprinkle over dough to within 1/2 in. of the edges. Roll up dough jelly-roll style, starting with a long side; pinch seam to seal. Place seam side down on a greased baking sheet; pinch the ends together to form a ring. Cover and let rise until doubled, about 1 hour. Brush with egg.

Bake at 375° for 25-30 minutes or until golden brown. Cool completely on a wire rack. For glaze, combine the confectioners' sugar, lemon juice and enough water to achieve desired consistency. Spread over cake. Sprinkle with colored sugars. **Yield:** 1 cake (12 slices).

Shrimp Gumbo

PREP: 30 min. **COOK:** 1 hour

It's just not Mardi Gras if you don't have gumbo. You're sure to enjoy this authentic, well–seasoned dish even if you don't hail from Cajun country. —Jo Ann Graham, Ovilla, Texas

- 1/4 cup all-purpose flour
- 1/4 cup canola oil
- 3 celery ribs, chopped
- 1 medium green pepper, chopped
- 1 medium onion, chopped
- 1 carton (32 ounces) chicken broth
- 3 garlic cloves, minced
- 1 teaspoon salt
- 1 teaspoon pepper
- 1/2 teaspoon cayenne pepper
- 2 pounds uncooked large shrimp, peeled and deveined
- 1 package (16 ounces) frozen sliced okra
- 4 green onions, sliced
- 1 medium tomato, chopped
- 1-1/2 teaspoons gumbo file powder

Hot cooked rice

In a Dutch oven over medium heat, cook and stir flour and oil until caramel-colored, about 12 minutes (do not burn). Add the celery, green pepper and onion; cook and stir for 5-6 minutes or until tender. Stir in chicken broth, garlic, salt, pepper and cayenne; bring to a boil. Reduce heat; cover and simmer for 30 minutes.

Stir in shrimp, okra, green onions and tomato. Return to a boil. Reduce heat; cover and simmer for 10 minutes or until shrimp turn pink. Stir in file powder. Serve with rice. **Yield:** 11 servings.

Editor's Note: Gumbo file powder is used to thicken and flavor Cajun and Creole recipes. If you can't find or do not want to use gumbo file powder, combine 2 tablespoons each cornstarch and water until smooth. Gradually stir into gumbo. Bring to a boil; cook and stir for 2 minutes or until thickened.

turkey sausage over mixture and mix well. Shape into four patties.

In a large skillet over medium heat, cook burgers for 5-7 minutes on each side or until a meat thermometer reads 165° and the juices run clear. Top with cheddar cheese slices; cover and cook for 1-2 minutes or until cheese is melted.

For remoulade, in a small bowl, combine the Miracle Whip, lemon juice, hot sauce, pickle relish and capers. Spread rolls with butter and sprinkle with remaining garlic powder. Broil 4 in. from the heat for 2-3 minutes or until lightly browned. Serve the burgers on rolls with remoulade. **Yield:** 4 servings.

Editor's Note: The following may be substituted for 1 teaspoon Creole seasoning: 1/4 teaspoon each salt, garlic powder and paprika; and a pinch each of dried thyme, ground cumin and cayenne pepper.

Bayou Burgers with Spicy Remoulade

(Pictured above and on page 158)

PREP/TOTAL TIME: 30 min.

I like to serve these slightly spicy, Southern-style burgers with sweet potato fries. For another great side, try red beans and rice.
—*Michele Claybrook-Lucas, Media, Pennsylvania*

- 1 **small onion, chopped**
- 2 **tablespoons olive oil**
- 1/4 **pound fully cooked andouille sausage link, casing removed, finely chopped**
- 1 **teaspoon Creole seasoning**
- 3/4 **teaspoon garlic powder, *divided***
- 1/4 **teaspoon salt**
- 1/4 **teaspoon pepper**
- 1 **pound ground turkey**
- 1/4 **pound Italian turkey sausage link, casing removed**
- 4 **slices cheddar cheese**
- 1/2 **cup Miracle Whip**
- 2 **tablespoons lemon juice**
- 1 **tablespoon hot pepper sauce**
- 2 **teaspoons sweet pickle relish**
- 1 **teaspoon capers, drained**
- 4 **kaiser rolls, split**
- 1 **tablespoon butter**

In a large skillet, saute the onion in oil until tender. Add andouille sausage; cook 1 minute longer. Transfer to a large bowl. Stir in the Creole seasoning, 1/4 teaspoon garlic powder, salt and pepper. Crumble the turkey and

Crawfish Beignets with Cajun Dipping Sauce

(Pictured below)

PREP: 20 min.   **COOK:** 5 min./batch

If you're only familiar with sweet beignets, you're sure to get a kick out of this savory version featuring crawfish, onions and a zippy dipping sauce. —*Donna Lanclos, Lafayette, Louisiana*

- 1 **egg, beaten**
- 1 **pound chopped cooked crawfish tail meat *or* shrimp**
- 4 **green onions, chopped**
- 1-1/2 **teaspoons butter, melted**
- 1/2 **teaspoon salt**
- 1/2 **teaspoon cayenne pepper**
- 1/3 **cup bread flour**
- **Oil for deep-fat frying**

3/4 cup mayonnaise
1/2 cup ketchup
1/4 teaspoon prepared horseradish, optional
1/4 teaspoon hot pepper sauce

In a large bowl, combine egg, crawfish, onions, butter, salt and cayenne. Stir in flour until blended.

In an electric skillet or deep-fat fryer, heat oil to 375°. Drop tablespoonfuls of the batter, a few at a time, into hot oil. Fry until golden brown on both sides. Drain on paper towels.

For the dipping sauce, in a small bowl, combine the mayonnaise, ketchup, horseradish if desired and hot pepper sauce. Serve with beignets. **Yield:** about 2 dozen (3/4 cup sauce).

Okra and Butter Bean Stew

PREP: 25 min. **COOK:** 45 min.

This stew is adapted from my mother's down-home Louisiana recipe. It will turn okra haters into okra lovers, guaranteed!
—Kaya Mack, Wichita Falls, Texas

7 bacon strips, chopped
1 pound smoked sausage, halved and thinly sliced
1 large onion, chopped
2 small green peppers, chopped
3 cups water
2 cans (16 ounces *each*) butter beans, rinsed and drained
1 can (14-1/2 ounces) diced tomatoes, undrained
1 can (12 ounces) tomato paste
1 teaspoon pepper
1/4 teaspoon salt
1 package (16 ounces) frozen sliced okra
Hot cooked rice, optional

In a Dutch oven, cook bacon and sausage over medium heat until bacon is crisp. Remove to paper towels; drain, reserving 2 tablespoons drippings.

Cook the onion and green peppers in drippings until tender. Stir in water, beans, tomatoes, tomato paste, pepper and salt. Bring to a boil. Reduce heat; simmer, uncovered, 10 minutes.

Add the cooked bacon and sausage; cook 10 minutes longer. Add the okra; cover and cook 8-10 minutes or until tender. Serve the stew with rice if desired. **Yield:** 12 servings (1 cup each).

Big-Batch Jambalaya

(Pictured above right)

PREP: 25 min. **COOK:** 55 min.

I fix this spicy dish every year for our annual Super Bowl party. The memory of a big bowlful leaves my mouth watering for the rest of the year. —*Kecia McCaffrey, South Dennis, Maryland*

1 boneless skinless chicken breast, cubed
3 tablespoons olive oil, *divided*
1/2 pound cubed fully cooked ham
1/2 pound smoked kielbasa *or* Polish sausage, cubed
2 medium green peppers, coarsely chopped
2 medium onions, coarsely chopped
6 garlic cloves, minced
2 cans (14-1/2 ounces *each*) beef broth
1 can (28 ounces) crushed tomatoes
1-1/2 cups water
3/4 cup Dijon mustard
1/4 cup minced fresh parsley
2 tablespoons Worcestershire sauce
1-1/2 to 2 teaspoons cayenne pepper
1/2 teaspoon dried thyme
1-1/2 cups uncooked long grain rice
1 pound uncooked medium shrimp, peeled and deveined

In a Dutch oven, cook chicken in 1 tablespoon oil until no longer pink; remove and set aside. In the same pan, cook and stir the ham, kielbasa, peppers and onions in remaining oil until onions are tender. Add garlic; cook 1 minute longer.

Stir in the broth, tomatoes, water, mustard, parsley, Worcestershire, cayenne and thyme. Bring to a boil. Reduce heat; cover and simmer for 10 minutes.

Add rice and return to a boil. Reduce heat; cover and simmer for 25-30 minutes or until rice is tender. Stir in shrimp and chicken; cook 2-4 minutes longer or until shrimp turn pink. **Yield:** 13 servings (1 cup each).

Fresh for July Fourth

ON INDEPENDENCE DAY, dining on fresh-air fare outdoors is practically a must (weather permitting!). If you're craving something deliciously different from the usual menu, look no further than the summery spread featured here.

Flag down friends and family members for picnic-perfect fare—Bacon-Blue Cheese Stuffed Burgers, Fruit Salad in a Pineapple Boat, Grilled Potato & Arugula Salad and Easy Garden Tomatoes.

Want a dessert with just as much spark? It's hard to beat warm-weather treats such as cool Ladyfinger Ice Cream Cake and crumb-topped Berry Delicious Tart.

Bacon-Blue Cheese Stuffed Burgers

(Pictured at left)

PREP: 30 min. **GRILL:** 10 min.

These loaded burgers are like a meal-in-one on a bun. Stuffed with a zippy filling of cheese and bacon, they're sure to satisfy the biggest appetites at a Fourth of July picnic or any get-together.
—Christine Keating, Norwalk, California

- 1-1/2 **pounds lean ground beef (90% lean)**
- 1 **package (3 ounces) cream cheese, softened**
- 1/3 **cup crumbled blue cheese**
- 1/3 **cup bacon bits**
- 1/2 **teaspoon salt**
- 1/2 **teaspoon garlic powder**
- 1/4 **teaspoon pepper**
- 1 **pound sliced fresh mushrooms**
- 1 **tablespoon olive oil**
- 1 **tablespoon water**
- 1 **tablespoon Dijon mustard**
- 4 **whole wheat hamburger buns, split**
- 1/4 **cup mayonnaise**
- 4 **romaine leaves**
- 1 **medium tomato, sliced**

Shape beef into eight thin patties. Combine the cream cheese, blue cheese and bacon bits; spoon onto the center of four patties. Top with remaining patties and press edges firmly to seal. Combine salt, garlic powder and pepper; sprinkle over patties.

Grill burgers, covered, over medium heat or broil 4 in. from the heat for 5-7 minutes on each side or until a meat thermometer reads 160° and juices run clear.

Meanwhile, in a large skillet, saute mushrooms in oil until tender. Stir in water and mustard.

Serve the burgers on buns with mayonnaise, romaine, tomato and mushroom mixture. **Yield:** 4 servings.

Grilled Potato & Arugula Salad

(Pictured at far left)

PREP: 30 min. **GRILL:** 15 min.

Looking for a new twist on an old picnic classic? This colorful potato salad has both sweet and Yukon Gold potatoes, plus fresh salad greens, some Cajun heat and a cool yogurt dressing.
—Nancee Melin, Tucson, Arizona

✓ **This recipe includes Nutrition Facts and Diabetic Exchanges.**

- 2 **medium sweet potatoes**
- 2 **medium Yukon Gold potatoes**
- 4-1/2 **teaspoons Cajun seasoning,** *divided*
- 1/4 **teaspoon salt,** *divided*
- 1/4 **teaspoon pepper,** *divided*
- 1/2 **cup plain yogurt**
- 4-1/2 **teaspoons lemon juice**
- 2 **garlic cloves, minced**
- 3 **cups fresh arugula** *or* **baby spinach**
- 1 **cup grape tomatoes**
- 1/2 **cup pitted Greek olives, sliced**
- 6 **green onions, chopped**

Pierce the sweet potatoes and Yukon Gold potatoes; microwave, uncovered, on high for 4 minutes, turning potatoes once.

When potatoes are cool enough to handle, peel and cut into 1/2-in. slices. Sprinkle with 4 teaspoons Cajun seasoning, 1/8 teaspoon salt and 1/8 teaspoon pepper.

Place potato slices on a grilling grid; transfer to grill rack. Grill, covered, over medium heat for 15-20 minutes or until tender, turning occasionally.

In a large bowl, combine the yogurt, lemon juice, garlic and remaining Cajun seasoning, salt and pepper. Gently fold in the arugula, tomatoes, olives, onions and potatoes. **Yield:** 8 servings.

Editor's Note: This recipe was tested in a 1,100-watt microwave.

Nutrition Facts: 1 cup equals 116 calories, 3 g fat (1 g saturated fat), 2 mg cholesterol, 535 mg sodium, 20 g carbohydrate, 2 g fiber, 3 g protein. **Diabetic Exchanges:** 1 starch, 1/2 fat.

SIMPLE STUFFING. The recipe for Bacon-Blue Cheese Stuffed Burgers (at left) calls for pressing together two thin beef patties around a filling to create each burger. Lightly moistening the edges of the patties will help seal them together.

Ladyfinger Ice Cream Cake

(Pictured above)

PREP/TOTAL TIME: 25 min. + freezing

On a hot summer day, this showstopper will melt all resistance to dessert—one cool, creamy slice at a time. Everyone will think you fussed.   —Barbara McCalley, Allison Park, Pennsylvania

- **2 packages (3 ounces *each*) ladyfingers, split**
- **3 cups vanilla ice cream, softened**
- **1 jar (16 ounces) hot fudge ice cream topping**
- **1 package (8 ounces) toffee bits**
- **3 cups chocolate ice cream, softened**
- **3 cups coffee ice cream, softened**

Arrange ladyfingers around the edge and on the bottom of a 9-inch springform pan coated with cooking spray.

  Spoon vanilla ice cream into prepared pan. Top with a third of the ice cream topping and toffee bits. Freeze 20 minutes. Repeat layers, using chocolate and coffee ice creams (pan will be full). Freeze overnight or until firm. **Yield:** 16 servings.

ICY IDEAS. Want to make luscious Ladyfinger Ice Cream Cake (recipe above) for your next event? Feel free to assemble it up to a week in advance and store it in the freezer. If you like, you could also try different flavors of ice cream...or replace the hot fudge topping with another variety.

Fruit Salad In a Pineapple Boat

(Pictured below)

PREP/TOTAL TIME: 50 min.

This sweet, summery treat looks as good as it tastes. No one will want to pass up this wholesome, refreshing salad chock-full of four kinds of fruit. It's presented in an easy-to-make pineapple boat and served alongside a creamy strawberry sauce.
—Amy Short, Lesage, West Virginia

☑ This recipe includes Nutrition Facts and Diabetic Exchange.

- **1 fresh pineapple**
- **2 cups cubed cantaloupe**
- **1 cup halved fresh strawberries**
- **1 cup fresh blueberries**
- **1 tablespoon lime juice**

SAUCE:
- **1 cup fresh strawberries, mashed**
- **1 cup (8 ounces) reduced-fat plain yogurt**
- **2 tablespoons honey**
- **1 tablespoon lime juice**
- **1-1/2 teaspoons grated lime peel**
- **1/2 teaspoon vanilla extract**

Stand the pineapple upright; vertically cut about a third from one side, leaving the top attached. Remove fruit and discard outer peel from the smaller section. Remove the fruit from the large section, leaving a 1/2-in. shell.

  Chop fruit; place in a large bowl. Add the cantaloupe, strawberries, blueberries and lime juice; toss to coat. Place in pineapple shell.

  In a small bowl, combine the sauce ingredients. Serve with fruit. **Yield:** 10 servings (1-1/3 cups sauce).

  Nutrition Facts: 2/3 cup fruit with 2 tablespoons sauce equals 81 calories, 1 g fat (trace saturated fat), 1 mg cholesterol, 21 mg sodium, 19 g carbohydrate, 2 g fiber, 2 g protein. **Diabetic Exchange:** 1 fruit.

Bake for 30-35 minutes or until bubbly and golden brown. Cool on a wire rack for 10 minutes. Carefully run a knife around edge of pan to loosen; cool 30 minutes longer. Serve the tart warm or cold. **Yield:** 12 servings.

Easy Garden Tomatoes

(Pictured below and on page 158)

PREP/TOTAL TIME: 15 min.

Simple as it is, this is one of my favorite dishes...and my family can't get enough of it either. I made three batches the first time, and a few olive slices were the only things left on the platter! The seasonings, onions and cheese only enhance the fresh tomatoes.
—*Heather Ahrens, Avon, Ohio*

- **3 large tomatoes, thinly sliced**
- **1 large red onion, thinly sliced**
- **1/3 cup olive oil**
- **1/4 cup red wine vinegar**
- **2 garlic cloves, minced**
- **1 tablespoon minced fresh basil *or* 1 teaspoon dried basil**
- **1-1/2 teaspoons minced fresh oregano *or* 1/2 teaspoon dried oregano**
- **3/4 cup crumbled feta cheese**
- **1 can (2-1/4 ounces) sliced ripe olives, drained**

Arrange tomatoes and onion on a serving platter. Whisk the oil, vinegar, garlic, basil and oregano; drizzle over the salad. Top with cheese and olives. Chill until serving. **Yield:** 6 servings.

Berry Delicious Tart

(Pictured above)

PREP: 25 min. **BAKE:** 35 min. + cooling

I love berries of all kinds, so I'm always trying to find something new to make with them. This is one of the recipes that resulted from my kitchen experiments. If you bring it to a picnic or party, prepare to hear rave reviews—and to get recipe requests!
—*Angela Moorhead, Cambridge, Ontario*

- **1 cup all-purpose flour**
- **1/3 cup plus 1/4 cup sugar, *divided***
- **1/2 cup cold butter**
- **1/2 cup seedless strawberry jam**
- **1 package (8 ounces) cream cheese, softened**
- **1 egg, lightly beaten**
- **1 teaspoon vanilla extract**
- **2 cups fresh *or* frozen unsweetened mixed berries, thawed and drained**

TOPPING:
- **3/4 cup packed brown sugar**
- **1/3 cup old-fashioned oats**
- **1/2 cup all-purpose flour**
- **1/4 cup cold butter**

In a small bowl, combine flour and 1/3 cup sugar; cut in butter until crumbly. Press onto the bottom and 1 in. up the sides of a greased 9-in. springform pan.

Place the pan on a baking sheet. Bake at 375° for 8-10 minutes or until the crust is lightly browned. Cool on a wire rack.

Spread the strawberry jam over the prepared crust. In a small bowl, beat the cream cheese and remaining sugar until smooth. Add the egg and vanilla; beat on low speed just until combined. Pour over the jam; sprinkle with berries.

In a small bowl, combine the brown sugar, oats and flour; cut in butter until crumbly. Sprinkle over filling.

Halloween Scene

SCARE UP a yummy time on October 31 with the festive treats here. They're more fun than frightful!

What kid or kid-at-heart wouldn't love cupcakes shaped like monsters? We've featured four of them from Karen Tack and Alan Richardson, authors of the book *What's New, Cupcake?*

Plus, you can dress up a favorite fall fruit with two recipes—Party Caramel Apples and Apple Nachos.

Eyes on You

(Pictured at left)

PREP/TOTAL TIME: 30 min.

With lots of red eyes dangling from long strands of black licorice, this kooky creature is guaranteed to get giggles from party guests.
—Karen Tack, Riverside, Connecticut

- 1 **can (16 ounces) vanilla frosting**
- **Neon green food coloring**
- 6 **chocolate *or* vanilla cupcakes baked in black foil liners**
- 1/4 **cup purple sprinkles**
- **Black licorice laces**
- 50 **mini marshmallows**
- 1 **tube (4.25 ounces) brown decorating frosting**
- 50 **red mini M&M's *or* red-hot candies**

Tint the vanilla frosting neon green with food coloring. Spread a generous mound of frosting on top of the cupcakes. While frosting is still wet, sprinkle the tops with the purple sprinkles.

Cut the black licorice laces into about 50 pieces about 3 to 5 in. long. Insert one end of the laces into the side of marshmallows. Pipe a small dot of brown decorating frosting on one flat end of the marshmallow and attach a red M&M to make an eyeball.

Insert 8 to 10 licorice laces as the eyes on top of a cupcake. Repeat with remaining licorice, marshmallow eyes and cupcakes. **Yield:** 6 cupcakes.

Orange You Spiky

(Pictured at right)

PREP/TOTAL TIME: 30 min.

You'll raise spirits with the high-rising eyeballs on these bright, googly-eyed delights. —Karen Tack, Riverside, Connecticut

- 6 **chocolate *or* vanilla cupcakes baked in black foil liners**
- 1 **can (16 ounces) plus 1 cup vanilla frosting**
- 1 **cup chow mein noodles**
- **Red and yellow food coloring**
- 12 **honey wheat sticks *or* pretzel sticks**
- 12 **mini marshmallows**
- 12 **brown M&M's**
- **Chocolate jimmies**

Spread the tops of the cupcakes with a small mound of vanilla frosting. Insert chow mein noodles into the cupcakes to look like spikes. Place in the freezer for about 15 minutes to firm up.

Spoon 3 tablespoons of the vanilla frosting into a small resealable bag and set aside.

Tint the remaining frosting bright orange with the food coloring and spoon into a glass microwave-safe bowl. Microwave the frosting, stirring frequently, until it is the texture of slightly whipped cream.

Holding foil liner of the slightly frozen cupcake, dip top of the cupcake up to the liner in the melted frosting to coat. Use a spoon to add more frosting if necessary. Allow excess frosting to drip off. Invert and transfer to a cookie sheet. Repeat with the remaining cupcakes.

Insert one end of a wheat stick into the side of a mini marshmallow. Repeat with remaining marshmallows and wheat sticks. Snip a small corner from the bag with the vanilla frosting. Pipe a dot of frosting on one flat side of a marshmallow. Add a brown candy as the pupil. Add a few chocolate jimmies on the top as eyelashes. Pipe a dot of vanilla frosting on the brown candy as the sparkle in the eyes.

Insert two marshmallow eyes on top of a frosted cupcake about 1 in. apart. Repeat with the remaining cupcakes. **Yield:** 6 cupcakes.

Purple People-Eater

(Pictured above)

PREP: 45 min. + standing

Beware—this goofy cupcake guy may try to gobble you up if you don't eat him first!   —Karen Tack, Riverside, Connecticut

   6 **chocolate *or* vanilla cupcakes baked in black foil liners**
   1 **can (16 ounces) vanilla frosting**
Neon purple food coloring
   9 **marshmallows**
  18 **thin pretzel sticks**
Black licorice laces
  12 **mini marshmallows**
  18 **brown mini M&M's**
   6 **pink fruit chews**

Spread the tops of the cupcakes with a mound of vanilla frosting. Spoon 1 tablespoon vanilla frosting into a small resealable bag. Tint the remaining vanilla frosting neon purple with the food coloring and place in a microwave-safe measuring cup.

Line a cookie sheet with waxed paper. Cut the large marshmallows in half crosswise with scissors. Insert a pretzel stick into the side of each marshmallow to create the eyes. Cut the black licorice laces into eighteen 2-in. pieces. Cut the mini marshmallows in half on the diagonal to make the teeth. Soften the pink fruit chews in the microwave for no more than 3 seconds.

Roll out each fruit chew into a 3-in. length. Cut into a long tongue with a rounded end. Press the back of a knife down the middle of the fruit chew to make the crease in the center of the tongue.

Place a wire rack over a cookie sheet lined with waxed paper. Heat the neon purple frosting in the microwave, stirring every 10 seconds, until the frosting is the consistency of slightly whipped cream, about 25 to 30 seconds total. Holding the frosted cupcakes by the foil liners, dip the cupcakes just up to the liners. Allow the excess frosting to drip off before inverting cupcake. Transfer to the wire rack to set.

Repeat with remaining cupcakes. If frosting becomes too thick, return to the microwave and heat for about 5 to 10 seconds longer, stirring well before dipping.

Holding the marshmallow eyes by the pretzel end, dip the top half of the marshmallows into the frosting to make the eyelids. Transfer the marshmallows to the waxed paper-lined cookie sheet. While the frosting is still wet, add black licorice lace along dipped edge for eyelid bottom. Repeat with remaining marshmallows. Snip a small corner from the bag with the vanilla frosting. Pipe a dot of frosting on the marshmallow area and add a brown M&M as a pupil. Let eyes set for about 30 minutes before assembling cupcakes.

Spoon some of remaining purple frosting on top of dipped cupcakes, allowing frosting to drip over the sides.

While frosting is still wet, add three to four cut mini marshmallow pieces as the teeth along one edge of the cupcakes. Insert three marshmallow eyes at different heights. Transfer to a serving platter and add the fruit chew tongue under the teeth. **Yield:** 6 cupcakes.

Apple Nachos

PREP/TOTAL TIME: 20 min.

A colorful and crisp treat, this nacho look–alike will please any sweet tooth.   —RaeAnn Gnatkowski, Carrollton, Michigan

☑ **This recipe includes Nutrition Facts and Diabetic Exchanges.**

  36 **caramels**
   1 **tablespoon water**
  30 **large marshmallows**
 1/3 **cup butter, cubed**
   4 **medium tart apples, peeled and cut into 1/4-inch slices**
 1/3 **cup chopped dry roasted peanuts**
 1/3 **cup miniature semisweet chocolate chips**
   3 **tablespoons Halloween sprinkles**

In a microwave-safe bowl, melt caramels with water; stir until smooth. Meanwhile, in a large saucepan, melt the marshmallows and butter. Arrange the apple slices on a large platter. Drizzle with caramel; top with the marshmallow mixture. Sprinkle with peanuts, chips and sprinkles. Serve immediately. **Yield:** 24 servings.

Nutrition Facts: 1 serving equals 149 calories, 6 g fat (3 g saturated fat), 8 mg cholesterol, 76 mg sodium, 25 g carbohydrate, 1 g fiber, 2 g protein. **Diabetic Exchanges:** 1-1/2 starch, 1 fat.

Party Caramel Apples

(Pictured above)

PREP: 30 min. **COOK:** 20 min. + standing

These dipped delights always get rave reviews. Sometimes I dress them up using miniature M&M's, jimmies or other candies.
—Natalie Bremson, Plantation, Florida

- 8 **medium Red Delicious apples**
- 8 **Popsicle sticks**
- 2-1/4 **cups packed brown sugar**
- 3/4 **cup butter, cubed**
- 1 **can (14 ounces) sweetened condensed milk**
- 3/4 **cup dark corn syrup**
- 1/2 **cup maple syrup**
- 1-1/2 **teaspoons molasses**

Dash salt
- 1/2 **teaspoon vanilla extract**

Chopped salted peanuts and red-hot candies
- 4 **ounces white baking chocolate, chopped**
- 4 **ounces semisweet chocolate, chopped**

Wash and dry apples; remove stems. Insert Popsicle sticks into the bottoms of apples. Place on a buttered baking sheet; refrigerate until ready to use.

In a large heavy saucepan, combine the brown sugar, butter, milk, corn syrup, maple syrup, molasses and salt. Stir with a wooden spoon over medium-low heat until sugar dissolves. Bring to a boil, stirring constantly, until a candy thermometer reads 248° (firm-ball stage). Remove from the heat; stir in vanilla.

Dip apples, one at a time, into caramel and then into an ice-water bath for 1-2 seconds to set caramel. Dip apples in peanuts; place on the buttered baking sheet. Press red-hot candies onto apples as desired.

In a microwave, melt the white chocolate; stir until smooth. Transfer to a small resealable plastic bag; cut a hole in a corner of the bag. Drizzle over apples. Repeat

with semisweet chocolate. Decorate with red-hot candies and additional nuts. Let stand until set. **Yield:** 8 caramel apples.

Editor's Note: We recommend that you test your candy thermometer before each use by bringing water to a boil; the thermometer should read 212°. Adjust your recipe temperature up or down based on your test.

Green-Eyed Monster

(Pictured below)

PREP/TOTAL TIME: 30 min.

A chocolate mint and marshmallow form the single eye on this funny fellow. —Karen Tack, Riverside, Connecticut

- 6 **marshmallows**
- 6 **chocolate** *or* **vanilla cupcakes baked in black foil liners**
- 1 **can (16 ounces) vanilla frosting**

Neon green food coloring
- 6 **small chocolate-coated mints**

Trim a corner from one short end of each marshmallow. Attach the marshmallows, cut side down, on top of the cupcakes with a dot of frosting.

Spoon 2 tablespoons of vanilla frosting into a small resealable bag; set aside.

Tint the remaining vanilla frosting neon green with the food coloring. Spoon the neon green frosting into a resealable 2-qt. freezer bag. Snip a very small corner (1/8 in.) from bag. Pipe dots of frosting along outer edge of cupcake with a "pipe, stop and pull" action to create spikes of frosting. Continue piping all over cupcakes to completely cover all but the flat side of marshmallow. Repeat with the remaining cupcakes and frosting.

Snip a very small (1/16 in.) corner from the bag with vanilla frosting. Pipe a dot of vanilla frosting in center of each marshmallow and attach the chocolate-coated mint. Pipe a small line to add the sparkle in the eye. **Yield:** 6 cupcakes.

Thanksgiving Gathering

FAMILY-PLEASING FOOD is at the heart of every Thanksgiving get-together. In this section, you will find extra-special dishes to make your holiday as memorable as can be.

What's a Turkey Day table without a turkey? We've featured a succulent bird recipe that's sure to make eyes light up and mouths water.

Enjoy all of the trimmings, too, from Cranberry Pecan Stuffing and Everything Bread to Honey-Thyme Butternut Squash and Roasted Harvest Vegetables. And everyone will want to save room for a can't-miss dessert—Upside-Down Apple Pie.

Plus, you'll find a fun-as-can-be Thanksgiving cupcake from Karen Tack and Alan Richardson, authors of the book *What's New, Cupcake?* Set one down at each place setting for an unforgettable treat.

Champagne-Basted Turkey

(Pictured at left and on page 158)

PREP: 20 min. **BAKE:** 3-1/2 hours + standing

I've served this moist, tender turkey every Thanksgiving for the past 15 years. The secret is to use lots of fresh parsley and to keep basting. —Sharon Hawk, Edwardsville, Illinois

        1 turkey (14 to 16 pounds)
    1/4 cup butter, softened
        1 teaspoon salt
        1 teaspoon celery salt
    3/4 teaspoon pepper
Fresh sage and parsley sprigs, optional
        2 cups Champagne *or* other sparkling wine
        2 medium onions, chopped
1-1/2 cups minced fresh parsley
        1 cup condensed beef consomme, undiluted
    1/2 teaspoon dried thyme
    1/2 teaspoon dried marjoram
GRAVY:
        1 tablespoon butter
        1 tablespoon all-purpose flour

Pat turkey dry. Combine the butter, salt, celery salt and pepper; rub over the outside and inside of turkey. Place sage and parsley sprigs in cavity if desired. Tuck wings under turkey; tie drumsticks together. Place breast side up on a rack in a roasting pan.

Bake, uncovered, at 325° for 30 minutes. In a large bowl, combine Champagne, onions, parsley, consomme, thyme and marjoram; pour into the pan. Bake for 3 to 3-1/2 hours longer or until a meat thermometer reads 180°, basting occasionally with the Champagne mixture. Cover loosely with foil if the turkey browns too quickly.

Cover and let stand for 20 minutes before slicing.

For gravy, strain the drippings into a small bowl. In a small saucepan, melt butter. Stir in flour until smooth; gradually add drippings. Bring to a boil; cook and stir for 2 minutes or until thickened. Serve with turkey. **Yield:** 14 servings (1-2/3 cups gravy).

Roasted Harvest Vegetables

(Pictured at left and on page 158)

PREP: 20 min. **BAKE:** 30 min.

With its herbal aroma and roasted flavor, this medley will be a hit—even with the kids. This is one of my "go-to" sides any time we have company. —Amy Logan, Mill Creek, Pennsylvania

☑ This recipe includes Nutrition Facts and Diabetic Exchanges.

        8 small red potatoes, quartered
        2 small onions, quartered
        1 medium zucchini, halved and sliced
        1 medium yellow summer squash, halved and sliced
    1/2 pound fresh baby carrots
        1 cup fresh cauliflowerets
        1 cup fresh broccoli florets
    1/4 cup olive oil
        1 tablespoon garlic powder
1-1/2 teaspoons dried rosemary, crushed
    1/2 teaspoon dried thyme
    1/4 teaspoon salt
    1/4 teaspoon pepper

Place the vegetables in a large bowl. Combine the remaining ingredients; drizzle over the vegetables and toss to coat. Transfer to two greased 15-in. x 10-in. x 1-in. baking pans.

Bake, uncovered, at 400° for 30-35 minutes or until tender, stirring occasionally. **Yield:** 9 servings.

Nutrition Facts: 3/4 cup equals 114 calories, 6 g fat (1 g saturated fat), 0 cholesterol, 97 mg sodium, 13 g carbohydrate, 3 g fiber, 2 g protein. **Diabetic Exchanges:** 1 vegetable, 1 fat, 1/2 starch.

TABLETOP TIP. The holidays are a perfect time to dress up your table with a special centerpiece. When selecting one, make sure it isn't too tall for guests to easily see one another across the table. As a general rule of thumb, the maximum acceptable height for a centerpiece is 10 to 12 inches.

Turkey Dinner Cupcakes

(Pictured above)

PREP: 1-1/2 hours

Delight the young and young–at–heart at your Thanksgiving table with these yummy treats resembling a turkey dinner.
—*Karen Tack, Riverside, Connecticut*

> **2 cans (16 ounces *each*) vanilla frosting**
> **Green and yellow food coloring**
> **2 cups cornflakes**
> **2-inch slice pound cake**
> **24 honey wheat sticks**
> **144 soft caramels**
> **24 vanilla cupcakes baked in orange foil liners**
> **Orange round candies (Sixlets)**
> **Yellow and purple candy-coated sunflower seeds**
>   **Ground cinnamon**

Tint 3 tablespoons of vanilla frosting light green with the green and yellow food coloring. Spoon the frosting into a resealable bag; set aside. Spoon 3 tablespoons vanilla frosting into a resealable bag; set aside.

Line a cookie sheet with waxed paper. Place the cornflakes in a large bowl. Tint 1/2 cup of the vanilla frosting green with the green food coloring. Heat green frosting in a microwave-safe bowl until liquid, about 10 to 15 seconds, stirring well. Pour frosting over cornflakes and toss until completely coated. Pour coated cornflakes onto prepared cookie sheet and spread out into a single layer. Allow cornflakes to dry, about 30 minutes.

Meanwhile, cut the pound cake into 1/8-in. cubes; cover until ready to use.

Cut the wheat sticks in half. Soften several caramels in the microwave for no more than 3 seconds. Flatten a caramel slightly and place one end of a wheat stick in the center of the flattened caramel.

Bring the caramel up and over the end of the wheat stick and shape into a drumstick. Trim the overhanging end of the wheat stick to 1/2 inch with a serrated knife. Continue to make 48 drumsticks.

Microwave four caramels at a time to soften, about 3 seconds. Press the caramels together and roll them out to a 3-1/2-in. diameter. Cut caramels into a 3-1/2-in. circle with a round cookie cutter or the opening of a glass. Cut out an opening for the stuffing about 1-1/2 in. wide and deep. Repeat with the remaining caramels to make 24 skins. Place caramel skins between sheets of waxed paper. (The drumsticks and skins can be made up to 4 days in advance and kept in an airtight container.)

Place a mound of vanilla frosting on top of a cupcake; top with a caramel turkey skin. Tuck the edge of the caramel in 1/4 in. from the edge of the cupcake. Use a small knife to push the caramel into the frosting; it will make the turkey look plumper and give room for the lettuce cornflakes. Pinch the ends of the caramel opening; some of the frosting will pop out. Press some of the cake cubes into the frosting as the stuffing.

Lightly brush one side of each drumstick with a bit of water. Press each drumstick to each side of the stuffing opening. Hold several seconds to secure. Repeat with the remaining drumsticks.

Snip a small corner from the bag with the vanilla frosting. Add green cornflakes around the edge of the cupcake to look like lettuce. Use some vanilla frosting if necessary to help secure. Pipe dots of vanilla frosting on the ends of wheat sticks to look like ends of turkey bones. Add more cake cubes as stuffing if desired.

Snip a small corner from the bag with the light green frosting. Pipe a few dots around the turkey and add the candies and seeds as fruit. Cluster the purple seeds as a bunch of grapes and pipe a dot of frosting on top as the stems. Sprinkle the top of the caramel turkey with some cinnamon. **Yield:** 2 dozen.

Everything Bread

PREP: 45 min. + rising **BAKE:** 25 min.

I love to make bread from scratch. This lovely braid has become one of our tried–and–true favorites to go with any meal, casual or formal.
—*Traci Wynne, Denver, Pennsylvania*

☑ **This recipe includes Nutrition Facts and Diabetic Exchanges.**

> **1 package (1/4 ounces) active dry yeast**
> **3/4 cup warm water (110° to 115°)**
> **1 cup warm 2% milk (110° to 115°)**
> **1/4 cup butter, softened**
> **2 tablespoons sugar**
> **1 egg yolk**

1-1/2 **teaspoons salt**
   4 **to 4-1/2 cups all-purpose flour**
   1 **egg white**
   2 **teaspoons water**
   1 **teaspoon coarse sea salt** *or* **kosher salt**
   1 **teaspoon dried minced onion**
   1 **teaspoon** *each* **sesame, caraway and poppy seeds**

In a large bowl, dissolve the yeast in warm water. Add the milk, butter, sugar, egg yolk, salt and 2 cups flour. Beat on medium speed for 3 minutes. Stir in enough remaining flour to form a firm dough.

   Turn onto a floured surface; knead until smooth and elastic, about 6-8 minutes. Place in a greased bowl, turning once to grease the top. Cover and let rise until doubled, about 1 hour.

   Punch the dough down. Turn onto a lightly floured surface; divide the dough into thirds. Shape each into a 20-in. rope. Place ropes on a large greased baking sheet and braid; pinch ends to seal and tuck under. Cover and let rise until doubled, about 45 minutes.

   Combine the egg white and water; brush over dough. Combine the salt, onion and seeds; sprinkle over bread. Bake at 375° for 22-28 minutes or until golden brown. Remove from pan to a wire rack to cool. **Yield:** 1 loaf (25 slices).

   Nutrition Facts: 1 slice equals 102 calories, 2 g fat (1 g saturated fat), 14 mg cholesterol, 237 mg sodium, 17 g carbohydrate, 1 g fiber, 3 g protein. **Diabetic Exchanges:** 1 starch, 1/2 fat.

Gorgonzola-Pear Mesclun Salad

(Pictured above)

PREP/TOTAL TIME: 10 min.

This elegant salad makes a refreshing addition to a holiday table. If you like, swap apples for the pears and pecans for the walnuts.
   —Joylyn Trickel, Helendale, California

   2 **large pears, sliced**
   1 **tablespoon lemon juice**
   6 **cups spring mix salad greens**
   1 **cup (4 ounces) crumbled Gorgonzola cheese**
   1 **cup chopped walnuts, toasted**
1/2 **cup raspberry vinaigrette**

In a salad bowl, toss pears with lemon juice. Add the salad greens, cheese, walnuts and vinaigrette; toss to coat. Serve immediately. **Yield:** 10 servings.

Green Beans in Yellow Pepper Butter

(Pictured below)

PREP/TOTAL TIME: 30 min.

It's hard to pass up these colorful, buttery beans. For an even fancier look, sprinkle more pine nuts on top before serving.
   —Judie White, Florien, Louisiana

   2 **medium sweet yellow peppers,** *divided*
   7 **tablespoons butter, softened,** *divided*
1/4 **cup pine nuts**
   1 **tablespoon lemon juice**
1/4 **teaspoon salt**
1/8 **teaspoon pepper**
1-1/2 **pounds fresh green beans, trimmed**

Finely chop one yellow pepper. In a small skillet, saute pepper in 1 tablespoon butter until tender. Set aside.

   Place nuts, lemon juice, salt, pepper and remaining butter in a food processor; cover and process until blended. Add cooked pepper; cover and process until blended. Set butter aside.

   Place beans in a large saucepan and cover with water. Cut remaining pepper into thin strips; add to the beans. Bring to a boil. Cover and cook for 5-7 minutes or until crisp-tender; drain. Place vegetables in a large bowl; add butter mixture and toss to coat. **Yield:** 8 servings.

Cranberry Pecan Stuffing

(Pictured below)

PREP: 30 min. **BAKE:** 40 min.

I love stuffing, but my family wasn't that fond of it—until I found this recipe. I added a few extra ingredients, and now they gobble it up. I think the cranberries give it that something special.
—*Robin Lang, Muskegon, Michigan*

- 1 cup orange juice
- 1/2 cup dried cranberries
- 1/2 pound bulk pork sausage
- 1/4 cup butter, cubed
- 3 celery ribs, chopped
- 1 large onion, chopped
- 1 teaspoon poultry seasoning
- 6 cups seasoned stuffing cubes
- 1 medium tart apple, peeled and finely chopped
- 1/2 cup chopped pecans
- 1/4 teaspoon salt
- 1/8 teaspoon pepper
- 3/4 to 1 cup chicken broth

In a small saucepan, bring orange juice and cranberries to a boil. Remove from the heat; let stand for 5 minutes. Meanwhile, in a large skillet, cook the sausage until no longer pink; drain. Transfer to a large bowl.

In the same skillet, melt butter. Add celery and onion; saute until tender. Stir in poultry seasoning.

Add to the sausage. Stir in the stuffing cubes, orange juice mixture, apple, pecans, salt, pepper and enough broth to reach desired moistness.

Transfer stuffing to a greased 13-in. x 9-in. baking dish. Cover and bake at 325° for 30 minutes. Uncover; bake

Honey-Thyme Butternut Squash

(Pictured above)

PREP/TOTAL TIME: 30 min.

Golden, honey-sweetened squash makes a tasty side for holiday turkey or any autumn entree. This dish can easily take the place of potatoes. —*Bianca Noiseux, Bristol, Connecticut*

☑ This recipe includes Nutrition Facts and Diabetic Exchanges.

- 1 large butternut squash (about 5 pounds), peeled and cubed
- 1/4 cup butter, cubed
- 3 tablespoons half-and-half cream
- 2 tablespoons honey
- 2 teaspoons dried parsley flakes
- 1/2 teaspoon salt
- 1/8 teaspoon dried thyme
- 1/8 teaspoon coarsely ground pepper

Place squash in a large saucepan and cover with water. Bring to a boil. Reduce the heat; cover and simmer for 8-10 minutes or until tender.

Drain. Mash squash with the remaining ingredients. **Yield:** 10 servings.

Nutrition Facts: 3/4 cup equals 145 calories, 5 g fat (3 g saturated fat), 14 mg cholesterol, 161 mg sodium, 26 g carbohydrate, 7 g fiber, 2 g protein. **Diabetic Exchanges:** 1-1/2 starch, 1 fat.

10-15 minutes longer or until lightly browned. **Yield:** 13 servings (3/4 cup each).

Editor's Note: This recipe makes enough stuffing to stuff a 14-pound turkey. Bake until a meat thermometer reads 180° for turkey and 165° for stuffing.

Cranberry-Apple Chutney

(Pictured on page 158)

PREP: 20 min. **COOK:** 35 min. + chilling

This tangy condiment, draped over slices of turkey, is a must for Thanksgiving dinner in our house. The chutney also makes a great appetizer spooned over cream cheese on Melba rounds.
—*Mary Ellen Gilbert, Franconia, New Hampshire*

  1-1/4 **cups sugar**
    1/2 **cup water**
      1 **package (12 ounces) fresh *or* frozen cranberries**
      2 **large tart apples, peeled and finely chopped**
      1 **medium onion, chopped**
    1/2 **cup golden raisins**
    1/2 **cup packed brown sugar**
    1/4 **cup cider vinegar**
      1 **teaspoon ground cinnamon**
    1/4 **teaspoon salt**
    1/8 **teaspoon ground allspice**
    1/8 **teaspoon ground cloves**
    1/2 **cup chopped walnuts, toasted**

In a large saucepan over medium heat, bring sugar and water to a boil. Reduce the heat; simmer, uncovered, for 3 minutes. Carefully stir in the cranberries, apples, onion, raisins, brown sugar, cider vinegar, cinnamon, salt, allspice and cloves.

Return to a boil. Reduce the heat; simmer, uncovered, for 20-25 minutes or until desired thickness, stirring occasionally. Just before serving, stir in walnuts. Serve warm or cold. **Yield:** 4 cups.

Upside-Down Apple Pie

(Pictured above right)

PREP: 1 hour + chilling **BAKE:** 1 hour + cooling

I combined two of my favorite recipes to create this sensational dessert, which won the local apple pie contest several years ago. I usually make two because we always end up wanting more.
—*Becky Berger, Deerfield, Illinois*

      3 **cups all-purpose flour**
      1 **tablespoon sugar**
      1 **teaspoon salt**
    3/4 **cup cold butter, cubed**
    1/3 **cup shortening, cubed**
      4 **to 6 tablespoons cold water**
PECANS:
    1/2 **cup packed brown sugar**

    1/4 **cup butter, melted**
      1 **cup pecan halves**
FILLING:
      1 **cup sugar**
    1/3 **cup all-purpose flour**
      2 **tablespoons butter, melted**
    1/4 **teaspoon ground cinnamon**
      8 **cups thinly sliced peeled tart apples**

In a food processor, combine flour, sugar and salt; cover and pulse until blended. Add the butter and shortening; pulse until the mixture resembles coarse crumbs. While processing, gradually add water until the dough forms a ball. Divide the dough in half so that one portion is slightly larger than the other; wrap each in plastic wrap. Refrigerate for 45 minutes or until easy to handle.

Coat a 9-in. deep-dish pie plate with cooking spray. Line bottom and sides of plate with parchment paper; coat paper with cooking spray and set aside.

In a small bowl, combine brown sugar and butter; stir in pecans. Arrange in the bottom of prepared pie plate with rounded sides of pecans facing down.

On a lightly floured surface, roll out larger portion of dough to fit bottom and sides of pie plate. Transfer to plate; press the crust firmly against pecans and sides of pie plate. Trim edges.

In a large bowl, combine the sugar, flour, butter and cinnamon. Add apples; toss to coat. Fill crust. Roll out remaining pastry to fit top of pie; place over filling. Trim and seal edges. Cut slits in pastry.

Place a foil-lined baking sheet on a rack below the pie to catch any spills. Bake pie at 375° for 60-70 minutes or until golden brown. Carefully loosen the parchment paper around edge of pie; invert hot pie onto a serving plate. Remove paper. Cool for at least 15 minutes before serving. **Yield:** 8 servings.

Merry Cookie Creations

CHRISTMAS just isn't the same without cute cutouts, special spritz and other sweet treats to share. This season, why not add something new to your Yuletide lineup? You're sure to find a number of irresistible options in this section.

Fill your holiday tray with Lemon Angel Wings... pack Pecan Meltaways into tins for a cookie exchange... or delight drop-in guests with Nutty Chocolate Batons. The hardest part isn't making the cookies—it's choosing which recipes to make!

You'll even learn how to turn sensational cream cheese cutout cookies into beautiful ornaments you can use to decorate the Christmas tree.

Nutty Chocolate Batons

(Pictured at left)

PREP: 45 min. + chilling **BAKE:** 10 min./batch + cooling

The great taste of a buttery cookie combines with chocolate and pistachios for these baton–shaped treats. The added bonus is that they look so elegant...people always think that I fussed.
—Angela Leinenbach, Mechanicsville, Virginia

☑ This recipe includes Nutrition Facts and Diabetic Exchange.

    3/4 cup butter, softened
    1/3 cup sugar
    1/3 cup almond paste
      1 egg yolk
  1-2/3 cups all-purpose flour
      1 cup (6 ounces) semisweet chocolate chips
    1/2 cup pistachios, finely chopped and toasted

In a small bowl, cream the butter, sugar and almond paste until light and fluffy. Beat in egg yolk. Gradually add flour and mix well. Shape into a ball, then flatten into a disk. Wrap in plastic wrap and refrigerate for 2 hours or until easy to handle.

Divide dough into eight equal portions; divide each portion in half. On a lightly floured surface, roll each half into a 12-in. rope; cut each rope into 2-in. lengths. Place 2 in. apart on greased baking sheets. Bake at 350° for 6-8 minutes or until the edges are lightly browned. Remove to wire racks to cool completely.

In a microwave, melt the semisweet chocolate chips; stir until smooth. Dip one end of each cookie in the melted chocolate, then in pistachios. Let the cookies stand on waxed paper until set. Store in an airtight container. **Yield:** 8 dozen.

Nutrition Facts: 1 cookie equals 39 calories, 3 g fat (1 g saturated fat), 6 mg cholesterol, 13 mg sodium, 4 g carbohydrate, trace fiber, 1 g protein. **Diabetic Exchange:** 1/2 starch.

Lemon Angel Wings

(Pictured below)

PREP: 20 min. + chilling **BAKE:** 20 min./batch + cooling

The light, lemony flavor of these delicate cookies is wonderful. Their unique shape also looks impressive on a holiday tray.
—Charlotte Westfall, Houston, Texas

  1-1/2 cups all-purpose flour
      1 cup cold butter
    1/2 cup sour cream
      1 teaspoon grated lemon peel
     10 tablespoons sugar, *divided*

Place flour in a large bowl; cut in butter until crumbly. Stir in sour cream and lemon peel until well blended. Place on a piece of waxed paper; shape into a 4-1/2-in. square. Wrap in plastic wrap and refrigerate for at least 2 hours.

Cut dough into four 2-1/4-in. squares. Place one square on a piece of waxed paper sprinkled with 2 tablespoons sugar. Cover with another piece of waxed paper. Keep remaining squares refrigerated. Roll out dough into a 12-in. x 5-in. rectangle, turning often to coat both sides with sugar.

Lightly mark center of 12-in. side. Starting with a short side, roll up jelly-roll style to the center mark, peeling the paper away while rolling. Repeat rolling from the other short side, so the two rolls meet in the center and resemble a scroll.

Wrap in plastic wrap and refrigerate. Repeat with the remaining squares, using 2 tablespoons sugar for each. Chill for 1 hour.

Unwrap dough and cut into 1/2-in. slices; dip each side in remaining sugar. Place 2 in. apart on foil-lined baking sheets. Bake at 375° for 14 minutes or until golden brown. Turn cookies over; bake 5 minutes longer. Remove to wire racks to cool. **Yield:** 3 dozen.

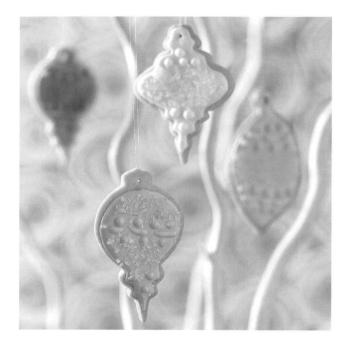

In a large bowl, cream butter, cream cheese and sugar until light and fluffy. Beat in the egg yolk and extracts. Combine flour, salt and baking soda; gradually add to creamed mixture and mix well. Cover and refrigerate for 3 hours or until easy to handle.

On a lightly floured surface, roll out dough to 1/8-in. thickness. Cut with a floured 2-1/2-in. cookie cutter. Place 1 in. apart on ungreased baking sheets. Bake at 375° for 8-10 minutes or until the edges begin to brown. Cool for 2 minutes before removing from pans to wire racks. Decorate as desired. **Yield:** 4 dozen.

Linzer Cookies

(Pictured below)

PREP: 20 min. + chilling **BAKE:** 10 min./batch

These pretty, sugar-sprinkled cookies filled with ruby-red jam may take a little extra effort, but the results are so worth it!
—Jane Pearcy, Verona, Wisconsin

      1-1/4 cups butter, softened
          1 cup sugar
          2 eggs
          3 cups all-purpose flour
          1 tablespoon baking cocoa
        1/2 teaspoon salt
        1/4 teaspoon ground cinnamon
        1/4 teaspoon ground nutmeg
        1/8 teaspoon ground cloves
          2 cups ground almonds
          6 tablespoons seedless raspberry jam
          3 tablespoons confectioners' sugar

In a large bowl, cream the butter and sugar until light and fluffy. Add eggs, one at a time, beating well after each addition. Combine the flour, cocoa, salt and spices;

Holiday Sugar Cookies

(Pictured above)

PREP: 40 min. **BAKE:** 10 min./batch + cooling

Cream cheese adds a rich flavor to these melt-in-your-mouth cookies. See the tip box below for turning them into lovely tree ornaments.   *—Julie Brunette, Green Bay, Wisconsin*

          1 cup butter, softened
          1 package (3 ounces) cream cheese, softened
          1 cup sugar
          1 egg yolk
        1/2 teaspoon vanilla extract
        1/4 teaspoon almond extract
      2-1/4 cups all-purpose flour
        1/2 teaspoon salt
        1/4 teaspoon baking soda
Tinted frosting, coarse sugar *and/or* colored sugar

HOLIDAY HOW-TO. Want to turn Holiday Sugar Cookies (recipe above) into ornaments? To firm up the batter, add an extra 1-3/4 cups of flour. After placing the cutout cookies on a baking sheet, poke a hole in each one so the cookie can hang. If the hole fills up during baking, carefully twist a toothpick in the correct spot to make the hole.

Frost the cookie ornaments with royal icing and use a pastry bag with a #5 tip to apply dots and dashes. For the final touches, sprinkle coarse sugar over the top and tie on hangers.

Walnut Horn Cookies

(Pictured below)

PREP: 40 min. **BAKE:** 35 min./batch

It takes just walnuts, cream cheese, sugar and a handful of other kitchen staples to create these elegant horn–shaped treats.
—*Loretta Stokes, Philadelphia, Pennsylvania*

> 1 **cup plus 1 teaspoon butter, softened,** *divided*
> 1 **package (8 ounces) cream cheese, softened**
> 3 **cups all-purpose flour**
> 4 **cups ground walnuts**
> 1-1/4 **cups sugar,** *divided*
> 1/2 **cup 2% milk**
> 1 **teaspoon vanilla extract**
> 1/8 **teaspoon salt**

In a large bowl, beat 1 cup butter and the cream cheese until light and fluffy. Gradually add flour, beating until mixture forms a ball. Divide dough into four portions; roll each into a 12-in. circle.

Melt the remaining butter. In a large bowl, combine the walnuts, 3/4 cup sugar, milk, vanilla, salt and melted butter. Spread over the circles. Cut each into 12 wedges. Roll up wedges, starting from the wide ends.

Place the point side down on greased baking sheets. Curve the ends to form crescents. Bake at 325° for 35-40 minutes or until lightly browned. Remove to wire racks.

Place remaining sugar in a small shallow bowl. Roll warm cookies in the sugar. **Yield:** 4 dozen.

gradually add to creamed mixture and mix well. Stir in almonds. Refrigerate for 1 hour or until easy to handle.

On a lightly floured surface, roll out dough to 1/8-in. thickness. Cut with a floured 2-1/2-in. round cookie cutter. From the center of half of the cookies, cut out a 1-1/2-in. shape.

Place on ungreased baking sheets. Bake at 350° for 10-12 minutes or until edges are golden brown. Remove to wire racks to cool.

Spread bottom of each solid cookie with 1/2 teaspoon jam. Sprinkle cutout cookies with confectioners' sugar; carefully place over jam. **Yield:** 3 dozen.

Pecan Goody Cups

(Pictured above and on page 158)

PREP: 35 min. + chilling **BAKE:** 20 min./batch

Pecan halves, a caramel–like filling and a buttery cream cheese crust make these tarts hard to resist. They bake in a miniature muffin pan.
—*Janice Hose, Hagerstown, Maryland*

> 3/4 **cup butter, softened**
> 2 **packages (3 ounces** *each***) cream cheese, softened**
> 2 **cups all-purpose flour**

FILLING:

> 1-1/2 **cups packed brown sugar**
> 2 **eggs**
> 1 **tablespoon butter, melted**
> 48 **pecan halves**

In a large bowl, beat butter and cream cheese until light and fluffy. Gradually add flour, beating until mixture forms a ball. Cover and refrigerate for 15 minutes. For filling, in a small bowl, combine the brown sugar, eggs and butter.

Roll dough into 1-in. balls. Press onto the bottoms and up the sides of greased miniature muffin cups. Spoon filling into cups; top each with a pecan half.

Bake at 350° for 20-25 minutes or until golden brown. Cool for 2-3 minutes before removing from pans to wire racks. **Yield:** 4 dozen.

Cinnamon Chocolate Minties

(Pictured below)

PREP: 45 min.   **BAKE:** 10 min./batch + cooling

These brownie–like cookies are so pretty with crushed candy and chocolate on top. —Barbara Estabrook, Rhinelander, Wisconsin

☑ **This recipe includes Nutrition Facts and Diabetic Exchanges.**

- 1/2 **cup butter, softened**
- 1/2 **cup sugar**
- 1/2 **cup packed brown sugar**
- 1 **egg**
- 1 **teaspoon vanilla extract**
- 1-1/2 **cups all-purpose flour**
- 1/3 **cup baking cocoa**
- 1 **teaspoon ground cinnamon**
- 1/4 **teaspoon baking soda**
- 1/3 **cup coarsely crushed soft peppermint candies**
- 1/3 **cup dark chocolate chips**

DRIZZLE:
- 1/2 **cup semisweet chocolate chips**
- 1/2 **teaspoon canola oil**
- 2 **teaspoons finely crushed soft peppermint candies**

In a small bowl, cream butter and sugars until light and fluffy. Beat in egg and vanilla. Combine the flour, cocoa, cinnamon and baking soda; gradually add to creamed mixture and mix well. Fold in the candies and dark chocolate chips.

Shape into 1-in. balls; place the balls 1 in. apart on greased baking sheets. Flatten slightly. Bake at 350° for 6-8 minutes or until set. Remove to wire racks to cool completely.

In a small bowl, melt semisweet chips with oil; stir until smooth. Drizzle over the cookies. Sprinkle with the candies. Let stand until set. Store cookies in an airtight container. **Yield:** about 4 dozen.

Nutrition Facts: 1 cookie equals 73 calories, 3 g fat (2 g saturated fat), 9 mg cholesterol, 23 mg sodium, 11 g carbohydrate, trace fiber, 1 g protein. **Diabetic Exchanges:** 1/2 starch, 1/2 fat.

Editor's Note: This recipe was tested with Bob's Sweet Stripes peppermint candies.

Candy Cane Cookies

(Pictured above)

PREP: 25 min.   **BAKE:** 10 min./batch + cooling

Children love these festive candy cane–shaped cookies that have peppermint sprinkles. —Tammy Schenk, Harlowton, Montana

- 1 **cup butter, softened**
- 1 **cup confectioners' sugar**
- 1 **egg**
- 1-1/2 **teaspoons almond extract**
- 2-1/2 **cups all-purpose flour**
- 1 **teaspoon salt**

Red food coloring
- 1/2 **cup crushed peppermint candy canes**
- 1/2 **cup sugar**

In a small bowl, cream butter and confectioners' sugar until light and fluffy. Beat in egg and extract. Combine flour and salt; gradually add to creamed mixture and mix well. Divide the dough in half; add 6-7 drops of food coloring to one half. Shape tablespoonfuls of each color of dough into 4-in. ropes. Place ropes side by side; lightly press the ends together and twist. Place on ungreased baking sheets; curve to form canes.

Bake at 375° for 9-12 minutes or until lightly browned. Combine crushed candy canes and sugar; immediately sprinkle over the cookies. Cool for 2 minutes before removing from pans to wire racks to cool. **Yield:** 3 dozen.

Touch-of-Gold Christmas Trees

(Pictured below)

PREP: 40 min. **BAKE:** 10 min./batch

If you prefer, you can enjoy these shimmering spritz evergreens individually—rather than as sandwich cookies with the hazelnut filling. But I think the filling makes them extra special.
—Linda Sweet, Cornwall, New York

✓ This recipe includes Nutrition Facts and Diabetic Exchanges.

- 1-1/2 cups butter, softened
- 1 cup sugar
- 1 egg
- 2 tablespoons 2% milk
- 1 teaspoon almond extract
- 1 teaspoon vanilla extract
- 3-1/2 cups all-purpose flour
- 1 teaspoon baking powder
- 2/3 cup chocolate hazelnut spread

Gold pearl dust

In a large bowl, cream butter and sugar until light and fluffy. Beat in the egg, milk and extracts. Combine flour and baking powder; gradually add to creamed mixture and mix well.

Using a cookie press fitted with the Christmas tree disk, press the dough 2 in. apart onto ungreased baking sheets. Bake at 375° for 8-10 minutes or until set (do not brown). Remove to wire racks to cool completely.

Spread the hazelnut spread on the bottoms of half of the cookies; top with the remaining cookies. Brush the tops with pearl dust. Store in an airtight container. **Yield:** 5-1/2 dozen.

Nutrition Facts: 1 cookie equals 89 calories, 5 g fat

(3 g saturated fat), 14 mg cholesterol, 38 mg sodium, 10 g carbohydrate, trace fiber, 1 g protein. **Diabetic Exchanges:** 1 fat, 1/2 starch.

Editor's Note: Pearl dust is available from Wilton Industries. Call 1-800/794-5866 or visit *www.wilton.com*.

Pecan Meltaways

(Pictured above)

PREP: 15 min. + chilling **BAKE:** 10 min./batch

These sugared, nut-filled balls are a tradition at our house at Christmastime, but they're great any time of year. You won't be able to eat just one! —Alberta McKay, Bartlesville, Oklahoma

- 1 cup butter, softened
- 1/2 cup confectioners' sugar
- 1 teaspoon vanilla extract
- 2-1/4 cups all-purpose flour
- 1/4 teaspoon salt
- 3/4 cup chopped pecans

Additional confectioners' sugar

In a large bowl, cream the butter, confectioners' sugar and vanilla until light and fluffy. Combine flour and salt; gradually add to creamed mixture and mix well. Stir in pecans. Refrigerate until chilled.

Roll into 1-in. balls and place on ungreased baking sheets. Bake at 350° for 10-12 minutes or until set. Roll warm cookies in additional confectioners' sugar; cool completely on wire racks. Roll cooled cookies again in confectioners' sugar. **Yield:** 4 dozen.

Homemade Gifts for Christmas

WHEN YOU want to warm hearts at holiday time, nothing beats from-scratch treats you've whipped up in the kitchen. Just take your pick of the guaranteed-to-please goodies here!

For chocolate lovers, you can't go wrong with Triple Chocolate Fudge or Chocolate-Covered Pretzels. And fans of old-fashioned confections will adore Cashew Brittle and Pecan Caramels.

Don't forget Caramel Corn with Nuts for all of the snackers on your list. And colorful Homemade Marshmallows make a fun addition to mugs of hot cocoa.

Cashew Brittle

(Pictured at left)

PREP: 10 min. **COOK:** 30 min. + cooling

I've made some changes to this recipe and have now been using it for 25 years. One year I whipped up over 170 pounds!
—Jim Merchant, Vinton, Iowa

- **1 tablespoon plus 1 cup butter,** *divided*
- **2 cups sugar**
- **1 cup light corn syrup**
- **1 cup water**
- **2-1/2 cups unsalted cashew halves**
- **1/4 teaspoon baking soda**

Butter a 15-in. x 10-in. x 1-in. pan with 1 tablespoon butter and set aside.

In a large saucepan, combine the sugar, corn syrup and water. Bring to a boil, stirring constantly. Reduce heat; cut remaining butter into cubes and carefully stir into the syrup. Cook and stir until a candy thermometer reads 280° (soft-crack stage).

Add the nuts; cook and stir until candy thermometer reads 295°. Remove from the heat; stir in baking soda. Immediately pour into prepared pan. Cool; break into pieces. Store in an airtight container. **Yield:** 2-1/4 pounds.

Editor's Note: We recommend that you test your candy thermometer before each use by bringing water to a boil; the thermometer should read 212°. Adjust your recipe temperature up or down based on your test.

STICKY SOLUTION. When making Cashew Brittle (recipe above) or other brittle, keep this hint in mind to avoid a sticky outcome. For best results, make candy when the humidity is below 60%. Also, use a candy thermometer to be sure ingredients are cooked to the proper temperature.

Pecan Caramels

(Pictured at left and below)

PREP: 30 min. **COOK:** 40 min. + standing

These chewy, nutty caramels may take a little bit of extra time to prepare, but it's worth it! —Darrell Brown, Lincoln, Nebraska

- **2 teaspoons plus 1 cup butter,** *divided*
- **1-1/4 cups sugar**
- **1-1/4 cups packed brown sugar**
- **1 cup dark corn syrup**
- **2 cups heavy whipping cream,** *divided*
- **2 pounds chopped pecans**
- **1 teaspoon vanilla extract**

Line a 13-in. x 9-in. pan with foil; grease the foil with 2 teaspoons butter and set aside.

In a large heavy saucepan, combine sugars, corn syrup, 1 cup cream and remaining butter. Cook and stir over medium heat until sugar is dissolved. Bring to a boil. Slowly stir in remaining cream. Cook, without stirring, until a candy thermometer reads 245° (firm-ball stage).

Remove from the heat; stir in pecans and vanilla. Pour into prepared pan (do not scrape saucepan). Let stand until firm. Using foil, lift candy out of pan. Discard foil; cut candy into 1-in. squares. Wrap individually in waxed paper; twist ends. **Yield:** 4-1/4 pounds.

Editor's Note: We recommend that you test your candy thermometer before each use by bringing water to a boil; the thermometer should read 212°. Adjust your recipe temperature up or down based on your test.

Triple Chocolate Fudge

(Pictured above and on page 188)

PREP: 20 min. **COOK:** 25 min. + chilling

This recipe makes more than enough creamy fudge to share with family, friends and neighbors. It's the ultimate gift!
—Linette Shepherd, Williamston, Michigan

- **4 teaspoons plus 1/2 cup butter, *divided***
- **4-1/2 cups sugar**
- **1 can (12 ounces) evaporated milk**
- **1 teaspoon salt**
- **16 ounces German sweet chocolate, chopped**
- **2 cups (12 ounces) semisweet chocolate chips**
- **1 package (11-1/2 ounces) milk chocolate chips**
- **2 jars (7 ounces *each*) marshmallow creme**
- **4 cups chopped pecans *and/or* walnuts, toasted**
- **2 teaspoons vanilla extract**

Line two 13-in. x 9-in. pans with foil; grease the foil with 4 teaspoons butter. In a heavy Dutch oven, combine the sugar, evaporated milk, salt and remaining butter. Bring to a boil over medium heat, stirring constantly. Cook, without stirring, until a candy thermometer reads 234° (soft-ball stage).

Remove from the heat. Stir in the German sweet chocolate and chocolate chips until smooth. Fold in the marshmallow creme, pecans and vanilla. Spread into prepared pans.

Refrigerate for 1 hour or until firm. Using foil, lift fudge out of the pan. Discard foil; cut fudge into 1-in. squares. Store in airtight containers. **Yield:** 6-3/4 pounds.

Homemade Marshmallows

(Pictured below)

PREP: 55 min. + standing

At Christmas, my grandpa always made marshmallows. These goodies are such treat. *—Diana Byron, New London, Ohio*

- **2 teaspoons butter**
- **3 envelopes unflavored gelatin**
- **1 cup cold water, *divided***
- **2 cups sugar**
- **1 cup light corn syrup**
- **1/8 teaspoon salt**
- **1 teaspoon clear vanilla extract**
- **Optional toppings: melted chocolate, hot fudge *and/or* caramel ice cream topping**
- **Optional garnishes: baking cocoa, confectioners' sugar, crushed candies, chopped nuts, colored sugars *and/or* sprinkles**

Line a 13-in. x 9-in. pan with foil and grease the foil with butter; set aside.

In a large metal bowl, sprinkle the gelatin over 1/2 cup water; set aside. In a large heavy saucepan, combine the sugar, corn syrup, salt and remaining water. Bring to a boil, stirring occasionally. Cook, without stirring, until a candy thermometer reads 240° (soft-ball stage).

Remove from the heat and gradually add to gelatin. Beat on high speed until the mixture is thick and the volume is doubled, about 15 minutes. Beat in vanilla. Spread into prepared pan. Cover and let stand at room temperature for 6 hours or overnight.

Using foil, lift marshmallows out of pan. With a knife or pizza cutter coated with cooking spray, cut into 1-in. squares. Dip or drizzle marshmallows with toppings if desired; coat with garnishes as desired. Roll the other marshmallows in desired garnishes. Store in an airtight container in a cool dry place. **Yield:** about 9-1/2 dozen.

Editor's Note: We recommend that you test your candy thermometer before each use by bringing water to a boil; the thermometer should read 212°. Adjust your recipe temperature up or down based on your test.

Caramel Corn with Nuts

(Pictured above)

PREP: 20 min. **BAKE:** 45 min.

This caramel corn far surpasses any store-bought variety I've tried. Adding mixed nuts makes it even better. I usually double the recipe for gifts. —Karen Scaglione, Nanuet, New York

- **10 cups popped popcorn**
- **1 cup packed brown sugar**
- **1/2 cup butter, cubed**
- **1/4 cup dark corn syrup**
- **1/4 teaspoon salt**
- **1/4 teaspoon baking soda**
- **1/2 cup mixed nuts**

Place popcorn in a large bowl; set aside. In a large heavy saucepan, combine the brown sugar, butter, corn syrup and salt. Cook over medium heat, stirring occasionally, until mixture comes to a rolling boil. Cook and stir until candy thermometer reads 238° (soft-ball stage). Remove from the heat; stir in baking soda (mixture will foam). Quickly pour over popcorn and mix well; stir in nuts.

Transfer to two greased 13-in. x 9-in. baking pans. Bake at 200° for 45 minutes, stirring once. Remove from pans and place on waxed paper to cool. Break into clusters. Store in airtight containers. **Yield:** 2-1/2 quarts.

Editor's Note: We recommend that you test your candy thermometer before each use by bringing water to a boil; the thermometer should read 212°. Adjust your recipe temperature up or down based on your test.

Chocolate-Covered Pretzels

(Pictured above)

PREP: 1 hour + chilling

These are addictive! A yummy variation is to replace the pretzels with an 18-ounce package of cream-filled cookies.
—Aimee Worth, Fair Oaks, California

- **12 ounces milk chocolate candy coating disks**
- **20 large sourdough pretzels,** *divided*
- **Colored sprinkles**
- **12 ounces white candy coating disks**

In a microwave, melt milk chocolate; stir until smooth. Dip 10 pretzels in chocolate, allowing the excess to drip off. Place on waxed paper. Decorate half of the pretzels with sprinkles. Chill for 10 minutes or until set.

Melt the white chocolate; stir until smooth. Dip the remaining pretzels in white chocolate, allowing excess to drip off. Place on waxed paper. Decorate half of the pretzels with sprinkles. Chill for 10 minutes or until set.

Drizzle the plain white-coated pretzels with melted milk chocolate. Drizzle the plain milk chocolate-coated pretzels with the melted white chocolate. Chill for 10 minutes or until set. Store in an airtight container. **Yield:** 20 pretzels.

'Mom's Best'

Six family cooks fondly recall their mothers' cooking...and share the recipes for their favorite made-by-mom meals and more.

Italian for the Holidays..................................194
   Lemon Broccoli with Garlic • Italian Christmas Turkey • Mom's Italian Bread • Iced Anise Cookies

Memories of India..198
   Curry Powder • Carrot Salad • Minted Rice with Garbanzo Curry • Cucumber Salad • Chicken Korma

South-of-the-Border Best 202
   Lavender Lemonade • Easy Enchiladas • Homemade Guacamole • Giant Flan

Slow Cooking on Sunday............................206
   Zucchini Relish • Beef Roast with Gravy • Honey Sweet Corn • Cake Roll with Berries

Home-Cooked History 210
   Dad's Baked Beans • Campers' Coleslaw • Barbecued Pork Sandwiches • Cream Puff Cake

Deliciously Diet-Friendly 214
   Penny's Apple-Brown Sugar Coffee Cake • Spaghetti and Meatballs with Garlic Crumbs • Grilled Peach BBQ Chicken Wings • Chocolate Chip-Banana Belgian Waffles

HOME-STYLE HIGHLIGHTS. Clockwise from upper left: Deliciously Diet-Friendly (p. 214), Memories of India (p. 198), Slow Cooking on Sunday (p. 206) and South-of-the-Border Best (p. 202).

LEMON BROCCOLI WITH GARLIC   MOM'S ITALIAN BREAD   ICED ANISE COOKIES

Italian
Christmas Turkey

Her Italian mother cooked almost everything from scratch and never used recipes. The result? Always an abundance of food...and room for one more at the dinner table.

By Linda Harrington, Hudson, New Hampshire

"ARE YOU hungry? Have you eaten yet?" Those are usually among the first words Italians will utter when you enter their home.

My mother, Elsie Laurenzo Palmer (above, at right), from Mechanicville, New York, was no different. Mom is 100% Italian and used to say, "We always have enough food for anyone who comes to visit."

"Food" often meant a traditional Italian meal. The first thing my husband, Jim, noticed when he met me was the constant aroma of garlic and Italian spices on our back porch!

I've shared one of Mom's best holiday dinners here. It started with Italian Christmas Turkey, which featured a favorite of mine—Mom's incredible sausage stuffing. Now, I rarely buy the sausage but make my own instead, like my relatives do.

There was always plenty of Mom's Italian Bread, too. I think she used to bake at least four of these tender loaves at once, and they never lasted long. She served the bread with every Italian meal.

Lemon Broccoli with Garlic was an easy, zesty way to use up leftover broccoli. That's what Mom did, and I tend to do the same thing today.

It was a tradition to have Iced Anise Cookies on Thanksgiving, Christmas and Easter. My grandmother always kept some on hand for her grandchildren. I'd help frost the fresh-baked cookies and put the sprinkles on top.

After my sister, brother and I started school, Mom worked as an executive secretary at a paper company. My dad, Louis, was a factory worker. As the oldest child, I was responsible for making dinner.

On weekends, Mom cooked, and I'd watch and help her. That's how I learned to cook.

I've always enjoyed making Mom's specialties for my own family. Jim and I have three grown daughters and two grandchildren. I even bake goodies for my students. I teach reading in grades six, seven and eight; Jim is a pastor.

I've started writing down recipes for Mom's dishes for our daughters, and I give them a few each Christmas. It hasn't been easy trying to calculate a handful of this and a pinch of that!

More than the wonderful taste and aroma of Mom's cooking, I cherish the memories of our family gathered around the dinner table, talking about our heritage. I hope I've passed that tradition on to our girls, too.

Lemon Broccoli with Garlic

PREP/TOTAL TIME: 20 min.

- 1 large bunch broccoli, cut into florets
- 1/2 cup olive oil
- 1/4 cup lemon juice
- 4 garlic cloves, minced
- 1/4 teaspoon salt
- 1/8 teaspoon pepper

Place broccoli in a steamer basket; place in a large saucepan over 1 in. of water. Bring to a boil; cover and steam for 6-8 minutes or until crisp-tender.

Meanwhile, in a small bowl, combine the remaining ingredients. Immediately place broccoli in ice water. Drain and pat dry. Place in a large bowl. Pour oil mixture over broccoli; toss to coat. Refrigerate until serving. **Yield:** 6 servings.

Italian Christmas Turkey

PREP: 40 min. **BAKE:** 3-3/4 hours + standing

1/2 cup butter, cubed
1 pound bulk Italian sausage
2 celery ribs, chopped
1 medium onion, chopped
1 package (14 ounces) seasoned stuffing cubes
1/4 cup egg substitute
2 to 3 cups hot water
1 turkey (16 pounds)
Salt and pepper to taste

In a large skillet over medium heat, melt butter. Add the sausage, celery and onion; cook and stir until meat is no longer pink. Transfer to a large bowl; stir in the stuffing cubes, egg substitute and enough hot water to reach desired moistness.

Just before baking, loosely stuff turkey with stuffing. Place remaining stuffing in a greased 2-qt. baking dish; cover and refrigerate. Remove from the refrigerator 30 minutes before baking.

Skewer turkey openings; tie drumsticks together. Place breast side up in a roasting pan. Rub with salt and pepper.

Bake, uncovered, at 325° for 3-3/4 to 4-1/4 hours or until a meat thermometer reads 180° for turkey and 165° for stuffing, basting occasionally with pan drippings. (Cover loosely with foil if turkey browns too quickly.)

Bake additional stuffing, covered, for 25-30 minutes. Uncover; bake 10 minutes longer or until a thermometer reads 160°. Cover turkey and let stand for 20 minutes before removing stuffing and carving turkey. If desired, thicken pan drippings for gravy. **Yield:** 16 servings (12 cups stuffing).

Mom's Italian Bread

PREP: 30 min. + rising **BAKE:** 20 min. + cooling

☑ This recipe includes Nutrition Facts and Diabetic Exchange.

1 package (1/4 ounce) active dry yeast
2 cups warm water (110° to 115°)
1 teaspoon sugar
2 teaspoons salt
5-1/2 cups all-purpose flour

In a large bowl, dissolve yeast in warm water. Add the sugar, salt and 3 cups flour. Beat on medium speed for 3 minutes. Stir in remaining flour to form a soft dough.

Turn onto a floured surface; knead until smooth and elastic, about 6-8 minutes. Place in a greased bowl, turning once to grease the top. Cover and let rise in a warm place until doubled, about 1 hour.

Punch dough down. Turn onto a floured surface; divide in half. Shape each portion into a loaf. Place each loaf seam side down on a greased baking sheet. Cover and let rise until doubled, about 30 minutes. With a sharp knife, make four shallow slashes across top of each loaf.

Bake at 400° for 20-25 minutes or until golden brown. Remove from pans to wire racks to cool. **Yield:** 2 loaves (12 slices each).

Nutrition Facts: 1 slice equals 106 calories, trace fat (trace saturated fat), 0 cholesterol, 197 mg sodium, 22 g carbohydrate, 1 g fiber, 3 g protein. **Diabetic Exchange:** 1-1/2 starch.

Iced Anise Cookies

PREP: 45 min. **BAKE:** 10 min./batch

✓ This recipe includes Nutrition Facts and Diabetic Exchange.

  2-2/3 **cups all-purpose flour**
    1/2 **cup sugar**
      3 **teaspoons baking powder**
      3 **eggs**
    1/2 **cup butter, melted**
    1/4 **cup 2% milk**
      2 **teaspoons anise extract**
ICING:
    1/4 **cup butter, softened**
      2 **cups confectioners' sugar**
      3 **tablespoons 2% milk**
    1/2 **teaspoon lemon extract**
Coarse and colored sugars, optional

In a large bowl, combine 2 cups flour, sugar and baking powder. In a small bowl, whisk the eggs, butter, milk and extract. Stir into dry ingredients until blended. Stir in remaining flour until dough forms a ball. Turn onto a floured surface; knead until smooth.

Shape dough by rounded teaspoonfuls into thin 6-in. ropes; twist each rope into a "Q" shape. Place on ungreased baking sheets. Bake at 350° for 8-10 minutes or until set. Remove from pans to wire racks to cool completely.

For the icing, in a small bowl, beat the butter until fluffy. Add the confectioners' sugar, milk and lemon extract; beat until smooth. Spread over the tops of the cookies; decorate with coarse and colored sugars if desired. **Yield:** 6 dozen.

Nutrition Facts: 1 cookie equals 56 calories, 2 g fat (1 g saturated fat), 14 mg cholesterol, 34 mg sodium, 8 g carbohydrate, trace fiber, 1 g protein. **Diabetic Exchange:** 1/2 starch.

CURRY POWDER

CUCUMBER SALAD

CARROT SALAD

CHICKEN KORMA

**Minted Rice with
Garbanzo Curry**

He can't recall a cooked-by-mom meal that the whole family didn't love. Today, his mother's traditional Indian cooking is still tops with everyone.

By Anand Madhavan, Omaha, Nebraska

IF THERE'S one thing I never forget to say to my mother after dinner it's, "Good food, Mom!"

Sometimes it may sound more automatic than genuine, but I can't remember my mother ever making a bad meal. It's the best Indian food I've ever tasted.

My mother, Jemima (Jemy) Madhavan (above, at right), along with my father, my older brother and I, came to the U.S. in 1985. For the most part, it has been only the four of us living in the States, so we have an extremely deep bond.

When my brother, Deepak, and I were children, Mom would make anything we asked for. As we got more into American culture, she'd mix in American foods for us but always stayed true to Indian cooking.

Among my favorite dishes are Chicken Korma, Minted Rice with Garbanzo Curry, Cucumber Salad and Carrot Salad. I've shared those recipes here, as well as her unbeatable homemade curry powder (below).

I'm now 27 and a marketing professional, and my brother is a neurologist. Mom still makes our favorites when we come home to Lincoln, Nebraska, where my father is a biochemistry professor. Deepak and I live in Omaha, so we try to eat as a family on weekends.

Cooking is just one of Mom's wonderful talents. I cannot truly express how much she means to me and our family.

One day I hope to repay all of the meals she made for me, the prayers she said for me and the tears she shed for me. For now, she knows her meals will be rewarded with a simple but heartfelt, "Good food, Mom."

Curry Powder

PREP/TOTAL TIME: 10 min.

- 3 cardamom seeds
- 2 teaspoons ground coriander
- 2 teaspoons ground cumin
- 1 teaspoon ground turmeric
- 1/2 teaspoon chili powder
- 1/2 teaspoon pepper
- 1/8 teaspoon fennel seed

Remove cardamom seeds from their pods if necessary. In a spice grinder or with a mortar and pestle, combine all ingredients; grind until mixture becomes a powder. Store in an airtight container for up to one year. **Yield:** 2 tablespoons.

Carrot Salad

PREP: 15 min. + chilling

- 2 medium carrots, grated
- 1 medium tomato, seeded and chopped
- 1/2 cup plain yogurt
- 1/2 cup sour cream
- 1/4 cup raisins
- 1/4 cup finely chopped red onion
- 1/2 teaspoon salt

Fresh cilantro leaves and coarsely ground pepper, optional

In a small bowl, combine the first seven ingredients. Cover and refrigerate until chilled. Garnish with cilantro and pepper if desired. **Yield:** 4 servings.

In a large saucepan over medium heat, saute the cinnamon, cloves and cumin seeds in oil until aromatic, about 1-2 minutes. Add rice; cook and stir until lightly browned. Add water and mint. Bring to a boil. Reduce heat; cover and simmer for 15-20 minutes or until rice is tender.

Meanwhile, in a large skillet, saute onion and cinnamon in oil until onion is tender. Add the curry, garlic and ginger; cook 1 minute longer. Add the garbanzo beans, water, tomato sauce, lemon juice and salt; bring to a boil. Reduce heat; simmer, uncovered, for 4-6 minutes or until slightly thickened. Discard cinnamon; stir in cilantro.

Fluff rice with a fork. Discard cinnamon and cloves. Serve with garbanzo curry. **Yield:** 3 servings.

Cucumber Salad

PREP/TOTAL TIME: 15 min.

- 1/2 **cup plain yogurt**
- 1/2 **cup sour cream**
- 1/4 **teaspoon salt**
- 1-1/2 **cups chopped cucumbers**
- 1 **medium onion, chopped**
- 1 **medium tomato, seeded and chopped**
- 1 **tablespoon chopped seeded jalapeno pepper**

Fresh cilantro leaves, optional

In a small bowl, combine the yogurt, sour cream and salt. Add the cucumbers, onion, tomato and jalapeno; stir until blended. Garnish with cilantro if desired. **Yield:** 6 servings.

Editor's Note: When cutting hot peppers, disposable gloves are recommended. Avoid touching your face.

Minted Rice with Garbanzo Curry

PREP: 20 min. **COOK:** 20 min.

- 1 **cinnamon stick (3 inches)**
- 2 **whole cloves**
- 1/8 **teaspoon cumin seeds**
- 2 **teaspoons canola oil**
- 1 **cup uncooked long grain rice**
- 2 **cups water**
- 1/2 **cup minced fresh mint**

GARBANZO CURRY:

- 1 **medium onion, chopped**
- 1 **cinnamon stick (3 inches)**
- 1 **tablespoon canola oil**
- 1 **teaspoon curry powder**
- 1 **garlic clove, minced**
- 1/4 **teaspoon minced fresh gingerroot**
- 1 **can (15 ounces) garbanzo beans or chickpeas, rinsed and drained**
- 1 **cup water**
- 1 **can (8 ounces) tomato sauce**
- 2 **tablespoons lemon juice**
- 1/2 **teaspoon salt**
- 1/2 **cup minced fresh cilantro**

Chicken Korma

PREP: 20 min. COOK: 25 min.

- 1 **large potato, peeled and cut into 1/2-inch cubes**
- 1 **large onion, chopped**
- 1 **cinnamon stick (3 inches)**
- 1 **bay leaf**
- 3 **whole cloves**
- 1 **tablespoon canola oil**
- 1 **pound boneless skinless chicken breasts, cut into 1/2-inch cubes**
- 1 **garlic clove, minced**
- 1 **teaspoon curry powder**
- 1/2 **teaspoon minced fresh gingerroot**
- 2 **medium tomatoes, seeded and chopped**
- 1 **teaspoon salt**
- 1/2 **cup sour cream**

Hot cooked rice

Place potato in a small saucepan and cover with water. Bring to a boil. Reduce heat; cover and cook for 10-15 minutes or until tender. Drain.

In a large skillet, saute the onion, cinnamon, bay leaf and cloves in oil until onion is tender. Add the chicken, garlic, curry and ginger; cook and stir 1 minute longer. Stir in the tomatoes, salt and potato.

Cover and cook for 10-15 minutes or until chicken is no longer pink. Remove from the heat; discard cinnamon, bay leaf and cloves. Stir in sour cream. Serve with rice. **Yield:** 4 servings.

LAVENDER LEMONADE   GIANT FLAN   HOMEMADE GUACAMOLE

Easy Enchiladas

When it comes to her mother's Southwestern-style cooking, family members ask for the whole enchilada—and get it. Then they request a second helping!

By Mariah Hilton, Las Vegas, Nevada

FAMILY FUN at our house often revolves around cooking. My mom and dad, four sisters and I love to experiment with new dishes and desserts, substituting and changing things to find the perfect combination.

My mom, Nanette Hilton (above, at left), instilled that love of cooking in her daughters. She started cooking for her family when she was a teenager. Now, she can whip up something quick and tasty but also can carefully plan and prepare a breathtaking meal with wonderful and different flavors.

She makes as many meals from scratch as time and energy allow. Mom is a Master Gardener and grows an abundance of fruit, vegetables and herbs in her garden. She's also an illustrator and writer, but has always worked from home.

There are 18 years between my oldest and youngest sisters, and I'm in the middle. Mom taught us just about everything we know about cooking, simply by having us work alongside her in the kitchen.

One of our family's favorite styles of cooking is Mexican. While living in Dallas, Texas, where my dad, Paul, attended dental school, my parents fell in love with Mexican food. That love was fostered by a move to Phoenix, Arizona, and later to Las Vegas, where Mexican food thrives.

For my grandma's 60th birthday, we celebrated with a Mexican fiesta. Mom loves to throw a party! Special meals for holidays and birthdays are planned well in advance, and everyone pitches in.

On Sundays, Mom prefers the meal to be simple but satisfying, so she relies on dishes that can simmer in the slow cooker or bake in the oven while we're at church.

I'm sharing one of our favorite meals here. It starts with Easy Enchiladas, made with a yummy salsa and yogurt sauce. This cheesy entree can be assembled ahead and frozen...or made meatless by using refried beans in place of chicken.

Guacamole and tortilla chips are always a great side to a Mexican feast. We sometimes call Mom's Homemade Guacamole "five-finger" guacamole to remember that it's made with only five ingredients.

A classic finale, Giant Flan has a delicious sauce that's to die for. To make this caramel custard even more special, top it off with whipped cream.

Wonderfully aromatic, Lavender Lemonade is so refreshing—a great complement to this spicy Mexican meal. I hope you like it as much as we do!

Lavender Lemonade

PREP: 15 min. + chilling

2-1/2 cups water
1 cup sugar
1 tablespoon dried lavender flowers
2-1/2 cups cold water
1 cup lemon juice
Ice cubes

In a large saucepan, bring water and sugar to a boil. Remove from the heat; add lavender. Cover and let stand for 1 hour.

Strain, discarding lavender. Stir in cold water and lemon juice. Serve over ice. **Yield:** 4 servings.

Editor's Note: Look for dried lavender flowers in specialty spice shops. If using lavender from the garden, confirm that it hasn't been treated with chemicals.

Easy Enchiladas

PREP: 20 min. BAKE: 30 min.

2 cups cubed cooked chicken
1 package (8 ounces) cream cheese, softened
8 flour tortillas (8 inches)
1 cup (8 ounces) plain yogurt *or* sour cream
1 cup salsa
2 cups (8 ounces) shredded cheddar cheese
1 can (2-1/4 ounces) sliced ripe olives, drained
Shredded lettuce and chopped tomatoes, optional

In a small bowl, combine chicken and cream cheese. Spoon about 1/4 cup chicken mixture down the center of each tortilla; roll up tightly. Place seam side down in a greased 13-in. x 9-in. baking dish.

In a small bowl, combine the plain yogurt and salsa; spread over the tortillas. Bake, uncovered, at 350° for 20 minutes. Sprinkle with cheddar cheese and ripe olives. Bake 10-15 minutes longer or until the cheese is melted. Serve with lettuce and tomatoes if desired. **Yield:** 8 servings.

Homemade Guacamole

PREP/TOTAL TIME: 10 min.

3 medium ripe avocados, peeled
1/4 cup finely chopped onion
1/4 cup minced fresh cilantro
2 tablespoons lime juice
1/8 teaspoon salt
Tortilla chips

In a small bowl, mash avocados with a fork. Stir in the onion, cilantro, lime juice and salt. Refrigerate until serving. Serve with chips. **Yield:** 2 cups.

AVOCADO ADVICE. Keep these helpful hints in mind when using avocados to prepare a batch of mouthwatering Homemade Guacamole (above) or other recipes:
• To quickly ripen an avocado, place it in a paper bag with an apple. Poke the bag with a toothpick in several spots and leave it at room temperature. The avocado should be ripe in 1 to 3 days.
• To remove the pit, wash the avocado and cut it in half lengthwise, cutting around the seed. Twist the halves in opposite directions to separate them. Slip a tablespoon under the seed to loosen it from the fruit.
• To remove the peel from a pitted avocado, scoop out the flesh from each avocado half with a large metal spoon, staying close to the peel.

Giant Flan

PREP: 15 min. + chilling

- **2 cups sugar,** *divided*
- **3-1/2 cups whole milk**
- **6 eggs**
- **1/2 teaspoon salt**
- **3 teaspoons vanilla extract**

In a heavy saucepan over medium-low heat, cook 1 cup sugar until melted, about 20 minutes. Do not stir. Reduce heat to low; cook for 5 minutes or until syrup is golden brown, stirring occasionally. Quickly pour into an ungreased shallow 10-in. round baking dish, tilting to coat bottom of dish. Place dish in a large baking pan; let stand for 10 minutes.

In a large saucepan, heat milk until bubbles form around sides of pan. Remove from the heat. In a large bowl, whisk the eggs, salt and remaining sugar. Stir 1 cup warm milk into egg mixture; return all to the pan and mix well. Stir in vanilla. Slowly pour into prepared baking dish.

Add 3/4 in. hot water to the large baking pan. Bake at 325° for 35-40 minutes or until the center is just set (the mixture will jiggle). Remove the flan to a wire rack; cool for 1 hour. Chill overnight. Run a knife around the edge to loosen; invert flan onto a rimmed serving dish. **Yield:** 4 servings.

BEEF ROAST WITH GRAVY

ZUCCHINI RELISH

CAKE ROLL WITH BERRIES

Honey Sweet Corn

Her family has a standing invitation to share Mom's Sunday dinner featuring specialties such as slow-cooked beef roast...and are only too happy to accept.

By Paula Montijo, Lebanon, Pennsylvania

BY THE AGE of 10, my mom, Nancy Kreiser (above, at right), was taking on much of the family cooking so her parents could work the farm. She even helped her mother can and freeze the harvest from their garden.

Even after Mom married my dad, Paul, they helped on the farm and kept a garden there. I remember our freezer always stocked with beef, corn and strawberries, and the basement shelves lined with jars of canned vegetables and fruit.

Mom loved cooking for our family of six. My dad is a postmaster in nearby Hamburg; my older brother Craig, my sister Patty and I live nearby, and my younger sister, Rebecca, is still at home and is a big help to Mom.

When we were kids, my mother had a delicious dinner on the table every night, and we enjoyed eating together as a family. The meal I've shared here is one of her most memorable.

Beef Roast with Gravy is a main course I always asked Mom to fix for special occasions—and not just for the taste. I loved to smell the aroma of the rich gravy as it cooked.

There's nothing that says summer quite like fresh sweet corn, and Mom's Honey Sweet Corn is such a treat. The honey butter makes the ears even sweeter.

When zucchini is in season and Dad's little patch has produced to excess, Mom likes to make Zucchini Relish. It's crisp, tangy and colorful.

Fresh-baked desserts were a staple on our table every week. We all loved the fresh strawberries and cream filling in delectable Cake Roll with Berries. Now I make that dessert myself for company or to take to church potlucks.

We have a standing invitation for Sunday dinner, and my mother is never satisfied with a casual spread. Although she can no longer do the cooking herself for health reasons, she supervises Dad and us girls.

All of us pitch in on the canning, too, while Mom gives instructions. My dad and brother pick fruit so Dad can freeze it or make jelly to share, which delights the 10 grandkids.

Mom still likes poring over new recipes and planning menus. It's not unusual for one of us to call and pick her brain about a recipe or dish she has made.

Over the years, I've really enjoyed learning to cook from her and making her special recipes for my husband and our four children. Maybe her recipes will become favorites in your household, too.

Zucchini Relish

PREP: 20 min. + standing **COOK:** 15 min. + chilling

- 4 cups diced zucchini
- 1 large onion, thinly sliced
- 2 celery ribs, sliced
- 2 medium carrots, sliced
- 1 medium sweet red pepper, sliced
- 2 tablespoons salt
- 3/4 cup sugar
- 1/2 cup water
- 1/2 cup cider vinegar
- 1/2 teaspoon celery seed

Dash onion salt
Dash ground turmeric

In a large bowl, combine the vegetables; sprinkle with salt and cover with cold water. Let stand for 3 hours; rinse and drain.

In a large saucepan, bring the remaining ingredients to a boil. Stir in zucchini mixture and return to a boil. Reduce heat; simmer, uncovered, for 5 minutes. Transfer to a large bowl; cool to room temperature. Cover and refrigerate for at least 2 days. **Yield:** 4 cups.

Beef Roast with Gravy

PREP: 10 min. **COOK:** 6 hours

- 1 pound fresh baby carrots
- 1 can (4 ounces) mushroom stems and pieces, drained
- 1 beef rump roast *or* bottom round roast (3 pounds)
- 1/2 teaspoon garlic powder
- 1/4 teaspoon pepper
- 1 tablespoon canola oil
- 1 jar (12 ounces) beef gravy
- 1 can (10-3/4 ounces) condensed cream of mushroom soup, undiluted
- 1 cup water
- 1 envelope onion soup mix

Place the carrots and mushrooms in a 4- or 5-qt. slow cooker. Sprinkle roast with garlic powder and pepper. In a large skillet, brown roast in oil on all sides. Transfer to slow cooker.

Combine the beef gravy, cream of mushroom soup, water and onion soup mix; pour over the roast. Cover and cook on low for 6-8 hours or until meat is tender. Skim fat from gravy if necessary; serve gravy with beef. **Yield:** 8 servings.

Honey Sweet Corn

PREP/TOTAL TIME: 15 min.

- 6 medium ears sweet corn
- 1/4 cup butter, melted
- 1 teaspoon honey
- Ground pepper, optional

Place the corn in a Dutch oven or stockpot; cover with water. Bring to a boil; cover and cook for 5-10 minutes or until tender. Drain. In a small bowl, combine butter and honey; brush over corn. Sprinkle with pepper if desired. **Yield:** 6 servings.

CORN CLUE. Remember these hints when making Honey Sweet Corn (above):
- When selecting fresh corn, look for ears with bright green, tightly closed husks and golden-brown silk. The kernels should be plump, milky and in closely spaced rows all the way to the tip.
- As soon as corn is picked, the sugar gradually begins to convert to starch, reducing its natural sweetness. So corn is best cooked and served the same day it's picked and purchased.
- The exact cooking time will depend on the type of corn and its maturity. Very fresh or super-sweet corn may require a shorter cooking time while older corn may require a longer one.

Cake Roll with Berries

PREP: 40 min. **BAKE:** 15 min. + chilling

- 3 **eggs**
- 1 **cup sugar**
- 1/3 **cup water**
- 1 **teaspoon vanilla extract**
- 3/4 **cup all-purpose flour**
- 1 **teaspoon baking powder**
- 1/4 **teaspoon salt**

Confectioners' sugar

FILLING:
- 1/2 **cup all-purpose flour**
- 1 **cup milk**
- 1/2 **cup butter, softened**
- 1/2 **cup shortening**
- 1 **cup sugar**
- 1 **teaspoon vanilla extract**
- 1/4 **teaspoon salt**

BERRIES:
- 3 **cups sliced fresh strawberries**
- 1/4 **cup sugar**

Line a greased 15-in. x 10-in. x 1-in. baking pan with waxed paper and grease the paper; set aside.

In a large bowl, beat eggs on high speed for 3 minutes. Gradually add sugar, beating until mixture becomes thick and lemon-colored. Beat in water and vanilla. Combine the flour, baking powder and salt; fold into egg mixture. Spread batter into prepared pan.

Bake at 375° for 12-15 minutes or until cake springs back when lightly touched. Cool for 5 minutes. Invert onto a kitchen towel dusted with confectioners' sugar. Gently peel off waxed paper. Roll up cake in the towel jelly-roll style, starting with a short side. Cool completely on a wire rack.

Meanwhile, for filling, combine flour and milk in a small saucepan until smooth. Cook and stir over medium heat until mixture comes to a boil; cook and stir 2 minutes longer (mixture will be very thick). Transfer to a bowl; press waxed paper onto surface of mixture. Cool completely.

In a large bowl, cream the butter, shortening and sugar until light and fluffy. Beat in vanilla and salt. Gradually beat in milk mixture; beat for 5 minutes or until filling is light and fluffy.

Unroll cake; spread filling over cake to within 1/2 in. of edges. Roll up again. Place seam side down on a serving platter. Sprinkle with confectioners' sugar. Combine strawberries and sugar; refrigerate cake and berries for 1 hour before serving. **Yield:** 10 servings.

DAD'S BAKED BEANS

CAMPERS' COLESLAW

CREAM PUFF CAKE

Barbecued Pork Sandwiches

With an unwritten history of good cooking, her mother doesn't need written recipes in order to pass on the family's flavorful traditions to new generations.

By Kim Wallace, Dennison, Ohio

FOR AS LONG as I can remember, my mom, Bertha Meese (above, at left), has spent much of her time in the kitchen preparing meals for family, friends, business associates and others. When my brother, Billy, and I were kids, we sat down to her home-cooked dinners every night. Everything she made was delicious.

Good cooking has been passed down in our family from generation to generation. My grandmother and great-grandmother shared their skills with Mom and then me. I hope to pass on what I've learned to my son and two daughters.

There's only one problem: Few things Mom makes have a recipe! She cooks from scratch, using a pinch of this and a dash of that, with a smattering of several other ingredients tossed in. That makes my job as a *Taste of Home* Field Editor harder because, before sending in a recipe, I have to make it, writing down each ingredient and step along the way.

Although my brother and I now have our own families, we make time to get together with Mom and our dad, Bill, for meals. We all live close by, on land that's been in our family for more than 100 years. My brother's house is on one side of Mom and Dad, and I'm on the other side, just across the road.

Our children know that Grandma's house is a great place to go for good food. Sometimes Billy and I find out that they've eaten at home but have also eaten at our parents' house!

Mom's cooking is popular with the square dance crowd, too. My parents own a dance hall, and my dad, who's an electrician, is also a square dance caller. So at least twice a month, Mom throws together a new dish for a potluck at the hall. She's always asked for her recipe, and I have to laugh because I know she has no clue what exactly she used to make it!

The meal I've shared here wins rave reviews with the whole family—and I actually have the recipes! The menu starts with saucy Barbecued Pork Sandwiches, great for a hungry crowd and easy to prepare. Once the meat is cooked, transfer it to a slow cooker to keep it warm until serving time.

I always use the recipe for Dad's Baked Beans when I need baked beans for any occasion; they're the best I've ever had. And crunchy Campers' Coleslaw is a traditional, no-fuss slaw that makes a refreshing side dish for summer picnics and parties.

With its light, golden crust and yummy filling, Cream Puff Cake is a definite crowd-pleaser. Be prepared to get lots of requests for the recipe!

Dad's Baked Beans

PREP: 15 min. **BAKE:** 1 hour

- **3** cans (15-1/2 ounces *each*) great northern beans, rinsed and drained
- **5** hot dogs, sliced
- **1-1/2** cups ketchup
- **1/2** cup packed brown sugar
- **2** tablespoons molasses
- **1** medium onion, chopped
- **1/2** teaspoon ground mustard
- **1/4** teaspoon salt
- **1/4** teaspoon pepper

In an ungreased 2-quart baking dish, combine all ingredients. Cover and bake at 350° for 1 to 1-1/2 hours or until heated through. **Yield:** 8 servings.

Campers' Coleslaw

PREP: 20 min. + chilling

☑ This recipe includes Nutrition Facts and Diabetic Exchanges.

    1-1/2 cups sugar
      3/4 cup white vinegar
      3/4 cup olive oil
        3 teaspoons salt
        1 teaspoon celery seed
        1 medium head cabbage, shredded
        1 large onion, chopped
        1 medium green pepper, chopped

In a small saucepan, combine the first five ingredients. Bring to a boil; boil for 1-2 minutes or until the sugar is dissolved. Remove from the heat; cool to room temperature.

In a large bowl, combine the cabbage, onion and pepper; add dressing and toss to coat. Refrigerate until chilled. Serve with a slotted spoon. **Yield:** 12 servings (3/4 cup each).

Nutrition Facts: 3/4 cup equals 121 calories, 6 g fat (1 g saturated fat), 0 cholesterol, 274 mg sodium, 17 g carbohydrate, 2 g fiber, 1 g protein. **Diabetic Exchanges:** 1 starch, 1 fat.

Barbecued Pork Sandwiches

PREP: 25 min. COOK: 2-1/2 hours

        1 boneless pork shoulder butt roast (3 pounds)
        1 medium onion, chopped
        1 tablespoon butter
        1 can (15 ounces) tomato puree
      1/2 cup packed brown sugar
      1/4 cup Worcestershire sauce
        2 tablespoons lemon juice
      1/2 teaspoon salt
       10 hard rolls, split

Place pork on a rack in a roasting pan; bake, uncovered, at 350° for 2 hours or until tender.

In a Dutch oven, saute onion in butter until tender. Stir in the tomato puree, brown sugar, Worcestershire sauce, lemon juice and salt. Bring to a boil. Reduce heat; simmer, uncovered, for 30 minutes. Shred the pork; add to the sauce and heat through. Serve on buns. **Yield:** 10 servings.

GOING DUTCH. A Dutch oven can easily go from stovetop to oven to table. If you worry that your food will stick to the pot, heat it over medium heat before adding the food. To clean a Dutch oven, fill it with water and boil it until the food releases. Drain the water and scrub with a ball of aluminum foil to remove any burned-on food.

Cream Puff Cake

PREP: 25 min. **BAKE:** 25 min. + chilling

- **1 cup water**
- **1/2 cup butter, cubed**
- **1 cup all-purpose flour**
- **4 eggs**

FILLING:
- **1 package (8 ounces) cream cheese, softened**
- **2-1/2 cups 2% milk**
- **3 packages (3.3 ounces *each*) instant white chocolate *or* vanilla pudding mix**
- **1 carton (8 ounces) frozen whipped topping, thawed**

In a large saucepan, bring the water and butter to a boil. Add the flour all at once and stir until a smooth ball forms. Continue beating until the mixture is smooth and shiny.

Remove the mixture from the heat; let stand for 5 minutes. Add the eggs, one at a time, beating well after each addition.

Transfer to a greased 13-in. x 9-in. baking dish. Bake at 400° for 22-26 minutes or until puffed and golden brown. Cool completely on a wire rack.

For the filling, in a large bowl, beat the cream cheese, milk and white chocolate pudding mixes until smooth. Spread over the baked crust; refrigerate for 20 minutes. Spread with whipped topping. Chill until serving. **Yield:** 15 servings.

SPAGHETTI AND MEATBALLS
WITH GARLIC CRUMBS

PENNY'S APPLE-BROWN SUGAR
COFFEE CAKE

CHOCOLATE CHIP-BANANA
BELGIAN WAFFLES

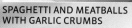

**Grilled Peach
BBQ Chicken Wings**

When this teen discovered he was gluten- and dairy-sensitive, his mom wrote the cookbook that set him free with delicious foods that suit his special diet.

By Isaiah Nardone, Brooklyn, New York

EVERYONE KNOWS that my mom, Silvana Nardone (above, at left), knows her way around the kitchen, but no one more than me. I've watched her cook and bake ever since I could stand on my SpongeBob stepstool and peek over the kitchen countertop to see what she was making.

I was her helper—cracking eggs, mixing batters, mashing bananas. The first thing we cooked together was fluffy banana pancakes. I think it's safe to say I'm still the best flipper in the house.

But that was just the beginning. Next, I was her meatball shaper and cookie scooper, and I loved every minute of it.

When my mom opened a bakery, I was her official taste tester. She would pick me up from school and bring me back to the bakery, where I'd sit at the table and do my homework while she baked and packed all of the treats.

I especially loved the holidays, when there were cookies and other goodies everywhere I turned my head. I was in heaven.

Then, a couple of years ago, when I was 11, I was told that I was sensitive to gluten and dairy. I wasn't sure if I'd ever eat any of my favorite foods again.

Luckily for me, my mom stopped at nothing until she figured out how to make my favorites not only look good but taste good—just like before. She spent months developing new recipes for our book, *Cooking for Isaiah: Gluten-Free & Dairy-Free Recipes for Easy, Delicious Meals*, available at bookstores everywhere.

Now, I'm pretty much eating everything I want. I've shared some of my favorite recipes here.

One of them is a wonderful homemade waffle. Mom uses gluten-free pancake mix, rice milk, lots of bananas and hot fudge ice cream topping to make Chocolate Chip-Banana Belgian Waffles.

Grilled Peach BBQ Chicken Wings are cooked low and slow for crispy skin and moist, tender chicken every time. You can swap 1 cup of fresh pineapple for the peaches, if you like.

Not all apple cakes are the same, as Penny's Apple-Brown Sugar Coffee Cake proves. It's the perfect mix of sweet apple and spiced chocolate crumb.

Garlic crumbs add a nice crunch to Spaghetti and Meatballs with Garlic Crumbs. No one would guess this hearty, Italian-style favorite is gluten-free.

I hope you enjoy these recipes as much as I do!

Penny's Apple-Brown Sugar Coffee Cake

PREP: 25 min. **BAKE:** 30 min. + cooling

- 1 cup plus 2 teaspoons gluten-free all-purpose flour, *divided*
- 2 teaspoons baking powder
- 1/4 teaspoon salt
- 3/4 cup packed light brown sugar, *divided*
- 1/4 cup mini chocolate chips (1-1/2 ounces)
- 1/2 cup chopped walnuts
- 1 teaspoon cinnamon
- 2 large eggs, at room temperature
- 1/2 cup granulated sugar
- 1/2 cup vegetable oil
- 2 teaspoons pure vanilla extract
- 2 large apples—cored, peeled and cut into 1/2-inch pieces

Preheat oven to 375°. Lightly grease a 9-in. round baking or springform pan. In a large bowl, whisk together 1 cup flour, baking powder and salt. In a small bowl, stir together the remaining 2 teaspoons flour, 1/2 cup brown sugar, chocolate chips, nuts and cinnamon.

In another small bowl, whisk together the eggs, granulated sugar and remaining 1/4 cup brown sugar until smooth. Whisk in the oil and vanilla. Stir into the flour mixture until just combined. Pour half the batter into prepared pan; top with half the apples and half the crumb mixture. Repeat with the remaining batter, apples and crumb mixture. Bake until a toothpick inserted in the center comes out clean, 30-35 minutes. **Yield:** 8 servings.

Spaghetti and Meatballs With Garlic Crumbs

PREP: 15 min. COOK: 40 min.

- 1 **pound ground beef chuck**
- 1 **small onion, grated**
- 5 **cloves garlic—1 chopped, 2 smashed and 2 grated**
- 1 **cup rice cereal crumbs,** *divided*
- 1/2 **cup rice milk**
- 1 **large egg**
- 6 **tablespoons chopped flat-leaf parsley,** *divided*

Salt

- 2 **tablespoons extra-virgin olive oil,** *divided*
- 2 **(28-ounces) cans crushed tomatoes**
- 1 **(12-ounces) package corn or rice spaghetti**
- 1/2 **teaspoon crushed red pepper flakes,** *or* **to taste**

In a large bowl, combine the beef, onion, chopped garlic, 1/2 cup cereal crumbs, milk, egg, 2 tablespoons parsley and 1 teaspoon salt; shape into eight 2-in. balls.

In a large saucepan, heat 1 tablespoon olive oil over medium heat. Add the smashed garlic and cook until golden, about 2 minutes. Add the tomatoes and bring to a simmer, stirring occasionally. Submerge the meatballs in the sauce; bring to a simmer and cook, covered and stirring occasionally, for 20 minutes. Season with about 1 teaspoon salt.

In a large pot of boiling salted water, cook the spaghetti until al dente, about 15 minutes; drain and toss with the sauce.

To make the garlic crumbs, heat the remaining 1 tablespoon olive oil in a small skillet over medium heat. Add the grated garlic, remaining 1/2 cup cereal crumbs, red pepper flakes and 1/4 teaspoon salt. Cook until toasted, 1 to 2 minutes. Let cool, then stir in remaining 1/4 cup parsley. To serve, divide the spaghetti among shallow bowls and top with meatballs and garlic crumbs. **Yield:** 4 servings.

Editor's Note: Read all ingredient labels for possible gluten and dairy content prior to use. Ingredient formulas can change, and production facilities vary among brands. If you're concerned that your brand may contain gluten or dairy, contact the company.

Grilled Peach BBQ Chicken Wings

PREP: 20 min. + marinating COOK: 30 min.

- 2 **cups store-bought barbecue sauce**
- 2 **cloves garlic, finely chopped,** *divided*
- 2 **peaches, peeled, pitted and chopped**

Salt and pepper

- 24 **chicken wings, separated at the joint and tips discarded**
- 1 **cup peach jam, such as Smuckers**
- 1/4 **cup apple cider vinegar**
- 2 **tablespoons hot sauce, such as Frank's Red Hot,** *or* **to taste**

Scallions, green parts only, thinly sliced, for topping

In a food processor, combine the barbecue sauce and half of the garlic. Add the peaches and process until finely chopped; season with about 1-1/2 teaspoons salt and about 1/4 teaspoon pepper. Reserve 1/2 cup for basting. In a resealable plastic bag, toss together the chicken wings and remaining peach barbecue sauce; refrigerate for about 30 minutes.

Meanwhile, combine peach jam, vinegar, remaining garlic, hot sauce and 1/2 teaspoon salt in a small saucepan. Cook over medium heat until slightly thickened, about 5 minutes; let cool.

Preheat a grill or grill pan to low. Grill the chicken wings with the grill cover down, turning and basting occasionally with the reserved barbecue sauce, until cooked through, about 30 minutes. Top with the scallions and serve with the peach jam dipping sauce. **Yield:** 4 servings.

Editor's Note: Read all ingredient labels for possible gluten and dairy content prior to use. Ingredient

formulas can change, and production facilities vary among brands. If you're concerned that your brand may contain gluten or dairy, contact the company.

Chocolate Chip-Banana Belgian Waffles

PREP: 20 min. COOK: 25 min.

- 2 **cups store-bought gluten-free pancake mix, such as Cherrybrook Kitchen**
- 1/2 **teaspoon salt**
- 1/2 **teaspoon ground cinnamon**
- 1 **large egg, at room temperature**
- 2 **tablespoons vegetable oil**
- 1-1/2 **cups rice milk**
- 3 **bananas, 1 mashed and 2 diagonally sliced 1/4 inch thick**
- 1 **tablespoon pure vanilla extract**
- 1/2 **cup mini chocolate chips**

Toppings: chopped walnuts and hot fudge ice cream topping

Preheat a Belgian waffle iron to medium-high. In a large bowl, whisk together the pancake mix, salt, cinnamon, egg, oil, milk, mashed banana and vanilla. Add the chocolate chips; stir until just combined.

Grease the waffle iron with nonstick cooking spray. Pour a heaping 1/3 cup batter into each waffle iron quarter, spreading the batter out to the edges. Close and cook until the waffle is crisp and the waffle iron stops steaming, about 4 minutes. Repeat with the remaining batter. To serve, top the waffles with banana slices, walnuts and hot fudge. **Yield:** 6 servings.

Editor's Note: Read all ingredient labels for possible gluten and dairy content prior to use. Ingredient formulas can change, and production facilities vary among brands. If you're concerned that your brand may contain gluten or dairy, contact the company.

BANANA BASICS. If you need ripe bananas for Chocolate Chip-Banana Belgian Waffles (recipe at left) but yours are too green, place them in a paper bag until they're ripe. Adding an apple to the bag will speed up the process.

Store ripe bananas at room temperature. To prevent bruises, use a banana hook or hanger.

Field Editor Favorites

Taste of Home is edited by 1,000 cooks across North America. Here, you'll "meet" six of them and see their family-favorite recipes.

A Burst of Sunshine 220
   Caribbean Chicken Caesar Salad • Citrus Fish • Upside-Down Orange French Toast • Florida Citrus Meringue Pie

Casual Comfort Food 224
   Sunflower Seed & Honey Wheat Bread • Hearty Meatless Minestrone • Chunky Blue Cheese Dressing • Chocolate Raspberry Cheesecake

A World of Flavor 228
   Frothy Mexi-Mocha Coffee • Honey-Orange Rice Pudding • Basil, Feta & Roasted Pepper Muffins • Potato & Red Onion Frittata

Homegrown Goodness 232
   Grilled Pork Chops • Marinated Veggie Beef Kabobs • Fabulous Green Beans • Blackberry Cobbler

Stirring Things Up 236
   Apple Bran Muffins • Super Low-Fat Granola Cereal • Butterhorns • Spiced Pudding Cake

Try and Try Again 240
   Lime-Buttered Broccoli • Honey-Glazed Hens with Fruit Stuffing • Cream of Walnut Soup • Banana Rum Sundaes

COOK'S BEST. Clockwise from top left: Homegrown Goodness (p. 232), Casual Comfort Food (p. 224), Homegrown Goodness (p. 232), A World of Flavor (p. 228) and Try and Try Again (p. 240).

UPSIDE-DOWN ORANGE
FRENCH TOAST

CARIBBEAN CHICKEN CAESAR
SALAD

CITRUS FISH

Florida Citrus Meringue Pie

A Burst of Sunshine

This Florida cook's backyard crop of fresh-picked fruit
promises family and friends a tangy feast.

By Barbara Carlucci, Orange Park, Florida

I GUESS you could say my middle name is "citrus!" I harvest those fruits by the wheelbarrow-full at the Orange Park, Florida home I share with my husband, Phil.

I work as a technical writer for a government contractor, and Phil is retired from the Navy. Whether mealtime involves just the two of us or guests such as our daughter, son-in-law and grandson, I enjoy finding ways to fit our backyard bounty into my cooking.

We get our bumper crop from Valencia orange, Meyer lemon, white grapefruit, tangerine and Buddha's Hand trees. I love the scent of the citrus blossoms!

Our fruit comes ripe around the holidays, and family and friends who visit go home with fresh fruit, a good citrus loaf and homemade jam or marmalade.

I squeeze and freeze lots of juice to keep on hand for homemade pound cake, lemon chicken, honey lemon tea and other favorites. We also have a huge garden, and I can like crazy!

As you'll see from the recipes I've shared here, citrus is really versatile. I like to serve Upside-Down Orange French Toast for breakfast when we have overnight guests or for a holiday brunch.

Carribean Chicken Caesar Salad and Citrus Fish always make tongue-tingling main courses. And thanks to orange and lemon, Florida Citrus Meringue Pie packs a bold, sweet-tart flavor.

If you love citrus fruit as much as I do, check out some of my best tips and ideas:

• To make fresh lemonade, remember 1-1-5. That is, one part lemon juice, one part sugar or sweetener and 5 parts water.

• Add citrus zest and/or juice near the end of a recipe's cooking time.

• Add a lemon wedge when cooking pasta to serve with recipes such as shrimp scampi, and choose an orange wedge for rice to accompany a chicken dish. Remove the citrus before serving.

• Coming down with a cold? Hot lemon tea with honey always makes me feel better!

• A few citrus rinds in the garbage disposal will clean it and leave a fresh scent.

• And one of my favorites: Whenever life gives you lemons...well, you know the rest!

Caribbean Chicken Caesar Salad

PREP/TOTAL TIME: 30 min.

- 1 **pound boneless skinless chicken breasts, cut into 1-inch pieces**
- 1/2 **cup thawed non-alcoholic pina colada mix, *divided***
- 1 **cup tangerine *and/or* mandarin orange segments**
- 1 **celery rib, chopped**
- 2 **tablespoons crushed pineapple**
- 1 **green onion, chopped**
- 4 **pitted ripe olives, sliced**
- 2 **tablespoons plus 2 teaspoons lemon juice**
- 4 **teaspoons mayonnaise**
- 2 **teaspoons grated Parmesan cheese**
- 1 **to 2 garlic cloves, minced**
- 1/8 **teaspoon salt**
- 1/8 **teaspoon pepper**
- 4 **cups torn romaine *and/or* iceberg lettuce**

Combine chicken and 1/4 cup pina colada mix. In a large skillet coated with cooking spray, cook and stir chicken mixture over medium heat until chicken is no longer pink. Remove from the heat; set aside.

Combine the tangerine segments, celery, pineapple, onion and olives in a large bowl. In a small bowl, combine the lemon juice, mayonnaise, cheese, garlic, salt, pepper and the remaining pina colada mix.

Add chicken and romaine to the tangerine mixture; drizzle with dressing and toss to coat. Serve salad immediately. **Yield:** 4 servings.

and lemon and orange peel. Drizzle with oil. Top with a second large piece of foil. Bring edges of foil together; crimp to seal, forming a large packet.

Bake at 450° for 15-20 minutes or until fish flakes easily with a fork. Open foil carefully to allow steam to escape. **Yield:** 4 servings.

Nutrition Facts: 5 oz. cooked fish equals 208 calories, 6 g fat (1 g saturated fat), 98 mg cholesterol, 193 mg sodium, 4 g carbohydrate, 1 g fiber, 33 g protein. **Diabetic Exchanges:** 5 lean meat, 1 fat.

Upside-Down Orange French Toast

PREP: 25 min. + chilling BAKE: 25 min.

- 1/2 **cup butter, melted**
- 1/2 **cup sugar**
- 1/4 **cup chopped pecans**
-   2 **tablespoons grated orange peel**
-   2 **teaspoons ground cinnamon**
- 12 **slices French bread (3/4 inch thick)**
-   4 **ounces cream cheese, cubed**
-   8 **eggs**
-   1 **cup orange juice**
-   1 **tablespoon orange liqueur, optional**
- 1/2 **teaspoon butter flavoring**

Place butter in a 13-in. x 9-in. baking dish. Combine the sugar, pecans, orange peel and cinnamon; sprinkle over butter. Arrange bread in dish. Dot with cream cheese. In a large bowl, whisk the eggs, orange juice, orange liqueur if desired and butter flavoring; pour over bread. Cover and refrigerate overnight.

Remove from the refrigerator 30 minutes before baking. Bake, uncovered, at 325° for 25-30 minutes or until a knife inserted near the center comes out clean. To serve, invert slices onto plates. **Yield:** 6 servings.

Citrus Fish

PREP/TOTAL TIME: 25 min. + chilling

✓ This recipe includes Nutrition Facts and Diabetic Exchanges.

- 1-1/2 **pounds haddock, cod *and/or* halibut fillets**
-   1/8 **teaspoon salt**
-   1/8 **teaspoon pepper**
-     1 **medium onion, chopped**
-   1/3 **cup minced fresh parsley**
-     2 **teaspoons grated lemon peel**
-     2 **teaspoons grated orange peel**
-     4 **teaspoons canola oil**

Place an 18-in. x 12-in. piece of heavy-duty foil on a large baking sheet. Arrange fillets in a single layer on foil; sprinkle with salt and pepper. Top with onion, parsley,

SIMPLE SWAP. A great way to add a twist to your favorite French toast recipe is to simply use different breads. Try day-old banana, apple, zucchini or pumpkin bread. Don't forget to slice up cinnamon-raisin bread or even loaves dotted with chocolate chips. You can even slice a few croissants and substitute them for the bread. When in a pinch, try leftover hot dog or hamburger buns.

Florida Citrus Meringue Pie

PREP: 30 min. **BAKE:** 15 min. + chilling

Pastry for single-crust pie (9 inches)
- 1 **cup sugar**
- 5 **tablespoons cornstarch**
- 1/2 **teaspoon salt**
- 1 **cup water**
- 1 **cup orange juice**
- 4 **egg yolks, beaten**
- 1/2 **cup lemon juice**
- 2 **tablespoons butter**
- 1 **teaspoon grated lemon peel**
- 1 **teaspoon grated orange peel**

MERINGUE:
- 3 **egg whites**
- 1 **teaspoon vanilla extract**
- 6 **tablespoons sugar**

Roll out pastry to fit a 9-in. pie plate. Transfer pastry to pie plate. Trim pastry to 1/2 in. beyond edge of plate; flute edges. Line unpricked pastry with a double thickness of heavy-duty foil. Bake at 450° for 8 minutes. Remove foil; bake 5-7 minutes longer or until lightly browned. Cool on a wire rack. Reduce heat to 350°.

Meanwhile, in a large saucepan, combine the sugar, cornstarch and salt. Gradually stir in water and orange juice until smooth. Cook and stir over medium-high heat until thickened and bubbly. Reduce heat; cook and stir 2 minutes longer (mixture will be thick).

Remove from the heat. Stir a small amount of the hot mixture into the egg yolks; return all to the pan, stirring constantly. Bring to a gentle boil; cook and stir 2 minutes longer. Remove from the heat. Gently stir in the lemon juice, butter, and lemon and orange peel. Pour into prepared crust.

In a large bowl, beat the egg whites and vanilla on medium speed until soft peaks form. Gradually beat in the sugar, 1 tablespoon at a time, on high until stiff peaks form. Spread meringue over hot filling, sealing edges to crust.

Bake at 350° for 12-15 minutes or until the meringue is golden brown. Cool the pie on a wire rack for 1 hour. Refrigerate the pie for 1-2 hours before serving. **Yield:** 8 servings.

HEARTY MEATLESS MINESTRONE   CHUNKY BLUE CHEESE DRESSING   SUNFLOWER SEED & HONEY WHEAT BREAD

Chocolate Raspberry Cheesecake

Casual Comfort Food

Hearty soup-and-salad menu relects the down-home cooking style of this Oregon Field Editor.

By Mickey Turner, Grants Pass, Oregon

AS MUCH AS I love cooking, I don't consider myself to be a gourmet cook. And I must admit, I don't aspire to be one, either!

I prefer home-style cooking, although my style has changed a bit over the years. I now try to serve healthier foods and follow a low-glycemic diet.

My passion for cooking began after I met my husband, Jim, 40 years ago. We live in Grants Pass, Oregon and have four children and four grandchildren.

Jim works in marketing, and I work part-time for a small company that ships clock parts all over the world. Collecting recipes, quilting, Bible study, kayaking, camping and visiting the Pacific Ocean also keep me busy. But being a homemaker is where my heart has always been.

I home-schooled our children, which gave our three daughters—Tami, Amy and Anne—the chance to work in the kitchen. Each of us has entered many recipe contests and cook-offs, and we've collected some cash and prizes, too.

Our son, Scott, is also handy in the kitchen. One piece of cooking advice I gave to all of my children was to set out all ingredients before you begin and to clean up as you go. To me, the result is always a more pleasant cooking experience.

Living in southern Oregon, just 2 hours away from the ocean, we're blessed with lots of fresh fish. So that bounty often finds its way into my cooking. I use my slow cooker a lot, too.

I also enjoy making and eating hearty soups with homemade bread. I usually bake about 12 loaves at a time, freeze some and give some away. I even grind my own grain.

A friend gave me the recipe for Hearty Meatless Minestrone, part of the menu I've shared here. A bowlful is delicious with Sunflower Seed & Honey Wheat Bread, a staple in our home.

Chunky Blue Cheese Dressing is a mouthwatering finish for a tossed green salad. Sometimes I substitute gorgonzola cheese, which also works well.

I like to round out this satisfying meal with slices of Chocolate Raspberry Cheesecake. Chocolate and raspberries—it's a hard combination to beat!

Sunflower Seed & Honey Wheat Bread

PREP: 40 min. + rising **BAKE:** 35 min.

- 2 packages (1/4 ounce *each*) active dry yeast
- 3-1/4 cups warm water (110° to 115°)
- 1/4 cup bread flour
- 1/3 cup canola oil
- 1/3 cup honey
- 3 teaspoons salt
- 6-1/2 to 7-1/2 cups whole wheat flour
- 1/2 cup sunflower kernels
- 3 tablespoons butter, melted

In a large bowl, dissolve yeast in warm water. Add the bread flour, oil, honey, salt and 4 cups whole wheat flour. Beat until smooth. Stir in sunflower kernels and enough remaining flour to form a firm dough.

Turn onto a floured surface; knead until smooth and elastic, about 6-8 minutes. Place in a greased bowl, turning once to grease the top. Cover and let rise in a warm place until doubled, about 1 hour.

Punch dough down; divide into three portions. Shape into loaves; place in three greased 8-in. x 4-in. loaf pans. Cover and let rise until doubled, about 30 minutes. Bake at 350° for 35-40 minutes or until golden brown. Brush with melted butter. Remove from pans to wire racks to cool. **Yield:** 3 loaves (12 slices each).

Hearty Meatless Minestrone

PREP: 30 min. **COOK**: 40 min.

- 1 large onion, chopped
- 3 tablespoons olive oil
- 2 celery ribs, chopped
- 2 medium carrots, chopped
- 1 cup chopped cabbage
- 1 medium green pepper, chopped
- 1 medium zucchini, chopped
- 6 garlic cloves, minced
- 3-1/2 cups water
- 2 cans (14-1/2 ounces *each*) diced tomatoes, undrained
- 1 can (15 ounces) garbanzo beans *or* chickpeas, rinsed and drained
- 1 can (15 ounces) tomato puree
- 1 can (8 ounces) tomato sauce
- 3 tablespoons dried parsley flakes
- 2 teaspoons dried basil
- 2 teaspoons dried oregano
- 1 teaspoon salt
- 1/2 teaspoon pepper
- 1/4 teaspoon cayenne pepper
- 1/2 cup small pasta shells

Fresh basil leaves and shaved Parmesan cheese, optional

In a Dutch oven, saute onion in oil for 2 minutes. Add the celery, carrots, cabbage, green pepper, zucchini and garlic; saute 3 minutes longer.

Stir in the water, tomatoes, beans, tomato puree, tomato sauce and seasonings. Bring to a boil. Reduce heat; cover and simmer for 15 minutes.

Stir in pasta; cook 12-15 minutes longer or until tender. Garnish each serving with basil and cheese if desired. **Yield**: 8 servings (3 quarts).

Chunky Blue Cheese Dressing

PREP: 5 min. + chilling

- 1 cup (8 ounces) sour cream
- 1 cup (4 ounces) crumbled blue cheese
- 1/4 cup mayonnaise
- 1 tablespoon red wine vinegar
- 2 garlic cloves, minced

In a small bowl, combine all ingredients. Cover and refrigerate for at least 1 hour. **Yield**: 1-1/2 cups.

SOUP SAVVY. Soups are great to freeze for fast future meals. Here are some helpful hints:

- Most soups freeze nicely. The exceptions are soups made with cream and potatoes. Those are better when eaten fresh.
- Pasta in soup can get mushy in the freezer. It's best to add the pasta when ready to eat, not before freezing.
- To cool soup quickly before freezing, place the kettle in a sink filled with ice water. When cool, transfer to airtight freezer-safe containers, leaving 1/4-in. headspace for expansion.
- To help retain their fantastic flavor, don't freeze soups for longer than 3 months.

Chocolate Raspberry Cheesecake

PREP: 40 min. **BAKE:** 65 min. + chilling

- **1-1/2 cups cream-filled chocolate sandwich cookie crumbs**
- **2 tablespoons butter, melted**
- **4 packages (8 ounces *each*) cream cheese, softened**
- **1-1/4 cups sugar**
- **1 cup (8 ounces) sour cream**
- **1 teaspoon vanilla extract**
- **3 eggs, lightly beaten**
- **9 ounces semisweet chocolate, chopped**
- **1/2 cup seedless raspberry preserves**

TOPPING:
- **6 ounces semisweet chocolate, chopped**
- **1/3 cup heavy whipping cream**

Fresh raspberries and whipped cream, optional

Place a greased 9-in. springform pan on a double thickness of heavy-duty foil (about 18 in. square). Securely wrap foil around pan. Combine chocolate cookie crumbs and butter; press onto the bottom of prepared pan.

In a large bowl, beat cream cheese and sugar until smooth. Beat in sour cream and vanilla. Add eggs; beat on low speed just until combined. Set aside 1-1/2 cups; pour remaining batter over crust.

In a microwave, melt chocolate; stir in preserves until blended. Stir in reserved batter just until blended. Drop by tablespoonfuls over the plain batter (do not swirl). Place springform pan in a large baking pan; add 1 in. of hot water to larger pan.

Bake at 325° for 65-75 minutes or until the center is just set and top appears dull. Remove springform pan from water bath. Cool on a wire rack for 10 minutes. Carefully run a knife around edge of pan to loosen; cool 1 hour longer.

For topping, place chocolate in a small bowl. In a small saucepan, bring cream just to a boil. Pour over chocolate; whisk until smooth. Cool slightly. Spread over top of cheesecake. Refrigerate overnight. Garnish with raspberries and whipped cream if desired. **Yield:** 16 servings.

BASIL, FETA & ROASTED
PEPPER MUFFINS

HONEY-ORANGE RICE PUDDING

FROTHY MEXI-MOCHA COFFEE

Potato & Red Onion
Frittata

A World of Flavor

She blends cultural diversity and creativity in her Massachusetts kitchen to evoke memories and create new ones.

By Maria Regakis, Somerville, Massachusetts

ON ANY GIVEN DAY, my kitchen becomes a cantina, a taverna, a trattoria, a diner or a patisserie—depending on the food that is prepared and served.

To me, food is an opportunity to explore different cultures and share experiences. It's a common denominator among people.

A favorite breakfast/brunch menu of mine reflects my around-the-world cooking style. The main course is Potato & Red Onion Frittata, a delicious Italian classic.

I'm a fan of anything with basil, and it goes especially well with the salty cheese and sweet peppers in Basil, Feta & Roasted Pepper Muffins. The biscuit-like bites are always winners.

Arborio rice is the key to Honey-Orange Rice Pudding. During cooking, the rice becomes tender and absorbs the honey and citrus flavors.

Frothy Mexi-Mocha Coffee is a chocolaty spiced delight. Knowing that this beverage is waiting for me on the other side of the alarm clock makes for a great start to my morning!

Like many cooks, my earliest memories and experiences started in the kitchen. Growing up in the Greek and Italian culture, we ate a healthy and abundant Mediterranean diet. My mom prepared a homemade meal every evening.

Mom wasn't much of a baker, so I took the helm as soon as I was old enough to follow a recipe and navigate my way around the kitchen.

Now my cooking focuses on whatever looks fresh, evokes a memory or sparks creativity. I like to go back to basics and prepare soups with homemade stock or construct a trifle using from-scratch puddings, ice cream and sauces. Replicating restaurant dishes or those from my travels is always fun.

I find inspiration where I live, too. Somerville, just outside of Boston, is surrounded by many universities and colleges that bring diversity and ethnicity to the area. My family also owns a home on Cape Cod, where we fish for and eat local seafood.

When I'm not cooking, I enjoy event planning and fund-raising, sewing and clothing design, and home decorating and improvements. And do I love to talk—pretty much to anyone, especially if it's about food!

Frothy Mexi-Mocha Coffee

PREP/TOTAL TIME: 15 min.

- 1 cup packed brown sugar
- 4 ounces semisweet chocolate, chopped
- 2 orange peel strips (1 to 3 inches)
- 1/2 teaspoon ground cinnamon
- 1/4 teaspoon ground allspice
- 3 cups hot strong brewed coffee
- 1/2 cup half-and-half cream, warmed

Optional garnishes: cinnamon sticks, orange peel and whipped cream

Place the first five ingredients in a blender; cover and process until chocolate is finely chopped. Add coffee; cover and process for 1-2 minutes or until chocolate is melted. Transfer to a small saucepan; heat through.

Return mixture to blender; add cream. Cover and process until frothy. Strain, discarding solids; serve in mugs. Garnish with cinnamon sticks, orange peel and whipped cream if desired. **Yield:** 4 servings.

Honey-Orange Rice Pudding

PREP: 10 min. **COOK:** 35 min.

3-1/2 cups 2% milk
2/3 cup uncooked arborio rice
1/4 cup sugar
1/4 cup plus 2 tablespoons honey, *divided*
2 teaspoons grated orange peel
1/4 teaspoon salt
1 teaspoon vanilla extract
1/4 teaspoon ground cinnamon
1/3 cup pistachios

In a large saucepan, bring the milk, arborio rice, sugar, 1/4 cup honey, orange peel and salt to a boil. Reduce heat. Simmer, uncovered, for 30-35 minutes or until the rice is tender and the pudding is thickened, stirring occasionally.

Stir in vanilla, cinnamon and remaining honey. Serve warm or cold. Sprinkle with pistachios. **Yield:** 4 servings.

PUDDING POINTERS. Rice puddings are made with cooked rice, a custard mixture, flavoring and spices. Bread puddings are made with cubes or slices of bread baked in a custard mixture and may be accompanied by a sauce.

Rice and bread puddings are done when a knife inserted near the center comes out clean, and they may be served warm or cold. Store baked puddings in the refrigerator for 1 to 2 days.

Basil, Feta & Roasted Pepper Muffins

PREP: 20 min. **BAKE:** 20 min.

2 cups all-purpose flour
2 teaspoons baking powder
1/2 teaspoon salt
1/2 teaspoon baking soda
1 egg
1 cup buttermilk
1/4 cup olive oil
3/4 cup crumbled feta cheese
1/2 cup chopped roasted sweet red peppers
3 tablespoons minced fresh basil *or* 1 tablespoon dried basil

In a large bowl, combine the flour, baking powder, salt and baking soda. In another bowl, combine the egg, buttermilk and oil. Stir into dry ingredients just until moistened. Fold in the cheese, peppers and basil.

Fill greased muffin cups three-fourths full. Bake at 375° for 16-20 minutes or until a toothpick inserted near the center comes out clean. Cool for 5 minutes before removing from pan to a wire rack. Serve warm. **Yield:** 7 muffins.

Potato & Red Onion Frittata

PREP: 30 min. **BAKE:** 15 min.

- 1 **large red onion, chopped**
- 1/2 **teaspoon minced fresh rosemary *or***
  1/8 teaspoon dried rosemary, crushed
- 4 **tablespoons butter, *divided***
- 1 **garlic clove, minced**
- 1/2 **pound red potatoes (about 5 small), thinly**
  sliced
- 6 **eggs**
- 1/3 **cup 2% milk**
- 1/2 **teaspoon salt**
- 1/4 **teaspoon pepper**
- 1/2 **cup shredded Gruyere *or* Swiss cheese**

In a 10-in. ovenproof skillet, saute the onion and rosemary in 1 tablespoon butter until tender. Add the garlic; cook 1 minute longer. Remove from the pan and set aside.

In the same skillet, cook potatoes in 2 tablespoons butter until tender and golden brown. Remove and keep warm.

In a large bowl, whisk the eggs, milk, salt and pepper. Stir in the Gruyere cheese and onion mixture. Melt the remaining butter in the skillet; tilt the pan to evenly coat. Add the egg mixture. Bake at 350° for 8-10 minutes or until nearly set.

Top with potatoes; bake for 3-5 minutes or until eggs are completely set. Let stand for 5 minutes. Cut into wedges. **Yield:** 4 servings.

Blackberry Cobbler

GRILLED PORK CHOPS

MARINATED VEGGIE BEEF KABOBS

FABULOUS GREEN BEANS

Homegrown Goodness

The harvest of farm life brings fresh flavors to
this West Virginia Field Editor's cooking.

By Lori Daniels, Beverly, West Virginia

MY FAMILY and I relish our life on the farm—and it shows everyday in the meals I prepare.

Here in Beverly, West Virginia, we raise our own beef and chickens and maintain a large garden. My husband, Steve, is a real green thumb, so we eat fresh produce all summer and fall, then preserve the rest for the winter months.

We grow several kinds of vegetables, including squash, spinach, tomatoes, peas, corn and potatoes. We also have grapes, wild blackberries and a small apple orchard.

Steve and I follow the old-fashioned ways of growing, preserving and cooking our own food from scratch, and we're passing that tradition on to our daughters, Hannah and Heidi. Having the two children help with meal preparation instills responsibility, healthy eating habits and family togetherness.

Besides running our 42-acre farm, Steve works as a machinist and welder. I have a job as a licensed agent and customer service representative for an insurance company. I am also the leader for our daughters' Girl Scout troop, I sing and play handbells in church, and I'm involved in 4-H Club and several civic organizations.

But no matter how busy our lives get, sit-down dinners are a must. They give us time to reflect on our days and give thanks for our blessings.

Summer is my favorite time of year and a wonderful opportunity to prepare our favorite dishes fresh from the vine. It goes by quickly, yet I know when the crisp fall air says winter is coming, we'll be prepared for a long, hard winter in the mountains because of the bounty in our pantry and freezer.

When it comes to main courses, Grilled Pork Chops are always a popular choice. The marinade is so simple that I use it on all kinds of meat.

Marinated Beef Veggie Kabobs are a great way to showcase fresh veggies from the garden. Each bite is tender and flavorful, and the aroma is amazing.

My family loves the butter sauce in my Fabulous Green Beans. I've used it for sugar snap peas as well.

During winter, I pull our homegrown berries out of the freezer to make warm Blackberry Cobbler. Preparing this comforting dessert—and other dishes for my family—is truly one of life's simple pleasures.

Grilled Pork Chops

PREP: 10 min. + marinating GRILL: 10 min.

- 1/2 **cup packed brown sugar**
- 1/2 **cup soy sauce**
- 2 **garlic cloves, minced**
- 1/4 **teaspoon pepper**
- 4 **bone-in pork loin chops (1 inch thick and 8 ounces *each*)**

In a small bowl, combine the brown sugar, soy sauce, garlic and pepper. Pour marinade into a large resealable plastic bag. Add pork chops; seal bag and turn to coat. Refrigerate for 8 hours or overnight.

If grilling the chops, use long-handled tongs to dip a paper towel in cooking oil and lightly coat the grill rack. Drain and discard marinade. Grill chops, covered, over medium heat or broil 4 in. from the heat for 4-5 minutes on each side or until a meat thermometer reads 160°. **Yield:** 4 servings.

vegetables into 1-in. pieces; add to bag. Seal bag and turn to coat. Refrigerate beef and vegetables for at least 2 hours.

Using long-handled tongs, dip a paper towel in cooking oil and lightly coat the grill rack. Drain and discard marinade from beef. Drain the vegetables, reserving the marinade for basting. On eight metal or soaked wooden skewers, alternately thread beef and vegetables.

Grill, covered, over medium heat for 10-15 minutes or until the meat reaches desired doneness, basting frequently with reserved marinade and turning occasionally. **Yield:** 8 kabobs.

Fabulous Green Beans

PREP/TOTAL TIME: 20 min.

- 1 **pound fresh green beans, trimmed**
- 1/4 **cup butter, cubed**
- 1 **tablespoon olive oil**
- 1/2 **teaspoon salt**
- 1/2 **teaspoon Italian seasoning**
- 1/2 **teaspoon lemon juice**
- 1/4 **teaspoon grated lemon peel**

Place the beans in a steamer basket; place in a large saucepan over 1 in. of water. Bring to a boil; cover and steam for 8-10 minutes or until crisp-tender.

Meanwhile, in a small saucepan, heat the remaining ingredients until butter is melted. Transfer beans to a serving bowl; drizzle with butter mixture and toss to coat. **Yield:** 4 servings.

Marinated Veggie Beef Kabobs

PREP: 35 min. + marinating **GRILL:** 10 min.

- 1 **cup dry red wine**
- 1/2 **cup olive oil**
- 4 **teaspoons Worcestershire sauce**
- 4 **teaspoons Italian seasoning**
- 1 **tablespoon garlic powder**
- 2 **teaspoons seasoned salt**
- 2 **teaspoons pepper**
- 1 **teaspoon dried parsley flakes**
- 1 **beef top sirloin steak (1-1/2 pounds), cut into 1-inch cubes**
- 8 **cherry tomatoes**
- 1 **large red onion**
- 1 **medium green pepper**
- 1 **yellow summer squash**
- 1 **medium zucchini**

In a small bowl, combine first eight ingredients. Pour half the marinade into a large resealable plastic bag. Add the beef; seal bag and turn to coat.

Pour remaining marinade into another large resealable plastic bag; add tomatoes. Cut remaining

Blackberry Cobbler

PREP: 25 min. **BAKE:** 30 min.

- **3 cups fresh *or* frozen blackberries**
- **1 cup sugar**
- **1/4 teaspoon ground cinnamon**
- **3 tablespoons cornstarch**
- **1 cup cold water**
- **1 tablespoon butter**

BISCUIT TOPPING:
- **1-1/2 cups all-purpose flour**
- **1 tablespoon sugar**
- **1-1/2 teaspoons baking powder**
- **1/2 teaspoon salt**
- **1/2 cup cold butter**
- **1/2 cup 2% milk**
- **Whipped topping *or* vanilla ice cream, optional**

In a large saucepan, combine the blackberries, sugar and cinnamon. Cook and stir until mixture comes to a boil. Combine the cornstarch and water until smooth; stir into fruit mixture. Bring to a boil; cook and stir for 2 minutes or until thickened. Pour into a greased 8-in. square baking dish. Dot with butter.

For the topping, in a small bowl, combine the flour, sugar, baking powder and salt. Cut in the butter until the mixture resembles coarse crumbs. Stir in the milk just until moistened. Drop by tablespoonfuls onto hot berry mixture.

Bake, uncovered, at 350° for 30-35 minutes or until the filling is bubbly and the topping is golden brown. Serve warm with whipped topping or ice cream. **Yield:** 9 servings.

BERRY BEST. Blackberries will stay fresh for up to 2 days in the refrigerator. Or, they may be frozen for up to 1 year. To freeze, wash and blot dry the berries, then arrange them in a single layer on a jelly-roll pan. Freeze them until firm, then transfer them to a heavy-duty resealable plastic bag.

BUTTERHORNS

APPLE BRAN MUFFINS

SPICED PUDDING CAKE

**Super Low-Fat
Granola Cereal**

Stirring Things Up

For this Canadian Field Editor, baking provides relaxation and quality time with the kids.

By Kelly Kirby, Westville, Nova Scotia

LIFE here in Nova Scotia is pretty laid-back, but there's never a shortage of things to do. During the summer, for example, you can go to a festival just about every weekend. Many people take their vacations in July to attend the Pictou (County) Lobster Carnival.

Because my husband, Craig, and I work Monday through Friday, we really look forward to our weekends. Craig, the director of national accounting services for a grocery chain, likes to golf and barbecue. Our young daughters, Lauren and Regan, enjoy beachcombing for shells, rocks and beach glass.

I work as a service supervisor for an insurance company. On weekends, I stockpile our freezer with food for the week ahead and often put supper in the slow cooker on Sunday morning. I use produce that's in season and freeze fresh berries to use during the winter.

I find baking to be a great stress reliever and like to share what I make with others. I bake anything and everything, and love to try new recipes—so it's a good thing I work out about 6 days a week!

Lauren and Regan must have baking in their genes because every time I pull out my trusty mixer, they're by my side, measuring, mixing and tasting.

They especially like making Butterhorns, which my mom taught me to make when I was a young girl. We always have to double the recipe because they never last long. You can shape them any way you like, but to me, a crescent shape is so pretty.

My mom also taught me how to make moist, tasty Apple Bran Muffins. The recipe makes a big batch, so you can freeze the extras or share with friends.

I came across a recipe for Spiced Pudding Cake years ago and made a few changes. Now, my mom's church group serves it for dessert quite regularly.

Super Low-Fat Granola Cereal is another favorite—delicious with milk or sprinkled over yogurt. You could add chopped walnuts or pecans, too.

Fall has to be my absolute favorite time of year. The air is crisp and cool, and the colors paint such beautiful pictures. I look forward to baking more muffins and comfort foods such as crisps and casseroles this fall, especially since we recently renovated our kitchen. Now I love baking and cooking even more!

Apple Bran Muffins

PREP: 25 min. **BAKE:** 20 min. + cooling

    3 cups all-purpose flour
    2 teaspoons baking powder
    2 teaspoons ground cinnamon
    1 teaspoon salt
  1/2 teaspoon baking soda
  1/4 teaspoon ground nutmeg
1-1/2 cups 2% milk
    4 eggs
  2/3 cup packed brown sugar
  1/2 cup canola oil
    2 teaspoons vanilla extract
    3 cups All-Bran
    2 cups shredded peeled tart apples
    1 cup chopped walnuts
    1 cup raisins

In a large bowl, combine first six ingredients. In another bowl, combine the milk, eggs, brown sugar, oil and vanilla. Stir into dry ingredients just until moistened. Fold in remaining ingredients.

Fill greased or paper-lined muffin cups three-fourths full. Bake at 350° for 18-22 minutes or until a toothpick inserted in muffin comes out clean. Cool for 5 minutes before removing from pans to wire racks. **Yield:** 2 dozen.

Super Low-Fat Granola Cereal

PREP: 15 min. BAKE: 25 min. + cooling

- 8 cups old-fashioned oats
- 1 cup raisins
- 1/2 cup chopped dried apricots
- 1/2 cup dried cranberries
- 1-1/2 cups packed brown sugar
- 1/2 cup water
- 1 teaspoon salt
- 1 teaspoon maple flavoring
- 1 teaspoon vanilla extract

Milk *or* yogurt

In a large bowl, combine the oats, raisins, apricots and cranberries; set aside. In a small saucepan, combine the brown sugar, water and salt. Cook and stir over medium heat for 3-4 minutes or until brown sugar is dissolved. Remove from the heat; stir in maple flavoring and vanilla. Pour over oat mixture; stir to coat.

Transfer to two greased 15-in. x 10-in. x 1-in. baking pans. Bake at 350° for 25-30 minutes or until crisp, stirring every 10 minutes. Cool completely on wire racks. Store in an airtight container. Serve with milk or yogurt. **Yield:** 9 cups.

SWEET SUBSTITUTE. Out of brown sugar? For each 1 cup of firmly packed light brown sugar, use 1-1/2 tablespoons molasses plus 1 cup granulated sugar. For dark brown sugar, use 1/4 cup molasses and 1 cup granulated sugar. If the recipe doesn't specify light or dark, you may use either variety.

Butterhorns

PREP: 35 min. + rising BAKE: 10 min.

✓ This recipe includes Nutrition Facts and Diabetic Exchanges.

- 1 tablespoon active dry yeast
- 1 teaspoon plus 1/3 cup sugar
- 1/2 cup warm water (110° to 115°)
- 1/2 cup butter, softened
- 1/2 cup warm 2% milk (110° to 115°)
- 1 egg
- 3/4 teaspoon salt
- 4 cups all-purpose flour

In a large bowl, dissolve yeast and 1 teaspoon sugar in warm water. Add the butter, milk, egg, salt, remaining sugar and 2 cups flour. Beat until smooth. Stir in enough remaining flour to form a soft dough.

Turn onto a floured surface; knead until smooth and elastic, about 6-8 minutes. Place in a greased bowl, turning once to grease the top. Cover and let rise in a warm place until doubled, about 1 hour.

Punch dough down. Turn onto a lightly floured surface; divide in half. Roll each portion into a 12-inch circle; cut each circle into 12 wedges. Roll up wedges from the wide end and place point side down 2 inches apart on greased baking sheets. Curve ends to form crescents.

Cover and let rise in a warm place until doubled, about 30 minutes. Bake at 350° for 10-12 minutes or until golden brown. Remove the rolls from pans to wire racks. **Yield:** 2 dozen.

Nutrition Facts: 1 roll equals 128 calories, 4 g fat (3 g saturated fat), 19 mg cholesterol, 107 mg sodium, 19 g carbohydrate, 1 g fiber, 3 g protein. **Diabetic Exchanges:** 1 starch, 1 fat.

Spiced Pudding Cake

PREP: 25 min. BAKE: 35 min.

- 1/2 cup butter, softened
- 1/2 cup sugar
- 1 egg
- 1 cup molasses
- 2-1/2 cups all-purpose flour
- 1-1/2 teaspoons baking soda
- 1-1/2 teaspoons ground cinnamon
- 1-1/4 teaspoons ground ginger
- 1/2 teaspoon ground allspice
- 1/4 teaspoon ground nutmeg
- 1/4 teaspoon salt
- 1 cup water
- 2/3 cup packed brown sugar
- 1-1/2 cups water
- 1/4 cup butter, cubed
- **Whipped cream and ground cinnamon, optional**

In a large bowl, cream butter and sugar until light and fluffy. Add the egg; beat well. Beat in molasses. Combine the flour, baking soda, spices and salt; add to creamed mixture alternately with 1 cup water, beating well after each addition.

Transfer to an ungreased 13-in. x 9-in. baking pan; sprinkle with the brown sugar. In a microwave, heat 1-1/2 cups water and butter until butter is melted; carefully pour mixture over batter.

Bake at 350° for 35-40 minutes or until a toothpick inserted near the center comes out clean. Serve warm. Garnish cake with whipped cream and cinnamon if desired. **Yield:** 15 servings.

CREAM OF WALNUT SOUP

LIME-BUTTERED BROCCOLI

BANANA RUM SUNDAES

Honey-Glazed Hens
With Fruit Stuffing

Try and Try Again

This accomplished Illinois cook learned by trial and error. She still loves trying new things on a weekly basis.

By Denise Albers, Freeburg, Illinois

YOU COULD SAY a paper route got me interested in cooking. There were a lot of older ladies on my route, and when I'd go to collect payments on Saturday mornings, the most wonderful smells would come from their kitchens. I didn't care about a tip; I wanted a caramel roll!

Because I held jobs throughout school, and since I worked my way through college, I didn't get to spend time in the kitchen with my mom. So I didn't know much about cooking when I married my husband, Jim.

In order to become the cook I wanted to be, I decided to try two new recipes every week. Over 25 years later, I am still doing that.

I've also attended all sorts of cooking classes, from bread baking to gourmet dinners. I believe anyone can cook; the trick is to be able to look at a recipe and know if it will be a keeper.

Among my personal keepers are Honey-Glazed Hens with Fruit Stuffing and Lime-Buttered Broccoli. What a great meal to surprise your family with, particularly during the holidays! We also enjoy Cream of Walnut Soup on chilly winter nights, and nothing tops a homey meal like my Banana Rum Sundaes.

When I have extra time, I happily add baking to my to-do list. Favorites from my mom and grandmothers, such as rhubarb custard pie and cinnamon coffee cake, are sweets I turn to regularly. I also enjoy making salsa, jelly and homemade candies much to the delight of my two children, Catherine and Mitchell.

Cooking allows me to be creative and productive, while sharing what I make with friends, family and my staff. I own and operate a hospital supply company that my father started 26 years ago. I like to bring in lunches and desserts for my employees.

When I'm not trying new recipes in the kitchen, I'm checking out new eateries in our area. We live in a small town so we take advantage of all the wonderful restaurants and foods the city has to offer. Jim and I recently celebrated our 25th anniversary with a trip to Italy, and we enjoyed some of the best food we've ever tasted. You can bet that I'll be trying out new recipes with an Italian flavor at home. I hope to share a few with you sometime soon!

Lime-Buttered Broccoli

PREP/TOTAL TIME: 20 min.

☑ This recipe includes Nutrition Facts and Diabetic Exchanges.

- **8 cups fresh broccoli florets**
- **3 tablespoons butter, melted**
- **1 tablespoon lime juice**
- **1/4 teaspoon salt**
- **1/4 teaspoon pepper**

Place the broccoli in a steamer basket; place in a large saucepan over 1 in. of water. Bring to a boil; cover and steam for 3-4 minutes or until crisp-tender.

Meanwhile, in a small bowl, combine the remaining ingredients.

Drizzle the butter mixture over broccoli; toss to coat. **Yield:** 8 servings.

Nutrition Facts: 3/4 cup equals 58 calories, 5 g fat (3 g saturated fat), 11 mg cholesterol, 123 mg sodium, 4 g carbohydrate, 2 g fiber, 2 g protein. **Diabetic Exchanges:** 1 vegetable, 1/2 fat.

Loosely stuff hens with stuffing. Tuck wings under hens; tie drumsticks together. Sprinkle with salt and pepper. Place the breast side up on a rack in a shallow roasting pan. Combine the butter and honey; brush over the hens.

Bake, uncovered, at 350° for 1 to 1-1/2 hours or until a meat thermometer reads 180° for hens and 165° for stuffing, basting occasionally with pan drippings. Cover loosely with foil if hens brown too quickly. Cover and let stand for 10 minutes before serving. **Yield:** 4 servings.

Cream of Walnut Soup

PREP: 15 min. **COOK:** 40 min.

   3 cups chicken broth
   1 cup chopped walnuts
   2 tablespoons chopped onion
   2 tablespoons chopped celery
1/8 teaspoon ground nutmeg
   2 tablespoons butter
   2 tablespoons all-purpose flour
1/2 cup 2% milk
   1 cup half-and-half cream
Minced fresh parsley

In a small saucepan, combine the first five ingredients. Bring to a boil. Reduce the heat; cover and simmer for 30 minutes. Cool slightly. Transfer to a blender; cover and process until pureed. Strain.

In a large saucepan, melt butter over medium heat. Stir in flour until blended. Gradually whisk in milk. Bring to a boil; cook and stir for 1 minute or until thickened. Gradually stir in pureed mixture. Add the cream; heat through (do not boil). Garnish with parsley. **Yield:** 3 cups.

Honey-Glazed Hens With Fruit Stuffing

PREP: 30 min. **BAKE:** 1 hour + standing

1/2 cup butter, cubed
1/4 cup chopped onion
1/4 cup chopped celery
   4 cups cubed day-old bread
1/2 cup dried fruit bits
1/2 cup water
1/8 teaspoon ground allspice
CORNISH HENS:
   4 Cornish game hens (20 to 24 ounces *each*)
1/4 teaspoon salt
1/8 teaspoon pepper
   2 tablespoons butter, melted
   1 tablespoon honey

In a large skillet over medium heat, melt butter. Add onion and celery; cook and stir until tender. Stir in the bread, fruit bits, water and allspice; cover and cook for 2-3 minutes or until heated through.

Banana Rum Sundaes

PREP/TOTAL TIME: 20 min.

- **3 tablespoons butter**
- **3/4 cup packed brown sugar**
- **Dash ground nutmeg**
- **4 medium firm bananas, halved and sliced**
- **1/4 cup golden raisins**
- **1/4 cup rum**
- **2 tablespoons sliced almonds, toasted**
- **1 quart vanilla ice cream**

In a large nonstick skillet, melt butter over medium-low heat. Stir in brown sugar and nutmeg until blended.

Remove from the heat; add the bananas, raisins, rum and almonds. Cook over medium heat, stirring gently, for 3-4 minutes or until bananas are glazed and slightly softened. Serve with ice cream. **Yield:** 6 servings.

FAST FIX. Not only is this delightful sundae one of Denise Albers' favorite after-dinner delights, but it's so versatile, too. While it's scrumptious served over vanilla ice cream, you can prepare the sauce and serve it over the following as well:

- Pound cake
- Banana bread
- Angel food cake
- Biscuits
- Pancakes
- Coffee ice cream
- Chocolate ice cream
- Cheesecake
- French toast
- Bread pudding
- Cinnamon rolls

Quick Fixes

Home cooking doesn't have to take a lot of time. Scrumptious recipes such as Steak & New Potato Toss, Mini White Pizzas, French Onion Soup and Greek Chicken Pasta will be on the table in just 30 minutes—or less!

Salsa Verde....................246
Easy Parmesan Biscuits...................246
Scallops in Sage Cream 246
Crispy Taco Wings 247
Spicy Garlic Shrimp 247
Greek Deli Kabobs...................248
Dijon-Walnut Spinach Salad 248
Layered Pesto Cheese Spread 248
Cherry-Brandy Baked Brie...................249
Herbed Corn 249
Southwest Chicken Salad 250
Pad Thai Pizza 250
Honey-Lime Red Snapper...................251
Greek Chicken Pasta...................251
Blackberry-Sauced Pork Chops 252
Apricot Turkey Pinwheels 252
Blueberry Fruit Dip 252
Maple-Pecan Snack Mix 253

Coconut-Mango Mahi Mahi...................253
Sun-Dried Tomato Hummus...................254
Taco Salad...................254
Fast & Fabulous Thai Chicken Salad 255
Lemony Brussels Sprouts...................255
French Onion Soup 256
Tomato Tortellini Soup...................256
Shortcut Split Pea Soup 257
30-Minute Chicken Noodle Soup...................257
Hearty Cabbage Soup 258
Chicken Tortilla Chowder...................258
Steak & New Potato Toss...................259
Chicken Cordon Bleu Pizza...................259
Mini White Pizzas...................260
Bacon-Wrapped Breadsticks 260
Spicy Shrimp Kabobs...................260
Greek Islands Steak Salad...................261
Turkey & Fruit Salad...................261

SPEEDY SPECIALTIES. Clockwise from top left: Greek Deli Kabobs (p. 248), Crispy Taco Wings (p. 247), Chicken Cordon Bleu Pizza (p. 259), Greek Islands Steak Salad (p. 261) and Spicy Garlic Shrimp (p. 247).

Easy Parmesan Biscuits

PREP/TOTAL TIME: 15 min.

Rounding out your menu doesn't get any easier than these yummy biscuits. They're simple enough for children to help make.
—*Linda Becker, Olympia, Washington*

> 1 **tube (6 ounces) refrigerated buttermilk biscuits**
> 3 **tablespoons butter, melted**
> 1/2 **cup grated Parmesan cheese**

Dip both sides of each biscuit into melted butter, then into the cheese. Place 1 in. apart in a well-greased 9-in. round baking pan.

Bake at 400° for 8-11 minutes or until golden brown. Serve warm. **Yield:** 5 biscuits.

Scallops in Sage Cream

(Pictured below)

PREP/TOTAL TIME: 20 min.

I buy fresh scallops from a local fisherman, and I use everyday ingredients to showcase them. This is one of the recipes I go back to time and time again. It's so good and takes just 20 minutes.
—*Joan Churchill, Dover, New Hampshire*

> 1-1/2 **pounds sea scallops**
> 1/4 **teaspoon salt**
> 1/8 **teaspoon pepper**
> 3 **tablespoons olive oil,** *divided*
> 1/2 **cup chopped shallots**
> 3/4 **cup heavy whipping cream**
> 6 **fresh sage leaves, thinly sliced**
> **Hot cooked pasta, optional**

Salsa Verde

(Pictured above)

PREP: 15 min. + chilling

When you want a salsa that's a little different, try this one. It's fresh–tasting, creamy and full of flavor. Use it as a dip for your favorite tortilla chips...or as a condiment for tacos and other Mexican dishes. You can adjust the spiciness to suit your family.
—*Paul and Nanette Hilton, Las Vegas, Nevada*

> 8 **tomatillos, husks removed**
> 1 **medium ripe avocado, peeled and pitted**
> 1 **small onion, halved**
> 1 **jalapeno pepper, seeded**
> 1/3 **cup fresh cilantro leaves**
> 1/2 **teaspoon salt**
> **Tortilla chips**

In a large saucepan, bring 4 cups water to a boil. Add the tomatillos. Reduce heat; simmer, uncovered, for 5 minutes. Drain.

Place the avocado, onion, jalapeno, cilantro, salt and tomatillos in a food processor. Cover and process until blended. Refrigerate until chilled. Serve with chips. **Yield:** 2-1/2 cups.

Editor's Note: When cutting hot peppers, disposable gloves are recommended. Avoid touching your face.

In a large shallow bowl, combine the flour and taco seasoning. Add wings, a few at a time, and coat. Place butter and corn chips in separate shallow bowls. Dip wings in butter, then coat with chips.

Transfer to a greased 15-in. x 10-in. x 1-in. baking pan. Bake, uncovered, at 350° for 30-40 minutes or until juices run clear. **Yield:** 2 dozen.

Editor's Note: Uncooked chicken wing sections (wingettes) may be substituted for whole chicken wings.

Spicy Garlic Shrimp

(Pictured below and on page 244)

PREP/TOTAL TIME: 25 min.

Zesty and spicy yet fuss–free, these lip–smacking shrimp are perfect for a party. If you prefer a bit more fire, just substitute minced fresh hot chili peppers for the red pepper flakes.
—*Jasmin Baron, Livonia, New York*

> 1 **pound uncooked medium shrimp**
> 3 **garlic cloves, minced**
> 1/2 **teaspoon crushed red pepper flakes**
> 3 **tablespoons butter**
> 1/2 **cup white wine**

Peel and devein the shrimp, leaving the tails on.

In a large skillet over medium heat, cook garlic and pepper flakes in butter for 1 minute. Add shrimp; cook and stir until shrimp turn pink. Remove from the pan and set aside. Add wine to the pan; cook until liquid is reduced by half. Return shrimp to skillet; heat through. **Yield:** about 2-1/2 dozen.

Sprinkle the scallops with salt and pepper. In a large skillet, saute scallops in 2 tablespoons oil for 1-1/2 to 2 minutes on each side or until firm and opaque. Remove and keep warm.

In the same skillet, saute shallots in the remaining oil until tender. Add cream; bring to a boil. Cook and stir for 30 seconds or until slightly thickened.

Return scallops to the pan; heat through. Stir in sage. Serve with pasta if desired. **Yield:** 4 servings.

Crispy Taco Wings

(Pictured above and on page 244)

PREP: 15 min. **BAKE:** 30 min.

These wings are everything you love about chicken—a crispy, tasty outside with a tender, moist center—plus Southwest zip.
—*Blanche Gibson, Gordon, Wisconsin*

> 1/2 **cup all-purpose flour**
> 1 **envelope taco seasoning**
> 2-1/2 **pounds chicken wingettes and drummettes**
> 1/2 **cup butter, melted**
> 1-3/4 **cups crushed corn chips**

SUREFIRE SHRIMP. Plan to make Spicy Garlic Shrimp (recipe above right)? When shopping for the ingredients, keep in mind that fresh shrimp should have a firm texture with a mild odor. Uncooked shrimp will have shells that range in color from gray or brown to pink or red.

Greek Deli Kabobs

(Pictured above and on page 244)

PREP: 30 min. + marinating

These pretty skewers turn marinated mozzarella cheese, veggies and salami into a fun, hearty appetizer that's a snap to make.
—Vikki Spengler, Ocala, Florida

- 2 jars (7-1/2 ounces *each*) roasted sweet red peppers, drained
- 1 pound part-skim mozzarella cheese, cut into 1/2-inch cubes
- 24 fresh broccoli florets
- 24 slices hard salami
- 1/2 cup Greek vinaigrette

Cut the red peppers into 24 strips; place in a large resealable plastic bag. Add the remaining ingredients. Seal the bag and turn to coat; refrigerate for 4 hours or overnight.

Drain and discard the marinade. Thread the cheese, vegetables and meat onto frilled toothpicks or short skewers. **Yield:** 2 dozen.

Dijon-Walnut Spinach Salad

PREP/TOTAL TIME: 10 min.

After one bite of this special salad, you'll be amazed at how much flavor you get from so few ingredients. It's a family favorite that also has lots of different textures and can be tossed together in a heartbeat. For variety, change the dressing to honey mustard.
—Chris DeMontravel, Mohegan Lake, New York

- 1 package (9 ounces) fresh baby spinach
- 1 package (4 ounces) crumbled feta cheese
- 1 cup dried cranberries
- 1 cup walnut halves, toasted
- 1/2 cup honey Dijon vinaigrette

In a large salad bowl, combine the spinach, feta cheese, dried cranberries and walnuts. Drizzle with the honey Dijon vinaigrette; toss to coat. Serve immediately. **Yield:** 13 servings.

Layered Pesto Cheese Spread

(Pictured below)

PREP: 20 min. + chilling

My guests can never pass up this unique, fancy-looking layered spread. In fact, the combination of cream cheese, Parmesan, sun-dried tomatoes and pesto gets them coming back for more. The red and green colors make it festive for Christmastime.
—Denise Hruz, Germantown, Wisconsin

- 1 package (8 ounces) cream cheese, softened
- 1/2 cup butter, softened
- 1 jar (3-1/2 ounces) prepared pesto
- 1/4 cup grated Parmesan cheese
- 1/2 cup chopped oil-packed sun-dried tomatoes
Assorted crackers *or* baked pita chips

Line a 3-cup bowl with plastic wrap; set aside. In a small bowl, beat the cream cheese and butter until smooth. In another bowl, combine the pesto and Parmesan cheese.

Layer half of cream cheese mixture, pesto mixture and sun-dried tomatoes in prepared bowl. Repeat the layers. Cover and refrigerate for at least 1 hour.

Unmold onto a serving plate. Serve with the crackers. **Yield:** 2-1/2 cups.

Cherry-Brandy Baked Brie

(Pictured above)

PREP/TOTAL TIME: 20 min.

No one will believe this impressive appetizer is so easy to make. If you can't find dried cherries, substitute dried cranberries or apricots. You could also replace the brandy with apple juice.
—Kevin Phebus, Katy, Texas

- 1 **round (8 ounces) Brie cheese**
- 1/2 **cup dried cherries**
- 1/2 **cup chopped walnuts**
- 1/4 **cup packed brown sugar**
- 1/4 **cup brandy *or* unsweetened apple juice**

French bread baguette, sliced and toasted *or* assorted crackers

Place cheese in a 9-in. pie plate. Combine the cherries, walnuts, brown sugar and brandy; spoon over cheese.

Bake at 350° for 15-20 minutes or until the cheese is softened. Serve with baguette. **Yield:** 8 servings.

Herbed Corn

PREP/TOTAL TIME: 25 min.

Red onion and a pleasant blend of herbs enhance this fast but yummy side. It's our family's preferred way of eating fresh corn.
—Tania Bikerman, Pittsburgh, Pennsylvania

- 8 **cups fresh *or* frozen corn, thawed**
- 1 **cup finely chopped red onion**
- 12 **garlic cloves, minced**
- 3/4 **cup butter, cubed**
- 4 **to 6 teaspoons herbes de Provence *or* Italian seasoning**
- 1 **teaspoon salt**

In a Dutch oven over medium-high heat, cook and stir the corn, onion and garlic in butter for 5 minutes. Add herbes de Provence and salt; cook 2-4 minutes longer or until vegetables are tender. **Yield:** 8 servings.

Editor's Note: Look for herbes de Provence in the spice aisle.

Southwest Chicken Salad

(Pictured below)

PREP/TOTAL TIME: 30 min.

My husband is a fan of salads, and this one is both nutritious and easy to fix. The recipe includes three different ways of serving it—over greens, tucked in a pita or rolled up in a tortilla.
—*Sara Hobbs, West Tawakoni, Texas*

✓ This recipe includes Nutrition Facts and Diabetic Exchanges.

    4 cups cubed rotisserie chicken
    2 cups frozen corn, thawed
    1 cup chopped roasted sweet red peppers
    1 cup chopped red *or* sweet onion
    1 cup minced fresh cilantro
DRESSING:
    3 tablespoons lime juice
    3 tablespoons olive oil
    4 teaspoons honey
    2 teaspoons ground cumin
    1 teaspoon salt
    1 teaspoon chili powder
  1/2 teaspoon coarsely ground pepper
SALADS:
Torn mixed salad greens and sliced almonds
PITAS:
Whole wheat pita breads, halved, and lettuce leaves
WRAPS:
Whole wheat tortillas and sliced ripe avocado

In a large bowl, combine the first five ingredients. In a small bowl, whisk the dressing ingredients; pour over the chicken mixture and toss to coat. Refrigerate until serving. Serve as desired.

  For salads: Top the salad greens with chicken salad; sprinkle with almonds.

  For pitas: Line the pita halves with lettuce leaves; fill with chicken salad.

  For wraps: Place the chicken salad off-center on the tortillas; top with avocado. Roll up. **Yield:** 6 cups.

  Nutrition Facts: 1/2 cup chicken salad (calculated without serving suggestions) equals 166 calories, 7 g fat (1 g saturated fat), 42 mg cholesterol, 316 mg sodium, 10 g carbohydrate, 1 g fiber, 15 g protein. **Diabetic Exchanges:** 2 lean meat, 1/2 starch, 1/2 fat.

Pad Thai Pizza

(Pictured above)

PREP/TOTAL TIME: 30 min.

A handy refrigerated pizza crust makes preparing this unusual, Thai-inspired pizza a snap. You'll love the combination of a slightly spicy peanut sauce, mozzarella, tender chicken and more.
—*Karen Shelton, Collierville, Tennessee*

    1 tube (11 ounces) refrigerated thin pizza crust
    2 tablespoons creamy peanut butter
    2 tablespoons teriyaki sauce
    1 tablespoon Thai chili sauce
    1 teaspoon honey
    2 cups shredded rotisserie chicken
    1 cup (4 ounces) shredded part-skim mozzarella cheese
  1/2 cup shredded carrot
  1/3 cup fresh bean sprouts
  1/4 cup chopped salted peanuts
  1/4 cup minced fresh cilantro
    2 green onions, thinly sliced

Unroll pizza crust dough into a greased 15-in. x 10-in. baking pan; flatten the dough and build up the edges slightly. Bake at 425° for 5-6 minutes or until edges are lightly browned.

Meanwhile, in a small bowl, whisk the peanut butter, teriyaki sauce, chili sauce and honey. Place chicken in another small bowl; add half of peanut butter mixture and toss to coat.

Spread remaining peanut butter mixture over crust; top with chicken and cheese. Bake for 10-15 minutes or until crust is golden brown. Sprinkle with the remaining ingredients. **Yield:** 6 pieces.

Honey-Lime Red Snapper

(Pictured below)

PREP: 5 min. + marinating **BROIL:** 15 min.

Here's a four–ingredient way of serving your family a delicious fish dinner. If you can't find snapper, you can substitute most any firm white fish. And if you don't have key lime juice, use regular lime juice. —Ken Hulme, Venice, Florida

- **3/4 cup key lime juice**
- **1/2 cup honey**
- **4 red snapper fillets (6 ounces *each*)**
- **2 teaspoons chili powder**

In a small bowl, combine the lime juice and honey. Pour 1/2 cup into a large resealable plastic bag; add the fish. Seal bag and turn to coat; refrigerate for up to 1 hour. Place remaining mixture in a small saucepan; set aside.

Drain fish and discard marinade. Sprinkle fillets with chili powder; place on a greased broiler pan.

Broil 4-6 in. from the heat for 12-15 minutes or until fish flakes easily with a fork. Meanwhile, bring reserved lime juice mixture to a boil. Reduce the heat; simmer, uncovered, until reduced by half. Spoon over the fillets. **Yield:** 4 servings.

Greek Chicken Pasta

(Pictured above)

PREP/TOTAL TIME: 25 min.

This hearty main dish, packed with penne pasta and chicken, has great Mediterranean flavor. I left out the olives, and my family still loved it. —Susan Stetzel, Gainesville, New York

- **2 cups uncooked penne pasta**
- **1/4 cup butter, cubed**
- **1 large onion, chopped**
- **1/4 cup all-purpose flour**
- **1 can (14-1/2 ounces) reduced-sodium chicken broth**
- **3 cups cubed rotisserie chicken**
- **1 jar (7-1/2 ounces) marinated quartered artichoke hearts, drained**
- **1 cup (4 ounces) crumbled feta cheese**
- **1/2 cup chopped oil-packed sun-dried tomatoes**
- **1/3 cup sliced pitted Greek olives**
- **2 tablespoons minced fresh parsley**

Cook the pasta according to the package directions.

Meanwhile, in a large ovenproof skillet, melt butter. Add the onion; saute until tender. Stir in the flour until blended; gradually add broth. Bring to a boil; cook and stir for 2 minutes or until thickened. Stir in the chicken, artichoke hearts, cheese, tomatoes and olives.

Drain the pasta; stir into the pan. Broil 3-4 in. from the heat for 5-7 minutes or until bubbly and golden brown. Sprinkle with parsley. **Yield:** 5 servings.

Blackberry-Sauced Pork Chops

(Pictured below)

PREP/TOTAL TIME: 30 min.

My family raved over this main dish the first time I served it, and they still request it for dinner. The mouthwatering pork chops are as good prepared in a skillet as they are grilled, so you can enjoy them all year long. The sauce also goes well with chicken.
—Priscilla Gilbert, Indian Harbour Beach, Florida

 1/2 cup seedless blackberry spreadable fruit
 1 tablespoon lemon juice
 1 tablespoon reduced-sodium soy sauce
Dash ground cinnamon
 4 boneless pork loin chops (5 ounces *each*)
 2 teaspoons steak seasoning
 2 teaspoons olive oil
 1 cup fresh blackberries

In a small saucepan, combine spreadable fruit, lemon juice, soy sauce and cinnamon. Cook and stir over low heat until spreadable fruit is melted. Remove from the heat; set aside.

Sprinkle both sides of the pork chops with the steak seasoning. In a large nonstick skillet coated with cooking spray, cook pork chops in oil over medium-high heat for 5-7 minutes on each side or until a meat thermometer reads 160°. Serve with prepared sauce and blackberries. **Yield:** 4 servings.

Editor's Note: This recipe was tested with McCormick's Montreal Steak Seasoning. Look for it in the spice aisle.

Apricot Turkey Pinwheels

(Pictured above)

PREP/TOTAL TIME: 30 min.

I created these five-ingredient pinwheels for a football game using ingredients I had on hand. The little baked spirals were a huge hit, and I love how quick and easy they are to fix.
—Melanie Foster, Blaine, Minnesota

 1 sheet frozen puff pastry, thawed
 1/4 cup apricot preserves
 1/2 teaspoon ground mustard
 1/2 cup shredded Monterey Jack cheese
 1/4 pound sliced deli turkey

Unfold pastry; layer with preserves, mustard, cheese and turkey. Roll up jelly-roll style. Cut into 16 slices. Place cut side down on a baking sheet.

Bake at 400° for 15-20 minutes or until golden brown. **Yield:** 16 pinwheels.

Blueberry Fruit Dip

PREP/TOTAL TIME: 10 min.

This makes a great snack for my kids. Fresh fruit and a creamy, sweet dip—what could be better after a long day at school?
—Renee Sevigny, Wayland, Michigan

 4 ounces cream cheese, softened
 1/2 cup confectioners' sugar
 1/2 teaspoon ground cinnamon
 1/2 teaspoon lemon juice
 1/2 cup fresh blueberries
Assorted fresh fruit, graham crackers *and/or* cookies

In a small bowl, beat the cream cheese, confectioners' sugar, cinnamon and lemon juice until smooth. Fold in blueberries. Serve with fruit, crackers and/or cookies. **Yield:** 1 cup.

Maple-Pecan Snack Mix

(Pictured below)

PREP/TOTAL TIME: 20 min.

When I need something healthy and portable for my children to carry in a bag to eat on the go, this yummy munch mix is perfect. We love blueberry pancakes, and this recipe incorporates some of that fruit flavor in a kid–pleasing but wholesome treat.
—Jackie Gregston, Hallsville, Texas

- **5 cups Honey Nut Chex**
- **1 cup granola without raisins**
- **1 cup chopped pecans, toasted**
- **1/4 cup butter, cubed**
- **1/4 cup brown sugar**
- **1/4 cup maple syrup**
- **1 package (3-1/2 ounces) dried blueberries**
- **3/4 cup semisweet chocolate chips, optional**

In a large microwave-safe bowl, combine cereal, granola and pecans; set aside.

In a small microwave-safe bowl, combine the butter, brown sugar and maple syrup. Microwave on high for 2 minutes, stirring once. Pour over the cereal mixture and toss to coat.

Microwave the mixture on high for 4 minutes, stirring every minute. Spread mixture onto waxed paper; cool for 5 minutes. Sprinkle with the dried blueberries and chocolate chips. Store the snack mix in an airtight container. **Yield:** 9 cups.

Editor's Note: This recipe was tested in a 1,100-watt microwave.

Coconut-Mango Mahi Mahi

(Pictured above)

PREP/TOTAL TIME: 30 min.

Whipping a bit of candied ginger into the sauce for these fish fillets really enhances the flavor. Try it—you're sure to like it!
—Don Thompson, Houston, Ohio

- **1/2 cup all-purpose flour**
- **2 eggs, beaten**
- **1 cup dry bread crumbs**
- **1 cup flaked coconut**
- **6 mahi mahi fillets (5 ounces *each*)**
- **2 tablespoons peanut *and/or* canola oil**
- **2 medium mangoes, peeled and cubed**
- **1/4 cup white wine *and/or* chicken broth**
- **2 tablespoons brown sugar**
- **1 garlic clove, halved**
- **1 teaspoon finely chopped crystallized ginger**
- **1 teaspoon soy sauce**
- **1/8 teaspoon pepper**
- **2 tablespoons minced fresh basil**

Place the flour and eggs in separate shallow bowls. In another shallow bowl, combine bread crumbs and coconut. Dip the fillets in the flour, eggs, then bread crumb mixture.

In a large skillet over medium heat, cook fish in oil for 4-5 minutes on each side or until golden brown on the outside and fish just turns opaque in the center.

Meanwhile, in a food processor, combine the mangoes, wine, brown sugar, garlic, ginger, soy sauce and pepper; cover and process until blended. Stir in basil. Serve with fish. **Yield:** 6 servings (1-1/2 cups sauce).

Sun-Dried Tomato Hummus

(Pictured above)

PREP/TOTAL TIME: 20 min.

Sun-dried tomatoes add eye-catching color and fantastic flavor to this smooth dip. It can be whipped up in minutes for drop-in guests or an impromptu neighborhood party. For dippers, fill a platter with baked pita chips or assorted fresh vegetables.
—*Todd Schmeling, Gurnee, Illinois*

 2 cans (15 ounces *each*) garbanzo beans *or*
   chickpeas, rinsed and drained
 1 jar (7 ounces) oil-packed sun-dried tomatoes,
   undrained
2/3 cup water
 3 tablespoons olive oil
 2 garlic cloves, halved
 1 teaspoon crushed red pepper flakes
1/2 teaspoon salt
1/4 teaspoon pepper
Chopped fresh basil, optional
Baked pita chips *and/or* assorted fresh vegetables

In a food processor, combine garbanzo beans, sun-dried tomatoes, water, oil, garlic, red pepper flakes, salt and pepper; cover and process until blended.
  Place hummus in a bowl; sprinkle with fresh basil if desired. Serve with baked pita chips and/or vegetables. **Yield:** 3-1/2 cups.

Taco Salad

(Pictured below)

PREP/TOTAL TIME: 30 min.

Even with my family's busy schedule, I like to cook from scratch. This 30-minute Southwestern main dish makes it easier and less time-consuming. If I don't fix this often enough, I get requests!
—*Sherry Duval, Baltimore, Maryland*

 1 pound ground pork *or* beef
 1 envelope taco seasoning
 1 can (16 ounces) kidney beans, rinsed and
   drained
3/4 cup water
 10 cups torn romaine
 2 medium tomatoes, chopped
1/3 cup chopped onion
 2 cups (8 ounces) shredded cheddar cheese
1/2 to 3/4 cup Western salad dressing
Tortilla chips, crushed
Sour cream and guacamole, optional

In a large skillet, cook pork over medium heat until no longer pink; drain. Stir in the taco seasoning, beans and water. Bring to a boil. Reduce heat; simmer, uncovered, for 5 minutes, stirring occasionally. Remove from the heat; cool for 10 minutes.
  In a large bowl, combine romaine, tomatoes, onion and cheese. Stir in the pork mixture. Drizzle with salad dressing and toss to coat. Sprinkle with tortilla chips. Serve immediately with sour cream and guacamole if desired. **Yield:** 6 servings.

Fast & Fabulous Thai Chicken Salad

(Pictured above)

PREP/TOTAL TIME: 20 min.

This delicious dinner may look complicated, but it's as simple as can be and comes together in less than half an hour. Aside from mixing, the only prep work is chopping a red pepper.
—*Elinor Ives, Sturbridge, Massachusetts*

- **1 package (16 ounces) coleslaw mix**
- **1/3 cup sesame ginger salad dressing**
- **2 cups cubed cooked chicken**
- **1/2 cup Thai peanut sauce**
- **1 medium sweet red pepper, julienned**
- **1/2 cup chow mein noodles**
- **2 green onions, chopped**

In a large bowl, combine the coleslaw mix and salad dressing. Transfer to a serving platter. Combine chicken and peanut sauce; place over coleslaw mixture. Top with the red pepper, noodles and onions. Serve immediately.
Yield: 6 servings.

Lemony Brussels Sprouts

PREP/TOTAL TIME: 25 min.

Here's a fast and refreshing way to serve little cabbages as a side dish. The buttery lemon sauce really brings out the taste of the sprouts. My youngest son is one of this recipe's biggest fans!
—*Joyce Guth, Mohnton, Pennsylvania*

- **1-1/2 pounds fresh brussels sprouts (about 2-1/2 cups), trimmed**
- **1 teaspoon lemon juice**
- **1/8 teaspoon salt**
- **1/8 teaspoon pepper**
- **1/3 cup butter, cubed**
- **2 garlic cloves, minced**

Cut an "X" in the core of each brussels sprout. Place in a saucepan; add 1 in. of water. Bring to a boil. Reduce the heat; cover and simmer for 10-12 minutes or until crisp-tender. Drain.

In a large skillet, saute the brussels sprouts, lemon juice, salt and pepper in butter for 2-3 minutes or until flavors are blended. Add garlic; cook 1 minute longer.
Yield: 6 servings.

Can-Do Soups

WHAT'S MORE comforting on a chilly day than a steaming bowl of warm-you-to-the-soul soup? The good news is you don't have to spend hours in front of a hot stove in order to enjoy one.

Instead, stir things up with an almost-homemade version that starts with a can. The recipes here are so good, you would never know they take advantage of a convenient store-bought shortcut.

Treat your family to a quick-but-delicious version of heartwarming chicken noodle, tomato tortellini, split pea or French onion soup. Chances are, everyone at the table will be clamoring for seconds!

French Onion Soup

(Pictured below)

PREP/TOTAL TIME: 30 min.

For a fuss-free meal, I sometimes make this savory, satisfying soup in a slow cooker. I use the low heat setting for 3 to 4 hours.
—Denise Hruz, Germantown, Wisconsin

- 1/4 cup butter, cubed
- 4 large onions, sliced
- 1/4 cup sugar
- 2 tablespoons all-purpose flour
- 2 cans (14-1/2 ounces *each*) reduced-sodium beef broth
- 2 cans (10-1/2 ounces *each*) condensed French onion soup
- 2 cups water
- 1/2 cup grated Parmesan cheese
- 9 slices French bread (1/2 inch thick)
- 9 tablespoons shredded part-skim mozzarella cheese

In a Dutch oven over medium-high heat, melt butter. Add onions; saute until tender. Add the sugar; cook and stir until lightly browned. Stir in flour until blended;

gradually add the broth, soup and water. Bring to a boil. Reduce heat; cover and simmer for 10 minutes. Stir in Parmesan cheese.

Meanwhile, place the bread on a baking sheet. Broil 4 in. from the heat for 2 minutes on each side or until toasted. Sprinkle with mozzarella; broil for 2 minutes or until cheese is melted. Ladle soup into bowls; top each with a cheese toast. **Yield:** 9 servings (2-1/4 quarts).

Tomato Tortellini Soup

(Pictured above)

PREP/TOTAL TIME: 25 min.

No one will guess you "cheated" by using a can to prepare this lovely, scrumptious cream soup. It tastes homemade all the way!
—Sandra Fick, Lincoln, Nebraska

- 1 package (9 ounces) refrigerated cheese tortellini
- 2 cans (10-3/4 ounces *each*) reduced-sodium condensed tomato soup, undiluted
- 2 cups vegetable broth
- 2 cups 2% milk
- 2 cups half-and-half cream

1/2 cup chopped oil-packed sun-dried tomatoes
1 teaspoon onion powder
1 teaspoon garlic powder
1 teaspoon dried basil
1/2 teaspoon salt
1/2 cup shredded Parmesan cheese
Additional shredded Parmesan cheese, optional

Cook the tortellini according to the package directions. Meanwhile, in a Dutch oven, combine the soup, broth, milk, cream, tomatoes and seasonings. Heat through, stirring frequently. Drain the tortellini; carefully add to soup. Stir in cheese. Sprinkle each serving with additional cheese if desired. **Yield:** 10 servings (2-1/2 quarts).

Shortcut Split Pea Soup

(Pictured below)

PREP/TOTAL TIME: 30 min.

The celery, carrots and thyme in this recipe dress up canned soup for a speedy lunch or light dinner. Just add a tossed salad and bread or crackers on the side. —Donna Noel, Gray, Maine

3 cups water
2 teaspoons reduced-sodium chicken bouillon granules
1/2 teaspoon dried thyme
4 celery ribs and leaves
2 medium carrots, thinly sliced
2 cans (11-1/2 ounces *each*) condensed split pea soup, undiluted
1 cup cubed fully cooked ham
Shaved Parmesan cheese, optional

In a large saucepan, bring the water, bouillon granules and thyme to a boil. Thinly slice celery ribs and finely chop the leaves; set leaves aside.

Add the celery ribs and carrots to the water mixture; simmer, uncovered, for 5-8 minutes or until tender. Stir in the soup, ham and celery leaves; heat through. Top each serving with cheese if desired. **Yield:** 5 servings.

30-Minute Chicken Noodle Soup

(Pictured above)

PREP/TOTAL TIME: 30 min.

This comforting, home-style soup is perfect for a cold day. It's also my favorite thing to eat when I'm not feeling well. Somehow it always makes me feel better! —Lacey Waadt, Payson, Utah

4 cups water
1 can (14-1/2 ounces) chicken broth
1-1/2 cups cubed cooked chicken breast
1 can (10-3/4 ounces) condensed cream of chicken soup, undiluted
3/4 cup sliced celery
3/4 cup sliced fresh carrots
1 small onion, chopped
1-1/2 teaspoons dried parsley flakes
1 teaspoon reduced-sodium chicken bouillon granules
1/4 teaspoon pepper
3 cups uncooked egg noodles

In a Dutch oven, combine the first 10 ingredients. Bring to a boil. Reduce heat; cover and simmer for 10 minutes or until vegetables are crisp-tender. Stir in the noodles; cook 5-7 minutes longer or until noodles and vegetables are tender. **Yield:** 6 servings.

In a large saucepan, cook beef and onion over medium heat until meat is no longer pink; drain. Add cabbage, zucchini and mushrooms; cook and stir 8 minutes longer. Stir in the soup, tomatoes, hot sauce, salt and pepper. Bring to a boil. Reduce heat; cover and simmer for 5 minutes. Sprinkle each serving with cheese. **Yield:** 6 servings.

Chicken Tortilla Chowder

(*Pictured below*)

PREP/TOTAL TIME: 30 min.

Strips of flour tortillas cook up like noodles in this thick, creamy Southwestern-style chowder. With some fresh bread on the side, it's a real treat. —*Dana Rood, Oreana, Illinois*

> 2 **cans (10-3/4 ounces *each*) condensed cream of potato soup, undiluted**
> 2 **cans (10-3/4 ounces *each*) condensed cream of chicken soup, undiluted**
> 2 **cups 2% milk**
> 1 **can (14-1/2 ounces) reduced-sodium chicken broth**
> 1 **can (11 ounces) Mexicorn, drained**
> 1 **package (10 ounces) ready-to-serve roasted chicken breast strips, chopped**
> 1 **can (4 ounces) chopped green chilies**
> 3 **flour tortillas (8 inches), cut into 2-inch x 1/2-inch strips**
> 1 **cup (4 ounces) shredded cheddar cheese**

Additional shredded cheddar cheese, optional

In a large saucepan, heat the soups, milk and broth, stirring frequently. Add corn, chicken and chilies; bring to a boil. Stir in the tortilla strips. Reduce heat; simmer, uncovered, for 5 minutes. Stir in cheddar cheese until melted. Sprinkle each serving with additional cheese if desired. **Yield:** 10 servings (2-1/2 quarts).

Hearty Cabbage Soup

(*Pictured above*)

PREP/TOTAL TIME: 30 min.

I didn't have time to make my favorite cabbage rolls one day, so I threw together this chunky, beefy soup instead. I loved it! —*Renee Leary, Citrus Springs, Florida*

> 1 **pound ground beef**
> 1 **medium onion, chopped**
> 3-1/2 **cups shredded cabbage**
> 1 **medium zucchini, halved and thinly sliced**
> 1 **cup sliced fresh mushrooms**
> 1 **carton (18.3 ounces) ready-to-serve sweet red pepper soup**
> 1 **can (10 ounces) diced tomatoes and green chilies, undrained**
> 1/4 **teaspoon hot pepper sauce**
> 1/4 **teaspoon salt**
> 1/4 **teaspoon pepper**
> 1/4 **cup grated Parmesan cheese**

SIMPLE SUBSTITUTIONS. Don't have the zucchini or mushrooms for Hearty Cabbage Soup (recipe above)? Use an equal amount of frozen mixed vegetables. For Chicken Tortilla Chowder (above right), you could substitute pork for the chicken.

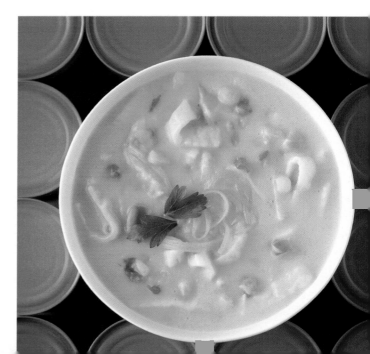

before thinly slicing across the grain.

Place broccoli florets in a steamer basket. Place in a saucepan over 1 in. of water. Bring to a boil. Cover and steam for 2-3 minutes or until crisp-tender. In a small bowl, combine vinaigrette ingredients.

Drain broccoli and potatoes; place in a bowl. Add the beef and red pepper; drizzle with vinaigrette and toss to coat. Serve warm or cold. **Yield:** 4 servings.

Chicken Cordon Bleu Pizza

(Pictured below and on page 244)

PREP/TOTAL TIME: 30 min.

I've made this for my family and also the teachers at my school. With chicken nuggets and Alfredo sauce, this pizza is different but very good. —*Justin Rippel, Colgate, Wisconsin*

- 1 tube (13.8 ounces) refrigerated pizza crust
- 1/2 cup Alfredo sauce
- 1/4 teaspoon garlic salt
- 1 cup (4 ounces) shredded Swiss cheese
- 1-1/2 cups cubed fully cooked ham
- 10 breaded chicken nuggets, thawed and cut into 1/2-inch pieces
- 1 cup (4 ounces) shredded part-skim mozzarella cheese

Unroll pizza crust dough into a greased 15-in. x 10-in. baking pan; flatten the dough and build up the edges slightly. Bake at 425° for 8-10 minutes or until the edges are lightly browned.

Spread the crust with Alfredo sauce; sprinkle with garlic salt and Swiss cheese. Top with ham, chicken nuggets and mozzarella cheese. Bake for 8-10 minutes or until crust is golden brown and cheese is melted. **Yield:** 6 pieces.

Steak & New Potato Toss

(Pictured above)

PREP/TOTAL TIME: 30 min.

I usually use leftover barbecued steak to prepare this fabulous main–dish salad. It's pretty, flavorful and always satisfying. —*Deyanne Davies, Rossland, British Columbia*

- 1 pound small red potatoes, scrubbed and cut into wedges
- 1-1/4 pounds beef top sirloin steak
- 3 cups fresh broccoli florets
- 1 medium sweet red pepper, chopped

VINAIGRETTE:
- 1/4 cup olive oil
- 2 tablespoons cider vinegar
- 2 green onions, thinly sliced
- 2 garlic cloves, minced
- 1/2 teaspoon ground mustard
- 1/2 teaspoon paprika
- 1/4 teaspoon pepper

Place the potatoes in a large saucepan and cover with water. Bring to a boil. Reduce heat; cover and cook for 10-15 minutes or until tender.

Grill steak, covered, over medium heat for 8-11 minutes on each side or until meat reaches desired doneness (for medium-rare, a meat thermometer should read 145°; medium, 160°; well-done, 170°). Let stand 10 minutes

Mini White Pizzas

(Pictured above)

PREP/TOTAL TIME: 20 min.

I like to assemble these yummy English–muffin pizzas ahead of time and freeze them. Then I can simply pop them in the oven whenever I need a last–minute snack or party appetizer.
—*Jocelyn Hook, Swoyersville, Pennsylvania*

- **1-1/3 cups shredded part-skim mozzarella cheese**
- **1/2 cup mayonnaise**
- **1-1/2 teaspoons dried oregano**
- **1/2 teaspoon garlic powder**
- **1/4 teaspoon salt**
- **1/4 teaspoon pepper**
- **4 English muffins, split**

In a small bowl, combine the first six ingredients. Spread over the English muffin halves; place on a baking sheet. Broil 3-4 in. from the heat for 5-8 minutes or until bubbly and golden brown. **Yield:** 8 mini pizzas.

Bacon-Wrapped Breadsticks

(Pictured above)

PREP/TOTAL TIME: 30 min.

I tasted these at a restaurant, and the owner was kind enough to share the recipe. The first time I served them to my family, not a crumb was left on the plate...and everyone was asking for more!
—*Wendy Domres, West Bend, Wisconsin*

- **24 bacon strips**
- **2 tubes (11 ounces *each*) refrigerated breadsticks**
- **1 cup grated Parmesan cheese**
- **2 teaspoons garlic powder**

Wrap a bacon strip around each breadstick; place on baking sheets. Bake at 375° for 15-20 minutes or until golden brown.

In a shallow bowl, combine cheese and garlic powder. Roll warm breadsticks in cheese mixture. **Yield:** 2 dozen.

Spicy Shrimp Kabobs

(Pictured below)

PREP/TOTAL TIME: 30 min.

These kabobs are so good, my guests always think I labored over the preparation. But really, you can make them in no time.
—*Marcia Pilgeram, Sandpoint, Idaho*

- **1/4 cup butter, cubed**
- **2 tablespoons lemon juice**
- **1 teaspoon ground coriander**
- **1 teaspoon ground cumin**
- **1/2 teaspoon paprika**
- **1/2 teaspoon grated lemon peel**
- **1/4 teaspoon salt**
- **1 pound uncooked large shrimp, peeled and deveined**

In a small saucepan, melt butter; add the lemon juice, spices, lemon peel and salt.

Thread shrimp onto eight metal or soaked wooden skewers. Place the skewers in a greased 15-in. x 10-in. baking pan.

Broil 3-4 in. from the heat for 3-4 minutes on each side or until shrimp turn pink, basting occasionally with butter mixture. **Yield:** 8 kabobs.

medium-rare, a meat thermometer should read 145°; medium, 160°; well-done, 170°). Let stand 5 minutes before slicing.

Divide the salad greens between two plates. Top with the tomatoes, cucumber, Greek olives, onion, steak and mushrooms. Sprinkle with the feta cheese. Drizzle with vinaigrette. Serve immediately. **Yield:** 2 servings.

Turkey & Fruit Salad

(Pictured below)

PREP/TOTAL TIME: 25 min.

We have our own turkeys, and I'm always on the lookout for recipes that are a little different. This one is a good way to use up leftover turkey. —Harriet Stichter, Milford, Indiana

    1/4 cup fat-free plain yogurt
    1/4 cup reduced-fat mayonnaise
      1 tablespoon honey
      1 tablespoon spicy brown mustard
    1/2 teaspoon dried marjoram
    1/8 teaspoon ground ginger
      3 cups cubed cooked turkey breast
      2 celery ribs, thinly sliced
      1 large red apple, finely chopped
    1/2 cup dried cranberries
    1/4 cup chopped walnuts, toasted

In a small bowl, combine the first six ingredients. In a large bowl, combine the turkey, celery, apple, cranberries and nuts. Add yogurt mixture; toss to coat. Refrigerate until serving. **Yield:** 5 servings.

Greek Islands Steak Salad

(Pictured above and on page 244)

PREP/TOTAL TIME: 25 min.

I came up with this dish while watching a film that was set in the Greek Isles. The steak, sauteed mushrooms and cheese make for a hearty meal. —Chris Wells, Lake Villa, Illinois

      1 boneless beef top loin steak (8 ounces)
      1 tablespoon A.1. steak sauce
MUSHROOMS:
  1-1/2 cups sliced fresh mushrooms
      2 tablespoons butter
      1 tablespoon sherry *or* chicken broth
    1/8 teaspoon salt
    1/8 teaspoon pepper
SALAD:
      4 cups torn mixed salad greens
     10 cherry tomatoes, halved
    2/3 cup thinly sliced cucumber
     10 pitted Greek olives
    1/4 cup finely chopped red onion
    1/2 cup crumbled feta cheese
    1/4 cup prepared balsamic vinaigrette

Rub steak on both sides with the steak sauce; let stand for 10 minutes.

Meanwhile, in a small skillet, saute the mushrooms in butter until golden brown. Add the sherry, salt and pepper. Cook 1-2 minutes or until liquid is evaporated. Set aside and keep warm.

Using long-handled tongs, dip a paper towel in cooking oil and lightly coat grill rack. Grill steak, covered, over medium heat or broil 4 in. from heat for 5-6 minutes on each side or until meat reaches desired doneness (for

Cooking Lighter

Who knew eating healthier could be so delicious? Even family members who aren't following a special diet will love the scrumptious specialties here.

✓ **All recipes in this chapter include Nutrition Facts. Most include Diabetic Exchanges.**

Chicken Florentine Meatballs 264
Broccoli-Ham Macaroni 264
Spicy Black Bean Soup 265
Chocolate Malt Desserts 265
Strawberry-Rhubarb Meringue Pie 266
Easy Chicken Potpie 266
Tangy Pulled Pork Sandwiches 266
Apricot-Glazed Pork Tenderloin 267
Curried Chicken Salad 267
Tropical Fusion Salad
    with Spicy Tortilla Ribbons 268
Mushroom Primavera Pasta Sauce 268
Chicken & Vegetable Stir-Fry 268
Light Sour Cream Coffee Cake 269
Grilled Stuffed Turkey Burgers 269
Grilled Tuna Bibb Salads 270
Halibut Soft Tacos 270
Citrus-Marinated Salmon 271
Shrimp and Scallop Couscous 271
Almond-Crusted Pork Loin 272
Nutty Wild Rice 272
Sweet-Hot Spiced Nuts 272
Summertime Orzo & Chicken 273
Sensational Tiramisu 273
Granola-to-Go Bars 274
A.M. Rush Espresso Smoothie 274
Mini Sweet Potato Muffins 274
Polynesian Parfaits 275
Sammie's Breakfast Burritos 275

GUILT-FREE FARE. Clockwise from top left: Chicken Florentine Meatballs (p. 264), Granola-to-Go Bars (p. 274), Tropical Fusion Salad with Spicy Tortilla Ribbons (p. 268) and Sensational Tiramisu (p. 273).

For the sauce, in a large nonstick skillet, saute the mushrooms in oil until tender. Stir in the remaining ingredients. Bring to a boil. Reduce heat; simmer, uncovered, for 8-10 minutes or until slightly thickened. Add meatballs and heat through.

When squash is cool enough to handle, use a fork to separate strands. Serve with meatballs and sauce. **Yield:** 6 servings.

Editor's Note: This recipe was tested in a 1,100-watt microwave.

Nutrition Facts: 3 meatballs with sauce and 2/3 cup squash equals 303 calories, 12 g fat (3 g saturated fat), 123 mg cholesterol, 617 mg sodium, 31 g carbohydrate, 7 g fiber, 22 g protein.

Chicken Florentine Meatballs

(*Pictured above and on page 262*)

PREP: 40 min. **COOK:** 20 min.

Served with spaghetti squash and a chunky tomato sauce, these tender ground–chicken meatballs are loaded with great flavor.
—*Diane Nemitz, Ludington, Michigan*

- 2 eggs, beaten
- 1 package (10 ounces) frozen chopped spinach, thawed and squeezed dry
- 1/2 cup dry bread crumbs
- 1/4 cup grated Parmesan cheese
- 1 tablespoon dried minced onion
- 1 garlic clove, minced
- 1/4 teaspoon salt
- 1/8 teaspoon pepper
- 1 pound ground chicken
- 1 medium spaghetti squash

SAUCE:
- 1/2 pound sliced fresh mushrooms
- 2 teaspoons olive oil
- 1 can (14-1/2 ounces) diced tomatoes, undrained
- 1 can (8 ounces) tomato sauce
- 2 tablespoons minced fresh parsley
- 1 garlic clove, minced
- 1 teaspoon dried oregano
- 1 teaspoon dried basil

In a large bowl, combine the first eight ingredients. Crumble chicken over mixture and mix well. Shape into 1-1/2-in. balls.

Place meatballs on a rack in a shallow baking pan. Bake, uncovered, at 400° for 20-25 minutes or until no longer pink. Meanwhile, cut squash in half lengthwise; discard seeds. Place the squash cut side down on a microwave-safe plate. Microwave, uncovered, on high for 15-18 minutes or until tender.

Broccoli-Ham Macaroni

(*Pictured below*)

PREP: 30 min. **BAKE:** 25 min.

Creamy and cheesy, this dressed–up version of mac and cheese provides all the goodness of comfort food without the extra fat.
—*Nancy Latulippe, Simcoe, Ontario*

- 1-1/2 cups uncooked elbow macaroni
- 4 cups fresh broccoli florets
- 1 large onion, finely chopped
- 1 cup cubed fully cooked ham
- 1 medium sweet red pepper, chopped
- 2 tablespoons butter, *divided*
- 1/3 cup all-purpose flour
- 4 cups fat-free milk
- 2-1/2 cups (10 ounces) shredded reduced-fat cheddar cheese
- 1/4 cup minced fresh parsley
- 2 teaspoons Dijon mustard
- 1/2 teaspoon garlic powder
- 1/2 teaspoon Italian seasoning
- 1/4 teaspoon pepper
- 1/4 cup dry bread crumbs

Cook macaroni according to the package directions. Meanwhile, place 1 in. of water in a large saucepan; add

broccoli. Bring to a boil. Reduce heat; cover and simmer for 4-5 minutes or until crisp-tender.

In a large saucepan, saute the onion, ham and red pepper in 1 tablespoon butter until vegetables are crisp-tender. Sprinkle with flour; stir until blended. Gradually stir in milk. Bring to a boil; cook and stir for 2 minutes or until thickened.

Stir in the cheese, parsley, mustard and seasonings until blended. Drain broccoli and macaroni; stir into cheese sauce. Transfer to a greased 2-qt. baking dish (dish will be full).

In a small skillet, melt remaining butter; stir in bread crumbs. Sprinkle over the macaroni mixture. Bake, uncovered, at 350° for 25-30 minutes or until heated through. **Yield:** 6 servings.

Nutrition Facts: 1-1/3 cups equals 389 calories, 16 g fat (10 g saturated fat), 57 mg cholesterol, 734 mg sodium, 39 g carbohydrate, 3 g fiber, 27 g protein.

Spicy Black Bean Soup

PREP: 25 min. **COOK:** 40 min.

A splash of sherry accents this hearty soup. For a milder version, remove the ribs and seeds from the jalapeno before dicing.
—Tia Musser, Hudson, Indiana

- 1 large red onion, chopped
- 1 medium sweet red pepper, chopped
- 1 jalapeno pepper, seeded and minced
- 2 tablespoons olive oil
- 3 garlic cloves, minced
- 3 cans (15 ounces *each*) black beans, rinsed and drained
- 3-1/2 cups vegetable broth
- 1 can (14-1/2 ounces) diced tomatoes with mild green chilies, undrained
- 1 can (4 ounces) chopped green chilies
- 1/3 cup sherry *or* additional vegetable broth
- 2 tablespoons minced fresh cilantro
- 1/2 cup fat-free sour cream
- 1/4 cup shredded cheddar cheese

In a Dutch oven, saute onion and peppers in oil until tender. Add garlic; cook 1 minute longer.

Stir in the beans, vegetable broth, tomatoes and green chilies. Bring to a boil. Reduce heat; simmer, uncovered, for 25 minutes. Add the sherry and cilantro; cook 5 minutes longer.

Remove from the heat; cool slightly. Place half of the soup in a blender; cover and process until pureed. Return to the pan and heat through. Top each serving with 2 teaspoons sour cream and 1 teaspoon cheese. **Yield:** 12 servings (3/4 cup each).

Editor's Note: When cutting hot peppers, wear disposable gloves. Avoid touching your face or eyes.

Nutrition Facts: 3/4 cup equals 150 calories, 3 g fat (1 g saturated fat), 4 mg cholesterol, 667 mg sodium, 23 g carbohydrate, 5 g fiber, 7 g protein.

Chocolate Malt Desserts

(Pictured above)

PREP: 10 min. **COOK:** 10 min. + chilling

I created this recipe after my mom gave me a container of malted milk powder. It's so rich tasting, you'd never believe it's light.
—Lisa Keys, Middlebury, Connecticut

- 1/2 cup malted milk powder
- 1/4 cup sugar
- 2 tablespoons baking cocoa
- 2 tablespoons cornstarch
- 1/2 teaspoon instant espresso powder
- 2 cups fat-free milk
- 2 ounces semisweet chocolate, finely chopped
- 1 teaspoon vanilla extract
- 3/4 cup reduced-fat whipped topping
- 6 malted milk balls, chopped
- 6 maraschino cherries

In a small saucepan, combine the first five ingredients. Stir in milk until smooth. Cook and stir over medium heat until mixture comes to a boil; cook 1-2 minutes longer or until thickened. Remove from the heat; stir in chocolate and vanilla until smooth.

Transfer to six dessert dishes, about 1/3 cup in each. Cover and refrigerate for at least 2 hours before serving.

Garnish each serving with 2 tablespoons whipped topping, 1/2 teaspoon chopped malted milk balls and a cherry. **Yield:** 6 servings.

Nutrition Facts: 1 serving equals 239 calories, 5 g fat (3 g saturated fat), 2 mg cholesterol, 87 mg sodium, 45 g carbohydrate, 1 g fiber, 6 g protein.

Strawberry-Rhubarb Meringue Pie

(Pictured below)

PREP: 55 min. **BAKE:** 40 min. + chilling

For us, this dessert is a rite of spring—one we've shared with many friends. We love that it's both sweet and tart, with a mild almond accent. —Jessie Grearson, Falmouth, Maine

- 1/2 cup all-purpose flour
- 1/4 cup whole wheat pastry flour
- 1/4 cup ground almonds
- 1/2 teaspoon salt
- 1/4 cup cold butter
- 2 tablespoons cold water

FILLING:
- 1 egg, beaten
- 3/4 cup sugar
- 2 tablespoons all-purpose flour
- 1/4 teaspoon ground cinnamon
- 2 cups chopped fresh *or* frozen rhubarb, thawed
- 1-1/2 cups sliced fresh strawberries

MERINGUE:
- 3 egg whites
- 1/4 teaspoon almond extract
- 6 tablespoons sugar

In a food processor, combine the all-purpose flour, pastry flour, almonds and salt; cover and pulse until blended. Add butter; cover and pulse until mixture resembles coarse crumbs. While processing, gradually add water until dough forms a ball.

Roll out pastry to fit a 9-in. pie plate. Transfer pastry to pie plate. Trim pastry to 1/2 in. beyond edge of plate; flute edges. In a large bowl, combine the egg, sugar, flour and cinnamon; stir in rhubarb and strawberries. Transfer to prepared crust. Bake at 375° for 35-40 minutes or until filling is bubbly. Remove pie from oven and place on a wire rack; keep warm. Reduce heat to 350°.

In a large bowl, beat egg whites and extract on medium speed until soft peaks form. Gradually beat in sugar, 1 tablespoon at a time, on high until stiff peaks form. Spread over hot filling, sealing edges to crust. Bake for 15 minutes or until golden brown. Cool on a wire rack for 1 hour; refrigerate for 1-2 hours before serving. **Yield:** 8 servings.

Nutrition Facts: 1 piece equals 255 calories, 8 g fat (4 g saturated fat), 41 mg cholesterol, 219 mg sodium, 42 g carbohydrate, 2 g fiber, 5 g protein.

Easy Chicken Potpie

PREP: 20 min. **BAKE:** 40 min.

I rely on a baking mix, canned soup and frozen vegetables for this heartwarming favorite. I often pair it with cranberry sauce. —Martha Evans, Omaha, Nebraska

- 1 can (10-3/4 ounces) reduced-fat reduced-sodium condensed cream of chicken soup, undiluted
- 1 can (10-3/4 ounces) reduced-fat reduced-sodium condensed cream of mushroom soup, undiluted
- 1/2 cup plus 2/3 cup fat-free milk, *divided*
- 1/2 teaspoon dried thyme
- 1/4 teaspoon pepper
- 1/8 teaspoon poultry seasoning
- 2 packages (16 ounces *each*) frozen mixed vegetables, thawed
- 1-1/2 cups cubed cooked chicken breast
- 1-1/2 cups reduced-fat biscuit/baking mix

In a large bowl, combine the soups, 1/2 cup milk, thyme, pepper and poultry seasoning. Stir in the vegetables and chicken.

Transfer to a 13-in. x 9-in. baking dish coated with cooking spray. In a small bowl, stir biscuit mix and remaining milk just until blended. Drop by 12 rounded tablespoonfuls onto chicken mixture.

Bake, uncovered, at 350° for 40-50 minutes or until filling is bubbly and biscuits are golden brown. **Yield:** 6 servings.

Nutrition Facts: 1-1/3 cups chicken mixture with 2 biscuits equals 342 calories, 5 g fat (2 g saturated fat), 36 mg cholesterol, 871 mg sodium, 53 g carbohydrate, 7 g fiber, 21 g protein. **Diabetic Exchanges:** 3 vegetable, 2-1/2 starch, 2 very lean meat.

Tangy Pulled Pork Sandwiches

PREP: 10 min. **COOK:** 4 hours

The slow cooker not only makes this an easy meal, but it also keeps the pork tender and loaded with flavor. It tastes anything but light! —Beki Kosydar–Krantz, Mayfield, Pennsylvania

- 1 pork tenderloin (1 pound)
- 1 cup ketchup
- 2 tablespoons plus 1-1/2 teaspoons brown sugar
- 2 tablespoons plus 1-1/2 teaspoons cider vinegar

basting occasionally with the pan juices. Let stand for 5 minutes before slicing. **Yield:** 6 servings.

Nutrition Facts: 4 ounces cooked pork equals 350 calories, 10 g fat (2 g saturated fat), 84 mg cholesterol, 338 mg sodium, 35 g carbohydrate, trace fiber, 30 g protein. **Diabetic Exchanges:** 4 lean meat, 2 starch, 1/2 fat.

- 1 tablespoon plus 1-1/2 teaspoons Worcestershire sauce
- 1 tablespoon spicy brown mustard
- 1/4 teaspoon pepper
- 4 kaiser rolls, split

Cut the tenderloin in half; place in a 3-qt. slow cooker. Combine ketchup, brown sugar, vinegar, Worcestershire sauce, mustard and pepper; pour over pork.

Cover; cook on low for 4-5 hours or until meat is tender. Remove meat; shred with two forks. Return to the slow cooker; heat through. Serve on rolls. **Yield:** 4 servings.

Nutrition Facts: 1 sandwich equals 402 calories, 7 g fat (2 g saturated fat), 63 mg cholesterol, 1,181 mg sodium, 56 g carbohydrate, 2 g fiber, 29 g protein. **Diabetic Exchanges:** 3-1/2 starch, 3 very lean meat, 1/2 fat.

Apricot-Glazed Pork Tenderloin

(*Pictured above*)

PREP: 15 min. **BAKE:** 25 min.

A simple glaze made with apricot preserves lends a delightful zest to this pork entree. It's so fuss–free and delicious, you'll make it again and again. —*Crystal Holsinger, Surprise, Arizona*

- 2 pork tenderloins (1 pound *each*)
- 2 tablespoons olive oil
- 1/2 teaspoon salt
- 1/4 teaspoon pepper
- 1 cup apricot preserves
- 3 tablespoons sherry *or* reduced-sodium chicken broth
- 1 tablespoon Dijon mustard
- 2 garlic cloves, minced
- 1 teaspoon minced fresh thyme *or* 1/4 teaspoon dried thyme

Place pork on a rack in a shallow roasting pan. Combine the oil, salt and pepper; rub over pork.

Bake at 450° for 15 minutes. In a small bowl, combine the remaining ingredients; spoon over pork. Bake 10-15 minutes longer or until a meat thermometer reads 160°,

Curried Chicken Salad

(*Pictured below*)

PREP/TOTAL TIME: 15 min.

Curry and mustard complement the fruit and nuts in this special salad. I like it served on greens or whole wheat toast...or scooped up with apple slices. —*Joanna Perdomo, Miami, Florida*

- 3 cups cubed cooked chicken breast
- 1 medium apple, finely chopped
- 1/4 cup slivered almonds, toasted
- 2 tablespoons golden raisins
- 2 tablespoons dried cranberries
- 1/2 cup fat-free plain Greek yogurt
- 1/4 cup apricot preserves
- 2 tablespoons curry powder
- 1 tablespoon Dijon mustard
- 1/2 teaspoon salt
- 1/4 to 1/2 teaspoon pepper

Lettuce leaves

In a small bowl, combine the first five ingredients. Add the yogurt, preserves, curry, mustard, salt and pepper; toss to coat. Serve on lettuce leaves. **Yield:** 4 servings.

Editor's Note: If Greek yogurt is not available, line a strainer with a coffee filter and place over a bowl. Place 1 cup fat-free yogurt in prepared strainer; refrigerate overnight. Discard liquid from bowl; proceed as directed.

Nutrition Facts: 1 cup equals 323 calories, 7 g fat (1 g saturated fat), 81 mg cholesterol, 477 mg sodium, 30 g carbohydrate, 3 g fiber, 36 g protein. **Diabetic Exchanges:** 4 lean meat, 1 starch, 1/2 fruit, 1/2 fat.

Tropical Fusion Salad with Spicy Tortilla Ribbons

(Pictured above and on page 263)

PREP/TOTAL TIME: 30 min.

The fresh taste of this colorful salad makes it a perfect choice for a spring or summer meal. Served with spicy tortilla strips, it's special enough for company.   —Jennifer Fisher, Austin, Texas

- 2 cups cubed peeled papaya
- 1 can (15 ounces) black beans, rinsed and drained
- 1 medium ripe avocado, peeled and cubed
- 1 cup frozen corn, thawed
- 1/2 cup golden raisins
- 2 serrano peppers, seeded and chopped
- 1/4 cup minced fresh cilantro
- 1/4 cup orange juice
- 2 tablespoons lime juice
- 1 tablespoon cider vinegar
- 2 garlic cloves, minced
- 2 teaspoons ground ancho chili pepper, *divided*
- 1/4 teaspoon sugar
- 1/4 teaspoon salt
- 2 corn tortillas (6 inches), cut into 1/4-inch strips

In a large bowl, combine the papaya, beans, avocado, corn, raisins, peppers, cilantro, orange juice, lime juice, vinegar, garlic, 1/2 teaspoon chili pepper, sugar and salt.

Place tortilla strips on a baking sheet coated with cooking spray; sprinkle with remaining chili pepper. Bake at 350° for 8-10 minutes or until crisp. Serve with salad. **Yield:** 4 servings.

Editor's Note: When cutting hot peppers, wear disposable gloves. Avoid touching your face or eyes.

Nutrition Facts: 1-1/4 cups salad with about 10 tortilla ribbons equals 321 calories, 8 g fat (1 g saturated fat), 0 cholesterol, 380 mg sodium, 58 g carbohydrate, 11 g fiber, 9 g protein.

Mushroom Primavera Pasta Sauce

PREP: 50 min. **COOK:** 45 min.

This meatless dish has plenty of mushrooms and vegetables in a rich tomato sauce. I sprinkle a little shredded Parmesan on top.
    —Cindy Adams, Tracy, California

- 1 large onion, chopped
- 1 tablespoon olive oil
- 1 whole garlic bulb, peeled and minced
- 15 plum tomatoes, peeled and chopped
- 2 medium zucchini, grated
- 2 medium carrots, grated
- 1 medium green pepper, chopped
- 1 medium sweet red pepper, chopped
- 1/4 cup water
- 1 teaspoon salt
- 1/4 teaspoon pepper
- 1 pound fresh mushrooms, quartered
- **Hot cooked multigrain pasta**
- **Shredded Parmesan cheese**

In a large saucepan, saute onion in oil until tender. Add garlic; cook 1 minute longer. Add tomatoes, zucchini, carrots, peppers, water, salt and pepper. Bring to a boil.

Reduce heat; cover and simmer for 20-25 minutes or until vegetables are tender, stirring occasionally. Stir in mushrooms; cook 10 minutes longer or just until mushrooms are tender. Serve over pasta. Sprinkle with cheese. **Yield:** 6 servings.

Nutrition Facts: 3/4 cup (calculated without pasta and cheese) equals 85 calories, 2 g fat (trace saturated fat), 0 cholesterol, 321 mg sodium, 15 g carbohydrate, 4 g fiber, 4 g protein. **Diabetic Exchange:** 3 vegetable.

Chicken & Vegetable Stir-Fry

PREP: 20 min. **COOK:** 15 min.

When you want a light entree that's filling and flavor-packed, it's hard to beat a stir-fry. Pepper flakes give this one some zip.
    —Samuel Onizuk, Elkton, Maryland

- 4 teaspoons cornstarch
- 1 cup reduced-sodium chicken broth
- 2 tablespoons reduced-sodium soy sauce
- 1 pound boneless skinless chicken breasts, cut into 1/4-inch strips
- 2 tablespoons olive oil, *divided*
- 1-1/2 cups fresh cauliflowerets
- 1-1/2 cups fresh broccoli florets

    2 medium carrots, sliced
    1 small sweet red pepper, julienned
    1 small onion, halved and sliced
    1 garlic clove, minced
  1/2 teaspoon salt
  1/2 teaspoon pepper
  1/4 to 1/2 teaspoon crushed red pepper flakes
2-1/2 cups hot cooked rice
Minced fresh cilantro

Combine cornstarch, broth and soy sauce until smooth; set aside.

In a large nonstick skillet or wok, stir-fry chicken in 1 tablespoon oil until no longer pink. Remove; keep warm.

Stir-fry cauliflower, broccoli, carrots, red pepper and onion in remaining oil until crisp-tender. Add the garlic, salt, pepper and pepper flakes; cook 1 minute longer.

Stir cornstarch mixture and add to the pan. Bring to a boil; cook and stir for 2 minutes or until thickened. Add chicken; heat through. Serve with rice. Sprinkle each serving with cilantro. **Yield:** 5 servings.

Nutrition Facts: 1 cup stir-fry with 1/2 cup rice equals 297 calories, 8 g fat (1 g saturated fat), 50 mg cholesterol, 670 mg sodium, 32 g carbohydrate, 3 g fiber, 23 g protein. **Diabetic Exchanges:** 2 lean meat, 1-1/2 starch, 1 vegetable, 1 fat.

Light Sour Cream Coffee Cake

PREP: 25 min. BAKE: 30 min. + cooling

Begin your day delightfully with a piece of this reduced-fat coffee cake. It's moist and yummy, with a band of cinnamon through the center. —*Amy McBride, Columbia, Missouri*

    2 cups all-purpose flour
1-1/2 cups sugar
    1 teaspoon baking powder
  1/2 teaspoon salt
  1/2 teaspoon ground cinnamon
    2 eggs, beaten
    1 cup (8 ounces) reduced-fat sour cream
  1/2 cup vanilla yogurt
  1/2 cup butter, melted
    1 teaspoon vanilla extract
STREUSEL:
  1/2 cup packed brown sugar
  1/3 cup all-purpose flour
    2 tablespoons butter, melted
    1 teaspoon ground cinnamon

In a large bowl, combine first five ingredients. In another bowl, combine eggs, sour cream, yogurt, butter and vanilla. Stir into dry ingredients just until moistened.

In a small bowl, combine the streusel ingredients. Spoon half of the batter into a 13-in. x 9-in. baking pan coated with cooking spray; sprinkle with half of the streusel. Top with remaining batter and streusel. Bake at 350° for 30-35 minutes or until a toothpick inserted near the center comes out clean. Place pan on a wire rack to cool. **Yield:** 20 servings.

Nutrition Facts: 1 piece equals 210 calories, 7 g fat (4 g saturated fat), 40 mg cholesterol, 140 mg sodium, 33 g carbohydrate, trace fiber, 3 g protein. **Diabetic Exchanges:** 2 starch, 1 fat.

Grilled Stuffed Turkey Burgers

(Pictured below)

PREP/TOTAL TIME: 25 min.

Your taste buds will love every bite of these hearty burgers. Never tried ground turkey? This recipe will definitely make you a fan! —*Megan Crow, Lincoln, Nebraska*

    2 tablespoons onion soup mix
  1/2 teaspoon garlic powder
  1/2 teaspoon Worcestershire sauce
  1/8 teaspoon salt
Dash pepper
1-1/4 pounds lean ground turkey
  1/2 cup finely chopped sweet red pepper
  1/2 cup shredded part-skim mozzarella cheese
    5 whole wheat hamburger buns, split

In a small bowl, combine the first five ingredients. Crumble turkey over mixture and mix well. Shape into 10 thin patties. Spoon red pepper and cheese onto center of five patties; top with remaining patties and press edges firmly to seal.

Grill burgers, covered, over medium heat or broil 4 in. from heat for 5-7 minutes on each side or until a meat thermometer reads 165° and juices run clear. Serve on buns. **Yield:** 5 servings.

Nutrition Facts: 1 burger equals 325 calories, 13 g fat (4 g saturated fat), 96 mg cholesterol, 674 mg sodium, 25 g carbohydrate, 4 g fiber, 27 g protein.

Catch of the Day

YOU'LL GET HOOKED on seafood—and good nutrition at the same time—when you fix these delicious main dishes for your family.

Halibut Soft Tacos wrap a refreshing combination of fish and fruit inside flour tortillas. Prefer tuna? Grilled Tuna Bibb Salads mix that ingredient with fresh vegetables and top it off with reduced-fat ranch dressing to keep things on the lighter side.

Featuring a homemade marinade, Citrus-Marinated Salmon is sure to tingle everyone's taste buds. And shrimp lovers will fall hook, line and sinker for nicely seasoned Shrimp and Scallop Couscous.

Grilled Tuna Bibb Salads

(Pictured above)

PREP/TOTAL TIME: 30 min.

This quick, refreshing salad starts on the grill for great flavor. It's terrific served with a French baguette or on toasted crackers.
—*Wolfgang Hanau, West Palm Beach, Florida*

    1 pound tuna steaks (3/4 inch thick)
    2 teaspoons lime juice
 1/4 teaspoon salt
 1/4 teaspoon pepper
    2 celery ribs
    1 small sweet red pepper
    1 small sweet yellow pepper
    1 small red onion
    4 cups torn Bibb *or* Boston lettuce
 1/4 cup thinly sliced fresh basil leaves
    1 teaspoon minced fresh rosemary
Whole Bibb *or* Boston lettuce leaves
 1/2 cup reduced-fat ranch salad dressing

Sprinkle tuna with lime juice, salt and pepper. Using long-handled tongs, dip a paper towel in cooking oil and lightly coat grill rack. For medium-rare, grill the tuna, covered, over high heat for 3-4 minutes on each side or until slightly pink in the center. Cut into 1-in. pieces.

Finely chop the celery, peppers and onion; place in a large bowl. Add the torn lettuce, tuna, basil and rosemary; toss to combine.

Arrange lettuce leaves on four plates; top each with 2 cups tuna mixture. Drizzle with ranch salad dressing. **Yield:** 4 servings.

Nutrition Facts: 2 cups salad with 2 tablespoons dressing equals 228 calories, 8 g fat (1 g saturated fat), 59 mg cholesterol, 513 mg sodium, 9 g carbohydrate, 2 g fiber, 28 g protein. **Diabetic Exchanges:** 4 lean meat, 1 vegetable, 1 fat.

Halibut Soft Tacos

PREP/TOTAL TIME: 25 min.

Here's one of my summer "go-to" recipes. The tacos are colorful and full of nutrients. Sometimes I serve them wrapped in lettuce instead of tortillas. —*Kristin Kossak, Bozeman, Montana*

    1 medium mango, peeled and cubed
 1/2 cup cubed avocado
 1/4 cup chopped red onion
    2 tablespoons chopped seeded jalapeno pepper
    1 tablespoon minced fresh cilantro
    3 teaspoons olive oil, *divided*
    1 teaspoon lemon juice
    1 teaspoon honey
    1 pound halibut steaks (3/4 inch thick)
 1/2 teaspoon salt
 1/4 teaspoon pepper
    4 Bibb lettuce leaves
    4 flour tortillas (6 inches), warmed
    4 teaspoons sweet Thai chili sauce

In a small bowl, combine the mango, avocado, onion, jalapeno, cilantro, 2 teaspoons oil, lemon juice and honey; set aside. Brush halibut with remaining oil; sprinkle with salt and pepper.

Using long-handled tongs, dip a paper towel in cooking oil and lightly coat grill rack. Grill halibut, covered, over high heat or broil 3-4 in. from the heat for 3-5 minutes on each side or until fish flakes easily with a fork.

Place lettuce leaves on tortillas; top with fish and mango mixture. Drizzle with sauce. **Yield:** 4 servings.

Editor's Note: When cutting hot peppers, disposable gloves are recommended. Avoid touching your face.

Nutrition Facts: 1 taco with 1/3 cup mango mixture equals 330 calories, 12 g fat (1 g saturated fat), 36 mg cholesterol, 648 mg sodium, 28 g carbohydrate, 2 g fiber, 28 g protein. **Diabetic Exchanges:** 3 lean meat, 2 starch, 1 fat.

Citrus-Marinated Salmon

PREP: 10 min. + marinating **GRILL:** 5 min.

For this excellent entree, I prepare the marinade in the morning and put the fish in when I get home from work. In 30 minutes, it's on the grill. —Joan Hallford, North Richland Hills, Texas

- 3 tablespoons orange juice
- 2 tablespoons lemon juice
- 2 tablespoons olive oil
- 4 teaspoons reduced-sodium soy sauce
- 2 teaspoons lime juice
- 3 red onion rings
- 2 garlic cloves
- 1 fresh thyme sprig
- 1 bay leaf
- 2 teaspoons minced fresh gingerroot
- 1/8 teaspoon fennel seed
- 1/8 teaspoon coarsely ground pepper
- 4 salmon fillets (6 ounces *each*)

In a large resealable plastic bag, combine the first 12 ingredients. Add the salmon; seal bag and turn to coat. Refrigerate for 30 minutes, turning occasionally.

Drain and discard the marinade. Using long-handled tongs, dip a paper towel in cooking oil and lightly coat grill rack. Grill salmon, covered, over high heat or broil 4 in. from the heat for 5-10 minutes or until fish flakes easily with a fork. **Yield:** 4 servings.

Nutrition Facts: 1 fillet equals 351 calories, 22 g fat (4 g saturated fat), 100 mg cholesterol, 202 mg sodium, 2 g carbohydrate, trace fiber, 34 g protein.

Shrimp and Scallop Couscous

(*Pictured at right*)

PREP/TOTAL TIME: 30 min.

When it comes to pleasing dinner guests, this tasty seafood skillet is a "shore" thing! Round out the meal with garlic breadsticks.
—Marvin Meuser Jr., Princeton, Indiana

- 2 medium zucchini, julienned
- 1 medium green pepper, julienned
- 2 tablespoons olive oil
- 3 plum tomatoes, chopped
- 4 green onions, chopped
- 1 tablespoon minced fresh basil *or* 1 teaspoon dried basil
- 3 teaspoons chili powder
- 1 garlic clove, minced
- 1/2 teaspoon dried oregano
- 1/2 pound uncooked medium shrimp, peeled and deveined
- 1/2 pound bay scallops
- 1/4 teaspoon salt
- 1/8 teaspoon pepper

Hot cooked couscous *or* rice
Thinly sliced fresh basil leaves, optional

In a large skillet, saute the zucchini and green pepper in oil until tender. Add the tomatoes, onions, basil, chili powder, garlic and oregano. Bring to a boil. Reduce heat; simmer, uncovered, for 5 minutes.

Stir in the shrimp, scallops, salt and pepper. Return to a boil. Reduce heat; simmer, uncovered, for 5 minutes or until shrimp turn pink and scallops are opaque. Serve with couscous. Garnish with sliced basil if desired. **Yield:** 4 servings.

Nutrition Facts: 1 cup seafood mixture (calculated without couscous) equals 201 calories, 9 g fat (1 g saturated fat), 88 mg cholesterol, 342 mg sodium, 11 g carbohydrate, 3 g fiber, 21 g protein. **Diabetic Exchanges:** 3 very lean meat, 1-1/2 fat, 1 vegetable.

Almond-Crusted Pork Loin

(Pictured above)

PREP: 35 min. **BAKE:** 1 hour + standing

Paired with a zesty homemade salsa and coated with ground almonds, this mouthwatering pork loin bursts with great flavor. The recipe comes from the Almond Board of California.

Vegetable oil spray
- 6 ounces slivered California almonds (1-1/4 cups chopped)
- 2 medium garlic cloves, crushed

Salt and pepper to taste
- 2 egg whites
- 1-1/2 pounds boneless pork loin

SALSA:
- 2 medium tomatoes, diced (about 2 cups)
- 1/2 cup diced red onion
- 1 jalapeno pepper, seeded and chopped
- 1 teaspoon ground cumin
- 2 tablespoons lime juice
- 1/4 cup chopped fresh cilantro

Salt and freshly ground pepper to taste, optional

Preheat oven to 375°F. Line a roasting pan with foil; place a meat rack on the foil. Spray with vegetable oil spray. Coarsely grind nuts in a food processor. Mix nuts, garlic and salt and pepper to taste in a bowl. Set aside.

Whip egg whites to form soft peaks. Remove fat from the pork. Roll the pork in the egg whites and then in the nut mixture. Roll once more in the egg whites and in the nut mixture again. Place the pork on the rack; press any remaining nuts onto the pork.

Roast 1 hour or until a meat thermometer reads 160°F. Remove from the oven and let rest 15 minutes.

Mix salsa ingredients together. Taste for seasoning; add salt and pepper if needed. Serve salsa with pork. **Yield:** 4 servings (2 cups salsa).
Nutrition Facts: 1 serving equals 499 calories, 30 g fat (5.9 g saturated fat), 85 mg cholesterol, 140 mg sodium, 14 g carbohydrate, 6 g fiber, 46 g protein.

Nutty Wild Rice

(Pictured at left)

PREP: 15 min. **COOK:** 50 min.

Crunch! You'll go wild for this nutty side dish. It's a treat to eat with nearly any entree. —Heather Webb, Channelview, Texas

- 2-1/2 cups water
- 1/2 cup uncooked wild rice
- 1 tablespoon reduced-sodium soy sauce
- 6 green onions, sliced
- 1 tablespoon butter
- 2/3 cup sliced almonds, toasted
- 1/4 cup sunflower kernels
- 3 tablespoons sesame seeds, toasted
- 1/4 teaspoon salt

In a large saucepan, bring water, rice and soy sauce to a boil. Reduce heat; cover and simmer for 45-60 minutes or until rice is tender.

Meanwhile, in a small skillet, saute onions in butter until tender. Stir in the remaining ingredients; heat through. Remove from the heat.

Drain the rice if necessary. Stir in the onion mixture. **Yield:** 5 servings.
Nutrition Facts: 3/4 cup equals 236 calories, 15 g fat (3 g saturated fat), 6 mg cholesterol, 314 mg sodium, 21 g carbohydrate, 4 g fiber, 8 g protein.

Sweet-Hot Spiced Nuts

PREP: 10 min. **BAKE:** 20 min. + cooling

Put some kick in your holiday gathering with this well-spiced snack. It also makes a terrific hostess gift packed in a festive tin. —Carla Hutton, Lakeside, Montana

- 1 egg white
- 2 cups unblanched almonds
- 2 teaspoons canola oil
- 1/3 cup sugar
- 3/4 teaspoon cayenne pepper
- 1/2 teaspoon salt
- 1/2 teaspoon ground coriander
- 1/4 teaspoon ground cinnamon
- 1/8 teaspoon ground allspice

In a large bowl, beat egg white until frothy. Add nuts and oil; stir gently to coat. Combine the remaining ingredients; add to egg white mixture and stir to coat.

Spread into a 15-in. x 10-in. x 1-in. baking pan coated with cooking spray. Bake at 300° for 18-22 minutes or until lightly browned, stirring once. Cool completely. Store in an airtight container. **Yield:** 2 cups.

Nutrition Facts: 1/4 cup equals 257 calories, 20 g fat (1 g saturated fat), 0 cholesterol, 165 mg sodium, 16 g carbohydrate, 4 g fiber, 8 g protein.

Summertime Orzo & Chicken

(Pictured below)

PREP/TOTAL TIME: 30 min.

This 30-minute chicken and pasta entree is good enough to become a dinner staple. A sprinkling of feta cheese adds richness.
—Fran MacMillan, West Melbourne, Florida

>   3/4 **cup uncooked orzo pasta**
>   1 **pound boneless skinless chicken breasts, cut into 1-inch pieces**
>   1 **medium cucumber, chopped**
>   1 **small red onion, chopped**
>   1/4 **cup minced fresh parsley**
>   2 **tablespoons lemon juice**
>   1 **tablespoon olive oil**
>   1 **teaspoon salt**
>   1/4 **teaspoon pepper**
>   1/4 **cup crumbled reduced-fat feta cheese**

Cook the pasta according to the package directions. Meanwhile, in a large skillet coated with cooking spray, cook chicken over medium heat for 6-8 minutes or until no longer pink.

In a large bowl, combine the cucumber, onion, parsley and chicken. Drain pasta; stir into chicken mixture. In a small bowl, whisk juice, oil, salt and pepper. Pour over chicken mixture; toss to coat. Serve warm or cold. Just before serving, sprinkle with cheese. **Yield:** 4 servings.

Nutrition Facts: 1-1/4 cups orzo mixture with 1 tablespoon cheese equals 323 calories, 7 g fat (2 g saturated fat), 65 mg cholesterol, 742 mg sodium, 33 g carbohydrate, 2 g fiber, 30 g protein. **Diabetic Exchanges:** 3 lean meat, 2 starch, 1 vegetable, 1 fat.

Sensational Tiramisu

(Pictured above and on page 262)

PREP: 25 min. **COOK:** 10 min. + chilling

This light take on the classic Italian dessert is moist and creamy, and it cuts perfectly into luscious layered squares that are pretty enough for a party.
—Mary Walters, Westerville, Ohio

>   1 **package (8 ounces) reduced-fat cream cheese**
>   2/3 **cup confectioners' sugar**
> 1-1/2 **cups reduced-fat whipped topping,** *divided*
>   1/2 **cup plus 1 tablespoon sugar**
>   3 **egg whites**
>   1/4 **cup water**
>   2 **packages (3 ounces *each*) ladyfingers, split**
>   1/2 **cup boiling water**
>   2 **tablespoons Kahlua**
>   1 **tablespoon instant coffee granules**
>   1/2 **teaspoon baking cocoa**

In a small bowl, beat cream cheese and confectioners' sugar until smooth. Fold in 1 cup whipped topping; set mixture aside.

Combine 1/2 cup sugar, egg whites and water in a small heavy saucepan over low heat. With a hand mixer, beat on low speed for 1 minute. Continue beating on low over low heat until mixture reaches 160°, about 8-10 minutes. Pour into a large bowl. Beat on high until stiff peaks form, about 7 minutes. Fold into cream cheese mixture.

Arrange half of ladyfingers in an ungreased 11-in. x 7-in. dish. Combine the boiling water, Kahlua, coffee granules and remaining sugar; brush half of mixture over ladyfingers. Top with half of cream cheese mixture. Repeat layers. Spread remaining whipped topping over the top; sprinkle with cocoa. Refrigerate for 2 hours before serving. **Yield:** 12 servings.

Nutrition Facts: 1 piece equals 223 calories, 7 g fat (4 g saturated fat), 62 mg cholesterol, 127 mg sodium, 34 g carbohydrate, trace fiber, 5 g protein. **Diabetic Exchanges:** 2 starch, 1 fat.

Granola-to-Go Bars

(Pictured below and on page 263)

PREP: 30 min. **BAKE:** 15 min. + cooling

Chewy and sweet, these fruity homemade granola bars will have you craving more—which is OK because they're good for you!
—*Sally Haen, Menomonee Falls, Wisconsin*

- 3-1/2 cups quick-cooking oats
- 1 cup chopped almonds
- 1 egg, beaten
- 2/3 cup butter, melted
- 1/2 cup honey
- 1 teaspoon vanilla extract
- 1/2 cup sunflower kernels
- 1/2 cup flaked coconut
- 1/2 cup chopped dried apples
- 1/2 cup dried cranberries
- 1/2 cup packed brown sugar
- 1/2 teaspoon ground cinnamon

Combine oats and almonds in a 15-in. x 10-in. x 1-in. baking pan coated with cooking spray. Bake at 350° for 15 minutes or until toasted, stirring occasionally.

In a large bowl, combine the egg, butter, honey and vanilla. Stir in the sunflower kernels, coconut, apples, cranberries, brown sugar and cinnamon. Stir in the oat-almond mixture.

Press into a 15-in. x 10-in. x 1-in. baking pan coated with cooking spray. Bake at 350° for 13-18 minutes or until set and edges are lightly browned. Cool on a wire rack. Cut into bars. Store in an airtight container. **Yield:** 3 dozen.

Nutrition Facts: 1 bar equals 130 calories, 7 g fat (3 g saturated fat), 15 mg cholesterol, 40 mg sodium, 16 g carbohydrate, 2 g fiber, 2 g protein.

A.M. Rush Espresso Smoothie

(Pictured above)

PREP/TOTAL TIME: 10 min.

Want a morning pick-me-up that's wholesome, too? Fruit and flaxseed give this sweet espresso plenty of flavor and nutrition.
—*Aimee Wilson, Clovis, California*

- 1/2 cup cold fat-free milk
- 1 tablespoon vanilla flavoring syrup
- 1 cup ice cubes
- 1/2 medium banana, cut up
- 1 to 2 teaspoons instant espresso powder
- 1 teaspoon ground flaxseed
- 1 teaspoon baking cocoa

In a blender, combine all ingredients; cover and process for 1-2 minutes or until smooth. Pour into a chilled glass; serve immediately. **Yield:** 1 serving.

Editor's Note: This recipe was tested with Torani brand flavoring syrup. Look for it in the coffee section.

Nutrition Facts: 1-1/2 cups equals 148 calories, 2 g fat (trace saturated fat), 2 mg cholesterol, 54 mg sodium, 31 g carbohydrate, 3 g fiber, 6 g protein.

Mini Sweet Potato Muffins

PREP: 35 min. **BAKE:** 10 min./batch

I'm always looking for ways to make recipes healthier, and my husband then critiques my creations. He loves the light texture, buttery streusel and spice of these miniature muffins.
—*Meredith Hedeen, New Kensington, Pennsylvania*

- 1 cup all-purpose flour
- 3/4 cup whole wheat flour

1/2 cup sugar
1/2 cup packed brown sugar
1 teaspoon baking powder
1 teaspoon ground cinnamon
1 teaspoon ground allspice
1/2 teaspoon salt
1/4 teaspoon baking soda
2 eggs, beaten
1 cup mashed sweet potatoes
1/2 cup water
1/4 cup canola oil
3 tablespoons unsweetened applesauce
STREUSEL:
2 tablespoons biscuit/baking mix
2 tablespoons quick-cooking oats
1 tablespoon sugar
1 tablespoon brown sugar
1-1/2 teaspoons cold butter
1 tablespoon finely chopped crystallized ginger

In a large bowl, combine the first nine ingredients. In another bowl, combine the eggs, potatoes, water, oil and applesauce. Stir into the dry ingredients just until moistened.

Coat miniature muffin cups with cooking spray or use paper liners; fill two-thirds full. For streusel, combine the baking mix, oats and sugars; cut in the butter until crumbly. Stir in ginger. Sprinkle over batter.

Bake at 350° for 10-12 minutes or until a toothpick inserted near the center comes out clean. Cool muffins for 5 minutes before removing from pans to wire racks. **Yield:** 4-1/2 dozen.

Nutrition Facts: 1 muffin equals 51 calories, 1 g fat (trace saturated fat), 8 mg cholesterol, 45 mg sodium, 9 g carbohydrate, trace fiber, 1 g protein. **Diabetic Exchange:** 1/2 starch.

Polynesian Parfaits

PREP/TOTAL TIME: 15 min.

Here's a lighter recipe that tastes like a real treat. Whip one up to enjoy on your afternoon break or on a hot, lazy summer day.
—*Janice Mitchell, Aurora, Colorado*

2 cups (16 ounces) pineapple yogurt
1 tablespoon sugar
1/8 teaspoon ground nutmeg
1 cup granola without raisins
1 can (11 ounces) mandarin oranges, drained
3/4 cup unsweetened pineapple tidbits
1/3 cup fresh raspberries

Combine the yogurt, sugar and nutmeg; spoon into four dishes. Top with granola and fruit. **Yield:** 4 servings.

Nutrition Facts: 1 parfait equals 293 calories, 5 g fat (1 g saturated fat), 6 mg cholesterol, 79 mg sodium, 57 g carbohydrate, 6 g fiber, 11 g protein.

Sammie's Breakfast Burritos

(Pictured below)

PREP/TOTAL TIME: 20 min.

This recipe is a healthier version of popular fast-food breakfast burritos. If you prefer, replace the sausage with ham or bacon.
—*Sandra Ward, Tulsa, Oklahoma*

4 eggs
1/4 cup salsa
1/8 teaspoon chili powder
1/8 teaspoon ground cumin
1/8 teaspoon pepper
3 breakfast turkey sausage links, casings removed
1/4 cup shredded reduced-fat cheddar cheese
4 fat-free flour tortillas (6 inches), warmed

In a small bowl, whisk eggs, salsa, chili powder, cumin and pepper; set aside.

Crumble the sausage into a large skillet; cook over medium heat until no longer pink. Drain. Push sausage to the sides of pan. Pour egg mixture into center of pan. Cook and stir until set. Sprinkle cheese over the top. Remove from the heat; cover and let stand until cheese is melted.

Place 1/2 cup mixture on each tortilla; roll up. **Yield:** 4 servings.

Nutrition Facts: 1 burrito equals 211 calories, 11 g fat (4 g saturated fat), 233 mg cholesterol, 510 mg sodium, 16 g carbohydrate, 1 g fiber, 13 g protein.

Entrees on a Budget

It's true—delicious, wholesome dinners don't have to empty your wallet. All of the mouthwatering main dishes in this chapter cost less than $2 per serving!

Mushroom Lasagna..278
Baked Stew with Root Vegetables 278
Tuna Mac and Cheese Bake 279
Cassoulet for Today 279
Sara's Summer Rolls 280
Corn, Rice & Bean Burritos.................................280
Creamy Pasta Primavera 280
Greek Meat Loaves 281
Presto Chicken Tacos 281
Enchilada Lasagna...282
Louisiana Red Beans and Rice 282
Perfect Brunch Omelets 283
Italian Pork Stew 284
Macaroni 'n' Cheese Pizza..................................284
Rainbow Quiche...285
Chiles Rellenos Casserole 285
Slow Cooker Tamale Pie......................................286
White Chili..286
Roast Pork with Apples & Onions 286
Brie-and-Veggie Brunch Strata............................287
Skillet Tacos...287

FRUGAL FAVORITES. Clockwise from upper left: Sara's Summer Rolls (p. 280), Rainbow Quiche (p. 285), Louisiana Red Beans and Rice (p. 282) and Mushroom Lasagna (p. 278).

Spread 1 cup sauce in a greased 13-in. x 9-in. baking dish. Layer with three noodles, 1-1/3 cups sauce, and a scant 1/4 cup each of mozzarella and Parmesan. Repeat layers twice. In a small bowl, combine the cream, milk and remaining cheeses; spoon over the top.

Cover and bake at 350° for 30 minutes. Uncover; bake 10 minutes longer or until cheese is melted. Let stand for 10 minutes before cutting. **Yield:** 12 servings.

Nutrition Facts: 1 piece equals 230 calories, 11 g fat (5 g saturated fat), 25 mg cholesterol, 279 mg sodium, 23 g carbohydrate, 3 g fiber, 10 g protein. **Diabetic Exchanges:** 2 fat, 1 starch, 1 lean meat, 1 vegetable.

Baked Stew with Root Vegetables

(*Pictured below*)

PREP: 35 min. **BAKE:** 2-1/2 hours

Tender beef and a medley of chunky veggies make this hearty stew a real family pleaser.   —*Barb Templin, Norwood, Minnesota*

- 1 cup all-purpose flour, *divided*
- 3/4 teaspoon salt
- 1/2 teaspoon pepper
- 2 pounds boneless beef chuck roast, cut into 1-inch cubes
- 1/4 cup canola oil
- 1 large onion, chopped
- 3 tablespoons butter
- 2 garlic cloves, minced
- 5 cups beef broth
- 1 bay leaf
- 3 celery ribs
- 3 medium parsnips, peeled
- 3 medium carrots
- 1 small rutabaga, peeled

Mushroom Lasagna

(*Pictured above and on page 276*)

PREP: 45 min. **BAKE:** 40 min. + standing

Two types of mushrooms and a hint of wine provide savory flavor for this creamy lasagna. It's delicious and feeds a crowd.
—*Gary Bachara, Wilson, North Carolina*

✓ This recipe includes Nutrition Facts and Diabetic Exchanges.

- 9 uncooked lasagna noodles
- 1 pound sliced fresh mushrooms
- 2 cups chopped baby portobello mushrooms
- 1 large sweet onion, chopped
- 3 tablespoons olive oil
- 1/2 cup minced fresh parsley
- 2 thin slices prosciutto *or* deli ham, chopped
- 2 garlic cloves, minced
- 1-1/2 teaspoons Italian seasoning
- 2/3 cup white wine *or* chicken broth
- 2 cans (14-1/2 ounces *each*) diced tomatoes, drained
- 1 cup (4 ounces) shredded part-skim mozzarella cheese, *divided*
- 1 cup shredded Parmesan cheese, *divided*
- 1/2 cup heavy whipping cream
- 1/4 cup milk

Cook noodles according to package directions. Meanwhile, in a Dutch oven, cook and stir the mushrooms and onion in oil until tender. Add the parsley, prosciutto, garlic and Italian seasoning; cook 2 minutes longer. Add wine; cook and stir until liquid is evaporated. Add tomatoes and heat through.

In a resealable plastic bag, combine 3/4 cup flour, salt and pepper. Add beef, a few pieces at a time; shake to coat. In an ovenproof Dutch oven, brown beef in oil in batches. Remove; keep warm.

In same pan, saute onion in butter until tender. Stir in garlic, then remaining flour until blended. Gradually add broth; stir in bay leaf and beef. Bring to a boil.

Cover; bake at 350° for 1 hour. Cut vegetables into 1-in. pieces; stir into stew. Cover; bake 1-1/2 to 2 hours longer or until beef is tender. Skim fat and discard bay leaf. **Yield:** 8 servings (3 quarts).

Tuna Mac and Cheese Bake

PREP: 15 min. **BAKE:** 30 min.

Tuna lovers are bound to gobble up this no-fuss casserole. And chances are, you already have the ingredients in your pantry.
—Bonnie Hord, Lee's Summit, Missouri

- 1 **package (7-1/4 ounces) macaroni and cheese dinner mix**
- 1 **can (12 ounces) light water-packed tuna, drained and flaked**
- 1 **can (10-3/4 ounces) condensed cream of mushroom soup, undiluted**
- 1-1/3 **cups 2% milk**
- 2 **packages (9 ounces *each*) frozen peas and pearl onions**
- 1 **can (4 ounces) mushroom stems and pieces, drained**
- 1 **can (2.8 ounces) French-fried onions, *divided***

Prepare the macaroni and cheese according to package directions. Add the tuna, mushroom soup, milk, peas, mushrooms and half of the fried onions. Place in a greased 11-in. x 7-in. baking dish. Bake, uncovered, at 325° for 25 minutes.

Sprinkle with remaining fried onions; bake 5 minutes longer or until heated through. **Yield:** 8 servings.

Cassoulet for Today

(Pictured above right)

PREP: 40 min. **BAKE:** 55 min.

Traditionally cooked for hours, this version of the rustic French dish offers the same home-style taste in less time. It's easy on the wallet, too! —Virginia Anthony, Jacksonville, Florida

- 6 **boneless skinless chicken thighs (about 1-1/2 pounds)**
- 1/4 **teaspoon salt**
- 1/4 **teaspoon coarsely ground pepper**
- 1 **tablespoon olive oil, *divided***
- 1 **large onion, chopped**
- 2 **garlic cloves, minced, *divided***
- 1/2 **cup white wine *or* chicken broth**
- 1 **can (14-1/2 ounces) diced tomatoes, drained**
- 1 **bay leaf**

- 1 **teaspoon minced fresh rosemary *or* 1/4 teaspoon dried rosemary, crushed**
- 1 **teaspoon minced fresh thyme *or* 1/4 teaspoon dried thyme**
- 2 **cans (15 ounces *each*) white kidney *or* cannellini beans, rinsed and drained**
- 1/4 **pound smoked turkey kielbasa, chopped**
- 3 **bacon strips, cooked and crumbled**
- 1/2 **cup soft whole wheat bread crumbs**
- 1/4 **cup minced fresh parsley**

Sprinkle chicken with salt and pepper. In an ovenproof Dutch oven, brown the chicken in 2 teaspoons oil in batches. Remove and keep warm.

In the same pan, saute onion in remaining oil until crisp-tender. Add 1 garlic clove; cook 1 minute longer. Add wine, stirring to loosen browned bits from pan. Stir in the tomatoes, bay leaf, rosemary, thyme and chicken; bring to a boil.

Cover and bake at 325° for 30 minutes. Add beans and kielbasa; cover and bake 20-25 minutes longer or until chicken is tender. Discard bay leaf. Stir in bacon.

Combine the bread crumbs, parsley and remaining garlic; sprinkle over cassoulet. Broil 3-4 in. from the heat for 2-3 minutes or until bread crumbs are golden brown. **Yield:** 6 servings.

Sara's Summer Rolls

(Pictured below and on page 276)

PREP: 30 min. **COOK:** 15 min.

My daughter, Sara, saw Elmo create summer rolls on a "Sesame Street" DVD and wanted to give them a try. I tweaked this recipe to suit her tastes. She made them—and loved them.
—Beth McGee, Pinckney, Michigan

- 1/2 **pound boneless skinless chicken breast, finely chopped**
- 1/4 **cup water**
- 1/4 **cup light coconut milk**
- 1/4 **cup creamy peanut butter**
- 3 **tablespoons soy sauce**
- 1 **green onion, sliced**
- 1 **tablespoon minced fresh gingerroot**
- 1 **garlic clove, minced**
- 1 **teaspoon lime juice**
- 2 **cups bean sprouts**
- 1 **cup fresh sugar snap peas, trimmed and chopped**
- 1/2 **cup shredded carrot**
- 2 **ounces uncooked thick rice noodles**
- 12 **spring roll wrappers** *or* **rice papers (8 inch)**
- 1/2 **cup shredded red cabbage**

In a large skillet, combine the first nine ingredients. Bring to a boil. Reduce heat; simmer, uncovered, for 8-10 minutes or until chicken is no longer pink. Set aside.

In a large saucepan, bring 8 cups water to a boil. Add bean sprouts, peas and carrot; cover and boil for 3-4 minutes or just until tender. Drain and immediately place vegetables in ice water. Drain and pat dry. Cook noodles according to package directions; drain.

Soak a spring roll wrapper in cool water for 30 seconds; place on a flat surface and pat dry. Place 1 heaping tablespoonful of chicken down the center of the wrapper; top with a scant 3 tablespoons vegetable mixture. Top with noodles and cabbage.

Fold both ends over filling; fold one long side over the filling, then roll up tightly. Place seam side down on a plate. Repeat. Cover with damp paper towels until serving. Cut summer rolls in half. **Yield:** 1 dozen.

Corn, Rice & Bean Burritos

PREP/TOTAL TIME: 30 min.

No one will miss the meat when you serve up these satisfying, wholesome burritos bursting with a fresh-tasting filling. They're fast to fix, delicious and won't put a dent in your wallet.
—Sharon Bickett, Chester, South Carolina

☑ This recipe includes Nutrition Facts.

- 1-1/3 **cups fresh** *or* **frozen corn, thawed**
- 1 **medium onion, chopped**
- 1 **medium green pepper, sliced**
- 1 **tablespoon canola oil**
- 2 **garlic cloves, minced**
- 1-1/2 **teaspoons chili powder**
- 1/2 **teaspoon ground cumin**
- 1 **can (15 ounces) black beans, rinsed and drained**
- 1-1/2 **cups cooked brown rice**
- 8 **flour tortillas (8 inches), warmed**
- 3/4 **cup shredded reduced-fat cheddar cheese**
- 1/2 **cup reduced-fat plain yogurt**
- 2 **green onions, sliced**
- 1/2 **cup salsa**

In a large skillet, saute the corn, onion and pepper in oil until tender. Add the garlic, chili powder and cumin; cook 1 minute longer. Add beans and rice; heat through.

Spoon 1/2 cup filling off center on each tortilla. Top with cheese, yogurt and green onions. Fold sides and ends over the filling and roll up. Serve with salsa. **Yield:** 8 servings.

Nutrition Facts: 1 burrito with 1 tablespoon salsa equals 326 calories, 8 g fat (2 g saturated fat), 8 mg cholesterol, 500 mg sodium, 52 g carbohydrate, 4 g fiber, 13 g protein.

Creamy Pasta Primavera

(Pictured above right)

PREP/TOTAL TIME: 30 min.

When I think of spring, asparagus comes to mind. I like using spiral pasta for this dish because the sauce doesn't slide off.
—Darlene Brenden, Salem, Oregon

- 2 **cups uncooked spiral pasta**
- 1 **pound fresh asparagus, trimmed and cut into 2-inch pieces**

In a large bowl, combine the first 10 ingredients. Crumble beef over mixture and mix well. Pat into two greased 8-in. x 4-in. loaf pans.

Bake, uncovered, at 350° for 50-60 minutes or until no pink remains and a meat thermometer reads 160°. Let stand for 5 minutes. Transfer to a serving plate; sprinkle with cheese. **Yield:** 2 loaves (6 servings each).

Presto Chicken Tacos

(Pictured below)

PREP: 20 min. **COOK:** 25 min.

Slowly cooking the chicken strips with the seasonings is the key to perfection with this dish. The chicken mixture also makes a great salad topping. —Nanette Hilton, Las Vegas, Nevada

- **3 pounds boneless skinless chicken breasts, cut into strips**
- **2 tablespoons canola oil**
- **1 garlic clove, minced**
- **2 cans (14-1/2 ounces *each*) diced tomatoes, undrained**
- **1 teaspoon ground cumin**
- **1 teaspoon chili powder**
- **12 corn tortillas (6 inches), warmed**
- **Optional toppings: shredded lettuce, shredded cheddar cheese, diced tomatoes, fresh cilantro leaves, sour cream and cubed avocado**

In a Dutch oven, brown chicken in oil in batches. Add garlic; cook 1 minute longer. Add the tomatoes, cumin and chili powder. Bring to a boil. Reduce heat; cover and simmer for 15-20 minutes or until chicken is no longer pink, stirring occasionally. Fill each tortilla with about 1/2 cup chicken mixture. Serve with toppings of your choice. **Yield:** 12 servings.

- **3 medium carrots, cut into strips**
- **2 teaspoons canola oil**
- **2 cups cherry tomatoes, halved**
- **1 garlic clove, minced**
- **1/2 cup grated Parmesan cheese**
- **1/2 cup heavy whipping cream**
- **1/4 teaspoon pepper**

Cook the pasta according to package directions. In a large skillet, saute asparagus and carrots in oil until crisp-tender. Add tomatoes and garlic; cook 1 minute longer. Stir in cheese, cream and pepper. Drain pasta; toss with asparagus mixture. **Yield:** 6 servings.

Greek Meat Loaves

PREP: 20 min. **BAKE:** 50 min.

Flavored with sun-dried tomatoes and Greek olives, this twist on traditional meat loaf is sure to be a hit—especially if you round out the menu with a Greek salad and crusty bread. —Radelle Knappenberger, Oviedo, Florida

- **2 eggs, beaten**
- **1/2 cup ketchup**
- **1/4 cup 2% milk**
- **1 large red onion, finely chopped**
- **3/4 cup quick-cooking oats**
- **1/3 cup oil-packed sun-dried tomatoes, patted dry and finely chopped**
- **1/3 cup pitted Greek olives, chopped**
- **2 garlic cloves, minced**
- **1 teaspoon salt**
- **1 teaspoon pepper**
- **2 pounds lean ground beef (90% lean)**
- **1/2 cup crumbled feta cheese**

Enchilada Lasagna

(Pictured above)

PREP: 45 min. **BAKE:** 30 min. + standing

Whenever I make this cheesy layered casserole, my guests ask for the recipe. I serve it with French bread or toasted garlic bread.
—*Charlene Griffin, Minocqua, Wisconsin*

1-1/2 **pounds ground beef**
   1 **medium onion, chopped**
   1 **garlic clove, minced**
   1 **can (14-1/2 ounces) stewed tomatoes, undrained**
   1 **can (10 ounces) enchilada sauce**
   1 **to 2 teaspoons ground cumin**
   1 **egg, beaten**
1-1/2 **cups (12 ounces) 4% cottage cheese**
   3 **cups (12 ounces) shredded Mexican cheese blend**
   8 **flour tortillas (8 inches), cut in half**
   1 **cup (4 ounces) shredded cheddar cheese**

In a large skillet, cook the beef, onion and garlic over medium heat until meat is no longer pink; drain. Stir in the tomatoes, enchilada sauce and cumin. Bring to a boil. Reduce heat; simmer, uncovered, for 20 minutes.

In a small bowl, combine egg and cottage cheese; set aside. Spread a third of the meat sauce into a greased 13-in. x 9-in. baking dish. Layer with half of the Mexican cheese blend, tortillas, cottage cheese mixture and remaining meat sauce. Repeat layers. Sprinkle with cheddar cheese.

Cover and bake at 350° for 20 minutes. Uncover; bake 10 minutes longer or until bubbly. Let stand for 15 minutes before cutting. **Yield:** 12 servings.

Louisiana Red Beans and Rice

(Pictured below and on page 277)

PREP: 20 min. **COOK:** 8 hours

Smoked turkey sausage and red pepper flakes bring zip to this saucy, slow-cooked version of the New Orleans classic. If you prefer extra heat, add hot pepper sauce at the table.
—*Julia Bushree, Georgetown, Texas*

   4 **cans (16 ounces *each*) kidney beans, rinsed and drained**
   1 **can (14-1/2 ounces) diced tomatoes, undrained**
   1 **package (14 ounces) smoked turkey sausage, sliced**
   1 **cup chicken broth**
   3 **celery ribs, chopped**
   1 **large onion, chopped**
   1 **medium green pepper, chopped**
   1 **small sweet red pepper, chopped**
   6 **garlic cloves, minced**
   1 **bay leaf**
1/2 **teaspoon crushed red pepper flakes**
   2 **green onions, chopped**
Hot cooked rice

In a 4-qt. slow cooker, combine the first 11 ingredients. Cover and cook on low for 8-10 hours or until heated through. Stir before serving. Discard bay leaf.

Sprinkle each serving with onions. Serve with rice.
Yield: 9 servings.

Perfect Brunch Omelets

(Pictured above)

PREP/TOTAL TIME: 30 min.

Homemade salsa makes these cheesy omelets a special morning treat. They're even better if you prepare the salsa a day ahead to let the flavors blend. —Francis Garland, Anniston, Alabama

2 medium tomatoes, chopped
1-1/2 teaspoons chopped red onion
1-1/2 teaspoons *each* chopped green, sweet red and yellow pepper
1 teaspoon chopped seeded jalapeno pepper
1-1/2 teaspoons lime juice
1 teaspoon minced fresh cilantro
1 small garlic clove, minced
1/8 teaspoon dried oregano
1 tablespoon butter, *divided*

6 eggs
1/4 cup 2% milk
1/4 teaspoon *each* salt and pepper
1 cup (4 ounces) shredded cheddar cheese

In a small bowl, combine the tomatoes, onion, peppers, lime juice, cilantro, garlic and oregano; set aside.

In small nonstick skillet, melt 1 teaspoon butter over medium-high heat. Whisk eggs, milk, salt and pepper. Add 2/3 cup egg mixture to skillet (mixture should set immediately at edges).

As eggs set, push cooked edges toward the center, letting uncooked portion flow underneath. When the eggs are set, spoon 1/3 cup tomato mixture on one side and sprinkle with 1/3 cup cheese; fold other side over filling. Slide omelet onto a plate. Repeat. **Yield:** 3 servings.

Editor's Note: When cutting hot peppers, disposable gloves are recommended. Avoid touching your face.

Place flour in a large resealable plastic bag. Add pork, a few pieces at a time, and shake to coat. In a Dutch oven, brown pork in 3 tablespoons oil in batches. Remove and keep warm.

In same pan, saute onion in remaining oil until tender. Add garlic; cook 1 minute longer. Add tomatoes, wine, bay leaves, cinnamon, tomato paste, vinegar, anchovy, herbs, salt, red pepper flakes, pepper and pork; bring to a boil.

Reduce heat; cover and simmer for 1-1/2 hours, stirring occasionally. Stir in parsley. Cover and cook 30-60 minutes longer or until meat is tender. Skim fat; discard bay leaves and cinnamon. Serve with pasta; sprinkle with cheese. **Yield:** 8 servings (2 quarts).

Macaroni 'n' Cheese Pizza

PREP: 25 min. **BAKE:** 10 min. + standing

Here's a fun and flavorful way to combine two perennial family favorites—pizza and mac 'n' cheese. Experiment with sausage, diced green peppers or any other pizza toppings you like.
— Andrew McDowell, Lake Villa, Illinois

- 1 **package (7-1/4 ounces) macaroni and cheese dinner mix**
- 2 **eggs, beaten**
- 1/2 **pound ground beef**
- 3/4 **cup chopped onion**
- 1-1/4 **cups pizza sauce**
- 1 **can (4 ounces) mushroom stems and pieces, drained**
- 28 **pepperoni slices**
- 1 **cup (4 ounces) shredded Mexican cheese blend**

Prepare macaroni and cheese according to package directions; gradually stir in eggs.

Spread onto a greased 12-in. pizza pan. Bake at 375° for 10 minutes. Meanwhile, in a large skillet, cook beef and onion over medium heat until meat is no longer pink; drain. Stir in pizza sauce.

Spread over the macaroni crust. Sprinkle with the mushrooms, pepperoni and cheese blend. Bake for 10-15 minutes or until a thermometer inserted in the crust reads 160° and the cheese is melted. **Yield:** 8 servings.

Italian Pork Stew

(Pictured above)

PREP: 30 min. **COOK:** 2-1/2 hours

For a meal that's different, try this bold, peppery combination. Anchovy paste adds wonderful, savory flavor without tasting particularly fishy.
— Lynne German, Norcross, Georgia

- 2/3 **cup all-purpose flour**
- 2 **pounds boneless pork loin, cut into 1-inch pieces**
- 4 **tablespoons olive oil,** *divided*
- 1 **large onion, chopped**
- 5 **garlic cloves, crushed**
- 1 **can (28 ounces) diced tomatoes, undrained**
- 1 **cup dry red wine** *or beef broth*
- 3 **bay leaves**
- 1 **cinnamon stick (3 inches)**
- 1 **tablespoon tomato paste**
- 1 **tablespoon red wine vinegar**
- 1 **teaspoon anchovy paste**
- 1 **teaspoon** *each* **dried oregano, basil and sage leaves**
- 1/2 **teaspoon salt**
- 1/2 **teaspoon crushed red pepper flakes**
- 1/4 **teaspoon pepper**
- 1/4 **cup minced fresh parsley**

Hot cooked bow tie pasta
Grated Parmesan cheese

GREAT GARLIC. Have fresh garlic left over from a recipe? Store whole or partial garlic bulbs in a cool, dry dark place in a well-ventilated container, such as a mesh bag, for up to 2 months. Leaving the cloves on the bulb with the papery skin attached will help prevent them from drying out.

The *Taste of Home* pros do not recommend freezing fresh garlic cloves. Also, avoid storing them in the refrigerator because they have a tendency to sprout, which can cause a bitter flavor.

Rainbow Quiche

(Pictured above and on page 277)

PREP: 20 min. **BAKE:** 45 min. + standing

With plenty of vegetables and a creamy egg-cheese filling, this tasty quiche gets two thumbs up from everyone who tries it.
—Molly Thompson, Oswego, New York

Pastry for single-crust pie (9 inches)
- 1-1/2 cups chopped fresh broccoli florets
- 1 small onion, finely chopped
- 1 cup sliced fresh mushrooms
- 1 *each* small green, sweet red and orange peppers, finely chopped
- 2 tablespoons butter
- 1 cup chopped fresh spinach
- 1 cup (4 ounces) shredded Mexican cheese blend
- 6 eggs
- 1-3/4 cups 2% milk
- 1/2 teaspoon salt

Line a 9-in. deep-dish pie plate with pastry; trim and flute edges. In a large skillet, saute the broccoli, onion, mushrooms and peppers in butter until tender. Stir in spinach. Spoon into prepared crust; sprinkle with cheese. In a large bowl, whisk the eggs, milk and salt; pour over cheese.

Bake at 350° for 45-55 minutes or until a knife inserted near the center comes out clean. Let quiche stand for 10 minutes before cutting. **Yield:** 8 servings.

Editor's Note: You may also use this recipe to fill two frozen deep-dish pie shells. Bake the quiches for 40-45 minutes. Each yields six servings.

Chiles Rellenos Casserole

(Pictured below)

PREP: 20 min. **BAKE:** 40 min. + standing

A friend gave me this simple take on a traditional Mexican dish about 35 years ago. I'm often asked to bring it to potlucks.
—Maggie Owen, Oceanside, California

- 7 cans (4 ounces *each*) whole green chilies, drained
- 3/4 pound Monterey Jack cheese, cut into strips
- 1 cup (4 ounces) shredded cheddar cheese
- 5 eggs
- 1-1/4 cups milk
- 1/4 cup all-purpose flour
- 1/4 teaspoon salt
- 1/4 teaspoon pepper
- 1/8 teaspoon hot pepper sauce

Split chilies lengthwise; rinse and remove seeds. Drain on paper towels; pat dry. Stuff chilies with cheese strips. Place half of chilies in a greased 11-in. x 7-in. baking dish; sprinkle with 1/2 cup cheddar cheese. Repeat layers.

In a small bowl, beat the eggs, milk, flour, salt, pepper and pepper sauce until smooth; pour over chilies. Bake, uncovered, at 350° for 40-45 minutes or until a knife inserted near the center comes out clean. Let stand for 10 minutes before serving. **Yield:** 8 servings.

Slow Cooker Tamale Pie

(Pictured below)

PREP: 25 min. **COOK:** 7 hours

Canned beans and corn bread/muffin mix speed up the prep for this crowd-pleasing main dish. It's perfect for busy evenings and carry-in dinners. —*Jill Pokrivka, York, Pennsylvania*

- **1 pound ground beef**
- **1 teaspoon ground cumin**
- **1/2 teaspoon salt**
- **1/2 teaspoon chili powder**
- **1/4 teaspoon pepper**
- **1 can (15 ounces) black beans, rinsed and drained**
- **1 can (14-1/2 ounces) diced tomatoes with mild green chilies, undrained**
- **1 can (11 ounces) whole kernel corn, drained**
- **1 can (10 ounces) enchilada sauce**
- **2 green onions, chopped**
- **1/4 cup minced fresh cilantro**
- **1 package (8-1/2 ounces) corn bread/muffin mix**
- **2 eggs**
- **1 cup (4 ounces) shredded Mexican cheese blend**

Sour cream and additional minced fresh cilantro, optional

In a large skillet, cook beef over medium heat until no longer pink; drain. Stir in the cumin, salt, chili powder and pepper. Transfer to a 4-qt. slow cooker; stir in the beans, tomatoes, corn, enchilada sauce, onions and cilantro. Cover and cook on low for 6-8 hours or until heated through.

In a small bowl, combine the corn bread/muffin mix and eggs; spoon over meat mixture. Cover and cook 1 hour longer or until a toothpick inserted near the center comes out clean.

Sprinkle with cheese; cover and let stand for 5 minutes. Serve with sour cream and additional cilantro if desired. **Yield:** 8 servings.

White Chili

PREP: 30 min. **COOK:** 3 hours

My friend Caroline Gray and I came up with this slow-cooked chicken chili. It's unique because it calls for Alfredo sauce. —*Cindi Mitchell, St. Marys, Kansas*

- **3 cans (15-1/2 ounces *each*) great northern beans, rinsed and drained**
- **3 cups cubed cooked chicken breast**
- **1 jar (15 ounces) Alfredo sauce**
- **2 cups chicken broth**
- **1 to 2 cans (4 ounces *each*) chopped green chilies**
- **1-1/2 cups frozen gold and white corn**
- **1 cup (4 ounces) shredded Monterey Jack cheese**
- **1 cup (4 ounces) shredded pepper Jack cheese**
- **1 cup sour cream**
- **1 small sweet yellow pepper, chopped**
- **1 small onion, chopped**
- **3 garlic cloves, minced**
- **1 tablespoon ground cumin**
- **1-1/2 teaspoons white pepper**
- **1 to 1-1/2 teaspoons cayenne pepper**

Salsa verde and chopped fresh cilantro, optional

In a 5- or 6-qt. slow cooker, combine the first 15 ingredients. Cover and cook on low for 3-4 hours or until heated though, stirring once. Serve chili with salsa verde and fresh cilantro if desired. **Yield:** 12 servings (1 cup each).

Roast Pork with Apples & Onions

(Pictured above right)

PREP: 25 min. **BAKE:** 1 hour + standing

Here's one of my family's favorite weekend dinners. The roasted onions and sweet apples really complement the moist pork. —*Lillian Julow, Gainesville, Florida*

- **1 boneless whole pork loin roast (2 pounds)**
- **1/4 teaspoon salt**
- **1/4 teaspoon pepper**
- **1 tablespoon olive oil**
- **3 large Golden Delicious apples, cut into wedges**
- **2 large onions, cut into wedges**
- **5 garlic cloves, peeled**
- **1 tablespoon minced fresh rosemary *and/or* 1 teaspoon dried rosemary, crushed**

In a large skillet, saute the onion, red pepper and potato in oil until tender.

In a greased 13-in. x 9-in. baking dish, layer half of the bread, onion mixture, Brie and Parmesan. Repeat layers. In a large bowl, whisk the remaining ingredients; pour over layers. Cover and refrigerate overnight.

Remove from refrigerator 30 minutes before baking. Bake, uncovered, at 350° for 45-50 minutes or until a knife inserted near the center comes out clean. Let stand for 10 minutes before cutting. **Yield:** 12 servings.

Skillet Tacos

(Pictured below)

PREP/TOTAL TIME: 20 min.

Busy day? Save time and money with this stovetop supper the whole family will love. It calls for handy convenience products.
—Kelly Roder, Fairfax, Virginia

  1 **pound ground beef**
  1 **small red onion, chopped**
  1 **can (15-1/4 ounces) whole kernel corn, drained**
 10 **corn tortillas (6 inches), cut into 1-inch pieces**
  1 **bottle (8 ounces) taco sauce**
1-1/4 **cups shredded cheddar cheese, *divided***
Hot pepper sauce, optional

In a large skillet, cook beef and onion over medium heat until the meat is no longer pink; drain. Add the corn, tortillas, taco sauce and 1 cup cheese; heat through. Sprinkle with remaining cheese. Serve with pepper sauce if desired. **Yield:** 6 servings.

Sprinkle roast with salt and pepper. In a large nonstick skillet, brown roast in oil on all sides. Place in a shallow roasting pan coated with cooking spray. Arrange apples, onions and garlic around roast; sprinkle with rosemary.

Bake, uncovered, at 350° for 1 to 1-1/4 hours or until a meat thermometer reads 160°, turning the apples, onions and garlic once. Let roast stand for 10 minutes before slicing. **Yield:** 8 servings.

Brie-and-Veggie Brunch Strata

PREP: 30 min. + chilling **BAKE:** 45 min. + standing

This filling strata is great for a morning gathering...and even for dinner. If you prefer, use 2 cups of Swiss cheese instead of Brie.
—Lee Elrod, Newnan, Georgia

1 **large onion, halved and thinly sliced**
1 **large sweet red pepper, chopped**
1 **large Yukon Gold potato, peeled and cubed**
2 **tablespoons olive oil**
1 **loaf sourdough bread (1 pound), cubed**
1 **round Brie cheese (8 ounces), rind removed, cut into 1/2-inch cubes**
1 **cup (4 ounces) shredded Parmesan cheese**
8 **eggs**
3 **cups 2% milk**
2 **tablespoons Dijon mustard**
1 **teaspoon seasoned salt**
1 **teaspoon pepper**

Getting in the Theme of Things

Whether you're hosting a baby shower or gathering around a campfire, invite friends and family to enjoy plenty of good company and festive food.

Italian Pasta Party...290
   Ragu Bolognese • Pasta Alla Puttanesca • Verde Sauce • Pesto Breadsticks

A Shower that Shines..292
   Candied Fruit Platter • Island Vacation Party Mix • Chocolate Peanut Butter Candy • Spiced Pineapple Cooler

Stir Crazy for Coffee!..294
   Coffee Toffee Cheesecake • Cappuccino Granita • Coffee-Nut Muffins • Coffee-Molasses Marinated Pork Chops

A Dreamy Ice Cream Social.......................................296
   Peach Gelato • Strawberry-Rhubarb Ice Cream • Cantaloupe Sorbet • Black Cherry Sherbet

Around the Campfire 298
   Marinated Ribeyes • Grilled Sweet Onions • Farmer's Country Breakfast • Potato-Sausage Foil Packs • Campfire Trout Dinner • Summertime Cooler • Hot Quick Banana Boats • Camping Haystacks

Thai in Your Kitchen 302
   Cashew Curried Beef • Peanut Butter Dipping Sauce • Thai Portobello Chicken Stir-Fry • Shrimp Pad Thai

GREAT GET-TOGETHERS. Clockwise from upper left: Thai in Your Kitchen (p. 302), A Shower that Shines (p. 292), Around the Campfire (p. 298) and A Dreamy Ice Cream Social (p. 296).

Italian Pasta Party

IN THE MOOD for something saucy? Invite friends over for a pasta party and let everyone indulge their love of Italian food.

Cook up a few different types of noodles and offer guests the mouthwatering sauces here, from Pasta Alla Puttanesca to Ragu Bolognese. We've also featured a recipe for the perfect side—golden Pesto Breadsticks.

To finish off your feast, add a tossed green salad and scoop up some Italian ice for dessert. You'll have everyone shouting, *Mangia!*

Ragu Bolognese

(Pictured above)

PREP: 25 min. **COOK:** 2 hours

My family loves homemade spaghetti sauce, and this one is a hit. I always make sure to serve it with plenty of garlic bread.
—*Kate Gaul, Dubuque, Iowa*

- 1 **pound ground beef**
- 1/2 **pound ground pork**
- 1/4 **pound bacon strips, diced**
- 2 **medium onions, chopped**
- 2 **celery ribs, chopped**
- 2 **small carrots, chopped**
- 4 **garlic cloves, minced**
- 1 **cup dry red wine** *or* **beef broth**

- 1 **can (28 ounces) crushed tomatoes**
- 1 **can (15 ounces) tomato sauce**
- 2 **tablespoons tomato paste**
- 2 **bay leaves**
- 2 **teaspoons sugar**
- 1 **teaspoon salt**
- 1/2 **teaspoon dried thyme**
- 1/2 **teaspoon dried oregano**
- 1/2 **teaspoon** *each* **ground cumin, nutmeg and pepper**
- 1/2 **cup heavy whipping cream**
- 2 **tablespoons butter**
- 2 **tablespoons minced fresh parsley**
- 1/2 **cup grated Parmesan cheese**

Hot cooked pasta and additional Parmesan cheese

In a Dutch oven, cook the beef, pork, bacon, onions, celery and carrots over medium heat until meat is no longer pink; drain. Add garlic; cook 2 minutes longer. Add wine; cook for 4-5 minutes or until liquid is reduced by half.

Stir in the tomatoes, tomato sauce, tomato paste, bay leaves, sugar and seasonings. Bring to a boil. Reduce heat; simmer, uncovered, for 1-1/2 to 2 hours or until thickened, stirring occasionally. Discard bay leaves. Add the cream, butter and parsley; cook 2 minutes longer. Sir in cheese. Serve with pasta and additional cheese.

Yield: 7-1/2 cups.

Pasta Alla Puttanesca

PREP: 15 min. **COOK:** 20 min.

This classic sauce promises a zesty meal. Adjust the amount of red pepper flakes to get the level of spiciness you desire.
—Katie Theken, Durham, North Carolina

- 3 anchovy fillets
- 3 tablespoons olive oil
- 1 garlic clove, minced
- 1 can (14-1/2 ounces) diced tomatoes, undrained
- 1-1/4 cups water
- 1 can (6 ounces) tomato paste
- 1 teaspoon dried basil
- 1 teaspoon dried parsley flakes
- 1/2 teaspoon salt
- 1/4 to 1/2 teaspoon crushed red pepper flakes
- 1/4 teaspoon dried oregano
- 1/4 teaspoon pepper
- 1/4 cup chopped pitted Greek olives
- 2 tablespoons capers, drained and chopped

Hot cooked pasta

In a large saucepan over medium heat, cook anchovy fillets in oil for 2 minutes. Add garlic; cook 1 minute longer. Stir in tomatoes, water, paste and seasonings.

Bring to a boil. Reduce heat; simmer, uncovered, for 10-15 minutes or until slightly thickened. Stir in the olives and capers; heat through. Serve with pasta. **Yield:** 3-1/2 cups.

Verde Sauce

(Pictured below)

PREP/TOTAL TIME: 25 min.

You'll love the robust garlic flavor of this hearty sauce. Try adding shrimp, chicken or homemade sausage for a fabulous meal.
—Ann Sheehy, Lawrence, Maryland

- 6 green onions, cut into thirds
- 5 garlic cloves, peeled
- 2 teaspoons grated lemon peel
- 3 cups loosely packed basil leaves
- 3 cups loosely packed parsley sprigs
- 1 jar (10 ounces) sliced green olives with pimientos, drained
- 1 jar (3-1/2 ounces) capers, drained
- 3 tablespoons lemon juice
- 1/4 teaspoon crushed red pepper flakes
- 1 cup grated Parmesan and Romano cheese blend
- 1 cup olive oil

Hot cooked pasta

Place the onions, garlic and lemon peel in a food processor; cover and pulse until chopped. Add half of the basil and parsley; cover and process until chopped. Add remaining basil and parsley; chop.

Add olives, capers, juice, pepper and cheese. Cover; process until blended. While processing, gradually add oil in a steady stream. Serve with pasta. **Yield:** 3 cups.

Pesto Breadsticks

(Pictured above)

PREP/TOTAL TIME: 20 min.

Our Test Kitchen created these breadsticks accented with garlic pepper and pesto. Whether you serve them with a pasta supper, bowl of soup or salad, these cute twists add fun to any menu.

- 1 tube (11 ounces) refrigerated breadsticks
- 2 tablespoons prepared pesto
- 1/4 teaspoon garlic pepper blend
- 1 tablespoon butter, melted
- 2 tablespoons shredded Parmesan cheese

Unroll and separate breadsticks; place on an ungreased baking sheet. Combine pesto and garlic pepper; brush over breadsticks. Twist each breadstick three times.

Brush with butter; sprinkle with cheese. Bake at 375° for 10-13 minutes or until golden brown. Serve warm. **Yield:** 1 dozen.

A Shower that Shines

EXPECT lots of compliments when you serve these dainty delights at a bridal or baby shower. They'll have guests happily munching all party long.

For fun finger foods and a great thirst-quencher, too, look no further than impressive Candied Fruit Platter, Chocolate Peanut Butter Candy, Island Vacation Party Mix and Spiced Pineapple Cooler.

Candied Fruit Platter

(Pictured above)

PREP: 1-1/4 hours

Luscious chocolate-dipped fruits make the perfect dessert and a pretty arrangement for your table. I especially like to serve them at brunches and buffets. —Dina Nicastro, Thornhill, Ontario

Assorted fruit: sliced apples and starfruit, peeled quartered kiwifruit, cubed fresh pineapple, dried apricots, dried sliced pineapple and apples, and fresh strawberries, grapes and sweet cherries

Caramels and Tootsie Roll Midgees
Pretzel dipping sticks
    1 package (11-1/2 ounces) milk chocolate chips
    3 tablespoons shortening, *divided*
    1 cup (6 ounces) semisweet chocolate chips
  1/2 pound white candy coating, chopped
Toasted coconut and finely chopped pecans, optional

Prepare fruit; pat dry with paper towels. Microwave unwrapped candies, one at a time, for 10 seconds each. Wrap softened candies around strawberries and pretzel sticks as desired.

In a microwave, melt the milk chocolate chips and 2 tablespoons shortening; stir until smooth. Repeat with the semisweet chocolate chips and remaining shortening. Melt candy coating; stir until smooth.

Dip the fruit and pretzel sticks into the melted coatings; decorate as desired. Sprinkle with coconut and pecans if desired. Place on waxed paper; let stand until set. **Yield:** varies.

Island Vacation Party Mix

PREP/TOTAL TIME: 15 min.

What's not to love about this taste of the tropics? With its convenient microwave method, you'll be munching in no time.
—Melissa Talbott, Peoria, Illinois

2-1/2 cups Corn Chex
2-1/2 cups Rice Chex
   2 cups macadamia nuts
  1/4 cup butter, cubed
   2 tablespoons sugar
   2 tablespoons corn syrup
   1 cup flaked coconut
   1 package (6 ounces) chopped dried pineapple
   1 cup white baking chips

In a large microwave-safe bowl, combine cereals and nuts; set aside. In a small microwave-safe bowl, combine the butter, sugar and corn syrup. Microwave, uncovered, on high for 2 minutes, stirring once. Pour over cereal mixture and toss to coat.

Cook the cereal mixture, uncovered, on high for 2 minutes, stirring once. Add coconut; cook 2 minutes longer, stirring once. Spread onto waxed paper to cool. Stir in pineapple and chips. Store in an airtight container. **Yield:** 3 quarts.

Editor's Note: This recipe was tested in a 1,100-watt microwave.

Chocolate Peanut Butter Candy

PREP: 25 min. **COOK:** 10 min. + standing

Have the kids roll up their sleeves and help make these crunchy, chocolaty bars. *—Kathy Mitchell, Brookfield, Wisconsin*

1-1/2 cups graham cracker crumbs
   1 cup sugar
  3/4 cup packed brown sugar
  3/4 cup butter, cubed
  1/3 cup 2% milk
   2 sleeves butter-flavored crackers (about 80 crackers)
   1 cup butterscotch chips
   1 cup (6 ounces) semisweet chocolate chips
  3/4 cup creamy peanut butter

In a saucepan, combine the cracker crumbs, sugars, butter and milk. Bring to a boil, stirring constantly; cook and stir 5 minutes longer.

Place a single layer of crackers in a greased 13-in. x 9-in. dish; top with half of crumb mixture. Repeat layers. Top with remaining crackers.

In a small saucepan, combine chips and peanut butter. Cook and stir until smooth. Pour over crackers. Let stand until set. **Yield:** 15 servings.

Editor's Note: This recipe was tested with Keebler Town House crackers.

Spiced Pineapple Cooler

(Pictured below and on page 289)

PREP: 10 min. **COOK:** 20 min. + chilling

I enjoy cooking, especially when I'm fixing something different. That's definitely the case with this refreshing party punch.
—Nancy Burford, Senatobia, Mississippi

✓ This recipe includes Nutrition Facts.

1-1/2 cups water
  2/3 cup sugar
   4 cinnamon sticks (3 inches)
  12 whole cloves
   1 can (46 ounces) unsweetened pineapple juice
1-1/2 cups orange juice
  1/2 cup lemon juice
   1 can (12 ounces) ginger ale, chilled
Ice cubes
Additional cinnamon sticks, optional

In a small saucepan, bring the water, sugar, cinnamon and cloves to a boil. Reduce heat; cover and simmer for 15 minutes. Strain. Cool to room temperature.

Pour into a large pitcher; stir in juices. Refrigerate until chilled. Just before serving, stir in ginger ale. Serve over ice. Garnish with additional cinnamon sticks if desired. **Yield:** 13 servings (3/4 cup each).

Nutrition Facts: 3/4 cup equals 119 calories, trace fat (trace saturated fat), 0 cholesterol, 4 mg sodium, 29 g carbohydrate, trace fiber, 1 g protein.

Stir Crazy for Coffee!

IF ESPRESSO, cappuccino or another bean beverage is your idea of heaven, invite members of your coffee klatch for some java-infused treats—or even a complete dinner! Brew up any of these perky recipes, from an entree of pork chops to a decadent cheesecake for dessert.

Coffee Toffee Cheesecake

(Pictured below)

PREP: 45 min. **BAKE:** 55 min. + chilling

When I served this chocolaty dessert on Thanksgiving, everybody raved over it.   —Tammy Baker, Bowling Green, Kentucky

- 2-1/2 **cups chocolate wafer crumbs**
- 1/2 **cup butter, melted**
- 2 **tablespoons sugar**

FILLING:
- 1 **cup (6 ounces) semisweet chocolate chips**
- 1/4 **cup heavy whipping cream**
- 4 **teaspoons instant coffee granules**
- 3 **packages (8 ounces *each*) cream cheese, softened**
- 1-1/3 **cups sugar**
- 1-1/2 **cups (12 ounces) sour cream**
- 1 **tablespoon vanilla extract**
- 1/8 **teaspoon salt**
- 3 **eggs, lightly beaten**
- 4 **Heath candy bars (1.4 ounces *each*), chopped**
- 1 **dark chocolate candy bar (1.45 ounces)**

Place a greased 9-in. springform pan on a double thickness of heavy-duty foil (about 18 in. square). Securely wrap foil around pan. In a small bowl, combine wafer crumbs, butter and sugar. Press onto bottom and 1 in. up the sides of prepared pan. Place pan on a baking sheet. Bake at 350° for 10 minutes. Cool on a wire rack.

In a microwave-safe bowl, melt chips and cream; stir until smooth. Stir in granules until dissolved. Set aside. In a large bowl, beat cream cheese and sugar until smooth.

Beat in sour cream, vanilla and salt; gradually beat in chocolate mixture. Add eggs; beat on low speed just until combined. Pour into crust. Place springform pan in a large baking pan; add 1-1/2 in. of hot water to large pan.

Bake at 350° for 55-65 minutes or until center is just set and top appears dull. Remove springform pan from water bath. Cool on a wire rack for 10 minutes. Sprinkle with Heath bars.

Carefully run a knife around edge of pan to loosen; cool 1 hour longer. Refrigerate overnight. Chop dark chocolate candy bar; melt in a microwave and stir until smooth. Drizzle over cheesecake. **Yield:** 12 servings.

Cappuccino Granita

PREP: 10 min. + freezing

I prepared this frozen dessert when a friend came to lunch during a heat wave. I sprinkle nuts on top and pair it with cookies.
—Sally Sibthorpe, Shelby Township, Michigan

☑ This recipe includes Nutrition Facts and Diabetic Exchanges.

- 1/4 **cup sugar**
- 1 **envelope unflavored gelatin**
- 2 **cups hot strong brewed coffee *or* cappuccino**
- 1/2 **cup refrigerated hazelnut nondairy creamer**
- 1/4 **cup chopped hazelnuts *or* walnuts**
- 6 **Pirouette cookies *or* cookies of your choice**

In a small bowl, combine the sugar and gelatin powder. Pour the coffee over the mixture; stir to dissolve. Stir in the hazelnut creamer.

Transfer the mixture to a 1-qt. dish; cool to room temperature. Freeze for 1 hour; stir with a fork. Freeze 4-5 hours longer or until completely frozen, stirring every 30 minutes. Stir granita with a fork just before serving; spoon into dessert dishes. Sprinkle with nuts; serve with cookies. **Yield:** 6 servings.

Editor's Note: This recipe was tested with Pepperidge Farm Pirouette cookies.

Nutrition Facts: 1 serving equals 156 calories, 7 g fat (1 g saturated fat), 1 mg cholesterol, 27 mg sodium, 23 g carbohydrate, 1 g fiber, 2 g protein. **Diabetic Exchanges:** 1-1/2 starch, 1/2 fat.

Coffee-Nut Muffins

(Pictured above)

PREP: 20 min. **BAKE:** 25 min.

There's nothing like a great cup of coffee—and one of these moist muffins to go with it! —Darla Germaux, Saxton, Pennsylvania

- 2 cups all-purpose flour
- 2/3 cup sugar
- 1-1/2 teaspoons baking powder
- 1 teaspoon salt
- 1/4 teaspoon baking soda
- 1 cup strong brewed coffee
- 1 tablespoon instant espresso powder
- 1/2 cup canola oil
- 1 egg, beaten
- 1/2 cup chopped walnuts
- 1/4 cup raisins
- 1/4 cup chopped dates

TOPPING:
- 1 tablespoon sugar
- 1/8 teaspoon ground cinnamon

DRIZZLE:
- 1/2 cup confectioners' sugar
- 1 tablespoon strong brewed coffee

In a large bowl, combine the first five ingredients. Combine coffee and espresso powder; cool to room temperature. Stir in oil and egg. Add coffee mixture to dry ingredients; stir just until moistened. Fold in the walnuts, raisins and dates.

Fill greased or paper-lined jumbo muffin cups three-fourths full. Combine sugar and cinnamon; sprinkle over the tops. Bake at 350° for 25-30 minutes or until a toothpick comes out clean. Cool for 5 minutes before removing from pan to a wire rack to cool completely.

Combine confectioners' sugar and coffee; drizzle over muffins. **Yield:** 6 muffins.

Coffee-Molasses Marinated Pork Chops

(Pictured below)

PREP: 10 min. + marinating **GRILL:** 10 min.

A friend gave me this fabulous recipe, and it's truly the best pork I've ever tasted. —Pam Moormann, Beverly, Maryland

- 1 cup strong brewed coffee
- 1/4 cup molasses
- 6 fresh thyme sprigs
- 2 tablespoons cider vinegar
- 1 tablespoon Dijon mustard
- 2 garlic cloves, minced
- 1/2 teaspoon salt
- 1/2 teaspoon lemon-pepper seasoning
- 1/2 teaspoon ground ginger
- 4 bone-in pork loin chops (1 inch thick)

In a large bowl, combine the first nine ingredients. Pour 1/2 cup marinade into a large resealable plastic bag; add the pork chops. Seal bag and turn to coat; refrigerate for at least 2 hours. Cover and refrigerate remaining coffee mixture until ready to cook.

For glaze, place remaining coffee mixture in a small saucepan. Bring to a boil; cook until liquid is reduced to about 1/2 cup.

If grilling the chops, use long-handled tongs to dip a paper towel in cooking oil and lightly coat the grill rack. Drain and discard marinade. Grill chops, covered, over medium heat or broil 4-6 in. from the heat for 4-5 minutes on each side or until a meat thermometer reads 160°. Spoon glaze over chops. **Yield:** 4 servings.

A Dreamy Ice Cream Social

I SCREAM, you scream, we all scream for ice cream... so create chills and thrills by hosting a party packed with from-the-freezer treats.

Guests will melt for refreshing Strawberry-Rhubarb Ice Cream, plus other cold confections—Cantaloupe Sorbet, Peach Gelato and Black Cherry Sherbet.

Peach Gelato

(Pictured above and on page 288)

PREP: 25 min. + chilling **PROCESS:** 20 min. + freezing

This heavenly, creamy gelato looks as good as it tastes. The mild but delightful peach flavor will make everyone a fan.
—Molly Haen, Baldwin, Wisconsin

  3 cups sliced peeled peaches
  2 cups whole milk
3/4 cup sugar
  4 egg yolks, beaten
  1 cup heavy whipping cream
  1 tablespoon peach schnapps liqueur, optional

Place the peaches and water in a large skillet; cook, uncovered, over medium heat until tender. Place in a food processor; cover and process until blended. Set peaches aside.

In a small saucepan, heat milk to 175°; stir in sugar until dissolved. Whisk a small amount of the hot mixture into egg yolks. Return all to the pan, whisking constantly. Cook and stir over low heat until mixture is slightly thickened. Remove from the heat. Cool quickly by placing pan in a bowl of ice water; stir for 2 minutes.

Stir in the cream, peaches and liqueur if desired. Press waxed paper onto surface of custard. Refrigerate for several hours or overnight.

Fill cylinder of ice cream freezer two-thirds full; freeze according to the manufacturer's directions. Transfer to a freezer container; freeze for 2-4 hours before serving. **Yield:** 1 quart.

Strawberry-Rhubarb Ice Cream

(Pictured below right)

PREP: 45 min. + cooling **PROCESS:** 20 min. + freezing

I served this at a party, and guests said it was the best ice cream they'd ever had. —Mary Ann Hansen, St. Cloud, Minnesota

> 2 cups diced fresh *or* frozen rhubarb, thawed
> 1-1/4 cups sugar, *divided*
> 1/2 cup water
> 2 tablespoons strawberry gelatin powder
> 1/2 teaspoon ground cinnamon
> 1/2 cup miniature marshmallows
> 1 cup whole milk
> 1/4 teaspoon salt
> 2 cups heavy whipping cream
> 1 teaspoon vanilla extract

In a small saucepan, bring the rhubarb, 1/2 cup sugar and water to a boil. Reduce heat; cover and simmer for 10-12 minutes or until rhubarb is tender. Remove from the heat; sprinkle gelatin and cinnamon over rhubarb mixture. Let stand for 1 minute. Stir until dissolved. Cool to room temperature. Stir in marshmallows.

In a large saucepan, heat the milk, salt and remaining sugar to 175°. Remove from the heat; stir in cream and vanilla. Refrigerate until chilled. Pour into cylinder of ice cream freezer; process for 10 minutes or until mixture begins to thicken. Add rhubarb mixture; freeze according to manufacturer's directions.

When the ice cream is frozen, transfer to a freezer container; freeze for 2-4 hours before serving. **Yield:** 5 cups.

Editor's Note: If using frozen rhubarb, measure rhubarb while still frozen, then thaw completely. Drain in a colander, but do not press liquid out.

Cantaloupe Sorbet

(Pictured at right)

PREP: 10 min. + chilling **PROCESS:** 20 min. + freezing

This sorbet is a refreshing summer dessert and palate-cleansing finale for a hearty meal. —Gena Persons, Severn, Maryland

☑ This recipe includes Nutrition Facts and Diabetic Exchange.

> 1 cup sugar
> 1 cup water
> 4 cups cubed cantaloupe
> 2 tablespoons lemon juice

In a small saucepan, bring sugar and water to a boil. Cook and stir until sugar is dissolved. Transfer to a small bowl; refrigerate until chilled.

Place the cantaloupe, lemon juice and sugar syrup in a food processor; cover and process for 2-3 minutes or until blended.

Fill cylinder of ice cream freezer; freeze according to the manufacturer's directions. Transfer to a freezer container; freeze for 4 hours or until firm. **Yield:** 1 quart.

Nutrition Facts: 1/2 cup equals 126 calories, trace fat (trace saturated fat), 0 cholesterol, 7 mg sodium, 32 g carbohydrate, 1 g fiber, 1 g protein. **Diabetic Exchange:** 2 starch.

Black Cherry Sherbet

(Pictured below)

PREP: 25 min. + chilling
PROCESS: 20 min./batch + freezing

When making this yummy recipe with the kids, I use caffeine-free soda—for obvious reasons! —Emily Evans, Roselle, Illinois

☑ This recipe includes Nutrition Facts.

> 4 cups fresh *or* frozen quartered pitted dark sweet cherries, thawed
> 1 cup sugar
> 2 liters black cherry soda, chilled
> 1 can (14 ounces) sweetened condensed milk
> 1 cup (6 ounces) miniature semisweet chocolate chips

In a large saucepan over medium heat, cook cherries and sugar for 15 minutes or until slightly thickened, stirring occasionally. Transfer to a large bowl; cool to room temperature. Refrigerate until chilled.

Stir in the soda, milk and chocolate chips. Fill cylinder of ice cream freezer two-thirds full; freeze according to manufacturer's directions. Refrigerate the remaining mixture until ready to freeze.

Transfer to a freezer container; freeze for 3 hours or until firm. **Yield:** 2-1/2 quarts.

Nutrition Facts: 1/2 cup equals 213 calories, 5 g fat (3 g saturated fat), 7 mg cholesterol, 39 mg sodium, 43 g carbohydrate, 1 g fiber, 2 g protein.

Around the Campfire

NATURAL WONDERS aren't the only rewards of spending time in the great outdoors. You can enjoy some great open-flame food, too—thanks to the recipes here!

To start off a day of wilderness adventure, get a fire going and cook up a morning meal of Farmer's Country Breakfast. Then for lunch and dinner, choose from hearty creations such as Potato-Sausage Foil Packs, Grilled Sweet Onions, Marinated Ribeyes and Hot Quick Banana Boats.

It's satisfying, fresh-air fare that'll make any camping trip even more enjoyable—Scout's honor!

Marinated Ribeyes

(Pictured above)

PREP: 10 min. + marinating **GRILL:** 10 min.

When we go camping, we place frozen steaks in the marinade in a sealed plastic container at the bottom of our cooler. By the second night, the meat is thawed, tender and ready to grill. It's great outdoor eating! —Louise Graybiel, Toronto, Ontario

1/2 cup barbecue sauce
  3 tablespoons olive oil
  3 tablespoons Worcestershire sauce
  2 tablespoons steak sauce
  1 tablespoon red wine vinegar
  1 tablespoon soy sauce
  2 teaspoons steak seasoning
  1 teaspoon hot pepper sauce
  1 garlic clove, minced
  4 beef ribeye steaks (8 ounces *each*)

In a large resealable plastic bag, combine the first nine ingredients. Add the steaks; seal bag and turn to coat. Refrigerate for 4 hours or overnight.

Drain and discard marinade. Grill steaks, covered, over medium-hot heat for 5-7 minutes on each side or until meat reaches desired doneness (for medium-rare, a meat thermometer should read 145°; medium, 160°; well-done, 170°). **Yield:** 4 servings.

Editor's Note: This recipe was tested with McCormick's Montreal Steak Seasoning. Look for it in the spice aisle.

Grilled Sweet Onions

(Pictured at left)

PREP: 15 min. **GRILL:** 30 min.

These onions are a summer requirement for our family. We enjoy the caramelized onions and garlic over steak or on their own.
—*Raeann Van Arsdall, Corvallis, Oregon*

- 4 large sweet onions, quartered
- 4 garlic cloves, crushed
- 1/4 cup butter
- 1 teaspoon seasoned salt

Place four onion wedges and a garlic clove on a double thickness of heavy-duty foil (about 12 in. square). Dot with butter and sprinkle with salt. Repeat.

Fold foil around onion mixture and seal tightly. Grill, covered, over medium heat for 30-35 minutes or until onions are tender. Open foil carefully to allow steam to escape. **Yield:** 4 servings.

Farmer's Country Breakfast

(Pictured below)

PREP/TOTAL TIME: 30 min.

When we're camping, we often eat a late breakfast. This hearty combination of sausage, hash browns and eggs is just right.
—*Bonnie Roberts, Newaygo, Michigan*

- 6 eggs
- 1/3 cup 2% milk
- 1/2 teaspoon dried parsley flakes
- 1/4 teaspoon salt
- 6 ounces bulk pork sausage
- 1-1/2 cups frozen cubed hash brown potatoes, thawed
- 1/4 cup chopped onion
- 1 cup (4 ounces) shredded cheddar cheese

Whisk the eggs, milk, parsley and salt; set aside. In a large skillet, cook sausage over medium heat until no longer pink; remove and drain. In the same skillet, cook the potatoes and onion for 5-7 minutes or until tender. Return sausage to the pan.

Add the egg mixture; cook and stir until almost set. Sprinkle with cheese. Cover and cook for 1-2 minutes or until cheese is melted. **Yield:** 4 servings.

Potato-Sausage Foil Packs

(Pictured above)

PREP: 20 min. **GRILL:** 30 min.

We had these all-in-one campfire bundles at a friend's house for dinner and loved the simplicity of this great summer meal.
—*Alissa Keith, Lynchburg, Virginia*

- 1 package (14 ounces) smoked turkey kielbasa, sliced
- 2 large potatoes, cut into wedges
- 1 *each* medium green, sweet red and yellow peppers, cut into 1-inch pieces
- 1 medium onion, chopped
- 4 teaspoons lemon juice
- 4 teaspoons olive oil
- 1/2 teaspoon garlic powder
- 1/2 teaspoon pepper
- 1/4 teaspoon salt

Divide the kielbasa, potatoes, peppers and onion among four double thicknesses of heavy-duty foil (about 18 in. x 12 in.). Drizzle with lemon juice and oil; sprinkle with garlic powder, pepper and salt.

Fold foil around kielbasa mixture and seal tightly. Grill, covered, over medium heat for 30-35 minutes or until potatoes are tender. Open foil carefully to allow steam to escape. **Yield:** 4 servings.

Campfire Trout Dinner

(Pictured above)

PREP: 20 min. **GRILL:** 20 min.

Your fresh catch will taste even better with this simple treatment that keeps fish moist. —Wendy McGowan, Fontana, California

        8 **bacon strips**
        4 **pan-dressed trout (about 1 pound *each*)**
        8 **lemon slices**
        2 **small onions, halved and sliced**
    1/2 **teaspoon salt**
    1/4 **teaspoon pepper**
CARROTS:
        8 **medium carrots, thinly sliced**
    1/4 **teaspoon salt**
    1/8 **teaspoon pepper**
        2 **tablespoons butter**

Cook bacon until partially cooked but not crisp; drain. Place each trout on a double thickness of heavy-duty foil (about 20 in. x 18 in.). Place lemon and onions in the trout cavities; sprinkle with salt and pepper. Wrap trout with bacon. Fold foil around trout and seal tightly.

Place carrots on a double thickness of heavy-duty foil (about 20 in. x 18 in.); sprinkle with salt and pepper. Dot with butter. Fold foil around carrots and seal tightly.

Grill carrots, covered, over medium heat for 10 minutes.

Add the trout packets to grill; cook 20-25 minutes longer or until fish flakes easily with a fork and carrots are tender. **Yield:** 4 servings.

Summertime Cooler

PREP: 10 min. + chilling

When the mercury rises, this pick-me-up punch from the Taste of Home Test Kitchen will cool you down in no time.

    1/2 **cup sugar**
        4 **cups cold water**
        2 **tablespoons lemon juice**
    1/2 **teaspoon minced fresh gingerroot**
    1/2 **teaspoon cider vinegar**

In a 1-1/2-qt. pitcher, combine all ingredients; chill. Stir before serving. **Yield:** 4 servings.

Hot Quick Banana Boats

(Pictured below)

PREP/TOTAL TIME: 20 min.

You can eat these delicious, warm bananas right out of the foil bowl. Cleanup is just as easy!   —Sheila Parker, Reno, Nevada

        4 **large unpeeled bananas**
        8 **teaspoons semisweet chocolate chips**
        8 **teaspoons trail mix**
    1/4 **cup miniature marshmallows**

Place each banana on a 12-in. square of foil; crimp and shape foil around bananas so they sit flat.

Cut each banana lengthwise about 1/2 in. deep, leaving 1/2 in. uncut at both ends. Gently pull each banana peel open, forming a pocket. Fill pockets with chocolate chips, trail mix and marshmallows.

Grill the bananas, covered, over medium heat for 4-5 minutes or until marshmallows are melted and golden brown. **Yield:** 4 servings.

Camping Haystacks

(Pictured above and on page 289)

PREP/TOTAL TIME: 15 min.

Try these haystacks for a quick and fuss-free meal after a day of hiking. I simply heat canned chili and layer it with corn chips, cheddar cheese and other favorite taco toppings. Everyone who likes Mexican will like this. —*Gaylene Anderson, Sandy, Utah*

   1 **can (15 ounces) chili with beans**
   2 **packages (1-1/2 ounces** *each*) **corn chips**
1/2 **cup shredded cheddar cheese**
1-1/2 **cups chopped lettuce**
   1 **small tomato, chopped**
1/2 **cup salsa**
   2 **tablespoons sliced ripe olives**
   2 **tablespoons sour cream**

In a small saucepan, heat chili. Divide corn chips between two plates; top with chili. Layer with cheese, lettuce, tomato, salsa, olives and sour cream. Serve immediately. **Yield:** 2 servings.

CLEVER CAMPING. Keep these tips in mind when taking food out into the great outdoors:
• Pack your cooler with frozen or already-cooled foods, and use blocks of ice. Freeze water in clean empty milk jugs—they last longer than ice cubes.
• Use a separate cooler for perishable foods, and open it only when necessary. Put food you'll use first near the top. The exception is raw meat, which should be double wrapped and stored near the bottom to prevent meat juices from dripping onto other foods.
• Plan to use perishable foods in the first 2 days. Pack non-perishable foods—things like peanut butter, canned tuna or meat, beef jerky, nuts or packaged convenience meals—for the last part of your camping trip.
• When ice has melted, throw away all perishables—it's an indication that your cooler is no longer cool enough to safely store food.

Thai in Your Kitchen

IS FAR-EAST CUISINE one of your favorites? Why not gather a few friends together for a delicious dinner of Thai-inspired dishes?

You don't have to go to a pricey restaurant in order to savor the exotic flavors of Thailand. The recipes featured here are easy to prepare in your own home kitchen using readily available ingredients and simple cooking techniques.

Cashew Curried Beef...Thai Portobello Chicken Stir-Fry...Shrimp Pad Thai...Peanut Butter Dipping Sauce...these mouthwatering specialties will give your menu a distinctively Asian accent.

Cashew Curried Beef

(Pictured above)

PREP: 20 min. **COOK:** 20 min.

This recipe is a favorite with my whole family. The ingredients are a wonderful combination of sweet, salty and spicy.
—Jennifer Fridgen, East Grand Forks, Minnesota

1 pound beef top sirloin steak, thinly sliced
2 tablespoons canola oil, *divided*
1 can (14 ounces) coconut milk, *divided*
1 tablespoon red curry paste
2 tablespoons packed brown sugar
2 tablespoons fish *or* soy sauce
8 cups chopped bok choy
1 small sweet red pepper, sliced
1/2 cup salted cashews
1/2 cup minced fresh cilantro
Hot cooked brown rice

In a large skillet, saute beef in 1 teaspoon oil until no longer pink. Remove from skillet and set aside.

Spoon 1/2 cup cream from top of coconut milk and place in the pan. Add remaining oil; bring to a boil. Add curry paste; cook and stir for 5 minutes or until oil separates from coconut milk mixture.

Stir in the brown sugar, fish sauce and remaining coconut milk. Bring to a boil. Reduce heat; simmer, uncovered, for 5 minutes or until slightly thickened. Add bok choy and red pepper; return to a boil. Cook and stir 2-3 minutes longer or until vegetables are tender.

Stir in the cashews, cilantro and beef; heat through. Serve with rice. **Yield:** 5 servings.

Peanut Butter Dipping Sauce

PREP/TOTAL TIME: 25 min.

Use this to toss with noodles, to marinate meat or as a dip for chicken wings. —Christine Omar, Harwich Port, Massachusetts

- 1 **medium onion, chopped**
- 2 **tablespoons canola oil**
- 2 **garlic cloves, minced**
- 1/2 **cup water**
- 1/4 **cup creamy peanut butter**
- 1 **tablespoon sugar**
- 1 **tablespoon chili powder**
- 2 **tablespoons lemon juice**
- 2 **tablespoons soy sauce**
- 1/4 **teaspoon salt**

In a small saucepan, saute onion in oil until tender. Add garlic; cook 1 minute longer. Add the water, peanut butter, sugar and chili powder. Bring to a boil. Cook and stir for 2-3 minutes or until slightly thickened.

Remove from the heat; stir in the lemon juice, soy sauce and salt. **Yield:** 1-1/3 cups.

Thai Portobello Chicken Stir-Fry

PREP: 25 min. **COOK:** 20 min.

My husband and I never met a mushroom we didn't like, so this dinner is a favorite. —Susan Bazan, Sequim, Washington

- 1/2 **cup Thai peanut sauce**
- 1/2 **cup teriyaki sauce**
- 1/4 **cup chunky peanut butter**
- 2 **teaspoons Worcestershire sauce**
- 3/4 **pound boneless skinless chicken breasts, cut into thin strips**
- 3 **tablespoons olive oil,** *divided*
- 1 **tablespoon sesame oil**
- 3 **cups chopped sweet onions**
- 4 **celery ribs, sliced diagonally**
- 2 **medium carrots, sliced diagonally**
- 1/2 **pound sliced baby portobello mushrooms**
- 4-1/2 **teaspoons minced fresh gingerroot**
- 3 **garlic cloves, minced**
- 1/3 **cup thinly sliced green onions**

Hot cooked rice

In a small bowl, combine peanut sauce, teriyaki sauce, peanut butter and Worcestershire sauce; set aside.

In a large skillet or wok, stir-fry chicken in 1 tablespoon olive oil and sesame oil until no longer pink. Remove and keep warm. Stir-fry sweet onions, celery and carrots in remaining oil for 4 minutes. Add the mushrooms, ginger and garlic; stir-fry 4-6 minutes longer or until vegetables are crisp-tender.

Stir sauce mixture and add to the pan. Bring to a boil; cook and stir for 2 minutes or until thickened. Add chicken; heat through. Sprinkle with green onions. Serve with rice. **Yield:** 6 servings.

Shrimp Pad Thai

(Pictured below and on page 288)

PREP/TOTAL TIME: 30 min.

For this tasty dish, look for chili garlic sauce and fish sauce in your grocery store's Asian foods aisle. —Elise Ray, Shawnee, Kansas

- 4 **ounces uncooked thick rice noodles**
- 1/2 **pound uncooked small shrimp, peeled and deveined**
- 2 **teaspoons canola oil**
- 1 **large onion, chopped**
- 1 **garlic clove, minced**
- 1 **egg, beaten**
- 3 **cups coleslaw mix**
- 4 **green onions, thinly sliced**
- 1/3 **cup rice vinegar**
- 1/4 **cup sugar**
- 3 **tablespoons reduced-sodium soy sauce**
- 2 **tablespoons fish sauce** *or* **additional reduced-sodium soy sauce**
- 2 to 3 **teaspoons chili garlic sauce**
- 2 **tablespoons chopped salted peanuts**

Chopped fresh cilantro leaves

Cook noodles according to package directions. In a large nonstick skillet or wok, stir-fry shrimp in oil until shrimp turn pink; remove and set aside.

Add onion and garlic to the pan. Make a well in the center of the onion mixture; add egg. Stir-fry for 2-3 minutes or until egg is completely set.

Add the coleslaw mix, green onions, vinegar, sugar, soy sauce, fish sauce, chili garlic sauce and peanuts; heat through. Return shrimp to the pan; heat through. Drain noodles; toss with shrimp mixture. Garnish with cilantro. **Yield:** 4 servings.

Substitutions & Equivalents

Equivalent Measures

3 teaspoons	= 1 tablespoon	16 tablespoons	= 1 cup
4 tablespoons	= 1/4 cup	2 cups	= 1 pint
5-1/3 tablespoons	= 1/3 cup	4 cups	= 1 quart
8 tablespoons	= 1/2 cup	4 quarts	= 1 gallon

Food Equivalents

Grains

Macaroni	1 cup (3-1/2 ounces) uncooked	= 2-1/2 cups cooked
Noodles, Medium	3 cups (4 ounces) uncooked	= 4 cups cooked
Popcorn	1/3 to 1/2 cup unpopped	= 8 cups popped
Rice, Long Grain	1 cup uncooked	= 3 cups cooked
Rice, Quick-Cooking	1 cup uncooked	= 2 cups cooked
Spaghetti	8 ounces uncooked	= 4 cups cooked

Crumbs

Bread	1 slice	= 3/4 cup soft crumbs, 1/4 cup fine dry crumbs
Graham Crackers	7 squares	= 1/2 cup finely crushed
Buttery Round Crackers	12 crackers	= 1/2 cup finely crushed
Saltine Crackers	14 crackers	= 1/2 cup finely crushed

Fruits

Bananas	1 medium	= 1/3 cup mashed
Lemons	1 medium	= 3 tablespoons juice, 2 teaspoons grated peel
Limes	1 medium	= 2 tablespoons juice, 1-1/2 teaspoons grated peel
Oranges	1 medium	= 1/4 to 1/3 cup juice, 4 teaspoons grated peel

Vegetables

Cabbage	1 head	= 5 cups shredded	Green Pepper	1 large	= 1 cup chopped
Carrots	1 pound	= 3 cups shredded	Mushrooms	1/2 pound	= 3 cups sliced
Celery	1 rib	= 1/2 cup chopped	Onions	1 medium	= 1/2 cup chopped
Corn	1 ear fresh	= 2/3 cup kernels	Potatoes	3 medium	= 2 cups cubed

Nuts

Almonds	1 pound	= 3 cups chopped	Pecan Halves	1 pound	= 4-1/2 cups chopped
Ground Nuts	3-3/4 ounces	= 1 cup	Walnuts	1 pound	= 3-3/4 cups chopped

Easy Substitutions

When you need...		Use...
Baking Powder	1 teaspoon	1/2 teaspoon cream of tartar + 1/4 teaspoon baking soda
Buttermilk	1 cup	1 tablespoon lemon juice *or* vinegar + enough milk to measure 1 cup (let stand 5 minutes before using)
Cornstarch	1 tablespoon	2 tablespoons all-purpose flour
Honey	1 cup	1-1/4 cups sugar + 1/4 cup water
Half-and-Half Cream	1 cup	1 tablespoon melted butter + enough whole milk to measure 1 cup
Onion	1 small, chopped (1/3 cup)	1 teaspoon onion powder *or* 1 tablespoon dried minced onion
Tomato Juice	1 cup	1/2 cup tomato sauce + 1/2 cup water
Tomato Sauce	2 cups	3/4 cup tomato paste + 1 cup water
Unsweetened Chocolate	1 square (1 ounce)	3 tablespoons baking cocoa + 1 tablespoon shortening *or* oil
Whole Milk	1 cup	1/2 cup evaporated milk + 1/2 cup water

Cooking Terms

HERE'S a quick reference for some of the cooking terms used in *Taste of Home* recipes:

Baste—To moisten food with melted butter, pan drippings, marinades or other liquid to add more flavor and juiciness.

Beat—A rapid movement to combine ingredients using a fork, spoon, wire whisk or electric mixer.

Blend—To combine ingredients until *just* mixed.

Boil—To heat liquids until bubbles form that cannot be "stirred down." In the case of water, the temperature will reach 212°.

Bone—To remove all meat from the bone before cooking.

Cream—To beat ingredients together to a smooth consistency, usually in the case of butter and sugar for baking.

Dash—A small amount of seasoning, less than 1/8 teaspoon. If using a shaker, a dash would comprise a quick flip of the container.

Dredge—To coat foods with flour or other dry ingredients. Most often done with pot roasts and stew meat before browning.

Fold—To incorporate several ingredients by careful and gentle turning with a spatula. Used generally with beaten egg whites or whipped cream when mixing into the rest of the ingredients to keep the batter light.

Julienne—To cut foods into long thin strips much like matchsticks. Used most often for salads and stir-fry dishes.

Mince—To cut into very fine pieces. Used often for garlic or fresh herbs.

Parboil—To cook partially, usually used in the case of chicken, sausages and vegetables.

Partially Set—Describes the consistency of gelatin after it has been chilled for a small amount of time. Mixture should resemble the consistency of egg whites.

Puree—To process foods to a smooth mixture. Can be prepared in an electric blender, food processor, food mill or sieve.

Saute—To fry quickly in a small amount of fat, stirring almost constantly. Most often done with onions, mushrooms and other chopped vegetables.

Score—To cut slits partway through the outer surface of foods. Often used with ham or flank steak.

Stir-Fry—To cook meats and/or vegetables with a constant stirring motion in a small amount of oil in a wok or skillet over high heat.

General Recipe Index

This handy index lists every recipe by food category, major ingredient and/or cooking method, so you can easily locate recipes to suit your needs.

APPETIZERS & SNACKS

Cold Appetizers
Chicken Salad Caprese, 10
Crab Puffs, 161
Fiesta Shrimp Cocktail, 11
Greek Deli Kabobs, 248
Pretty Stuffed Spring Peas, 10
Sara's Summer Rolls, 280
Seafood & Cream Cheese Stuffed
    Shells, 8

Dips
Blueberry Fruit Dip, 252
Fire-Roasted Tomato Salsa, 10
Homemade Guacamole, 204
Hot Wing Dip, 143
Salsa Verde, 246

Hot Appetizers
Apricot Turkey Pinwheels, 252
Asparagus, Brie & Parma Ham
    Crostini, 8
Blue Cheese and Bacon Stuffed
    Mushrooms, 15
Crawfish Beignets with Cajun
    Dipping Sauce, 166
Crispy Taco Wings, 247
Crunchy Potato Mounds, 137
Grilled Glazed Drummies, 7
Grilled Greek Crostini Topping, 14
Grilled Peach BBQ Chicken
    Wings, 216
Havarti Shrimp Quesadillas, 11
Hot Ham & Cheese Slices, 16
✓Mamma's Caponata, 6
Mini White Pizzas, 260
Onion, Garlic & Brie
    Bruschetta, 163
✓Savory Stuffed Figs, 9
Shrimp on Rosemary Skewers, 7
Smoked Gouda & Bacon
    Potatoes, 161
Spicy Garlic Shrimp, 247
Stuffed Artichoke Bottoms, 8
Tapas Meatballs with Orange
    Glaze, 6

Snacks
Buffalo Ranch Popcorn, 13
Chocolate-Covered Bacon, 14
Gingerbread Caramel Crunch, 12
Island Vacation Party Mix, 293
Kids' Favorite Pumpkin Seeds, 9
Maple-Pecan Snack Mix, 253
Rosemary-Parmesan Popcorn, 12
✓Sweet-Hot Spiced Nuts, 272
Sweet-Tooth Popcorn, 12
✓Tex-Mex Popcorn, 13

Spreads
Bacon Blue Cheese Appetizer, 7
Cherry-Brandy Baked Brie, 249
Layered Pesto Cheese Spread, 248
Sun-Dried Tomato Hummus, 254

APPLES
Apple & Blackberry Pie, 106
Apple-Brined Chicken Thighs, 56
Apple Bran Muffins, 237
Apple Cinnamon Rolls, 85
✓Apple Nachos, 174
Apple Pie Dessert, 152
Chocolate Mint Apple Fondue, 133
Cranberry-Apple Chutney, 181
Crisscross Apple Crowns, 81
Five-Fruit Pie, 109
Party Caramel Apples, 175
Penny's Apple-Brown Sugar Coffee
    Cake, 215
Perfect Winter Salad, 162
Roast Pork with Apples & Onions, 286
Slow-Cooked Stuffed Apples, 131
✓Spiced Cran-Apple Brisket, 60
Sweet Spiced Caramel Apples, 120
Upside-Down Apple Pie, 181

APRICOTS
Apricot Almond Torte, 108
✓Apricot-Glazed Pork Tenderloin, 267
Apricot Sunshine Coffee Cake, 83
Apricot Turkey Pinwheels, 252
✓Curried Apricot Pork Chops, 148
Ham with Orange-Apricot Sauce, 59
Mom's Gingered Apple Salad, 22
Tenderloin with Cremini-Apricot
    Stuffing, 162

ARTICHOKES
Chicken Salad Caprese, 10
Artichoke Hearts Romano, 48
Stuffed Artichoke Bottoms, 8

AVOCADOS
Fish Tacos with Avocado Sauce, 73
Homemade Guacamole, 204
Open-Faced Chicken Avocado
    Burgers, 32

BACON & CANADIAN BACON
Bacon Baklava, 121
Bacon Blue Cheese Appetizer, 7
Bacon-Blue Cheese Stuffed
    Burgers, 169
Bacon-Cheese Stuffed Shells, 144
Bacon Cheeseburger Pizza, 61
Bacon Potato Waffles, 59
Bacon Scones, 81
Bacon-Wrapped Breadsticks, 260
Beef & Bacon Stroganoff, 71
Blue Cheese and Bacon Stuffed
    Mushrooms, 15
Chicken Wrapped in Bacon, 150
Chocolate-Covered Bacon, 14
✓Savory Stuffed Figs, 9
Smoked Gouda & Bacon Potatoes, 161

BANANAS
Banana Pineapple Sundaes, 120
Banana Rum Sundaes, 243
Chocolate Banana Cream Cake, 111
Chocolate Chip-Banana Belgian
    Waffles, 217
Hot Quick Banana Boats, 300
Pumpkin Banana Bread, 80

BARLEY *(see Rice & Barley)*

BARS & BROWNIES
Cheesecake Brownies, 99
✓Chocolate Toffee Delights, 98
Cranberry-Port Fudge Brownies, 98
Ginger Cranberry Bars, 97
✓Granola-to-Go Bars, 274
Raspberry Walnut Bars, 103

BASIL *(also see Pesto)*
Basil Buttered Beans, 42
Basil, Feta & Roasted Pepper
    Muffins, 230
Lemon-Basil Frozen Yogurt, 120

✓ Recipe includes Nutrition Facts and Diabetic Exchanges.

Tomato-Basil Baked Fish, 156
Verde Sauce, 291

BEANS
Basil Buttered Beans, 42
Bean & Barley Salad, 27
Camping Haystacks, 301
✓Corn, Rice and Bean Burritos, 280
Dad's Baked Beans, 211
Fabulous Green Beans, 234
Green Beans in Yellow Pepper
    Butter, 179
Julia's Green Beans &
    Mushrooms, 154
Louisiana Red Beans and Rice, 282
Minted Rice with Garbanzo
    Curry, 200
New England Baked Beans, 48
Okra and Butter Bean Stew, 167
Sesame Green Beans, 49
✓Spicy Black Bean Soup, 265
Sun-Dried Tomato Hummus, 254
Turkey White Bean Soup, 38

BEEF *(also see Ground Beef)*
Chili
    Tex-Mex Chili, 141
Main Dishes
    Baked Stew with Root
        Vegetables, 278
    Beef Roast au Poivre with
        Caramelized Onions, 72
    Beef Roast with Gravy, 208
    Cashew Curried Beef, 302
    Genrose's Stuffed Beef
        Tenderloin, 66
    Herbed Standing Rib Roast, 68
    Marinated Ribeyes, 298
    Marinated Veggie Beef Kabobs, 234
    Sesame-Pepper Flank Steak, 66
    Slow Cooker Beef Stroganoff, 62
    Slow Cooker Beef with Red
        Sauce, 70
    ✓Spiced Cran-Apple Brisket, 60
    Steak & New Potato Toss, 259
    Tenderloin with Cremini-Apricot
        Stuffing, 162
Salads
    Grilled Steak and Mushroom
        Salad, 25
    Greek Islands Steak Salad, 261
Sandwiches
    Deli Beef Heroes, 138
    Double-Cheese Beef Panini, 36

BEVERAGES *(also see Coffee)*
✓A.M. Rush Espresso Smoothie, 274
Lavender Lemonade, 203
✓Spiced Pineapple Cooler, 293
Summertime Cooler, 300

BISCUITS & SCONES
Bacon Scones, 81
Chive Biscuits, 80
Chocolate Biscuit Puffs, 83
Easy Parmesan Biscuits, 246
Italian Drop Biscuits, 86
Onion & Cheddar Biscuits, 157

BLACKBERRIES
Apple & Blackberry Pie, 106
Blackberry Cobbler, 235
Blackberry-Sauced Pork Chops, 252
Four-Berry Spinach Salad, 26

BLUEBERRIES
Blueberry Cream Dessert, 122
Blueberry Dream Pie, 114
Blueberry Fruit Dip, 252
Cocoa Meringues with Berries, 125
Five-Fruit Pie, 109
Four-Berry Spinach Salad, 26
✓Kids' Favorite Blueberry Muffins, 79
Luscious Blueberry Jam, 50
Maple-Pecan Snack Mix, 253
Orange-Berry Jam, 49

BREADS *(see Biscuits & Scones; Coffee
Cakes; Corn Bread & Cornmeal;
Doughnuts & Danish; Muffins; Quick
Breads; Pancakes, Waffles & French
Toast; Rolls & Breadsticks; Yeast Breads)*

BROCCOLI
✓Baked Broccolini, 51
✓Broccoli-Ham Macaroni, 264
Broccoli Salad, 155
Cranberry Broccoli Salad, 18
Greek Deli Kabobs, 248
Lemon Broccoli with Garlic, 195
✓Lime-Buttered Broccoli, 241
Mac 'n' Cheese Soup, 35

**BURRITOS, TACOS &
ENCHILADAS**
✓Corn, Rice and Bean Burritos, 280
Easy Enchiladas, 204
Fish Tacos with Avocado Sauce, 73
✓Halibut Soft Tacos, 270

Havarti Shrimp Quesadillas, 11
Presto Chicken Tacos, 281
✓Sammie's Breakfast Burritos, 275
Skillet Tacos, 287
Tacoritos, 57
Texas Pork Burritos, 63

CABBAGE *(also see Coleslaw)*
Fast & Fabulous Thai Chicken
    Salad, 255
Hearty Cabbage Soup, 258

CAKES & TORTES *(also see
Cheesecakes; Coffee Cakes; Cupcakes)*
Apricot Almond Torte, 108
Brittle Torte, 110
Cake Roll with Berries, 209
Candy Explosion Cake, 106
Chocolate Banana Cream Cake, 111
Chocolate Lover's Delight Cake, 115
Chocolate Raspberry Tunnel
    Cake, 112
Chocolate Toffee Cake, 115
Chocolate Truffle Cake, 108
Cream Puff Cake, 213
Creative Cake, 106
Lemon-Rosemary Layer Cake, 113
"Give Me S'more" Cake, 113
Raspberry Chocolate Torte, 109
Rhubarb Cake with Lemon
    Sauce, 110
Spiced Pudding Cake, 239
Traditional New Orleans King
    Cake, 165
Truffle Cake with Candy Cane
    Cream, 111
White Chocolate Raspberry Torte, 116

CANDIES
Candied Fruit Platter, 292
Caramel Corn with Nuts, 191
Cashew Brittle, 189
Chocolate-Covered Pretzels, 191
Chocolate Peanut Butter Candy, 293
Crispy Peanut Butter Balls, 102
✓Go Nuts! Coconut Caramels, 99
✓Green Mint Bark, 98
Homemade Marshmallows, 190
Pecan Caramels, 189
Pinwheel Mints, 95
Rich Peanut Clusters, 136
Triple Chocolate Fudge, 190
White Chocolate Raspberry
    Truffles, 101

✓ *Recipe includes Nutrition Facts and Diabetic Exchanges.*

CARAMEL
✓Apple Nachos, 174
Caramel Corn with Nuts, 191
Caramel-Pecan Monkey Bread, 89
Gingerbread Caramel Crunch, 12
✓Go Nuts! Coconut Caramels, 99
Party Caramel Apples, 175
Pecan Caramels, 189
Sweet Spiced Caramel Apples, 120

CARROTS
Carrot Salad, 199
Red Curry Carrot Soup, 30

CASSEROLES
Bacon-Cheese Stuffed Shells, 144
Baked Mac & Cheese, 65
Bistro Mac & Cheese, 65
Brie-and-Veggie Brunch Strata, 287
Cassoulet for Today, 279
Chiles Rellenos Casserole, 285
Cowboy Casserole, 149
Cream Cheese and Swiss Lasagna, 74
Easy Enchiladas, 204
Enchilada Lasagna, 282
Hamburger Noodle Bake, 149
Hearty Macaroni Casserole, 59
Hot Tamale Casserole, 70
Meatball Sub Casserole, 66
✓Mushroom Lasagna, 278
Mushroom Turkey Tetrazzini, 69
The Best Eggplant Parmesan, 145
Tuna Mac and Cheese Bake, 279
Wake Up! Breakfast Casserole, 143

CHEESE *(also see Cheesecakes)*
Appetizers & Snacks
Asparagus, Brie & Parma Ham
    Crostini, 8
Bacon Blue Cheese Appetizer, 7
Blue Cheese and Bacon Stuffed
    Mushrooms, 15
Cherry-Brandy Baked Brie, 249
Chicken Salad Caprese, 10
Greek Deli Kabobs, 248
Grilled Greek Crostini Topping, 14
Havarti Shrimp Quesadillas, 11
Hot Ham & Cheese Slices, 16
Layered Pesto Cheese Spread, 248
Mini White Pizzas, 260
Onion, Garlic & Brie
    Bruschetta, 163
Pretty Stuffed Spring Peas, 10
Rosemary-Parmesan Popcorn, 12

Seafood & Cream Cheese Stuffed
    Shells, 8
Stuffed Artichoke Bottoms, 8
Breads
Basil, Feta & Roasted Pepper
    Muffins, 230
Easy Parmesan Biscuits, 246
Monterey Ranch Bread, 78
Onion & Cheddar Biscuits, 157
Desserts
Blueberry Dream Pie, 114
Cheesecake Brownies, 99
Cream Puff Cake, 213
Layered Lemon Pies, 139
Pinwheel Mints, 95
Pumpkin Cheesecake Pie, 107
✓Sensational Tiramisu, 273
Strawberries & Cream Pie, 114
White Chocolate Raspberry
    Truffles, 101
Main Dishes
Bacon-Cheese Stuffed Shells, 144
Bacon Cheeseburger Pizza, 61
✓Baked Fish with Cheese Sauce, 74
Baked Mac & Cheese, 65
Bistro Mac & Cheese, 65
Brie-and-Veggie Brunch Strata, 287
✓Broccoli-Ham Macaroni, 264
Caprese Chicken with Bacon, 67
Chiles Rellenos Casserole, 285
Cream Cheese and Swiss
    Lasagna, 74
Hearty Macaroni Casserole, 59
Macaroni 'n' Cheese Pizza, 284
Mascarpone-Pesto Chicken
    Rolls, 55
Ranch Mac & Cheese, 64
Roadside Diner Cheeseburger
    Quiche, 54
The Best Eggplant Parmesan, 145
Tuna Mac and Cheese Bake, 279
Salads and Dressings
Cheddar 'n' Pea Tossed Salad, 19
Chunky Blue Cheese Dressing, 226
Creamy Cranberry Gelatin, 26
Gorgonzola-Pear Mesclun
    Salad, 179
Sandwiches
Bacon-Blue Cheese Stuffed
    Burgers, 169
Chipotle Cheeseburgers, 37
Double-Cheese Beef Panini, 36
Ham 'n' Swiss Envelopes, 30
Herb & Cheese-Stuffed Burgers, 33

✓Philly Cheese Fakes, 37
Tomato-Pesto Cheddar Melts, 35
Soups and Side Dish
Artichoke Hearts Romano, 48
Cheddar Potato Soup, 36
Cheesy Cauliflower Soup, 31
Mac 'n' Cheese Soup, 35
Tomato Tortellini Soup, 256

CHEESECAKES
Chocolate Raspberry Cheesecake, 227
Classic Cheesecake, 152
Coffee Toffee Cheesecake, 294
Lavender Brownie Cheesecake, 131
Magnolia Dream Cheesecake, 163
Ricotta Cheesecake, 123

CHERRIES
✓Black Cherry Sherbet, 297
✓Celestial Cherry Conserve, 44
Cherry-Berry Streusel Pie, 116
Cherry-Brandy Baked Brie, 249
Cherry Wild Rice Salad, 21
✓Dried Cherry Biscotti, 103
Hot Cherry Sauce, 123
Overnight Cherry Danish, 78
Perfect Winter Salad, 162

CHICKEN
Appetizers & Snacks
Chicken Salad Caprese, 10
Crispy Taco Wings, 247
Grilled Glazed Drummies, 7
Grilled Peach BBQ Chicken
    Wings, 216
Hot Wing Dip, 143
Sara's Summer Rolls, 280
Main Dishes
Apple-Brined Chicken Thighs, 56
BBQ Chicken Baked Potatoes, 62
Caprese Chicken with Bacon, 67
Cassoulet for Today, 279
✓Chicken & Vegetable Stir-Fry, 268
✓Chicken Continental, 68
Chicken Cordon Bleu Pizza, 259
Chicken Dijon & Couscous, 58
Chicken Dinner Packets, 150
✓Chicken Florentine Meatballs, 264
Chicken Korma, 201
Chicken Mole Ole, 60
Chicken Wrapped in Bacon, 150
Curried Chicken Shepherd's Pie, 58
✓Easy Chicken Potpie, 266
Easy Enchiladas, 204

✓ Recipe includes Nutrition Facts and Diabetic Exchanges.

✓Ginger Chicken, 56
Greek Chicken Pasta, 251
Grilled Tomatillo Chicken, 62
✓Herbed Roast Chicken, 69
Jamaica-Me-Crazy Chicken
    Tropicale, 61
Kielbasa Chicken Kabobs, 57
Mascarpone-Pesto Chicken Rolls, 55
Pad Thai Pizza, 250
Pistachio-Crusted Chicken with
    Garden Spinach, 72
Presto Chicken Tacos, 281
Southern Fried Chicken Strips, 54
✓Summertime Orzo &
    Chicken, 273
Sunday's Best Chicken, 70
Thai Portobello Chicken
    Stir-Fry, 303

Salads
Caribbean Chicken Caesar
    Salad, 221
✓Curried Chicken Salad, 267
Fast & Fabulous Thai Chicken
    Salad, 255
Garden Cobb Salad, 19
Poppy Seed Chicken Salad, 24
✓Southwest Chicken Salad, 250
Spiced-Up Chicken Salad, 22

Sandwiches
Open-Faced Chicken Avocado
    Burgers, 32
Spicy Chicken Lettuce Wraps, 31
Zippy Chicken Wraps, 36

Soups and Chili
Big-Batch Jambalaya, 167
Chicken Tortilla Chowder, 258
Gnocchi Chicken Minestrone, 34
30-Minute Chicken Noodle
    Soup, 257
White Chili, 286

CHILI
Rootin'-Tootin' Cincinnati Chili, 33
Tex-Mex Chili, 141
White Chili, 286

CILANTRO
Cilantro Pesto, 46
Salsa Verde, 246

CHOCOLATE
Bars & Brownies
Cheesecake Brownies, 99
✓Chocolate Toffee Delights, 98

Cranberry-Port Fudge Brownies, 98
Breads
Chocolate Biscuit Puffs, 83
Chocolate Chip-Banana Belgian
    Waffles, 217
Chocolate Cinnamon Rolls, 86
White Chocolate Berry Muffins, 89
Cakes & Cupcakes
Box-of-Chocolates Cupcakes, 117
Candy Explosion Cake, 106
Chocolate Banana Cream Cake, 111
Chocolate Lover's Delight Cake, 115
Chocolate Raspberry Tunnel
    Cake, 112
Chocolate-Strawberry Celebration
    Cake, 107
Chocolate Toffee Cake, 115
Chocolate Truffle Cake, 108
Eyes on You, 173
"Give Me S'more" Cake, 113
Green-Eyed Monster, 175
Orange You Spiky, 173
Purple People-Eater, 174
Raspberry Chocolate Torte, 109
White Chocolate Raspberry
    Torte, 116
Candies
Candied Fruit Platter, 292
Chocolate-Covered Pretzels, 191
Chocolate Peanut Butter Candy, 293
Crispy Peanut Butter Balls, 102
✓Green Mint Bark, 98
Rich Peanut Clusters, 136
Triple Chocolate Fudge, 190
White Chocolate Raspberry
    Truffles, 101
Cookies
Chocolate-Dipped Orange
    Cookies, 95
Chunky Orange Marmalade
    Cookies, 102
✓Cinnamon Chocolate
    Minties, 186
German Chocolate Thumbprints, 94
Mocha Logs, 93
No-Bake Cookie Balls, 95
✓Nutty Chocolate Batons, 183
✓Touch-of-Gold Christmas
    Trees, 187
✓White Chocolate-Almond Dipped
    Cookies, 100
Desserts
✓Chocolate Malt Desserts, 265
Chocolate Mint Apple Fondue, 133

Chocolate Mousse with Cranberry
    Sauce, 130
Chocolate Raspberry
    Cheesecake, 227
Cocoa Meringues with
    Berries, 125
Coffee Toffee Cheesecake, 294
Hot Quick Banana Boats, 300
Ladyfinger Ice Cream Cake, 170
Lavender Brownie Cheesecake, 131
Party Caramel Apples, 175
Peanut Butter Brownie Trifle, 140
Peanut Ice Cream Delight, 126
Sweet Spiced Caramel
    Apples, 120
Toffee-Crunch Coffee Sundaes, 120
Tuxedo Cream Dessert, 124
Pies
Strawberries & Cream Pie, 114
Strawberry Cream Pie, 153
Snacks and Beverages
✓A.M. Rush Espresso
    Smoothie, 274
✓Apple Nachos, 174
Chocolate-Covered Bacon, 14
Frothy Mexi-Mocha Coffee, 229

COCONUT
Can't Miss Coconut Custard
    Pie, 116
Coconut Almond Bombs, 92
✓Coconut Macaroons, 102
Coconut-Mango Mahi Mahi, 253
German Chocolate Thumbprints, 94
✓Go Nuts! Coconut Caramels, 99
Island Vacation Party Mix, 293

COFFEE
✓Cappuccino Granita, 294
Coffee Barbecue Sauce, 44
Coffee-Molasses Marinated Pork
    Chops, 295
Coffee-Nut Muffins, 295
Coffee Toffee Cheesecake, 294
Frothy Mexi-Mocha Coffee, 229
Mocha Logs, 93
Toffee-Crunch Coffee Sundaes, 120

COFFEE CAKES
Apricot Sunshine Coffee Cake, 83
✓Light Sour Cream Coffee Cake, 269
Penny's Apple-Brown Sugar Coffee
    Cake, 215
Sour Cream Coffee Cake, 82

✓ Recipe includes Nutrition Facts and Diabetic Exchanges.

COLESLAW
✓Camper's Coleslaw, 212
Horseradish Coleslaw, 24
Pineapple Coleslaw, 26
✓Tangy Ginger Slaw, 18

CONDIMENTS *(see Relishes &*
Pickles; Sauces & Seasonings)

COOKIES *(also see Bars & Brownies)*
Cutout Cookies
  ✓Daria's Best-Ever Sugar
    Cookies, 100
  ✓Extra-Special Cashew
    Crescents, 92
  Holiday Sugar Cookies, 184
  Linzer Cookies, 184
  Walnut Horn Cookies, 185
Drop Cookies
  Brazil Nut Cookies, 93
  Chunky Orange Marmalade
    Cookies, 102
  Coconut Almond Bombs, 92
  ✓Coconut Macaroons, 102
  Soft Lemon-Ginger Cookies, 96
Refrigerator Cookies
  Lemon Angel Wings, 183
Shaped Cookies
  Candy Cane Cookies, 186
  Chocolate-Dipped Orange
    Cookies, 95
  ✓Cinnamon Chocolate
    Minties, 186
  ✓Cuccidati, 101
  ✓Dried Cherry Biscotti, 103
  German Chocolate Thumbprints, 94
  Holiday Spritz, 94
  ✓Iced Anise Cookies, 197
  ✓Mini Cinnamon Roll Cookies, 97
  Mocha Logs, 93
  ✓Molasses Cookies with a Kick, 96
  No-Bake Cookie Balls, 95
  ✓Nutty Chocolate Batons, 183
  Pecan Goody Cups, 185
  Pecan Meltaways, 187
  ✓Touch-of-Gold Christmas
    Trees, 187
  ✓White Chocolate-Almond Dipped
    Cookies, 100

CORN
✓Corn, Rice and Bean Burritos, 280
Herbed Corn, 249
Honey Sweet Corn, 208

CORN BREAD & CORNMEAL
Corn Bread Salad, 155
✓Creamy Pumpkin Polenta, 50
Hot Tamale Casserole, 70
Sloppy Jose Supper, 68

CORNISH GAME HENS
Berry-Port Game Hens, 154
Honey-Glazed Hens with Fruit
  Stuffing, 242

CRANBERRIES
Chocolate Mousse with Cranberry
  Sauce, 130
Cranberry-Apple Chutney, 181
Cranberry Broccoli Salad, 18
Cranberry Pecan Stuffing, 180
Cranberry-Port Fudge Brownies, 98
Cranburgers with Sweet Potato
  Fries, 39
Creamy Cranberry Gelatin, 26
Ginger Cranberry Bars, 97
Pumpkin Cranberry Bread
  Pudding, 132
✓Spiced Cran-Apple Brisket, 60

CUCUMBERS
Cucumber Salad, 200
✓Italian Cucumber Salad, 23

CUPCAKES
Box-of-Chocolates Cupcakes, 117
Eyes on You, 173
Green-Eyed Monster, 175
Orange You Spiky, 173
Purple People-Eater, 174
Turkey Dinner Cupcakes, 178

DESSERTS *(also see specific kinds)*
✓Apple Nachos, 174
Apple Pie Dessert, 152
Bacon Baklava, 121
Blackberry Cobbler, 235
Blueberry Cream Dessert, 122
✓Chocolate Malt Desserts, 265
Chocolate Mint Apple Fondue, 133
Citrus Tartlets, 124
Cocoa Meringues with Berries, 125
French Cream with Sugared
  Grapes, 126
Honey-Orange Rice Pudding, 230
Hot Cherry Sauce, 123
Hot Quick Banana Boats, 300
Lemon Sorbet Torte, 130

Party Caramel Apples, 175
Pomegranate Poached Pears, 128
✓Pretty Pumpkin Wontons, 143
Pumpkin Cranberry Bread
  Pudding, 132
Pumpkin Dessert Bars, 142
Roasted Pears in Pecan Sauce, 129
✓Sensational Tiramisu, 273
Slow-Cooked Stuffed Apples, 131
Strawberry Malted Mousse Cups, 127
✓Summertime Fruit Cones, 125
Sweet Riesling Pears, 129
Sweet Spiced Caramel Apples, 120
Tuxedo Cream Dessert, 124

DOUGHNUTS & DANISH
First-Prize Doughnuts, 82
✓Old-Time Cake Doughnuts, 87
Overnight Cherry Danish, 78
Spanish Fritters, 78

EGGS
Brie-and-Veggie Brunch Strata, 287
Farmer's Country Breakfast, 299
Perfect Brunch Omelets, 283
Potato & Red Onion Frittata, 231
Rainbow Quiche, 285
Roadside Diner Cheeseburger
  Quiche, 54
✓Sammie's Breakfast Burritos, 275
Wake Up! Breakfast Casserole, 143

EGGPLANT
✓Mamma's Caponata, 6
The Best Eggplant Parmesan, 145

FIGS
✓Cuccidati, 101
✓Savory Stuffed Figs, 9

FISH & SEAFOOD
Appetizers & Snacks
  Crab Puffs, 161
  Crawfish Beignets with Cajun
    Dipping Sauce, 166
  Fiesta Shrimp Cocktail, 11
  Havarti Shrimp Quesadillas, 11
  Seafood & Cream Cheese Stuffed
    Shells, 8
  Shrimp on Rosemary Skewers, 7
  Spicy Garlic Shrimp, 247
Main Dishes
  ✓Baked Fish with Cheese Sauce, 74
  Campfire Trout Dinner, 300

✓ Recipe includes Nutrition Facts and Diabetic Exchanges.

✓Citrus Fish, 222
✓Citrus-Marinated Salmon, 271
Coconut-Mango Mahi Mahi, 253
Fish Tacos with Avocado Sauce, 73
Fish with Fennel, 67
✓Halibut Soft Tacos, 270
Honey-Lime Red Snapper, 251
Lemon Scallop Linguine, 150
Pasta Alla Puttanesca, 291
Scallops in Sage Cream, 246
✓Shrimp & Shiitake Stir-Fry with
　　Crispy Noodles, 75
✓Shrimp and Scallop
　　Couscous, 271
Shrimp Pad Thai, 303
Spicy Shrimp Kabobs, 260
Tomato-Basil Baked Fish, 156
Tuna Mac and Cheese Bake, 279
Salads & Sandwiches
　Fiesta Tuna Salad Sandwiches, 141
　Ginger Salmon Salad, 20
　✓Grilled Tuna Bibb Salads, 270
Soups and Stews
　Big-Batch Jambalaya, 167
　✓Salmon Bisque, 38
　Shrimp Gumbo, 165

FRUIT (*also see specific kinds*)
Berry Delicious Tart, 171
Blueberry Fruit Dip, 252
Candied Fruit Platter, 292
French Cream with Sugared
　　Grapes, 126
✓Fruit Salad in a Pineapple Boat, 170
✓Granola-to-Go Bars, 274
Honey-Glazed Hens with Fruit
　　Stuffing, 242
✓Polynesian Parfaits, 275
Pomegranate Jelly, 44
✓Summertime Fruit Cones, 125
Super Low-Fat Granola Cereal, 238
✓Tropical Fusion Salad with Spicy
　　Tortilla Ribbons, 268
Turkey & Fruit Salad, 261

GRILLED & BROILED
Appetizers
　Grilled Glazed Drummies, 7
　Grilled Greek Crostini Topping, 14
　Grilled Peach BBQ Chicken
　　　Wings, 216
　Havarti Shrimp Quesadillas, 11
　Onion, Garlic & Brie
　　　Bruschetta, 163

✓Savory Stuffed Figs, 9
Shrimp on Rosemary Skewers, 7
Dessert
　Hot Quick Banana Boats, 300
Main Dishes
　Campfire Trout Dinner, 300
　✓Citrus-Marinated Salmon, 271
　Coffee-Molasses Marinated Pork
　　　Chops, 295
　Fish Tacos with Avocado Sauce, 73
　Grilled Pork Chops, 233
　Grilled Tomatillo Chicken, 62
　✓Halibut Soft Tacos, 270
　Honey-Lime Red Snapper, 251
　Kielbasa Chicken Kabobs, 57
　Marinated Ribeyes, 298
　Marinated Veggie Beef Kabobs, 234
　Potato-Sausage Foil Packs, 299
　Sesame-Pepper Flank Steak, 66
　Spicy Shrimp Kabobs, 260
　Steak & New Potato Toss, 259
Sandwiches
　Bacon-Blue Cheese Stuffed
　　　Burgers, 169
　Chipotle Cheeseburgers, 37
　✓Grilled Stuffed Turkey
　　　Burgers, 269
　Grilled Vegetable Sandwiches, 137
　Grilled Veggie Tortilla Wraps, 34
　Herb & Cheese-Stuffed Burgers, 33
　✓Philly Cheese Fakes, 37
Side Dish & Salads
　Ginger Salmon Salad, 20
　Grilled Steak and Mushroom
　　　Salad, 25
　Grilled Sweet Onions, 299
　✓Grilled Tuna Bibb Salads, 270

GROUND BEEF
Appetizer
　Tapas Meatballs with Orange
　　　Glaze, 6
Main Dishes
　Bacon Cheeseburger Pizza, 61
　Beef & Bacon Stroganoff, 71
　Cowboy Casserole, 149
　Cream Cheese and Swiss
　　　Lasagna, 74
　Enchilada Lasagna, 282
　Greek Meat Loaves, 281
　Hamburger Noodle Bake, 149
　Hawaiian Beef Dish, 148
　Hearty Macaroni Casserole, 59
　Hot Tamale Casserole, 70

Italian Shepherd's Pies, 54
Macaroni 'n' Cheese Pizza, 284
Meatball Sub Casserole, 66
Ragu Bolognese, 290
Roadside Diner Cheeseburger
　　Quiche, 54
Skillet Tacos, 287
Sloppy Jose Supper, 68
Slow Cooker Tamale Pie, 286
Spaghetti and Meatballs with Garlic
　　Crumbs, 216
Tacoritos, 57
Salads
　Layered Taco Salad, 139
　Taco Salad, 254
Sandwiches
　Bacon-Blue Cheese Stuffed
　　　Burgers, 169
　Chipotle Cheeseburgers, 37
　Herb & Cheese-Stuffed Burgers, 33
　Quick Pizza Sandwiches, 155
Soups
　Hearty Cabbage Soup, 258
　Red Curry Carrot Soup, 30
　Rootin'-Tootin' Cincinnati Chili, 33

HAM & PROSCIUTTO
Asparagus, Brie & Parma Ham
　　Crostini, 8
Big-Batch Jambalaya, 167
✓Broccoli-Ham Macaroni, 264
Chicken Cordon Bleu Pizza, 259
Crunchy Potato Mounds, 137
Ham 'n' Swiss Envelopes, 30
Ham with Orange-Apricot Sauce, 59
Hot Ham & Cheese Slices, 16
Mac 'n' Cheese Soup, 35
Nectarine, Prosciutto & Endive
　　Salad, 23
Shortcut Split Pea Soup, 257
Turkey Saltimbocca, 151
Tuscan Pork Medallions, 156

HONEY
Honey-Glazed Hens with Fruit
　　Stuffing, 242
Honey-Lime Red Snapper, 251
Honey-Mustard Turkey Salad, 20
Honey-Orange Rice Pudding, 230
Honey Sweet Corn, 208
✓Honey-Thyme Butternut
　　Squash, 180
Sunflower Seed & Honey Wheat
　　Bread, 225

✓ *Recipe includes Nutrition Facts and Diabetic Exchanges.*

ICE CREAM, SHERBET & SORBET
Banana Pineapple Sundaes, 120
Banana Rum Sundaes, 243
✓Black Cherry Sherbet, 297
Candy Bar Ice Cream, 132
✓Cantaloupe Sorbet, 297
✓Cappuccino Granita, 294
Grilled Pineapple Butterscotch
　Sundaes, 122
Ladyfinger Ice Cream Cake, 170
Lemon-Basil Frozen Yogurt, 120
Mexican Ice Cream, 121
Peach Gelato, 296
Peanut Ice Cream Delight, 126
Pear Sorbet, 128
Praline Crunch Ice Cream, 133
Strawberry-Rhubarb Ice Cream, 297
Toffee-Crunch Coffee Sundaes, 120
Watermelon Sorbet, 127

JAMS & JELLIES
✓Celestial Cherry Conserve, 44
Luscious Blueberry Jam, 50
Orange-Berry Jam, 49
Pear Marmalade, 51
Pomegranate Jelly, 44
Strawberry-Kiwi Jam, 50

LEMON & LIME
✓Citrus-Marinated Salmon, 271
Citrus Tartlets, 124
Florida Citrus Meringue Pie, 223
Honey-Lime Red Snapper, 251
Lavender Lemonade, 203
Layered Lemon Pies, 139
Lemon Angel Wings, 183
Lemon Broccoli with Garlic, 195
Lemon Delight Trifle, 140
Lemon Scallop Linguine, 150
Lemon Sorbet Torte, 130
Lemon-Basil Frozen Yogurt, 120
Lemon-Rosemary Layer Cake, 113
Lemony Brussels Sprouts, 255
✓Lime-Buttered Broccoli, 241
Rhubarb Cake with Lemon Sauce, 110
Soft Lemon-Ginger Cookies, 96
✓Summer Salad with Lemon
　Vinaigrette, 142

MARSHMALLOWS & MARSHMALLOW CREME
✓Apple Nachos, 174
Eyes on You, 173
Green-Eyed Monster, 175

Homemade Marshmallows, 190
Hot Quick Banana Boats, 300
Orange You Spiky, 173
Purple People-Eater, 174
Triple Chocolate Fudge, 190

MEAT LOAVES & MEATBALLS
✓Chicken Florentine Meatballs, 264
Greek Meat Loaves, 281
Spaghetti and Meatballs with Garlic
　Crumbs, 216
Tapas Meatballs with Orange Glaze, 6

MEAT PIES
Curried Chicken Shepherd's Pie, 58
✓Easy Chicken Potpie, 266
Italian Shepherd's Pies, 54
Roadside Diner Cheeseburger
　Quiche, 54

MELON
✓Cantaloupe Sorbet, 297
Watermelon Sorbet, 127

MUFFINS
Apple Bran Muffins, 237
Basil, Feta & Roasted Pepper
　Muffins, 230
Coffee-Nut Muffins, 295
✓Kids' Favorite Blueberry Muffins, 79
✓Mini Sweet Potato Muffins, 274
White Chocolate Berry Muffins, 89

MUSHROOMS
Beef & Bacon Stroganoff, 71
Blue Cheese and Bacon Stuffed
　Mushrooms, 15
Genrose's Stuffed Beef Tenderloin, 66
Grilled Steak and Mushroom
　Salad, 25
Havarti Shrimp Quesadillas, 11
Hot Ham & Cheese Slices, 16
Julia's Green Beans & Mushrooms, 154
✓Mushroom Lasagna, 278
✓Mushroom Primavera Pasta
　Sauce, 268
Mushroom Turkey Tetrazzini, 69
✓Philly Cheese Fakes, 37
Slow Cooker Beef Stroganoff, 62
✓Shrimp & Shiitake Stir-Fry with
　Crispy Noodles, 75
Tenderloin with Cremini-Apricot
　Stuffing, 162
Thai Portobello Chicken Stir-Fry, 303

NUTS & PEANUT BUTTER
Appetizers & Snacks
Maple-Pecan Snack Mix, 253
✓Sweet-Hot Spiced Nuts, 272
Breads
Almond-Filled Butterhorns, 88
Caramel-Pecan Monkey Bread, 89
Coffee-Nut Muffins, 295
Nut and Poppy Seed Rolls, 80
Candies
Caramel Corn with Nuts, 191
Cashew Brittle, 189
Chocolate Peanut Butter
　Candy, 293
Crispy Peanut Butter Balls, 102
✓Go Nuts! Coconut Caramels, 99
Pecan Caramels, 189
Rich Peanut Clusters, 136
Cookies & Bars
Brazil Nut Cookies, 93
Coconut Almond Bombs, 92
✓Cuccidati, 101
✓Extra-Special Cashew
　Crescents, 92
✓Granola-to-Go Bars, 274
✓Nutty Chocolate Batons, 183
Pecan Goody Cups, 185
Pecan Meltaways, 187
Raspberry Walnut Bars, 103
✓Touch-of-Gold Christmas
　Trees, 187
Walnut Horn Cookies, 185
✓White Chocolate-Almond
　Dipped Cookies, 100
Desserts
Apricot Almond Torte, 108
Peanut Butter Brownie Trifle, 140
Peanut Ice Cream Delight, 126
Praline Crunch Ice Cream, 133
Roasted Pears in Pecan
　Sauce, 129
Main Dishes
✓Almond-Crusted Pork Loin, 272
Cashew Curried Beef, 302
Pistachio-Crusted Chicken with
　Garden Spinach, 72
Side Dishes & Condiment
Almond Rice Pilaf, 49
Cranberry Pecan Stuffing, 180
✓Nutty Wild Rice, 272
Peanut Butter Dipping Sauce, 303
Soup & Salad
Cream of Walnut Soup, 242
Dijon-Walnut Spinach Salad, 248

✓ Recipe includes Nutrition Facts and Diabetic Exchanges.

OATS
✓Granola-to-Go Bars, 274
Super Low-Fat Granola Cereal, 238

OLIVES
Black & Green Olive Pesto, 47
Greek Chicken Pasta, 251
Greek Islands Steak Salad, 261
Greek Meat Loaves, 281

ONIONS & CHIVES
Beef Roast au Poivre with
    Caramelized Onions, 72
Chive Biscuits, 80
French Onion Soup, 256
Grilled Sweet Onions, 299
Onion & Cheddar Biscuits, 157
Onion, Garlic & Brie Bruschetta, 163
Potato & Red Onion Frittata, 231
Roast Pork with Apples & Onions, 286

ORANGE & NECTARINE
Chocolate-Dipped Orange Cookies, 95
Chunky Orange Marmalade
    Cookies, 102
✓Citrus-Marinated Salmon, 271
Citrus Tartlets, 124
Florida Citrus Meringue Pie, 223
Ham with Orange-Apricot Sauce, 59
Honey-Orange Rice Pudding, 230
Nectarine, Prosciutto & Endive
    Salad, 23
Orange-Berry Jam, 49
Tapas Meatballs with Orange Glaze, 6
Upside-Down Orange French
    Toast, 222

**PANCAKES, WAFFLES &
FRENCH TOAST**
Bacon Potato Waffles, 59
Chocolate Chip-Banana Belgian
    Waffles, 217
Pumpkin Pancakes with Cinnamon
    Brown Butter, 73
Upside-Down Orange French
    Toast, 222

PASTA & NOODLES
Appetizers
    Seafood & Cream Cheese Stuffed
        Shells, 8
Main Dishes
    Bacon-Cheese Stuffed Shells, 144
    Baked Mac & Cheese, 65

Balsamic Pork Scallopine, 144
Beef & Bacon Stroganoff, 71
Bistro Mac & Cheese, 65
✓Broccoli-Ham Macaroni, 264
Chicken Dijon & Couscous, 58
Cream Cheese and Swiss Lasagna, 74
Creamy Pasta Primavera, 280
Enchilada Lasagna, 282
Fire Island Ziti, 55
Greek Chicken Pasta, 251
Hamburger Noodle Bake, 149
Hearty Macaroni Casserole, 59
Lemon Scallop Linguine, 150
Macaroni 'n' Cheese Pizza, 284
✓Mushroom Lasagna, 278
✓Mushroom Primavera Pasta
    Sauce, 268
One-Skillet Pasta, 71
Pasta Alla Puttanesca, 291
Ragu Bolognese, 290
Ranch Mac & Cheese, 64
✓Shrimp and Scallop Couscous, 271
Slow Cooker Beef Stroganoff, 62
Spaghetti and Meatballs with Garlic
    Crumbs, 216
✓Summertime Orzo & Chicken, 273
Tuna Mac and Cheese Bake, 279
Verde Sauce, 291
Soups and Chili
    Gnocchi Chicken Minestrone, 34
    Hearty Meatless Minestrone, 226
    Mac 'n' Cheese Soup, 35
    Red Curry Carrot Soup, 30
    Rootin'-Tootin' Cincinnati Chili, 33
    30-Minute Chicken Noodle
        Soup, 257
    Tomato Tortellini Soup, 256

PEACHES
Grilled Peach BBQ Chicken
    Wings, 216
Magnolia Dream Cheesecake, 163
✓Peach Chutney, 42
Peach Gelato, 296
Streusel Peach Pie, 112
Tossed Salad with Peaches, 25

PEARS
Gorgonzola-Pear Mesclun Salad, 179
Pear Marmalade, 51
Pear Sorbet, 128
Pomegranate Poached Pears, 128
Roasted Pears in Pecan Sauce, 129
Sweet Riesling Pears, 129

PEAS
Cheddar 'n' Pea Tossed Salad, 19
Cherry Wild Rice Salad, 21
Poppy Seed Chicken Salad, 24
Pretty Stuffed Spring Peas, 10
Shortcut Split Pea Soup, 257

PEPPERS & CHILIES
Basil, Feta & Roasted Pepper
    Muffins, 230
Chiles Rellenos Casserole, 285
Green Beans in Yellow Pepper
    Butter, 179
Poblano Pesto, 47
Rainbow Pepper Medley, 136

PESTO
Black & Green Olive Pesto, 47
Cilantro Pesto, 46
Classic Pesto, 46
Layered Pesto Cheese Spread, 248
Mascarpone-Pesto Chicken
    Rolls, 55
Pesto Breadsticks, 291
Poblano Pesto, 47
Tomato-Pesto Cheddar Melts, 35

PIES & TARTS
Apple & Blackberry Pie, 106
Berry Delicious Tart, 171
Blueberry Dream Pie, 114
Can't Miss Coconut Custard
    Pie, 116
Cherry-Berry Streusel Pie, 116
Five-Fruit Pie, 109
Florida Citrus Meringue Pie, 223
Layered Lemon Pies, 139
Pumpkin Cheesecake Pie, 107
Strawberries & Cream Pie, 114
Strawberry Cream Pie, 153
✓Strawberry-Rhubarb Meringue
    Pie, 266
Streusel Peach Pie, 112
Upside-Down Apple Pie, 181

PINEAPPLE
Banana Pineapple Sundaes, 120
✓Fruit Salad in a Pineapple Boat, 170
Grilled Pineapple Butterscotch
    Sundaes, 122
Hawaiian Beef Dish, 148
Island Vacation Party Mix, 293
Pineapple Coleslaw, 26
✓Spiced Pineapple Cooler, 293

✓ *Recipe includes Nutrition Facts and Diabetic Exchanges.*

PIZZAS
Bacon Cheeseburger Pizza, 61
Chicken Cordon Bleu Pizza, 259
Macaroni 'n' Cheese Pizza, 284
Mini White Pizzas, 260
Pad Thai Pizza, 250

POPCORN & PRETZELS
Buffalo Ranch Popcorn, 13
Caramel Corn with Nuts, 191
Chocolate-Covered Pretzels, 191
Gingerbread Caramel Crunch, 12
Rosemary-Parmesan Popcorn, 12
Sweet-Tooth Popcorn, 12
✓Tex-Mex Popcorn, 13

PORK *(also see Bacon & Canadian Bacon; Ham & Prosciutto; Sausage & Pepperoni)*
✓Almond-Crusted Pork Loin, 272
✓Apricot-Glazed Pork Tenderloin, 267
Balsamic Pork Scallopine, 144
Barbecued Pork Sandwiches, 212
Blackberry-Sauced Pork Chops, 252
Coffee-Molasses Marinated Pork Chops, 295
✓Curried Apricot Pork Chops, 148
Grilled Pork Chops, 233
Italian Pork Stew, 284
Ragu Bolognese, 290
Roast Pork with Apples & Onions, 286
Sweet and Spicy Jerk Ribs, 63
✓Tangy Pulled Pork Sandwiches, 266
Texas Pork Burritos, 63
Tuscan Pork Medallions, 156

POTATOES *(also see Sweet Potatoes)*
Main Dishes
 Bacon Potato Waffles, 59
 BBQ Chicken Baked Potatoes, 62
 Chicken Dinner Packets, 150
 Cowboy Casserole, 149
 Farmer's Country Breakfast, 299
 Potato & Red Onion Frittata, 231
 Potato-Sausage Foil Packs, 299
 Steak & New Potato Toss, 259
 Wake Up! Breakfast Casserole, 143
Salads & Soup
 Cheddar Potato Soup, 36
 Greek Potato Salad, 21
 ✓Grilled Potato & Arugula Salad, 169
 Tangy Potato Salad, 27
 Three-Potato Salad, 18

Snacks
 Crunchy Potato Mounds, 137
 Smoked Gouda & Bacon Potatoes, 161

PUDDING, MOUSSE & CUSTARD
Chocolate Mousse with Cranberry Sauce, 130
Giant Flan, 205
Homemade Chocolate Pudding, 153

PUMPKIN & PUMPKIN SEEDS
✓Creamy Pumpkin Polenta, 50
✓Kids' Favorite Pumpkin Seeds, 9
✓Pretty Pumpkin Wontons, 143
Pumpkin Banana Bread, 80
Pumpkin Cheesecake Pie, 107
Pumpkin Cranberry Bread Pudding, 132
Pumpkin Dessert Bars, 142
Pumpkin-Filled Crescent Rolls, 136
Pumpkin Pancakes with Cinnamon Brown Butter, 73

QUICK BREADS
Crisscross Apple Crowns, 81
Herbed Bread Slices, 86
Homemade Croutons, 42
✓Homemade Tortillas, 79
Monterey Ranch Bread, 78
Pumpkin Banana Bread, 80

RASPBERRIES
Cherry-Berry Streusel Pie, 116
Chocolate Raspberry Cheesecake, 227
Chocolate Raspberry Tunnel Cake, 112
Cocoa Meringues with Berries, 125
Five-Fruit Pie, 109
Four-Berry Spinach Salad, 26
Linzer Cookies, 184
Orange-Berry Jam, 49
Raspberry Chocolate Torte, 109
Raspberry Walnut Bars, 103
White Chocolate Berry Muffins, 89
White Chocolate Raspberry Torte, 116
White Chocolate Raspberry Truffles, 101

RELISHES & PICKLES
✓Spiced Pickled Beets, 43
✓Strawberry Relish, 43
✓Zucchini Pickles, 45
Zucchini Relish, 207

RHUBARB
Five-Fruit Pie, 109
Lemon Sorbet Torte, 130
Rhubarb Cake with Lemon Sauce, 110
Strawberry-Rhubarb Ice Cream, 297
✓Strawberry-Rhubarb Meringue Pie, 266

RICE & BARLEY
Almond Rice Pilaf, 49
Bean & Barley Salad, 27
Cherry Wild Rice Salad, 21
✓Corn, Rice and Bean Burritos, 280
Honey-Orange Rice Pudding, 230
Louisiana Red Beans and Rice, 282
Minted Rice with Garbanzo Curry, 200
Mom's Fried Rice, 45
✓Nutty Wild Rice, 272
Veggie Rice Saute, 156
Wild Rice and Barley Soup Mix, 32

ROLLS & BREADSTICKS
Almond-Filled Butterhorns, 88
Apple Cinnamon Rolls, 85
Bacon-Wrapped Breadsticks, 260
✓Butterhorns, 238
Chocolate Cinnamon Rolls, 86
Little Snail Rolls, 87
Nut and Poppy Seed Rolls, 80
Pesto Breadsticks, 291
Pumpkin-Filled Crescent Rolls, 136

SALADS *(also see Coleslaw)*
Fruit & Gelatin Salads
 Creamy Cranberry Gelatin, 26
 ✓Fruit Salad in a Pineapple Boat, 170
 Mom's Gingered Apple Salad, 22
Green Salads
 Cheddar 'n' Pea Tossed Salad, 19
 Dijon-Walnut Spinach Salad, 248
 Four-Berry Spinach Salad, 26
 Gorgonzola-Pear Mesclun Salad, 179
 Nectarine, Prosciutto & Endive Salad, 23
 Perfect Winter Salad, 162
 ✓Summer Salad with Lemon Vinaigrette, 142
 ✓Tomato Tossed Salad, 24
 Tossed Salad with Peaches, 25
Main-Dish Salads
 Caribbean Chicken Caesar Salad, 221
 ✓Curried Chicken Salad, 267

✓ Recipe includes Nutrition Facts and Diabetic Exchanges.

Fast & Fabulous Thai Chicken
    Salad, 255
Garden Cobb Salad, 19
Ginger Salmon Salad, 20
Greek Islands Steak Salad, 261
Grilled Steak and Mushroom
    Salad, 25
✓Grilled Tuna Bibb Salads, 270
Honey-Mustard Turkey Salad, 20
Layered Taco Salad, 139
Poppy Seed Chicken Salad, 24
✓Southwest Chicken Salad, 250
Spiced-Up Chicken Salad, 22
Taco Salad, 254
Turkey & Fruit Salad, 261

Potato Salads
Greek Potato Salad, 21
✓Grilled Potato & Arugula
    Salad, 169
Tangy Potato Salad, 27
Three-Potato Salad, 18

Rice & Barley Salads
Bean & Barley Salad, 27
Cherry Wild Rice Salad, 21

Vegetable Salads
Broccoli Salad, 155
Carrot Salad, 199
Corn Bread Salad, 155
Cranberry Broccoli Salad, 18
Cucumber Salad, 200
Easy Garden Tomatoes, 171
✓Italian Cucumber Salad, 23
✓Pickled Veggie Salad, 138
Rainbow Pepper Medley, 136
Roasted Vegetable Salad, 140
✓Tropical Fusion Salad with Spicy
    Tortilla Ribbons, 268

SANDWICHES
Cold Sandwiches
Deli Beef Heroes, 138
Fiesta Tuna Salad Sandwiches, 141
✓Southwest Chicken Salad, 250
Turkey Salad Croissants, 30

Hot Sandwiches
Bacon-Blue Cheese Stuffed
    Burgers, 169
Barbecued Pork Sandwiches, 212
Bayou Burgers with Spicy
    Remoulade, 166
Chipotle Cheeseburgers, 37
Cranburgers with Sweet Potato
    Fries, 39
Double-Cheese Beef Panini, 36

✓Grilled Stuffed Turkey
    Burgers, 269
Grilled Vegetable Sandwiches, 137
Ham 'n' Swiss Envelopes, 30
Herb & Cheese-Stuffed Burgers, 33
Italian Sausage Grinders, 145
Open-Faced Chicken Avocado
    Burgers, 32
✓Philly Cheese Fakes, 37
Quick Pizza Sandwiches, 155
Spicy Chicken Lettuce Wraps, 31
✓Tangy Pulled Pork Sandwiches, 266
Tomato-Pesto Cheddar Melts, 35
Turkey Dijon Melts, 38
Zippy Chicken Wraps, 36

SAUCES & SEASONINGS
(also see Pesto)
Chunky Blue Cheese Dressing, 226
Coffee Barbecue Sauce, 44
Cranberry-Apple Chutney, 181
Curry Powder, 199
Foolproof Gravy, 51
✓Peach Chutney, 42
Peanut Butter Dipping Sauce, 303

SAUSAGE & PEPPERONI
Bayou Burgers with Spicy
    Remoulade, 166
Cream Cheese and Swiss Lasagna, 74
Farmer's Country Breakfast, 299
Fire Island Ziti, 55
Greek Deli Kabobs, 248
Italian Sausage Grinders, 145
Kielbasa Chicken Kabobs, 57
Okra and Butter Bean Stew, 167
Tacoritos, 57
Wake Up! Breakfast Casserole, 143

SEAFOOD *(see Fish & Seafood)*

SIDE DISHES *(also see Relishes &*
Pickles; Salads)
Baked Beans
    Dad's Baked Beans, 211
    New England Baked Beans, 48
Green Beans
    Basil Buttered Beans, 42
    Fabulous Green Beans, 234
    Green Beans in Yellow Pepper
        Butter, 179
    Julia's Green Beans &
        Mushrooms, 154
    Sesame Green Beans, 49

Miscellaneous
Artichoke Hearts Romano, 48
Cranberry Pecan Stuffing, 180
✓Creamy Pumpkin Polenta, 50
Rice
Almond Rice Pilaf, 49
Minted Rice with Garbanzo
    Curry, 200
Mom's Fried Rice, 45
✓Nutty Wild Rice, 272
Veggie Rice Saute, 156
Vegetables
✓Baked Broccolini, 51
Grilled Sweet Onions, 299
Herbed Corn, 249
✓Honey-Thyme Butternut
    Squash, 180
Lemon Broccoli with Garlic, 195
✓Lime-Buttered Broccoli, 241
✓Roasted Harvest Vegetables, 177
Twice-Baked Sweet Potatoes, 151

SLOW COOKER RECIPES
Beef Roast with Gravy, 208
Cheesy Cauliflower Soup, 31
Chicken Mole Ole, 60
Hot Wing Dip, 143
Jamaica-Me-Crazy Chicken
    Tropicale, 61
Louisiana Red Beans and Rice, 282
Pumpkin Cranberry Bread
    Pudding, 132
Rich Peanut Clusters, 136
Slow-Cooked Stuffed Apples, 131
Slow Cooker Beef Stroganoff, 62
Slow Cooker Beef with Red Sauce, 70
Slow Cooker Tamale Pie, 286
✓Spiced Cran-Apple Brisket, 60
Sweet and Spicy Jerk Ribs, 63
✓Tangy Pulled Pork Sandwiches, 266
Texas Pork Burritos, 63
Tex-Mex Chili, 141
Turkey White Bean Soup, 38
White Chili, 286

SOUPS *(also see Chili; Stews)*
Cheddar Potato Soup, 36
Cheesy Cauliflower Soup, 31
Chicken Tortilla Chowder, 258
Cream of Walnut Soup, 242
Creamy Butternut Squash Soup, 157
French Onion Soup, 256
Gnocchi Chicken Minestrone, 34
Hearty Cabbage Soup, 258

✓ *Recipe includes Nutrition Facts and Diabetic Exchanges.*

SOUPS (continued)
Hearty Meatless Minestrone, 226
Mac 'n' Cheese Soup, 35
Red Curry Carrot Soup, 30
✓Salmon Bisque, 38
Shortcut Split Pea Soup, 257
✓Spicy Black Bean Soup, 265
30-Minute Chicken Noodle Soup, 257
Tomato Tortellini Soup, 256
Turkey White Bean Soup, 38
Wild Rice and Barley Soup Mix, 32

SPINACH & ARUGULA
✓Chicken Florentine Meatballs, 264
Dijon-Walnut Spinach Salad, 248
Four-Berry Spinach Salad, 26
✓Grilled Potato & Arugula Salad, 169
Pistachio-Crusted Chicken with
    Garden Spinach, 72
Poppy Seed Chicken Salad, 24

SQUASH & ZUCCHINI
Creamy Butternut Squash Soup, 157
✓Honey-Thyme Butternut
    Squash, 180
✓Zucchini Pickles, 45
Zucchini Relish, 207

STEWS
Baked Stew with Root Vegetables, 278
Big-Batch Jambalaya, 167
Italian Pork Stew, 284
✓Moroccan Vegetarian Stew, 39
Okra and Butter Bean Stew, 167
Shrimp Gumbo, 165

STRAWBERRIES
Berry-Port Game Hens, 154
Cake Roll with Berries, 209
Chocolate-Strawberry Celebration
    Cake, 107
Creative Cake, 106
Five-Fruit Pie, 109
Four-Berry Spinach Salad, 26
Lemon Sorbet Torte, 130
Poppy Seed Chicken Salad, 24
Strawberries & Cream Pie, 114
Strawberry Cream Pie, 153
Strawberry Crumble Parfaits, 127
Strawberry-Kiwi Jam, 50

Strawberry Malted Mousse Cups, 127
✓Strawberry Relish, 43
Strawberry-Rhubarb Ice Cream, 297
✓Strawberry-Rhubarb Meringue
    Pie, 266
Tuxedo Cream Dessert, 124

STUFFING & DRESSING
Cranberry Pecan Stuffing, 180
Honey-Glazed Hens with Fruit
    Stuffing, 242
Tenderloin with Cremini-Apricot
    Stuffing, 162

SWEET POTATOES
Cranburgers with Sweet Potato
    Fries, 39
✓Grilled Potato & Arugula Salad, 169
✓Mini Sweet Potato Muffins, 274
Twice-Baked Sweet Potatoes, 151

TOMATILLOS
Chicken Mole Ole, 60
Grilled Tomatillo Chicken, 62
Salsa Verde, 246

TOMATOES
Caprese Chicken with Bacon, 67
Chicken Salad Caprese, 10
Easy Garden Tomatoes, 171
Fire Island Ziti, 55
Fire-Roasted Tomato Salsa, 10
Grilled Greek Crostini Topping, 14
Slow Cooker Beef with Red Sauce, 70
Sun-Dried Tomato Hummus, 254
Tomato-Basil Baked Fish, 156
Tomato-Pesto Cheddar Melts, 35
Tomato Tortellini Soup, 256
✓Tomato Tossed Salad, 24

TRIFLES & PARFAITS
Lemon Delight Trifle, 140
Peanut Butter Brownie Trifle, 140
✓Polynesian Parfaits, 275
Strawberry Crumble Parfaits, 127

TURKEY & TURKEY SAUSAGE
Apricot Turkey Pinwheels, 252
Cassoulet for Today, 279
Champagne-Basted Turkey, 177

Cranburgers with Sweet Potato
    Fries, 39
Honey-Mustard Turkey Salad, 20
✓Grilled Stuffed Turkey Burgers, 269
Italian Christmas Turkey, 196
Louisiana Red Beans and Rice, 282
Maui-Inspired Turkey Breast Roll, 74
Mushroom Turkey Tetrazzini, 69
One-Skillet Pasta, 71
Potato-Sausage Foil Packs, 299
✓Sammie's Breakfast Burritos, 275
Turkey Dijon Melts, 38
Turkey Salad Croissants, 30
Turkey Saltimbocca, 151
Turkey White Bean Soup, 38

VEGETABLES (also see specific kinds)
Asparagus, Brie & Parma Ham
    Crostini, 8
Baked Stew with Root Vegetables, 278
Brie-and-Veggie Brunch Strata, 287
Cheesy Cauliflower Soup, 31
✓Chicken & Vegetable Stir-Fry, 268
Creamy Pasta Primavera, 280
Grilled Vegetable Sandwiches, 137
Grilled Veggie Tortilla Wraps, 34
Hearty Meatless Minestrone, 226
Lemony Brussels Sprouts, 255
Marinated Veggie Beef Kabobs, 234
✓Moroccan Vegetarian Stew, 39
Okra and Butter Bean Stew, 167
Perfect Brunch Omelets, 283
✓Pickled Veggie Salad, 138
Rainbow Quiche, 285
✓Roasted Harvest Vegetables, 177
Roasted Vegetable Salad, 140
Sara's Summer Rolls, 280
✓Spiced Pickled Beets, 43
Veggie Rice Saute, 156

YEAST BREADS
Braided Wreath Bread, 84
Caramel-Pecan Monkey Bread, 89
Christmas Wreath Bread, 88
✓Everything Bread, 178
✓French Loaves, 83
✓Mom's Italian Bread, 196
Sunflower Seed & Honey Wheat
    Bread, 225
Toasted Sunflower Bread, 84

✓ Recipe includes Nutrition Facts and Diabetic Exchanges.

Alphabetical Recipe Index

This handy index lists every recipe in alphabetical order so you can easily find your favorites.

A

✓A.M. Rush Espresso Smoothie, 274
✓Almond-Crusted Pork Loin, 272
Almond-Filled Butterhorns, 88
Almond Rice Pilaf, 49
Apple & Blackberry Pie, 106
Apple Bran Muffins, 237
Apple-Brined Chicken Thighs, 56
Apple Cinnamon Rolls, 85
✓Apple Nachos, 174
Apple Pie Dessert, 152
Apricot Almond Torte, 108
✓Apricot-Glazed Pork Tenderloin, 267
Apricot Sunshine Coffee Cake, 83
Apricot Turkey Pinwheels, 252
Artichoke Hearts Romano, 48
Asparagus, Brie & Parma Ham
    Crostini, 8

B

Bacon Baklava, 121
Bacon Blue Cheese Appetizer, 7
Bacon-Blue Cheese Stuffed
    Burgers, 169
Bacon-Cheese Stuffed Shells, 144
Bacon Cheeseburger Pizza, 61
Bacon Potato Waffles, 59
Bacon Scones, 81
Bacon-Wrapped Breadsticks, 260
✓Baked Broccolini, 51
✓Baked Fish with Cheese Sauce, 74
Baked Mac & Cheese, 65
Baked Stew with Root Vegetables, 278
Balsamic Pork Scallopine, 144
Banana Pineapple Sundaes, 120
Banana Rum Sundaes, 243
Barbecued Pork Sandwiches, 212
Basil Buttered Beans, 42
Basil, Feta & Roasted Pepper
    Muffins, 230
Bayou Burgers with Spicy
    Remoulade, 166
BBQ Chicken Baked Potatoes, 62
Bean & Barley Salad, 27
Beef & Bacon Stroganoff, 71
Beef Roast au Poivre with Caramelized
    Onions, 72
Beef Roast with Gravy, 208
Berry Delicious Tart, 171

Berry-Port Game Hens, 154
Big-Batch Jambalaya, 167
Bistro Mac & Cheese, 65
Black & Green Olive Pesto, 47
✓Black Cherry Sherbet, 297
Blackberry Cobbler, 235
Blackberry-Sauced Pork Chops, 252
Blue Cheese and Bacon Stuffed
    Mushrooms, 15
Blueberry Cream Dessert, 122
Blueberry Dream Pie, 114
Blueberry Fruit Dip, 252
Box-of-Chocolates Cupcakes, 117
Braided Wreath Bread, 84
Brazil Nut Cookies, 93
Brie-and-Veggie Brunch Strata, 287
Brittle Torte, 110
✓Broccoli-Ham Macaroni, 264
Broccoli Salad, 155
Buffalo Ranch Popcorn, 13
✓Butterhorns, 238

C

Cake Roll with Berries, 209
✓Camper's Coleslaw, 212
Campfire Trout Dinner, 300
Camping Haystacks, 301
Candied Fruit Platter, 292
Candy Bar Ice Cream, 132
Candy Cane Cookies, 186
Candy Explosion Cake, 106
Can't Miss Coconut Custard Pie, 116
✓Cantaloupe Sorbet, 297
✓Cappuccino Granita, 294
Caprese Chicken with Bacon, 67
Caramel Corn with Nuts, 191
Caramel-Pecan Monkey Bread, 89
Caribbean Chicken Caesar Salad, 221
Carrot Salad, 199
Cashew Brittle, 189
Cashew Curried Beef, 302
Cassoulet for Today, 279
✓Celestial Cherry Conserve, 44
Champagne-Basted Turkey, 177
Cheddar 'n' Pea Tossed Salad, 19
Cheddar Potato Soup, 36
Cheesecake Brownies, 99
Cheesy Cauliflower Soup, 31
Cherry-Berry Streusel Pie, 116

Cherry-Brandy Baked Brie, 249
Cherry Wild Rice Salad, 21
✓Chicken & Vegetable Stir-Fry, 268
✓Chicken Continental, 68
Chicken Cordon Bleu Pizza, 259
Chicken Dijon & Couscous, 58
Chicken Dinner Packets, 150
✓Chicken Florentine Meatballs, 264
Chicken Korma, 201
Chicken Mole Ole, 60
Chicken Salad Caprese, 10
Chicken Tortilla Chowder, 258
Chicken Wrapped in Bacon, 150
Chiles Rellenos Casserole, 285
Chipotle Cheeseburgers, 37
Chive Biscuits, 80
Chocolate Banana Cream Cake, 111
Chocolate Biscuit Puffs, 83
Chocolate Chip-Banana Belgian
    Waffles, 217
Chocolate Cinnamon Rolls, 86
Chocolate-Covered Bacon, 14
Chocolate-Covered Pretzels, 191
Chocolate-Dipped Orange
    Cookies, 95
Chocolate Lover's Delight Cake, 115
✓Chocolate Malt Desserts, 265
Chocolate Mint Apple Fondue, 133
Chocolate Mousse with Cranberry
    Sauce, 130
Chocolate Peanut Butter Candy, 293
Chocolate Raspberry Cheesecake, 227
Chocolate Raspberry Tunnel
    Cake, 112
Chocolate-Strawberry Celebration
    Cake, 107
Chocolate Toffee Cake, 115
✓Chocolate Toffee Delights, 98
Chocolate Truffle Cake, 108
Christmas Wreath Bread, 88
Chunky Blue Cheese Dressing, 226
Chunky Orange Marmalade
    Cookies, 102
Cilantro Pesto, 46
✓Cinnamon Chocolate Minties, 186
✓Citrus Fish, 222
✓Citrus-Marinated Salmon, 271
Citrus Tartlets, 124
Classic Cheesecake, 152
Classic Pesto, 46

✓ Recipe includes Nutrition Facts and Diabetic Exchanges.

Cocoa Meringues with Berries, 125
Coconut Almond Bombs, 92
✓Coconut Macaroons, 102
Coconut-Mango Mahi Mahi, 253
Coffee Barbecue Sauce, 44
Coffee-Molasses Marinated Pork
   Chops, 295
Coffee-Nut Muffins, 295
Coffee Toffee Cheesecake, 294
Corn Bread Salad, 155
✓Corn, Rice and Bean Burritos, 280
Cowboy Casserole, 149
Crab Puffs, 161
Cranberry-Apple Chutney, 181
Cranberry Broccoli Salad, 18
Cranberry Pecan Stuffing, 180
Cranberry-Port Fudge Brownies, 98
Cranburgers with Sweet Potato
   Fries, 39
Crawfish Beignets with Cajun Dipping
   Sauce, 166
Cream Cheese and Swiss Lasagna, 74
Cream of Walnut Soup, 242
Cream Puff Cake, 213
Creamy Butternut Squash Soup, 157
Creamy Cranberry Gelatin, 26
Creamy Pasta Primavera, 280
✓Creamy Pumpkin Polenta, 50
Creative Cake, 106
Crispy Peanut Butter Balls, 102
Crispy Taco Wings, 247
Crisscross Apple Crowns, 81
Crunchy Potato Mounds, 137
✓Cuccidati, 101
Cucumber Salad, 200
✓Curried Apricot Pork Chops, 148
✓Curried Chicken Salad, 267
Curried Chicken Shepherd's Pie, 58
Curry Powder, 199

D_____

Dad's Baked Beans, 211
✓Daria's Best-Ever Sugar Cookies, 100
Deli Beef Heroes, 138
Dijon-Walnut Spinach Salad, 248
Double-Cheese Beef Panini, 36
✓Dried Cherry Biscotti, 103

E_____

✓Easy Chicken Potpie, 266
Easy Enchiladas, 204
Easy Garden Tomatoes, 171
Easy Parmesan Biscuits, 246
Enchilada Lasagna, 282

✓Everything Bread, 178
✓Extra-Special Cashew Crescents, 92
Eyes on You, 173

F_____

Fabulous Green Beans, 234
Farmer's Country Breakfast, 299
Fast & Fabulous Thai Chicken
   Salad, 255
Fiesta Shrimp Cocktail, 11
Fiesta Tuna Salad Sandwiches, 141
Fire Island Ziti, 55
Fire-Roasted Tomato Salsa, 10
First-Prize Doughnuts, 82
Fish Tacos with Avocado Sauce, 73
Fish with Fennel, 67
Five-Fruit Pie, 109
Florida Citrus Meringue Pie, 223
Foolproof Gravy, 51
Four-Berry Spinach Salad, 26
French Cream with Sugared Grapes, 126
✓French Loaves, 83
French Onion Soup, 256
Frothy Mexi-Mocha Coffee, 229
✓Fruit Salad in a Pineapple Boat, 170

G_____

Garden Cobb Salad, 19
Genrose's Stuffed Beef Tenderloin, 66
German Chocolate Thumbprints, 94
Giant Flan, 205
✓Ginger Chicken, 56
Ginger Cranberry Bars, 97
Ginger Salmon Salad, 20
Gingerbread Caramel Crunch, 12
"Give Me S'more" Cake, 113
Gnocchi Chicken Minestrone, 34
✓Go Nuts! Coconut Caramels, 99
Gorgonzola-Pear Mesclun Salad, 179
✓Granola-to-Go Bars, 274
Greek Chicken Pasta, 251
Greek Deli Kabobs, 248
Greek Islands Steak Salad, 261
Greek Meat Loaves, 281
Greek Potato Salad, 21
Green Beans in Yellow Pepper
   Butter, 179
Green-Eyed Monster, 175
✓Green Mint Bark, 98
Grilled Glazed Drummies, 7
Grilled Greek Crostini Topping, 14
Grilled Peach BBQ Chicken
   Wings, 216
Grilled Pineapple Butterscotch
   Sundaes, 122

Grilled Pork Chops, 233
✓Grilled Potato & Arugula Salad, 169
Grilled Steak and Mushroom Salad, 25
✓Grilled Stuffed Turkey Burgers, 269
Grilled Sweet Onions, 299
Grilled Tomatillo Chicken, 62
✓Grilled Tuna Bibb Salads, 270
Grilled Vegetable Sandwiches, 137
Grilled Veggie Tortilla Wraps, 34

H_____

✓Halibut Soft Tacos, 270
Ham 'n' Swiss Envelopes, 30
Ham with Orange-Apricot Sauce, 59
Hamburger Noodle Bake, 149
Havarti Shrimp Quesadillas, 11
Hawaiian Beef Dish, 148
Hearty Cabbage Soup, 258
Hearty Macaroni Casserole, 59
Hearty Meatless Minestrone, 226
Herb & Cheese-Stuffed Burgers, 33
Herbed Bread Slices, 86
Herbed Corn, 249
✓Herbed Roast Chicken, 69
Herbed Standing Rib Roast, 68
Holiday Spritz, 94
Holiday Sugar Cookies, 184
Homemade Chocolate Pudding, 153
Homemade Croutons, 42
Homemade Guacamole, 204
Homemade Marshmallows, 190
✓Homemade Tortillas, 79
Honey-Glazed Hens with Fruit
   Stuffing, 242
Honey-Lime Red Snapper, 251
Honey-Mustard Turkey Salad, 20
Honey-Orange Rice Pudding, 230
Honey Sweet Corn, 208
✓Honey-Thyme Butternut Squash, 180
Horseradish Coleslaw, 24
Hot Cherry Sauce, 123
Hot Ham & Cheese Slices, 16
Hot Quick Banana Boats, 300
Hot Tamale Casserole, 70
Hot Wing Dip, 143

I_____

✓Iced Anise Cookies, 197
Island Vacation Party Mix, 293
Italian Christmas Turkey, 196
✓Italian Cucumber Salad, 23
Italian Drop Biscuits, 86
Italian Pork Stew, 284
Italian Sausage Grinders, 145
Italian Shepherd's Pies, 54

✓ Recipe includes Nutrition Facts and Diabetic Exchanges.

J

Jamaica-Me-Crazy Chicken Tropicale, 61
Julia's Green Beans & Mushrooms, 154

K

✓Kids' Favorite Blueberry Muffins, 79
Kids' Favorite Pumpkin Seeds, 9
Kielbasa Chicken Kabobs, 57

L

Ladyfinger Ice Cream Cake, 170
Lavender Brownie Cheesecake, 131
Lavender Lemonade, 203
Layered Lemon Pies, 139
Layered Pesto Cheese Spread, 248
Layered Taco Salad, 139
Lemon Angel Wings, 183
Lemon-Basil Frozen Yogurt, 120
Lemon Broccoli with Garlic, 195
Lemon Delight Trifle, 140
Lemon-Rosemary Layer Cake, 113
Lemon Scallop Linguine, 150
Lemon Sorbet Torte, 130
Lemony Brussels Sprouts, 255
✓Light Sour Cream Coffee Cake, 269
✓Lime-Buttered Broccoli, 241
Linzer Cookies, 184
Little Snail Rolls, 87
Louisiana Red Beans and Rice, 282
Luscious Blueberry Jam, 50

M

Mac 'n' Cheese Soup, 35
Macaroni 'n' Cheese Pizza, 284
Magnolia Dream Cheesecake, 163
✓Mamma's Caponata, 6
Maple-Pecan Snack Mix, 253
Marinated Ribeyes, 298
Marinated Veggie Beef Kabobs, 234
Mascarpone-Pesto Chicken Rolls, 55
Maui-Inspired Turkey Breast Roll, 74
Meatball Sub Casserole, 66
Mexican Ice Cream, 121
✓Mini Cinnamon Roll Cookies, 97
✓Mini Sweet Potato Muffins, 274
Mini White Pizzas, 260
Minted Rice with Garbanzo Curry, 200
Mocha Logs, 93
✓Molasses Cookies with a Kick, 96
Mom's Fried Rice, 45
Mom's Gingered Apple Salad, 22
✓Mom's Italian Bread, 196

Monterey Ranch Bread, 78
✓Moroccan Vegetarian Stew, 39
✓Mushroom Lasagna, 278
✓Mushroom Primavera Pasta Sauce, 268
Mushroom Turkey Tetrazzini, 69

N

Nectarine, Prosciutto & Endive Salad, 23
New England Baked Beans, 48
No-Bake Cookie Balls, 95
Nut and Poppy Seed Rolls, 80
✓Nutty Chocolate Batons, 183
✓Nutty Wild Rice, 272

O

Okra and Butter Bean Stew, 167
✓Old-Time Cake Doughnuts, 87
One-Skillet Pasta, 71
Onion & Cheddar Biscuits, 157
Onion, Garlic & Brie Bruschetta, 163
Open-Faced Chicken Avocado Burgers, 32
Orange-Berry Jam, 49
Orange You Spiky, 173
Overnight Cherry Danish, 78

P

Pad Thai Pizza, 250
Party Caramel Apples, 175
Pasta Alla Puttanesca, 291
✓Peach Chutney, 42
Peach Gelato, 296
Peanut Butter Brownie Trifle, 140
Peanut Butter Dipping Sauce, 303
Peanut Ice Cream Delight, 126
Pear Marmalade, 51
Pear Sorbet, 128
Pecan Caramels, 189
Pecan Goody Cups, 185
Pecan Meltaways, 187
Penny's Apple-Brown Sugar Coffee Cake, 215
Perfect Brunch Omelets, 283
Perfect Winter Salad, 162
Pesto Breadsticks, 291
✓Philly Cheese Fakes, 37
✓Pickled Veggie Salad, 138
Pineapple Coleslaw, 26
Pinwheel Mints, 95
Pistachio-Crusted Chicken with Garden Spinach, 72
Poblano Pesto, 47

✓Polynesian Parfaits, 275
Pomegranate Jelly, 44
Pomegranate Poached Pears, 128
Poppy Seed Chicken Salad, 24
Potato & Red Onion Frittata, 231
Potato-Sausage Foil Packs, 299
Praline Crunch Ice Cream, 133
Presto Chicken Tacos, 281
✓Pretty Pumpkin Wontons, 143
Pretty Stuffed Spring Peas, 10
Pumpkin Banana Bread, 80
Pumpkin Cheesecake Pie, 107
Pumpkin Cranberry Bread Pudding, 132
Pumpkin Dessert Bars, 142
Pumpkin-Filled Crescent Rolls, 136
Pumpkin Pancakes with Cinnamon Brown Butter, 73
Purple People-Eater, 174

Q

Quick Pizza Sandwiches, 155

R

Ragu Bolognese, 290
Rainbow Pepper Medley, 136
Rainbow Quiche, 285
Ranch Mac & Cheese, 64
Raspberry Chocolate Torte, 109
Raspberry Walnut Bars, 103
Red Curry Carrot Soup, 30
Rhubarb Cake with Lemon Sauce, 110
Rich Peanut Clusters, 136
Ricotta Cheesecake, 123
Roadside Diner Cheeseburger Quiche, 54
Roast Pork with Apples & Onions, 286
✓Roasted Harvest Vegetables, 177
Roasted Pears in Pecan Sauce, 129
Roasted Vegetable Salad, 140
Rootin'-Tootin' Cincinnati Chili, 33
Rosemary-Parmesan Popcorn, 12

S

✓Salmon Bisque, 38
Salsa Verde, 246
✓Sammie's Breakfast Burritos, 275
Sara's Summer Rolls, 280
✓Savory Stuffed Figs, 9
Scallops in Sage Cream, 246
Seafood & Cream Cheese Stuffed Shells, 8
✓Sensational Tiramisu, 273
Sesame Green Beans, 49

✓ *Recipe includes Nutrition Facts and Diabetic Exchanges.*